Hello, Amélie here.
It's already been several months since
a newbie showed up at my house. She's
a pretty strange one. She makes these
sudden, unpredictable movements and yells
"waaaaaaaa!!" out of nowhere. And I think
she's getting bigger kinda fast... She's
insanely cute though! That said, I am going
to have to teach her one thing: the fact that
I'm the cutest one around here!!

—*Yūki Tabata's dog, 2020*

YŪKI TABATA

was born in Fukuoka Prefecture
and got his big break in the 2011
Shonen Jump Golden Future Cup
with his winning entry, *Hungry
Joker*. He started the magical fantasy
series *Black Clover* in 2015.

BLACK CLOVER
VOLUME 24
SHONEN JUMP Manga Edition

Story and Art by YŪKI TABATA

Translation ❋ TAYLOR ENGEL,
HC LANGUAGE SOLUTIONS, INC.

Touch-Up Art & Lettering ❋ ANNALIESE CHRISTMAN

Design ❋ KAM LI

Editor ❋ ALEXIS KIRSCH

BLACK CLOVER © 2015 by Yuki Tabata
All rights reserved.
First published in Japan in 2015 by SHUEISHA Inc., Tokyo.
English translation rights arranged by SHUEISHA Inc.

The stories, characters and incidents mentioned in
this publication are entirely fictional.

Printed in the U.S.A.

Published by VIZ Media, LLC
P.O. Box 77010
San Francisco, CA 94107

10 9 8 7 6 5 4 3 2 1
First printing, January 2021

PARENTAL ADVISORY
BLACK CLOVER is rated T for Teen and is
recommended for ages 13 and up. This volume
contains realistic and fantasy violence.

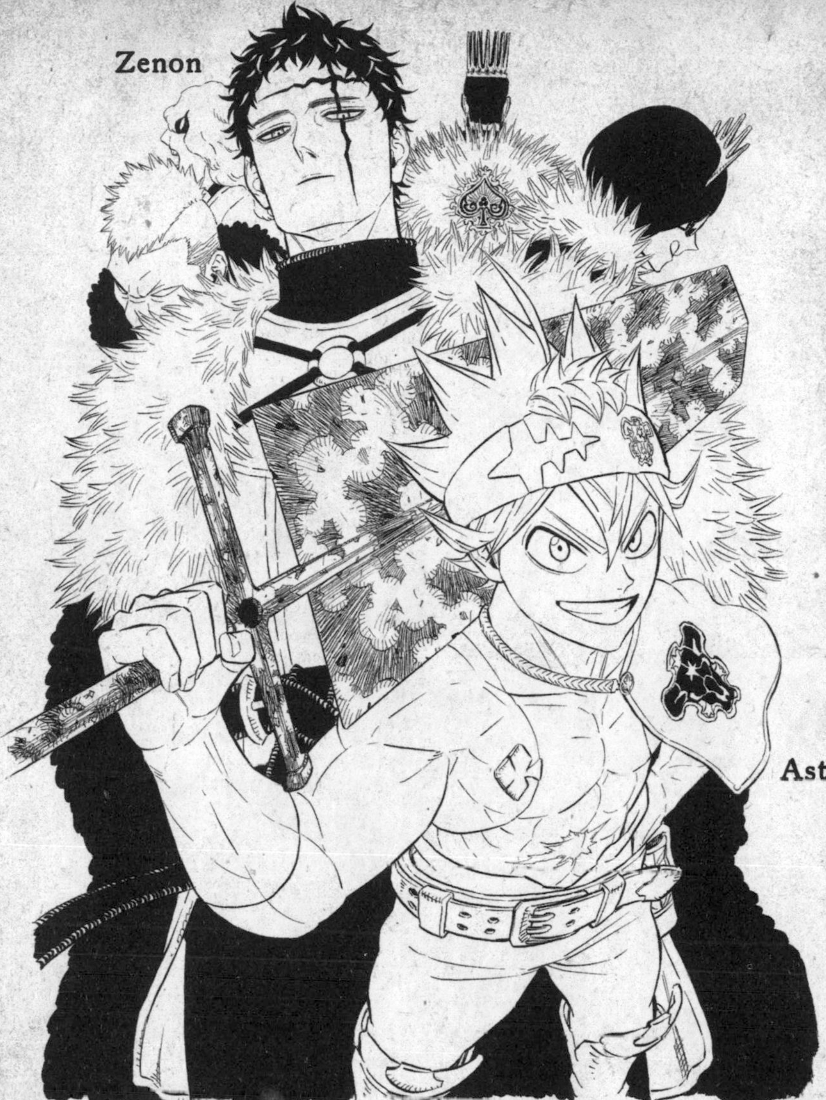
Zenon
Asta

Black Clover

YŪKI TABATA

24

THE BEGINNING OF
HOPE AND DESPAIR

Characters

Yuno

Member of: The Golden Dawn
Magic: Wind

Asta's best friend, and a good rival who's also been working to become the Wizard King. He controls Sylph, the spirit of wind.

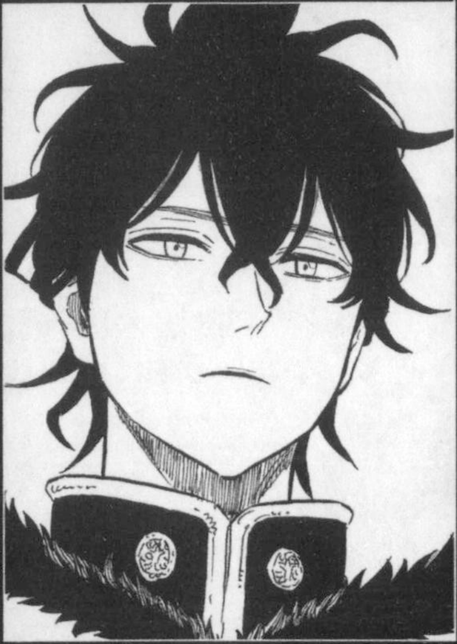

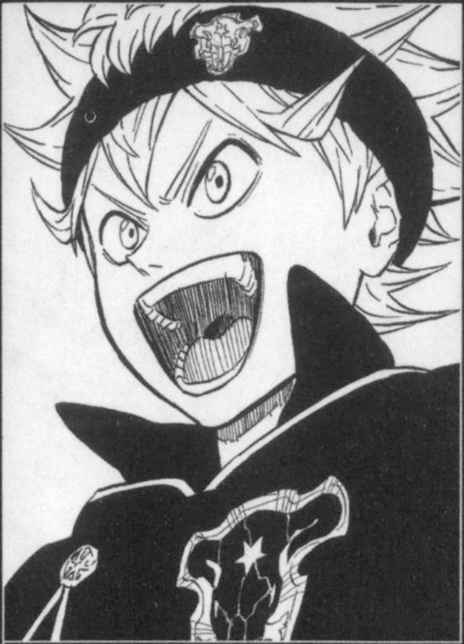

Asta

Member of: The Black Bulls
Magic: None (Anti-Magic)

He has no magic, but he's working to become the Wizard King through sheer guts and his well-trained body. He fights with anti-magic swords.

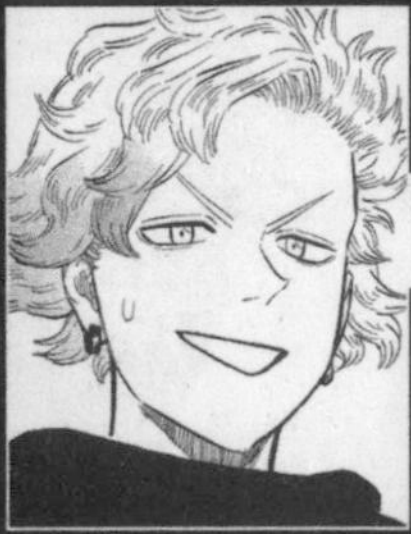

Finral Roulacase

Member of: The Black Bulls
Magic: Spatial

A playboy who immediately chats up any woman he sees. He can't attack, but he has high-level abilities.

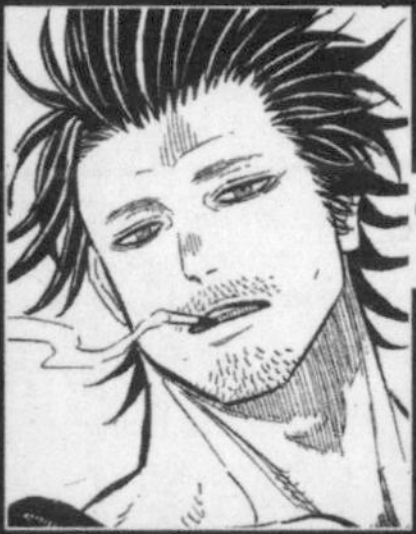

Yami Sukehiro

Member of: The Black Bulls
Magic: Dark

A captain who looks fierce, but is very popular with his brigade, which has a deep-rooted confidence in him. Heavy smoker.

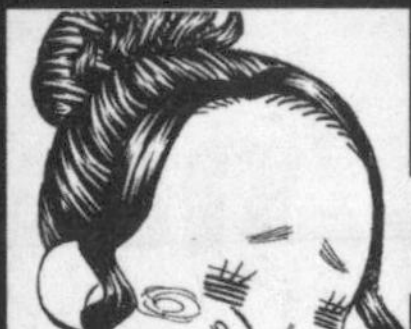

Charmy Pappitson

Member of: The Black Bulls
Magic: Cotton and Food

She eats like a maniac, and prizes food above all else. She's half dwarf. She has a big crush on Yuno.

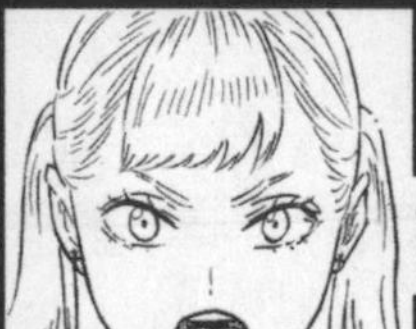

Noelle Silva

Member of: The Black Bulls
Magic: Water

A royal. She feels inferior to her brilliant siblings. Her latent abilities are an unknown quantity.

Secre Swallowtail (Nero)

Member of:
The Black Bulls
Magic: Sealing

She paid for using forbidden magic by becoming a bird 500 years ago. She watched over Licht's grimoire.

Luck Voltia

Member of:
The Black Bulls
Magic: Lightning

A battle maniac. Once he starts fighting, he gets totally absorbed in it. Smiles constantly.

Lolopechka

Magic: Water

The princess of the Heart Kingdom. She's fundamentally klutzy and clueless. She's been cursed by the devil Megicula.

Mimosa Vermillion

Member of:
The Golden Dawn
Magic: Plant

Noelle's cousin. She's ladylike and a bit of an airhead, but she can be rude. She just might like Asta…

Gaja

Magic: Lightning

Lolopechka's close adviser. He has Zero Stage magic and is one of the Heart Kingdom's spirit guardians.

Undine

Magic: Water Spirit

One of the four great spirits, she's contracted to Lolopechka, whom she adores.

STORY

In a world where magic is everything, Asta and Yuno are both found abandoned on the same day at a church in the remote village of Hage. Both dream of becoming the Wizard King, the highest of all mages, and they spend their days working toward that dream.

The year they turn 15, both receive grimoires, magic books that amplify their bearer's magic. They take the entrance exam for the Magic Knights, nine groups of mages under the direct control of the Wizard King. Yuno, whose magic is strong, joins the Golden Dawn, an elite group, while Asta, who has no magic at all, joins the Black Bulls, a group of misfits. With this, the two finally take their first step toward becoming the Wizard King…

In search of hints regarding the devils and curses that lurk in the shadows of the world, Asta and company went to the princess of the Heart Kingdom, Lolopechka. After learning of the threat of the devil Megicula, who has made his lair in the Spade Kingdom and is plotting to invade other countries, the Clover Kingdom decides to join forces with the Heart Kingdom. Asta and the others then spend half a year training with the spirit guardians, but what will the results be…?!

BLACK ✦ CLOVER

CONTENTS

PAGE 229 ❀ The Beginning of Hope and Despair 008

PAGE 230 ❀ I'll Crush You 027

PAGE 231 ❀ The Dark Triad 043

PAGE 232 ❀ Quiet Lakes and Forest Shadows 059

PAGE 233 ❀ Fate Begins to Move 073

PAGE 234 ❀ The Messenger from the Spade Kingdom 087

PAGE 235 ❀ Dark Disciples 103

PAGE 236 ❀ There's No Way We're The Same 119

PAGE 237 ❀ Sheer Obstinacy 135

PAGE 238 ❀ Zenon's Power 151

PAGE 239 ❀ Budding of Yggdrasil 167

BLACK ❀ CLOVER
24

Six months later

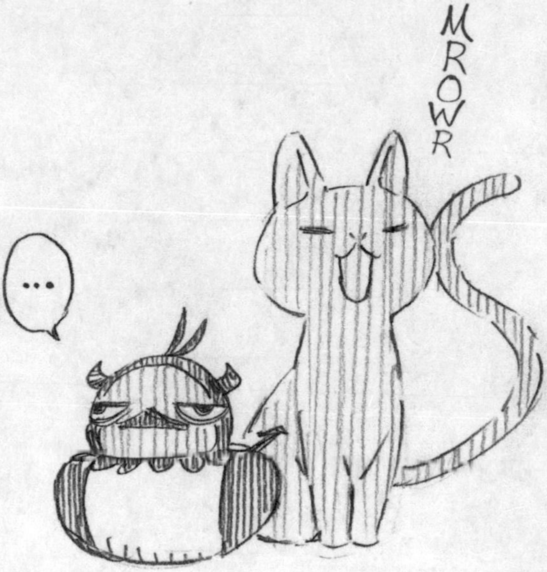

...
MROWR

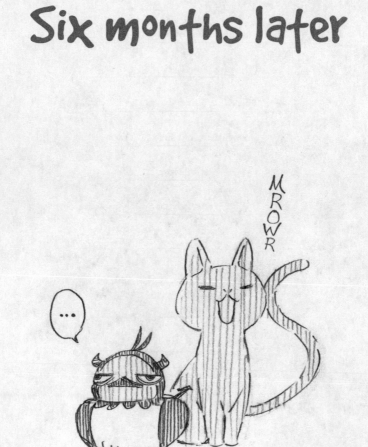

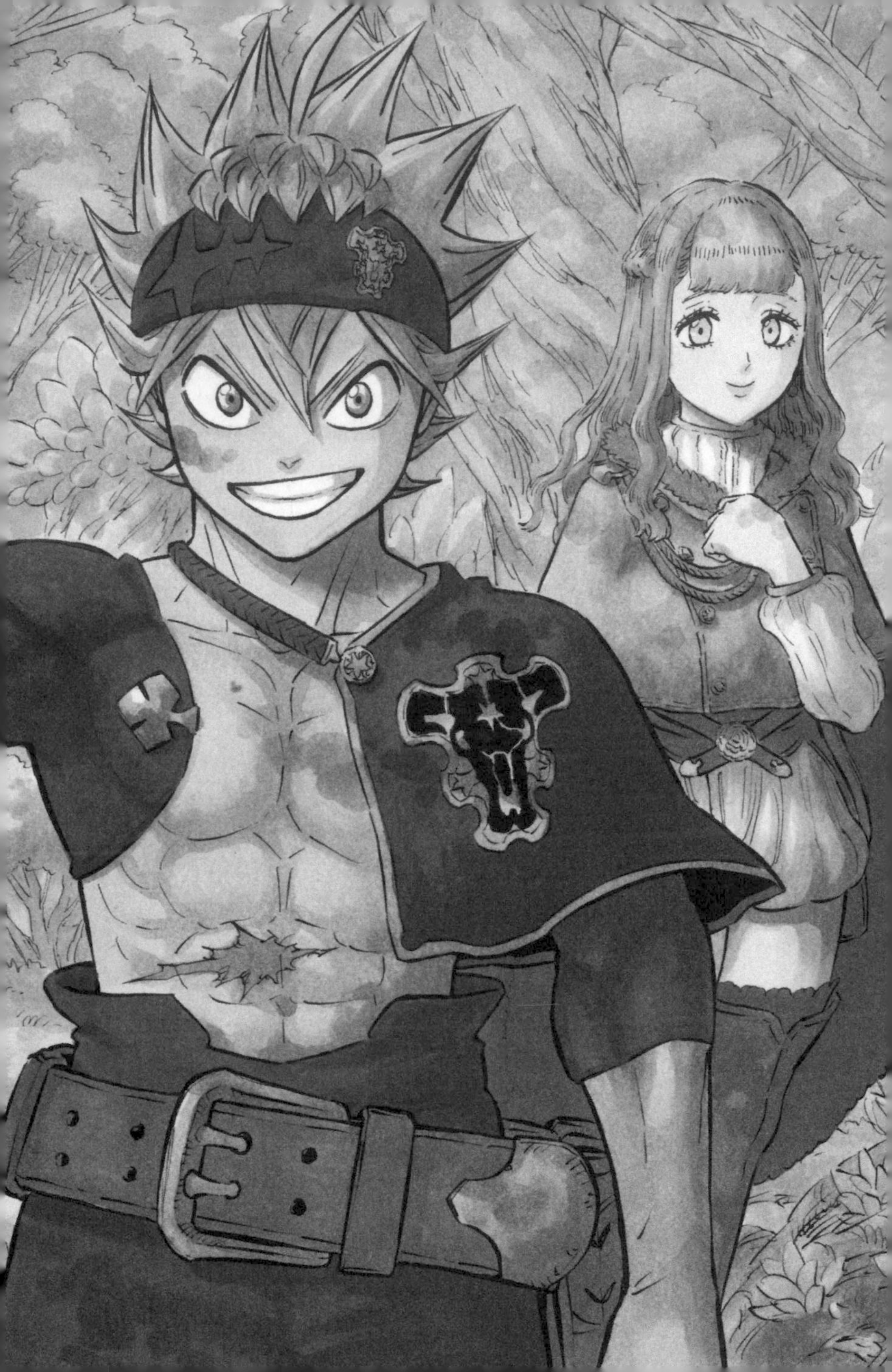

Page 229: The Beginning of Hope and Despair

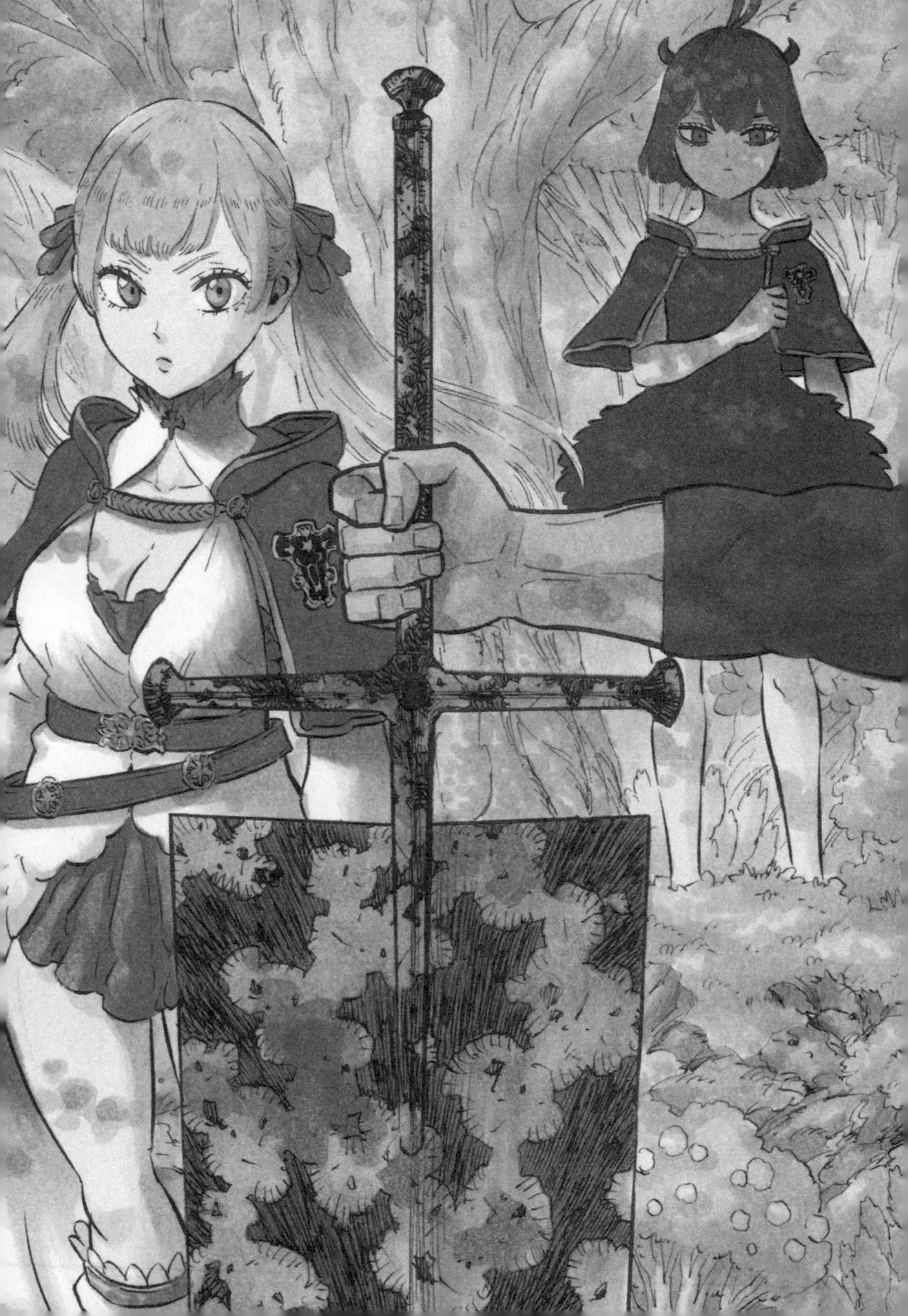

BLACK✤CLOVER

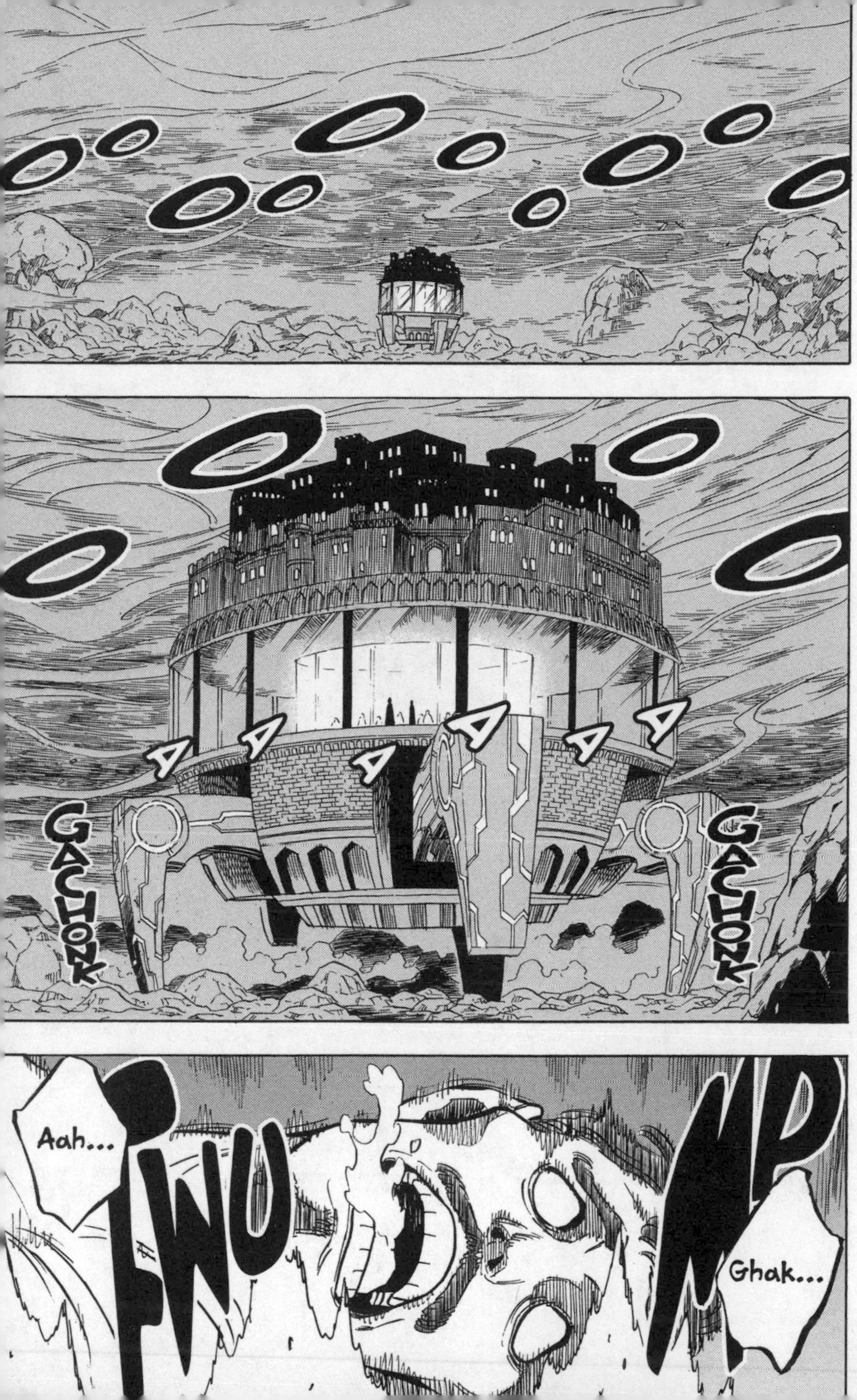
GACHONK
AAAAAA
GACHONK
Ghak...
FWUMP
Aah...

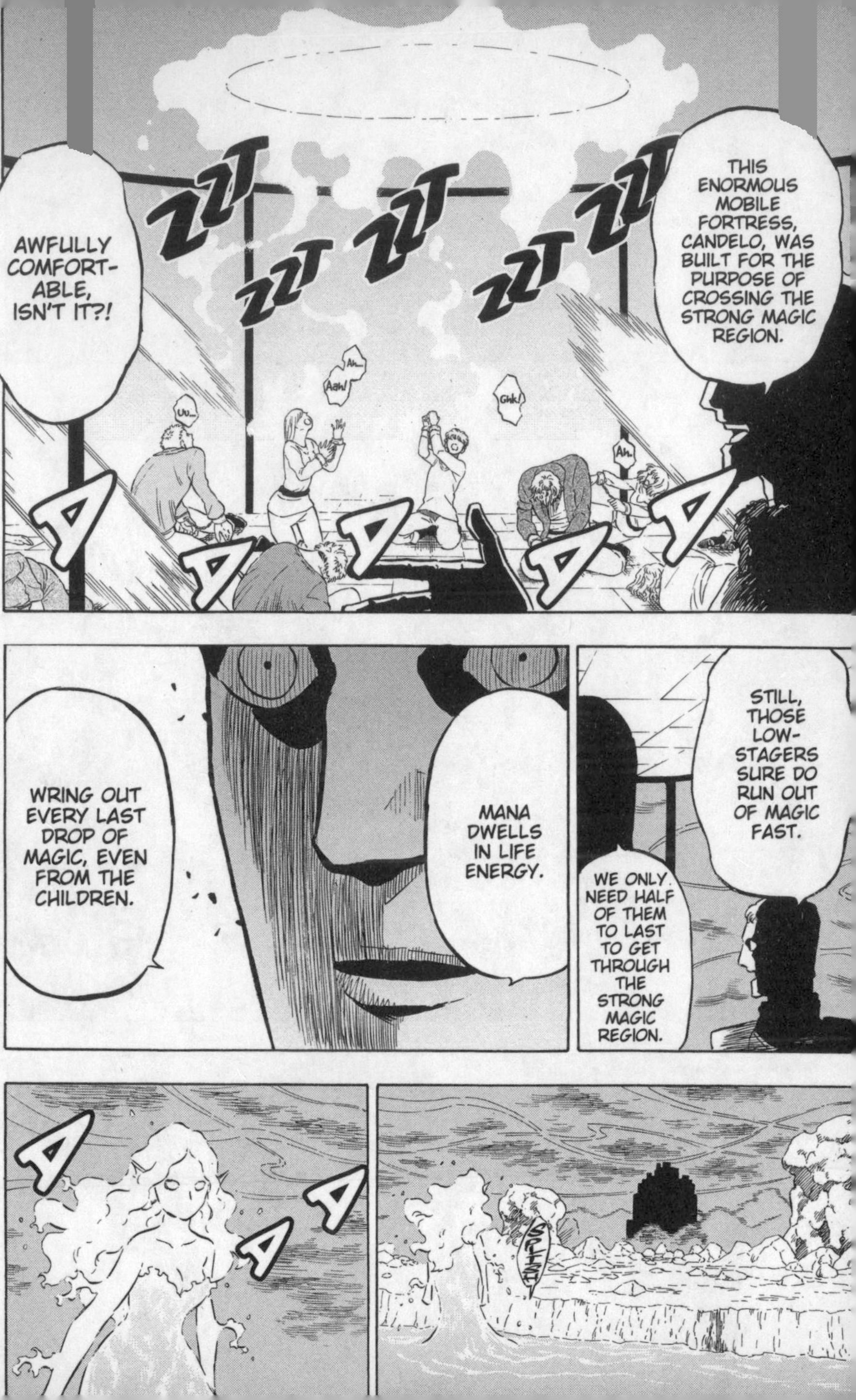
THIS ENORMOUS MOBILE FORTRESS, CANDELO, WAS BUILT FOR THE PURPOSE OF CROSSING THE STRONG MAGIC REGION.
ZZZT
ZZZT
ZZZT
ZZZT
AWFULLY COMFORTABLE, ISN'T IT?!
Ah.
Ghk!
Ah...
Aah!
Uu...
A
A
A
A
A
STILL, THOSE LOW-STAGERS SURE DO RUN OUT OF MAGIC FAST.
WE ONLY NEED HALF OF THEM TO LAST TO GET THROUGH THE STRONG MAGIC REGION.
MANA DWELLS IN LIFE ENERGY.
WRING OUT EVERY LAST DROP OF MAGIC, EVEN FROM THE CHILDREN.
SPLISH
A
A
A

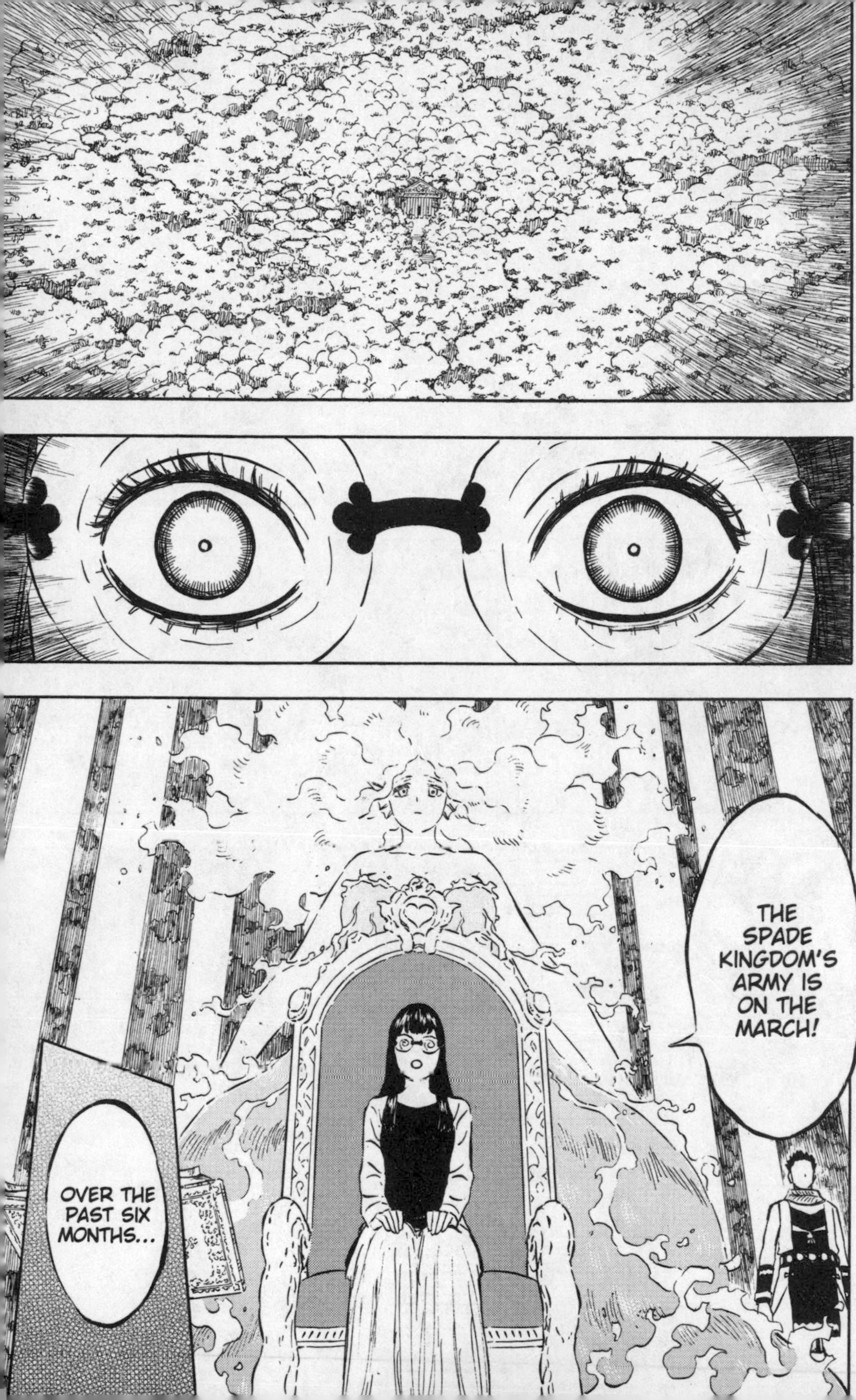
THE SPADE KINGDOM'S ARMY IS ON THE MARCH!
OVER THE PAST SIX MONTHS...

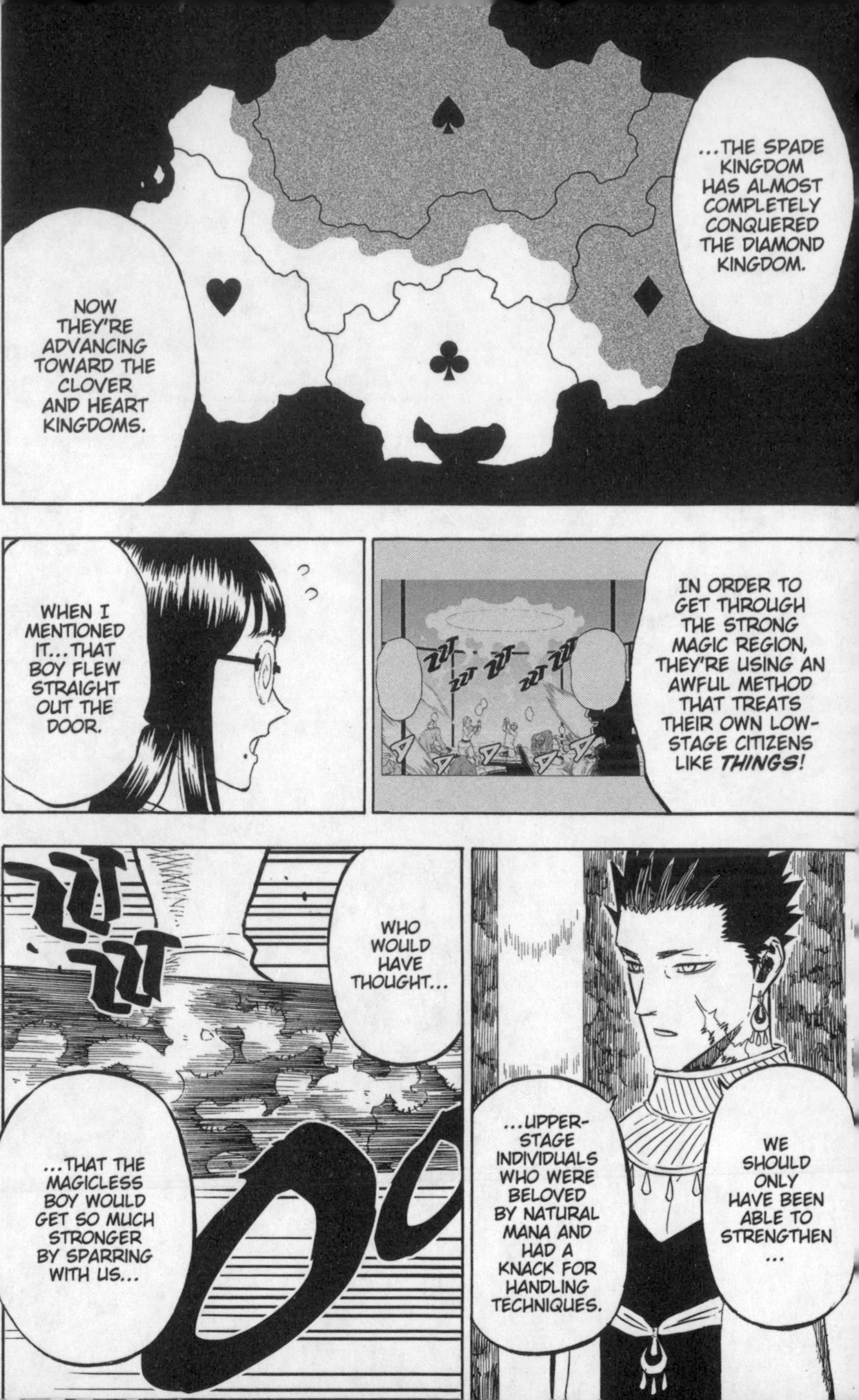
...THE SPADE KINGDOM HAS ALMOST COMPLETELY CONQUERED THE DIAMOND KINGDOM.
NOW THEY'RE ADVANCING TOWARD THE CLOVER AND HEART KINGDOMS.
IN ORDER TO GET THROUGH THE STRONG MAGIC REGION, THEY'RE USING AN AWFUL METHOD THAT TREATS THEIR OWN LOW-STAGE CITIZENS LIKE *THINGS!*
WHEN I MENTIONED IT...THAT BOY FLEW STRAIGHT OUT THE DOOR.
WE SHOULD ONLY HAVE BEEN ABLE TO STRENGTHEN...
...UPPER-STAGE INDIVIDUALS WHO WERE BELOVED BY NATURAL MANA AND HAD A KNACK FOR HANDLING TECHNIQUES.
WHO WOULD HAVE THOUGHT...
...THAT THE MAGICLESS BOY WOULD GET SO MUCH STRONGER BY SPARRING WITH US...

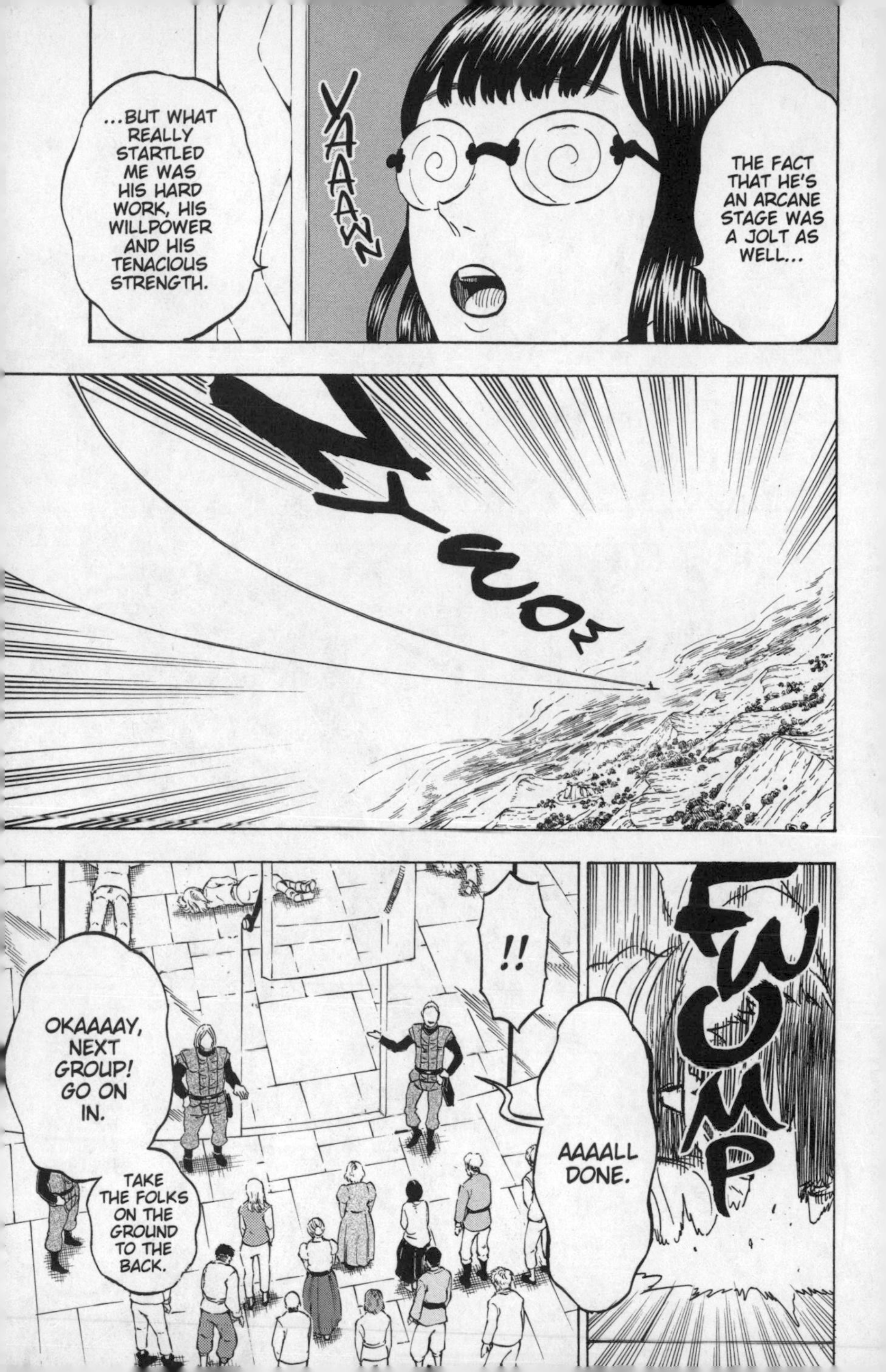
THE FACT THAT HE'S AN ARCANE STAGE WAS A JOLT AS WELL...
YAAAAWN
...BUT WHAT REALLY STARTLED ME WAS HIS HARD WORK, HIS WILLPOWER AND HIS TENACIOUS STRENGTH.
FWUMP
AAAALL DONE.
!!
OKAAAAY, NEXT GROUP! GO ON IN.
TAKE THE FOLKS ON THE GROUND TO THE BACK.

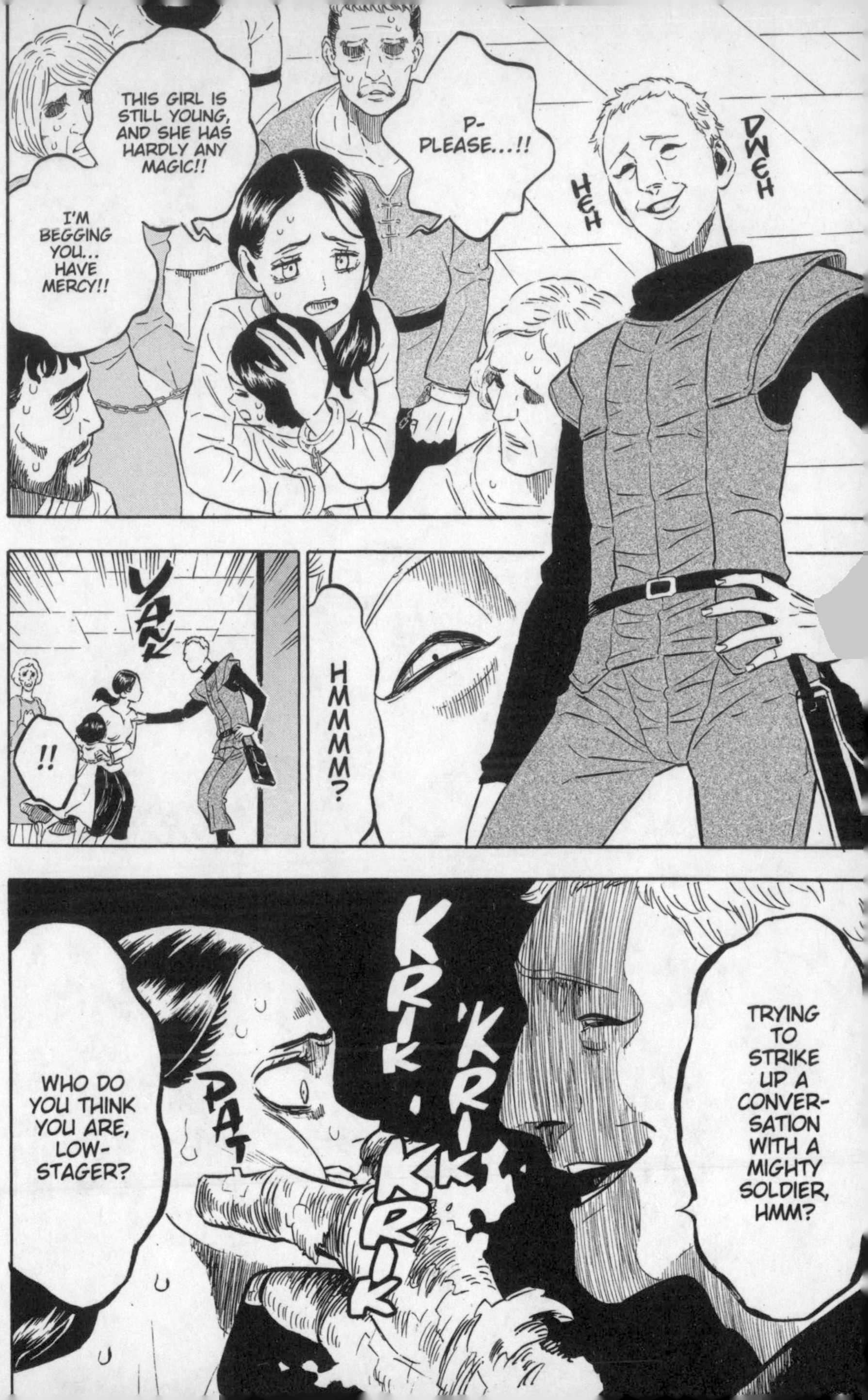
DWEH
HEH
P-PLEASE...!!
THIS GIRL IS STILL YOUNG, AND SHE HAS HARDLY ANY MAGIC!!
I'M BEGGING YOU... HAVE MERCY!!
HMMMMM?
YANK
!!
TRYING TO STRIKE UP A CONVERSATION WITH A MIGHTY SOLDIER, HMM?
KRIK
KRIK
KRIK
KRIK
PAT
WHO DO YOU THINK YOU ARE, LOW-STAGER?

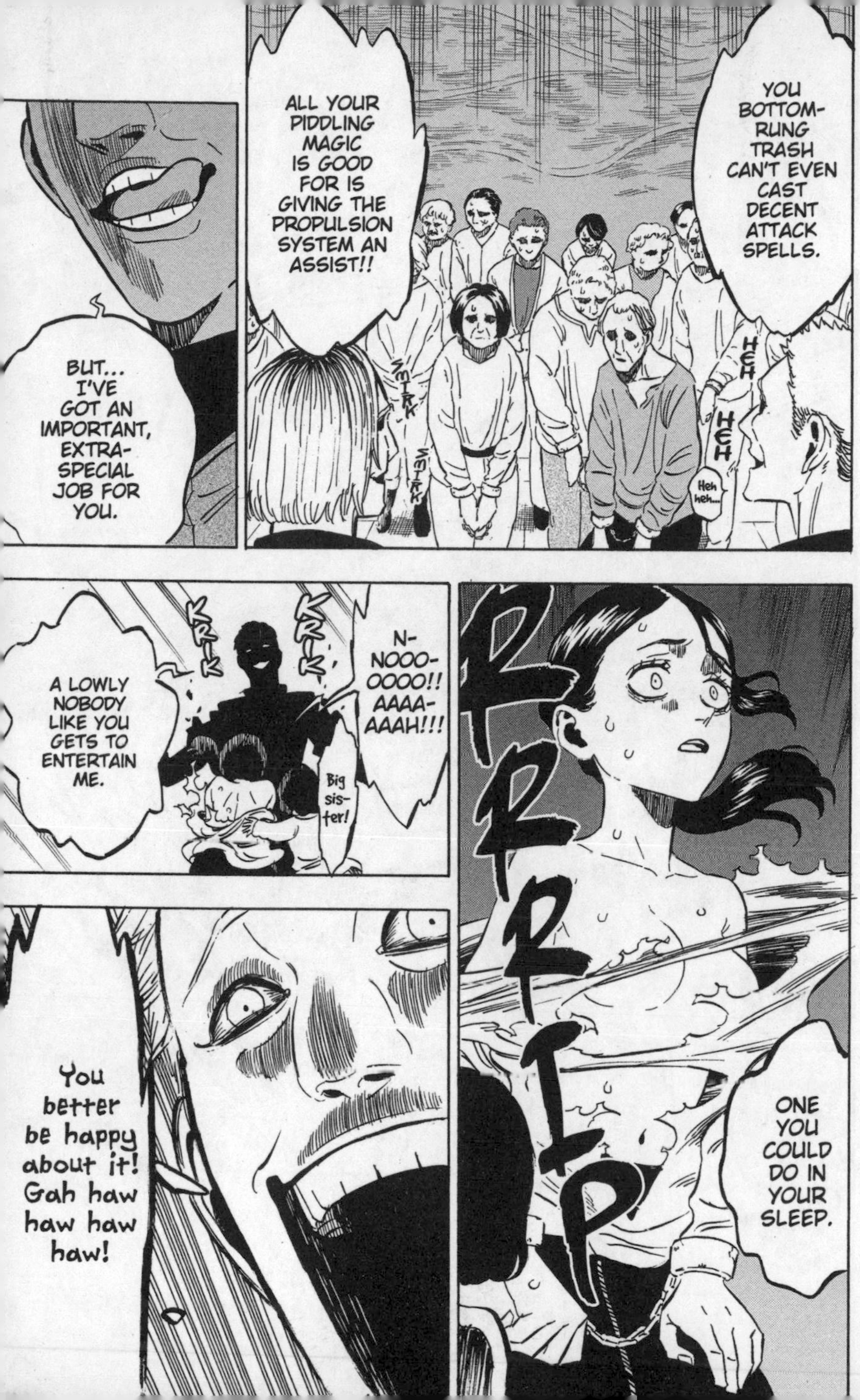
YOU BOTTOM-RUNG TRASH CAN'T EVEN CAST DECENT ATTACK SPELLS.
ALL YOUR PIDDLING MAGIC IS GOOD FOR IS GIVING THE PROPULSION SYSTEM AN ASSIST!!
HEH HEH
Heh heh...
SMIRK SMIRK
BUT... I'VE GOT AN IMPORTANT, EXTRA-SPECIAL JOB FOR YOU.
ONE YOU COULD DO IN YOUR SLEEP.
RRRIP
N-NOOOOOOO!! AAAAAAAH!!!
KRIK KRIK
Big sister!
A LOWLY NOBODY LIKE YOU GETS TO ENTERTAIN ME.
You better be happy about it! Gah haw haw haw haw!

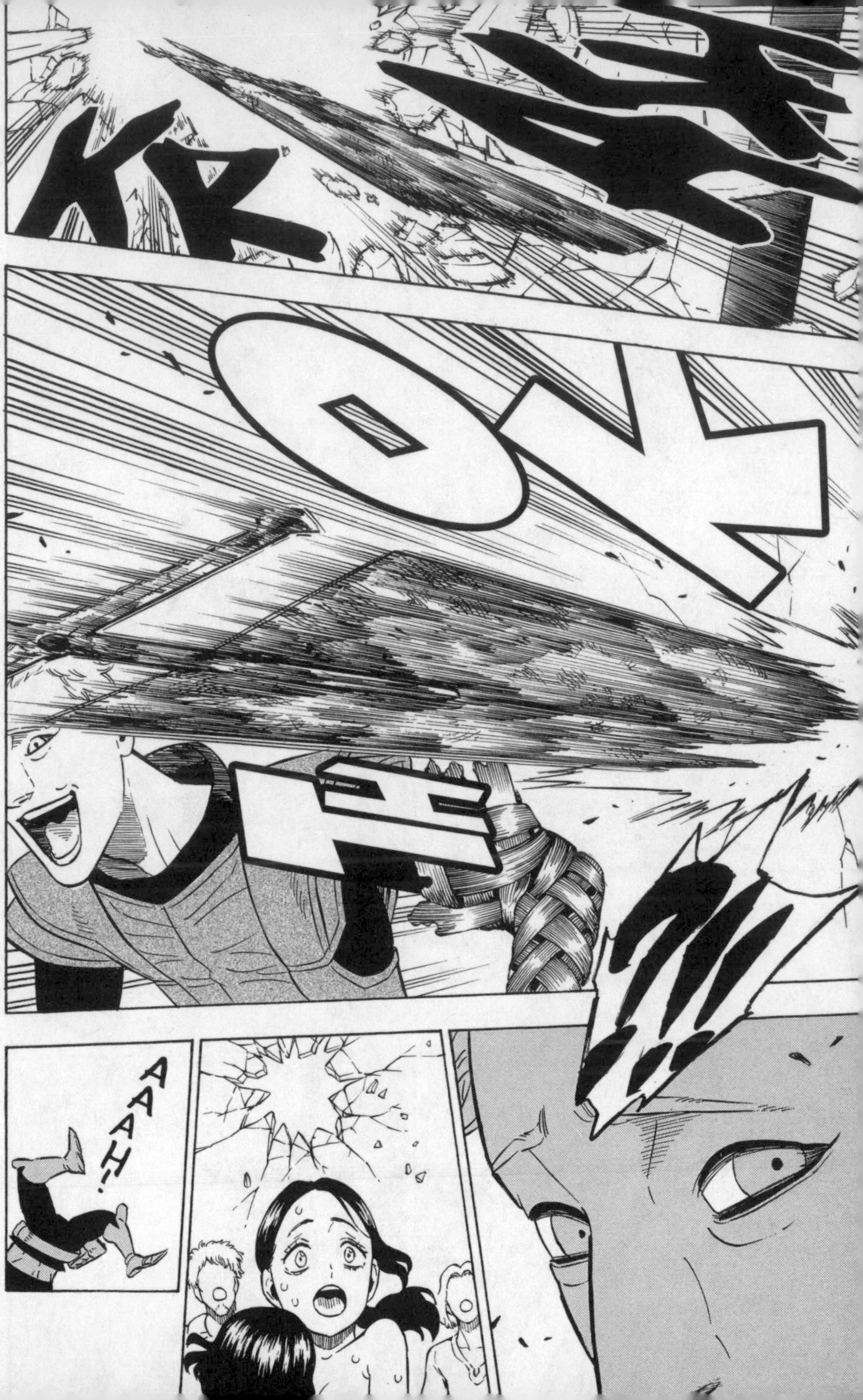
AAAH!

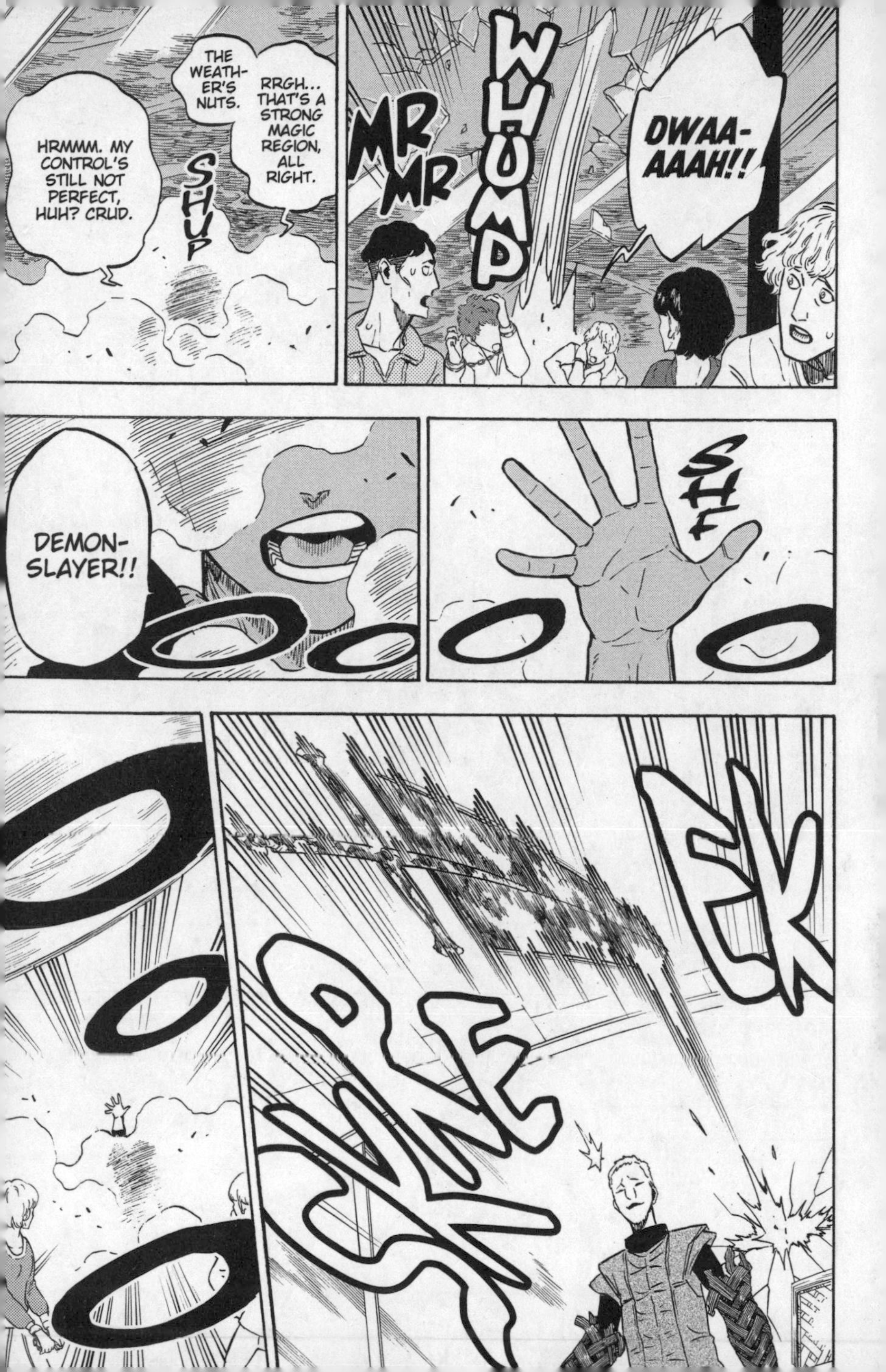
DWAA-AAAH!!
WHUMP
MR MR
RRGH... THAT'S A STRONG MAGIC REGION, ALL RIGHT.
THE WEATH-ER'S NUTS.
SHUP
HRMMM. MY CONTROL'S STILL NOT PERFECT, HUH? CRUD.
SHF
DEMON-SLAYER!!

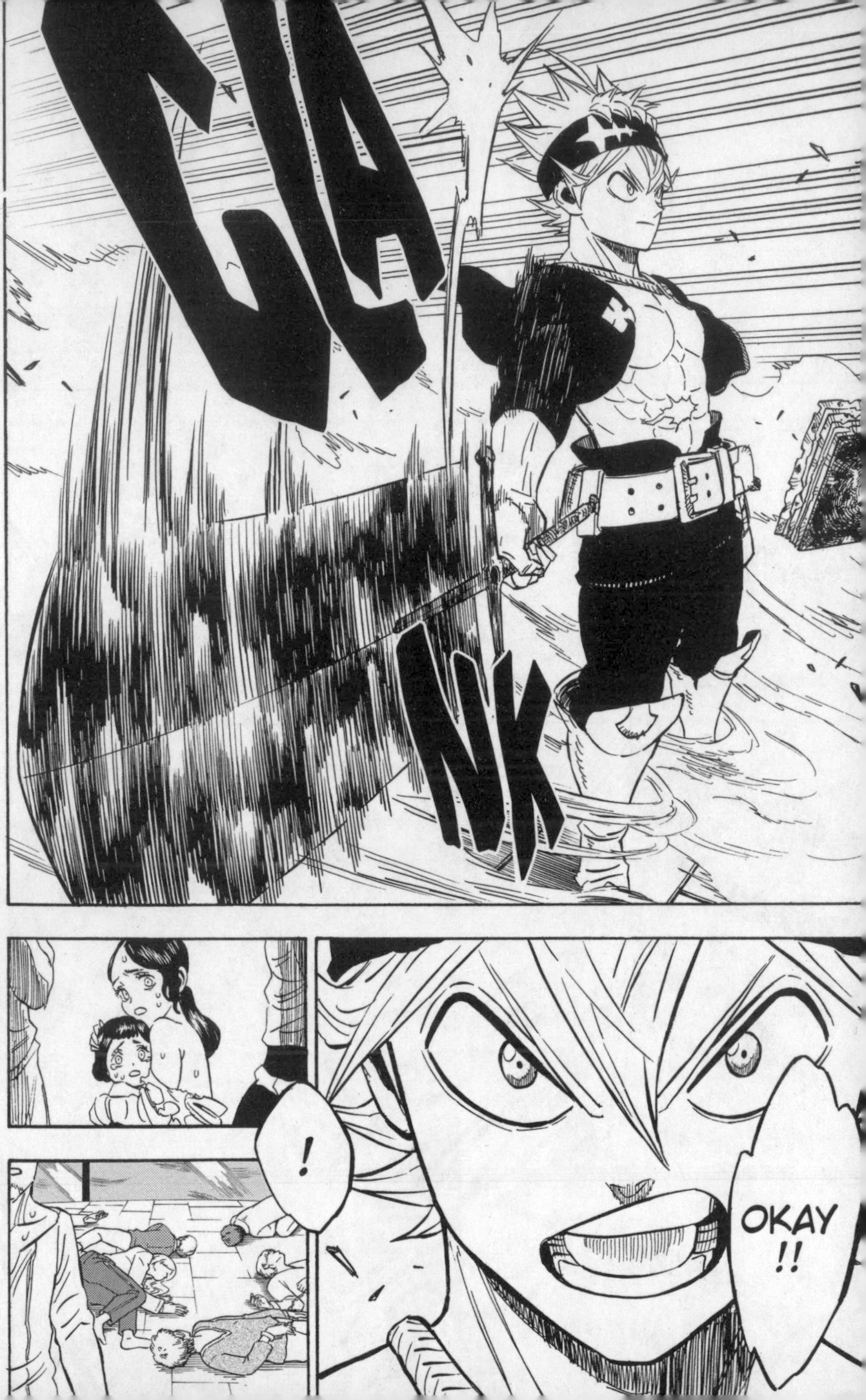
CLANK
OKAY !!
!

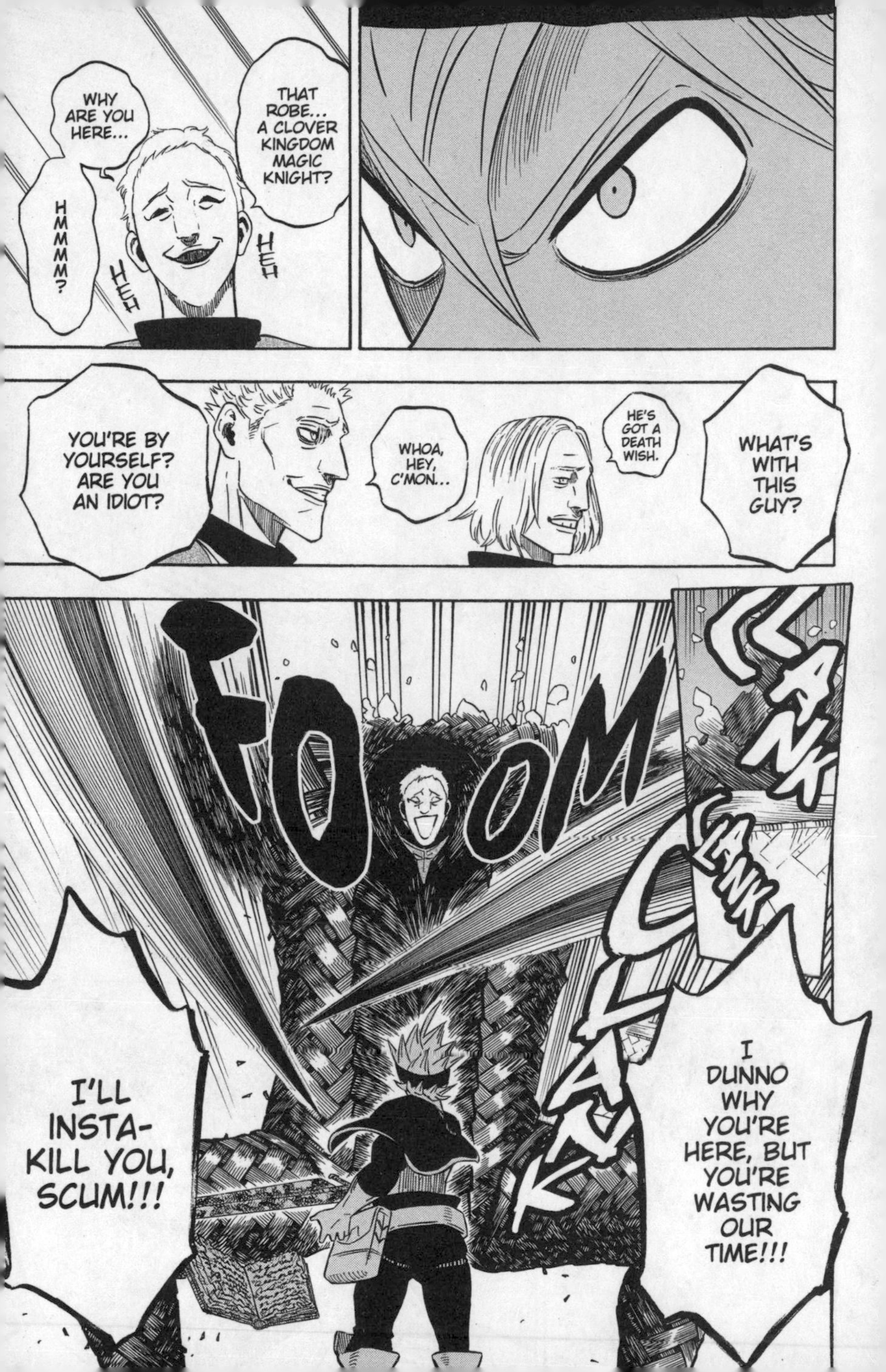
THAT ROBE... A CLOVER KINGDOM MAGIC KNIGHT?
WHY ARE YOU HERE...
HEH
HMMMMM?
HEH
WHAT'S WITH THIS GUY?
HE'S GOT A DEATH WISH.
WHOA, HEY, C'MON...
YOU'RE BY YOURSELF? ARE YOU AN IDIOT?
CLANK
CLANK
FOOOM
I DUNNO WHY YOU'RE HERE, BUT YOU'RE WASTING OUR TIME!!!
I'LL INSTA-KILL YOU, SCUM!!!

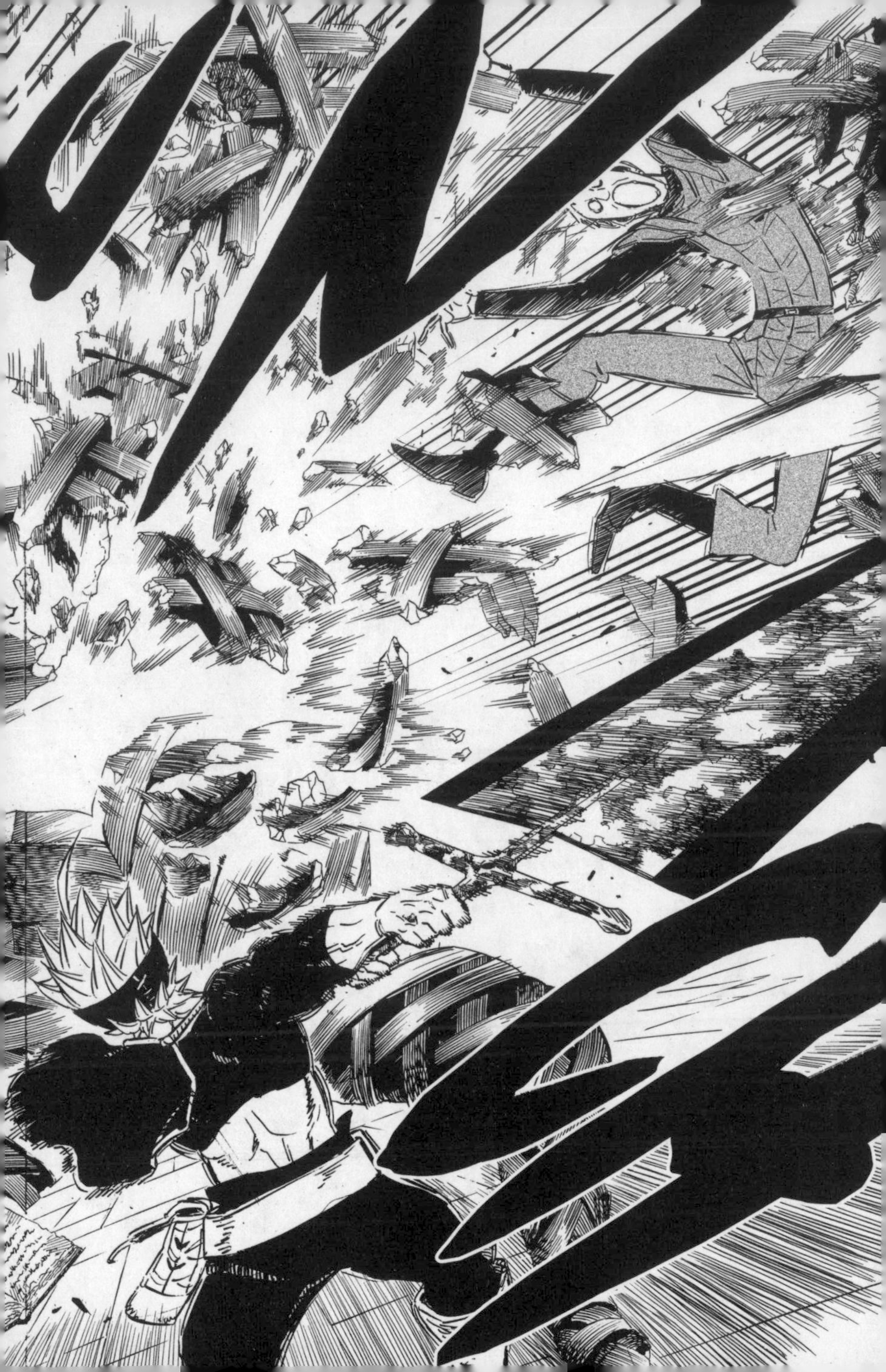

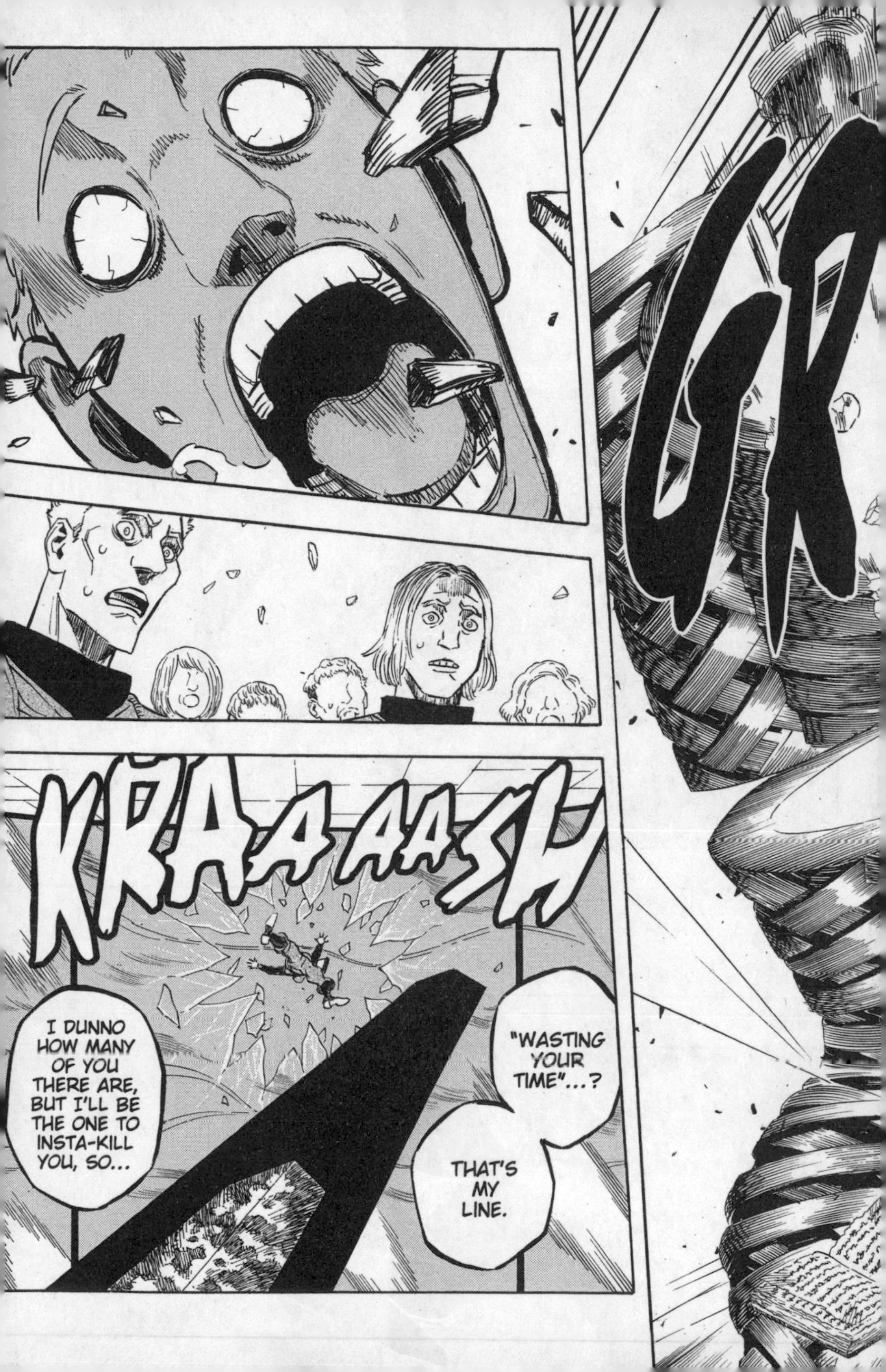
GR
KRAAAASH
"WASTING YOUR TIME"...?
THAT'S MY LINE.
I DUNNO HOW MANY OF YOU THERE ARE, BUT I'LL BE THE ONE TO INSTA-KILL YOU, SO...

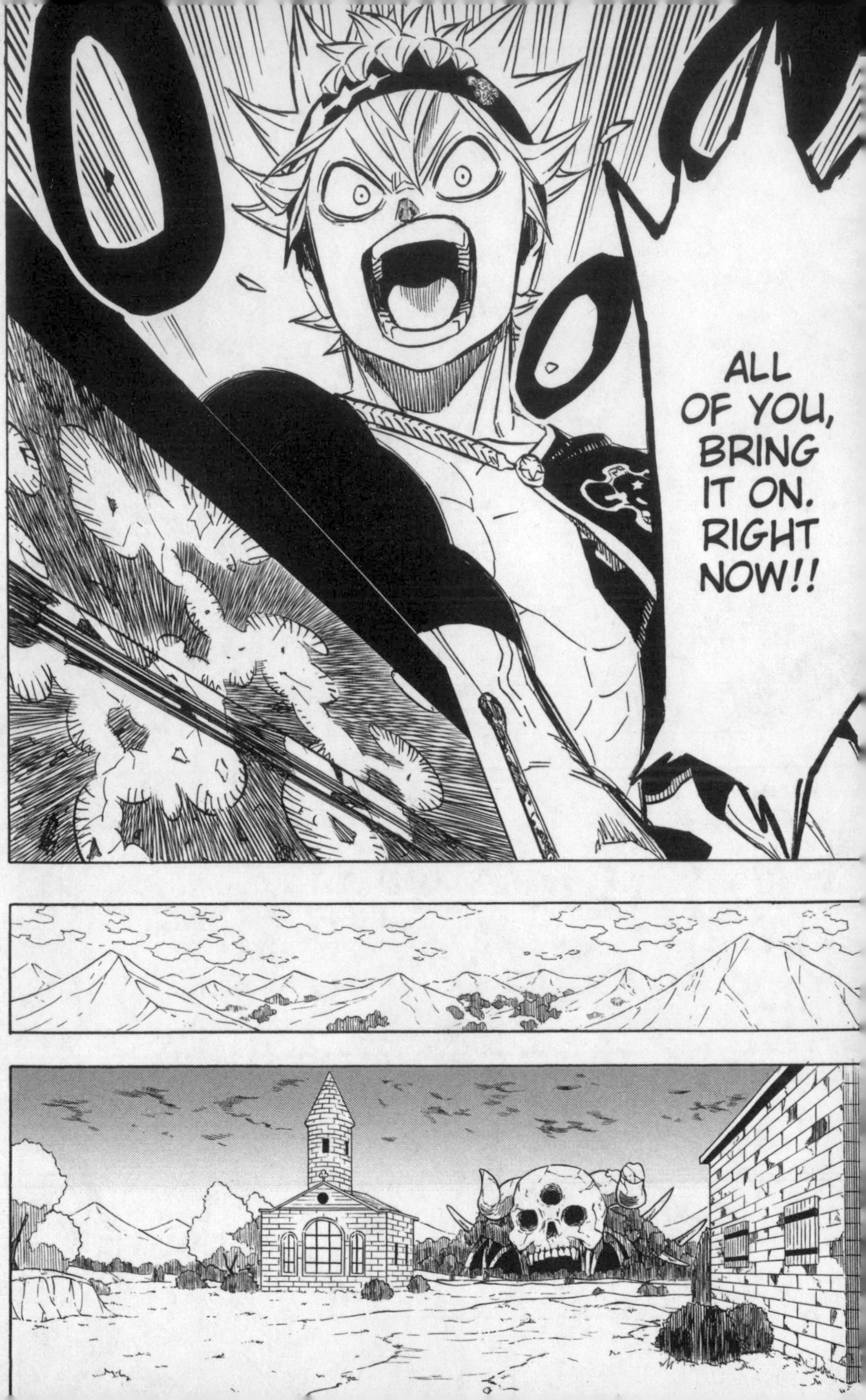
ALL OF YOU, BRING IT ON. RIGHT NOW!!

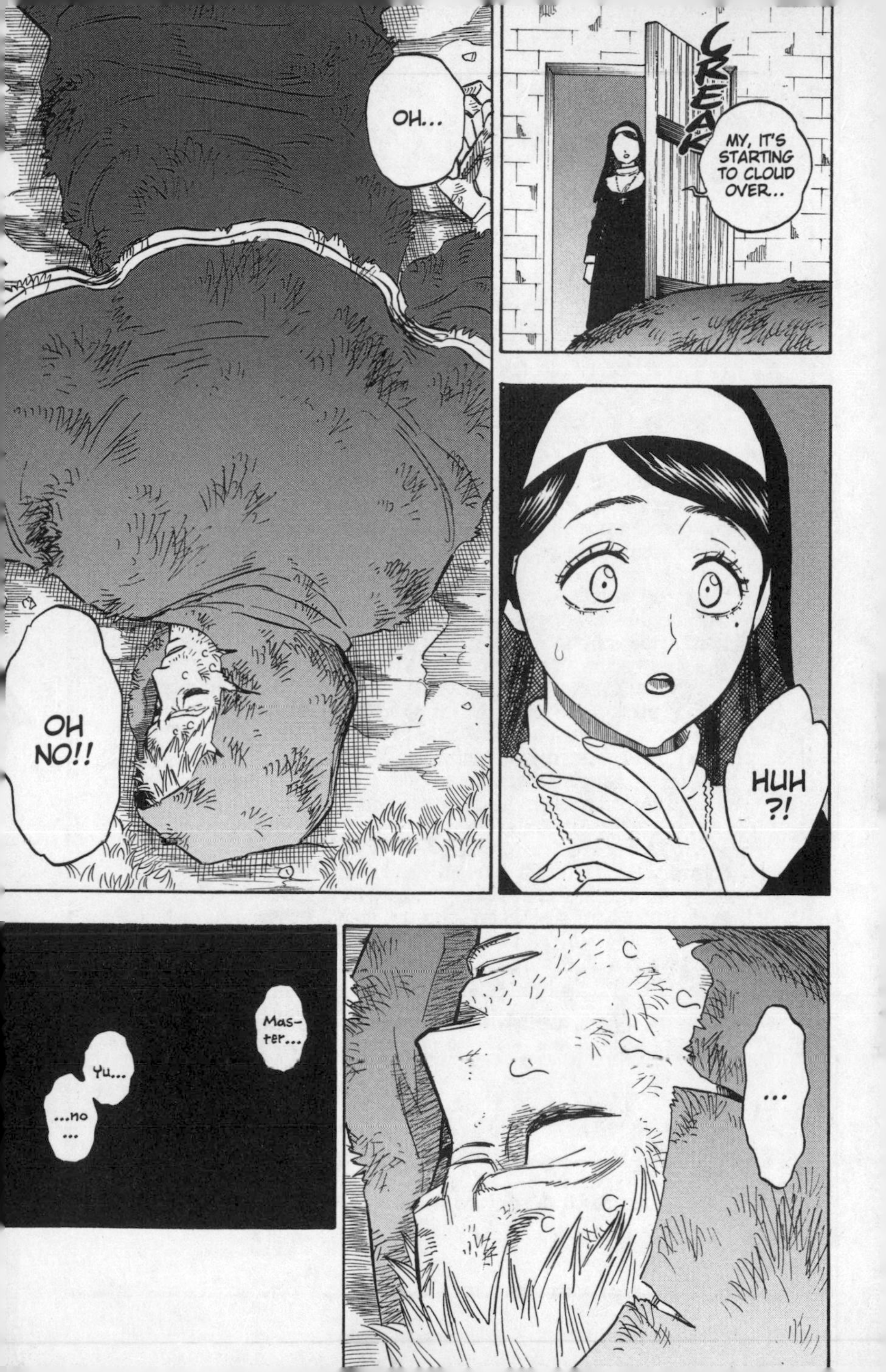
CREAK
MY, IT'S STARTING TO CLOUD OVER..
HUH ?!
OH...
OH NO!!
...
Mas-ter...
Yu...
...no ...

The Assorted Questions Brigade

Good day! Good evening! Good morning!

It's time for the letters corner.

Sharp-eyed readers have spotted a few things!
Let's go right to the questions!!

Q: When exactly did the seal on the word soul devil get broken "500 years later," and when and where did he possess Ronne? Please tell me what he was doing up until his first appearance. (*Time Garden*, Tokyo)

A: I wasn't able to draw that properly. I'm really sorry!! As the word soul devil was being sealed by Secre's spell, Eternal Prison, he cast the forbidden spell Noad Nephesh, which would bring about the elves' reincarnation around the time that his seal would break. In other words, around the time Patry took up residence in William's body, the word soul devil also started to regain his mobility. (Although he was only a soul at the time.) After that, he just waited and watched until Patry's group gathered the magic stones and the Shadow Palace appeared. Then, in the middle of the battle for Clover Castle, he took over David's (Baval) body. (Those who harbor malice, like elves driven by revenge, are easy to take over.) At the House of Vermillion, when David faced off against Mimosa, Kirsch and En, he'd already been taken over and that was the word soul devil acting like him. (He used his Word Soul Magic to re-create the Dice Magic.) After that, he infiltrated the Shadow Palace, went to the upper right-hand room where Ronne had been stationed and jumped from David's body into Ronne's. He then went to join the others in the room where he used Yuno's magic stone pendant to manifest. And that's about the size of it. Apologies for the long response!!!

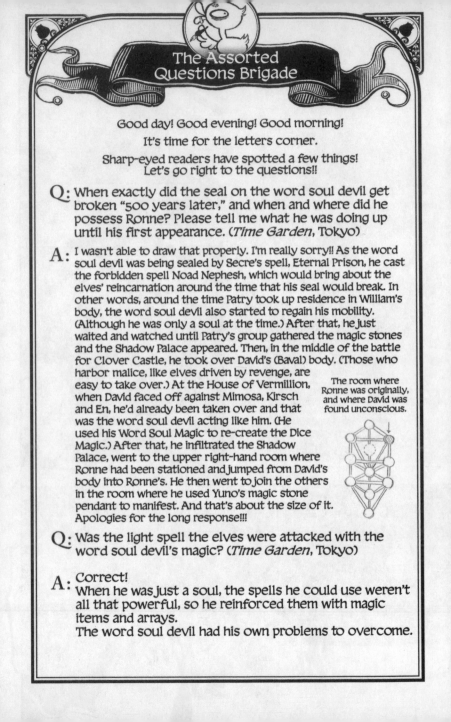

The room where Ronne was originally, and where David was found unconscious.

Q: Was the light spell the elves were attacked with the word soul devil's magic? (*Time Garden*, Tokyo)

A: Correct!
When he was just a soul, the spells he could use weren't all that powerful, so he reinforced them with magic items and arrays.
The word soul devil had his own problems to overcome.

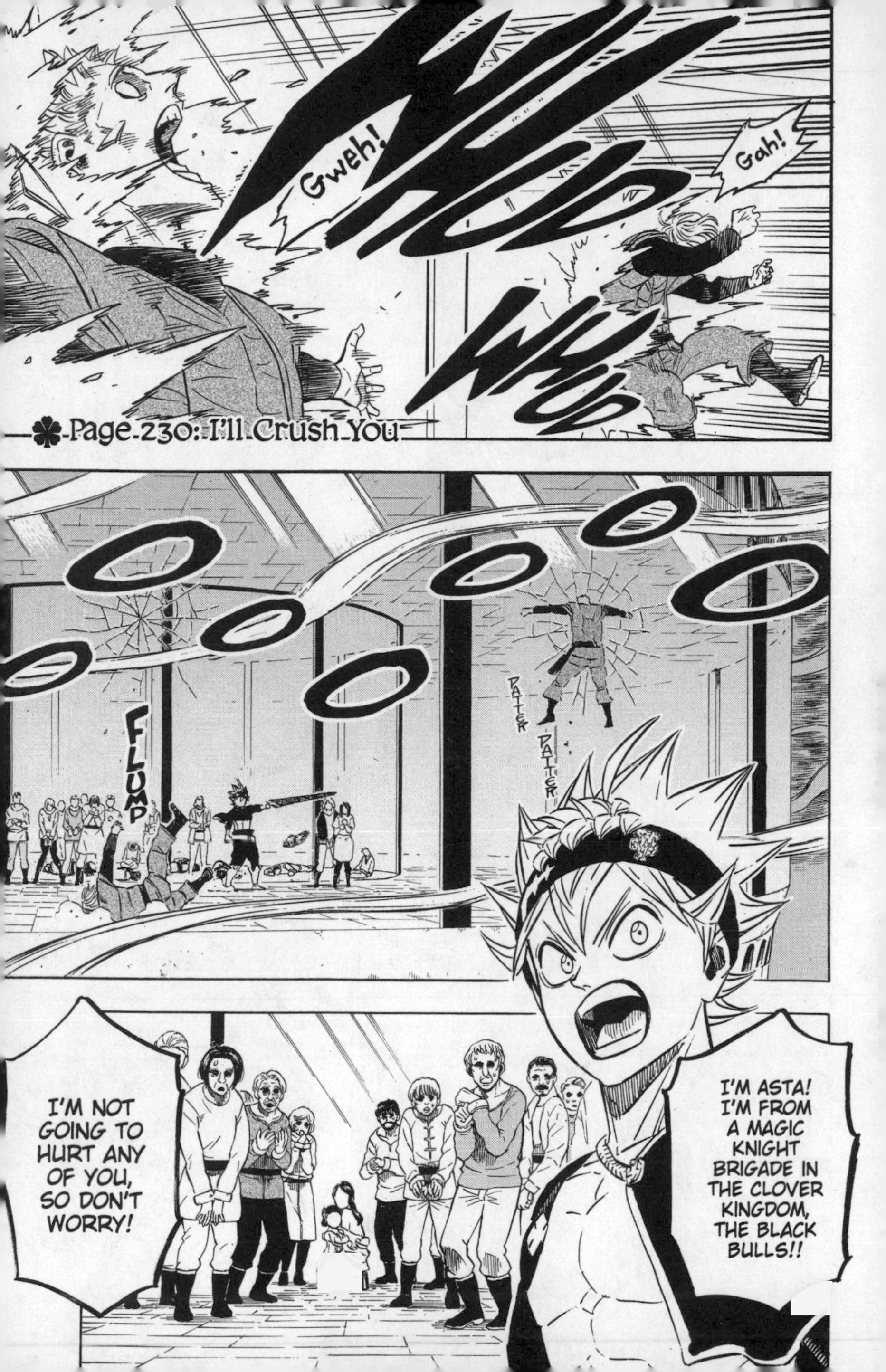
Gah!
Gweh!
Page 230: I'll Crush You
PATTER
PATTER
FLUMP
I'M ASTA! I'M FROM A MAGIC KNIGHT BRIGADE IN THE CLOVER KINGDOM, THE BLACK BULLS!!
I'M NOT GOING TO HURT ANY OF YOU, SO DON'T WORRY!

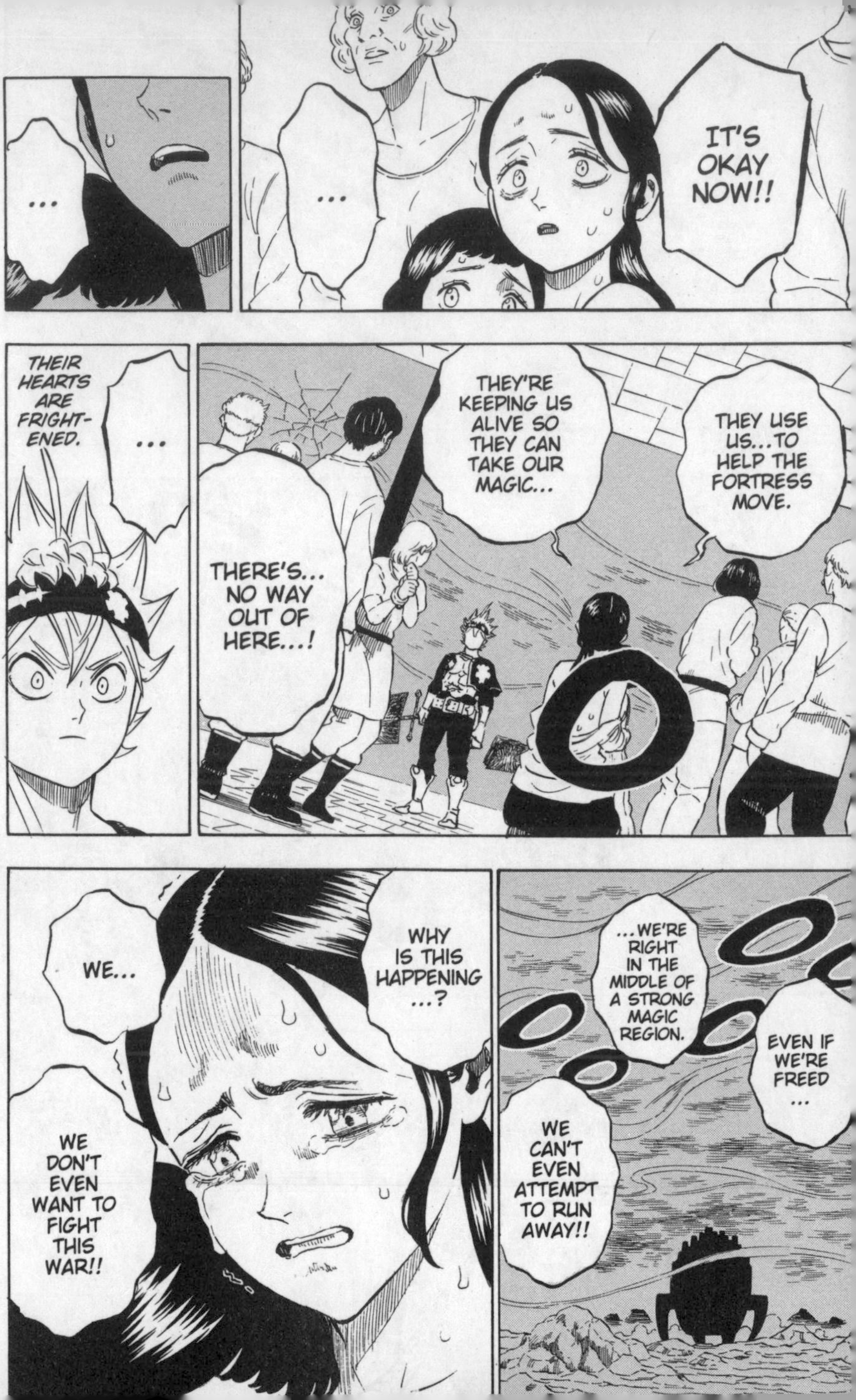
IT'S OKAY NOW!!
...
...
THEY USE US...TO HELP THE FORTRESS MOVE.
THEY'RE KEEPING US ALIVE SO THEY CAN TAKE OUR MAGIC...
THERE'S... NO WAY OUT OF HERE...!
...
THEIR HEARTS ARE FRIGHT-ENED.
...WE'RE RIGHT IN THE MIDDLE OF A STRONG MAGIC REGION.
EVEN IF WE'RE FREED...
WE CAN'T EVEN ATTEMPT TO RUN AWAY!!
WHY IS THIS HAPPENING...?
WE...
WE DON'T EVEN WANT TO FIGHT THIS WAR!!

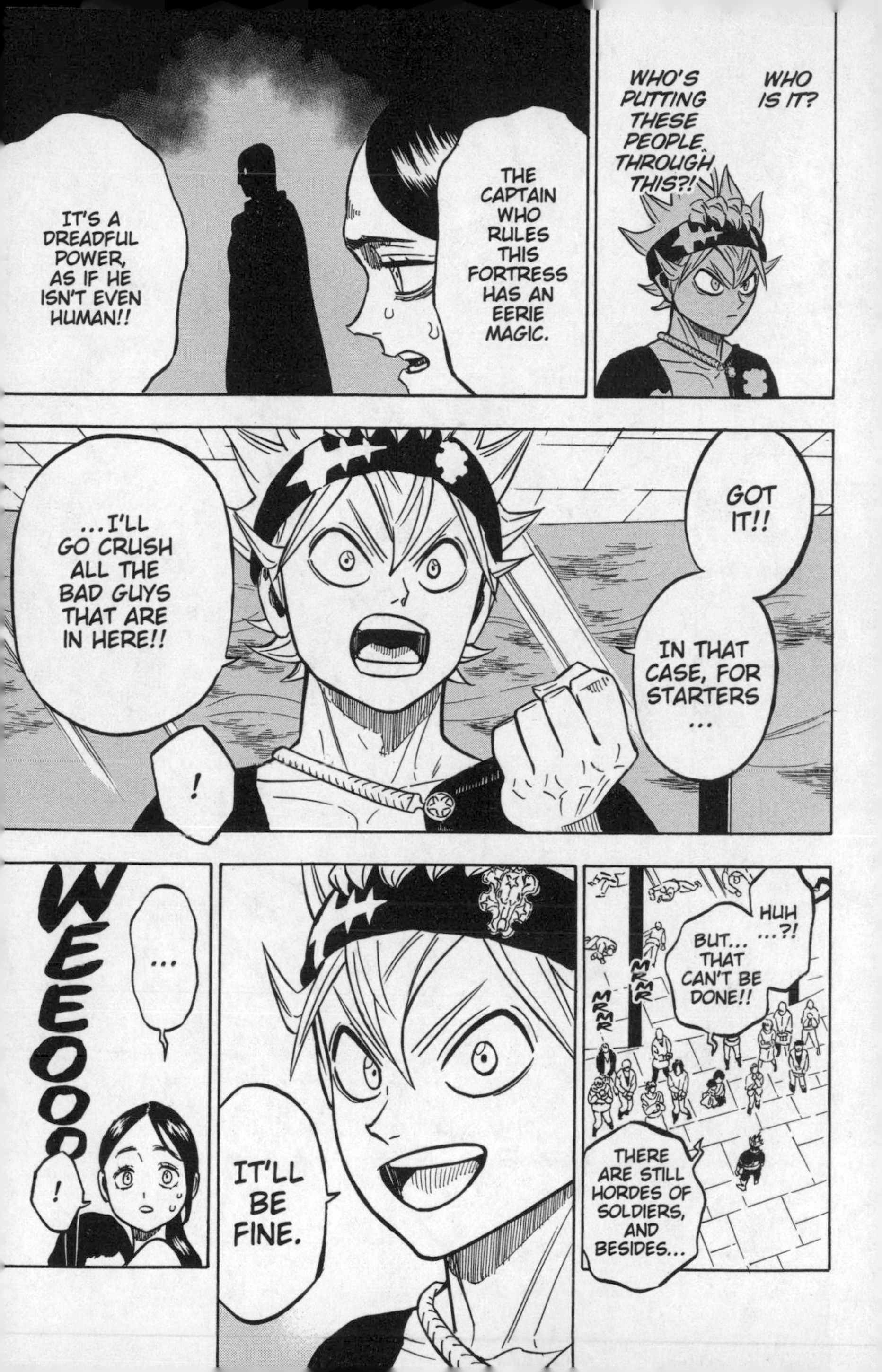
WHO IS IT?
WHO'S PUTTING THESE PEOPLE THROUGH THIS?!
THE CAPTAIN WHO RULES THIS FORTRESS HAS AN EERIE MAGIC.
IT'S A DREADFUL POWER, AS IF HE ISN'T EVEN HUMAN!!
GOT IT!!
IN THAT CASE, FOR STARTERS ...
...I'LL GO CRUSH ALL THE BAD GUYS THAT ARE IN HERE!!
!
HUH ...?!
BUT... THAT CAN'T BE DONE!!
MRMR
MRMR
THERE ARE STILL HORDES OF SOLDIERS, AND BESIDES...
IT'LL BE FINE.
WEEOOO
...
!

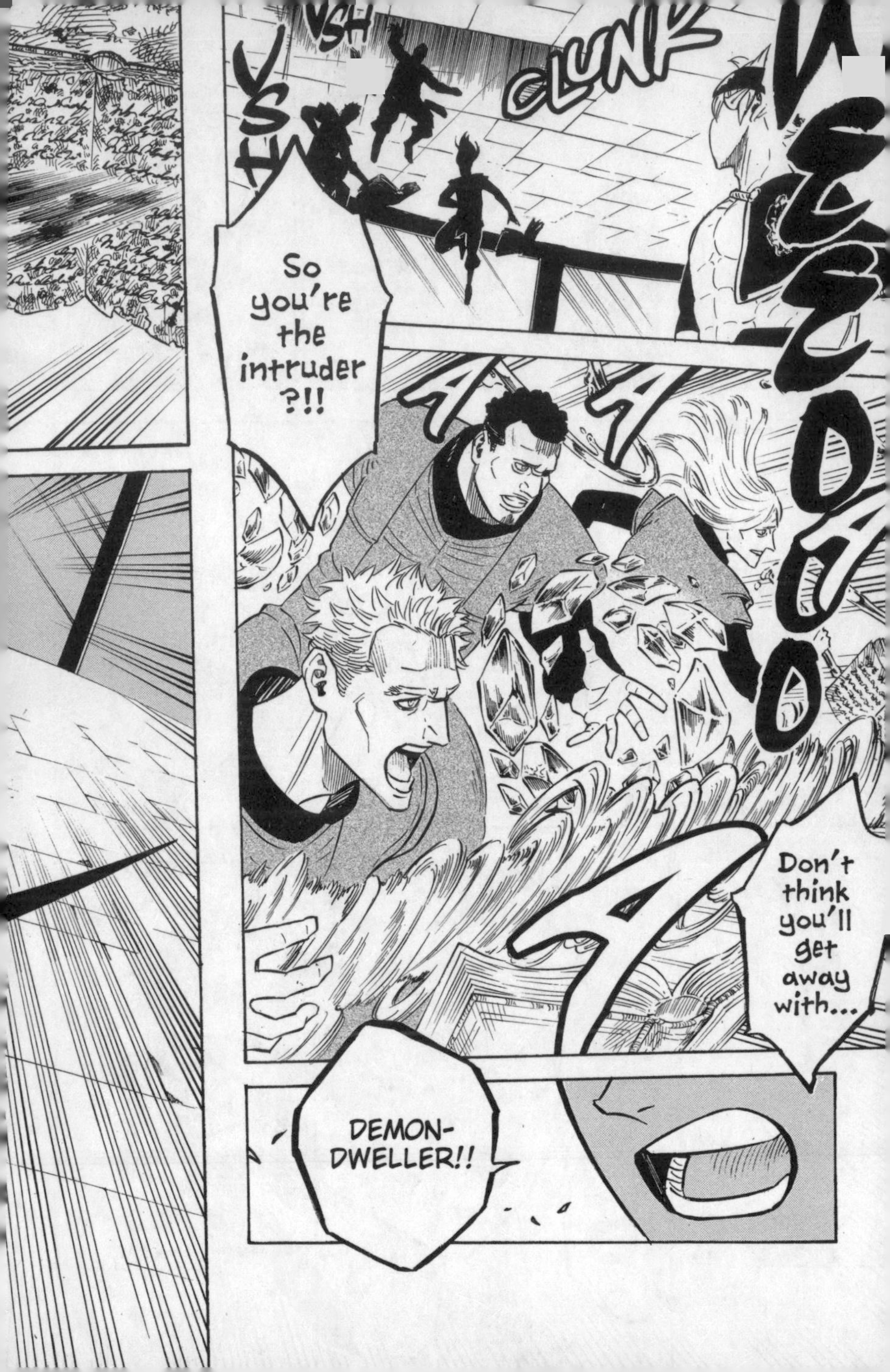
VSH
VSH
CLUNK
So you're the intruder?!!
Don't think you'll get away with...
DEMON-DWELLER!!

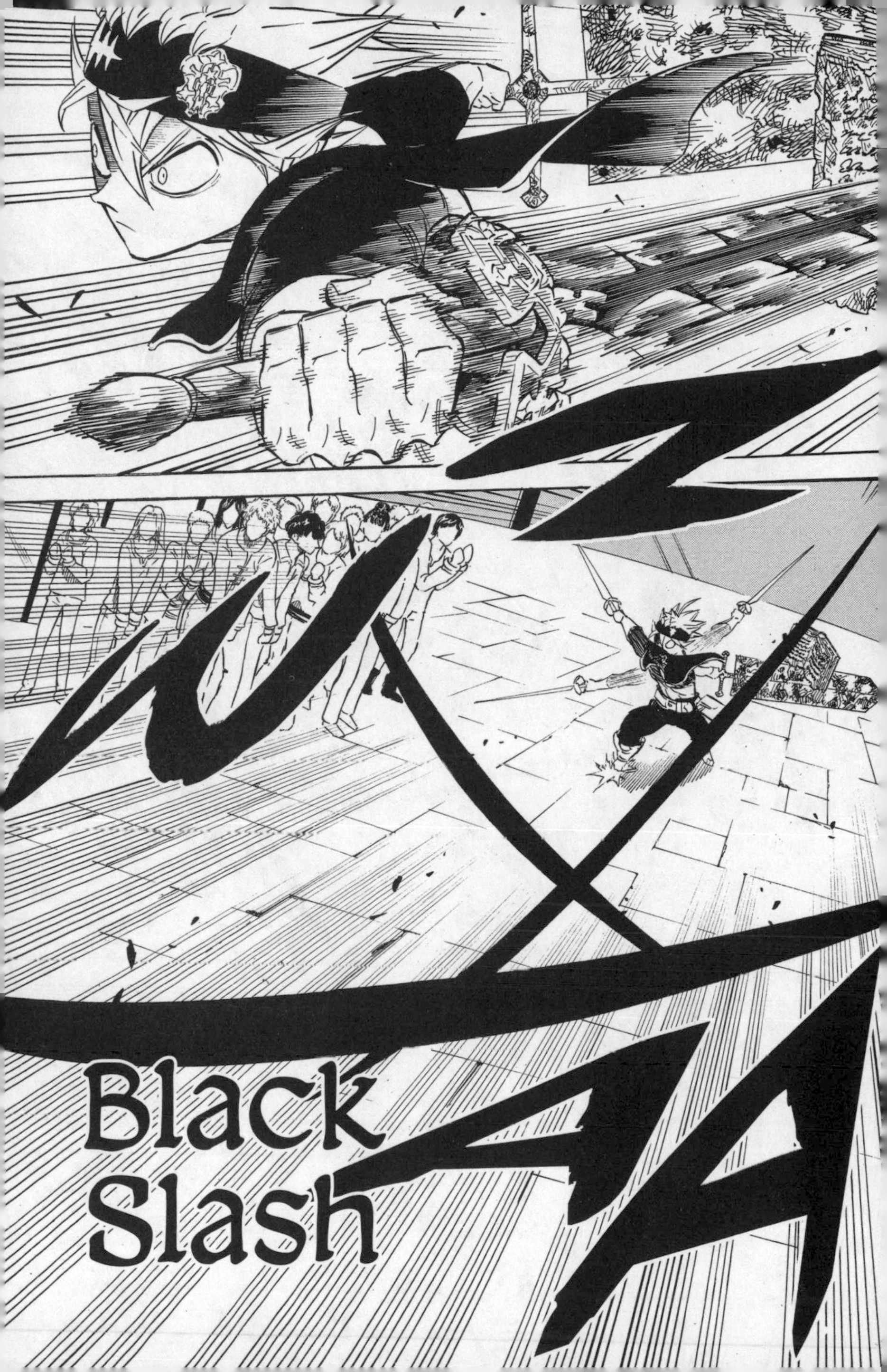
Black Slash

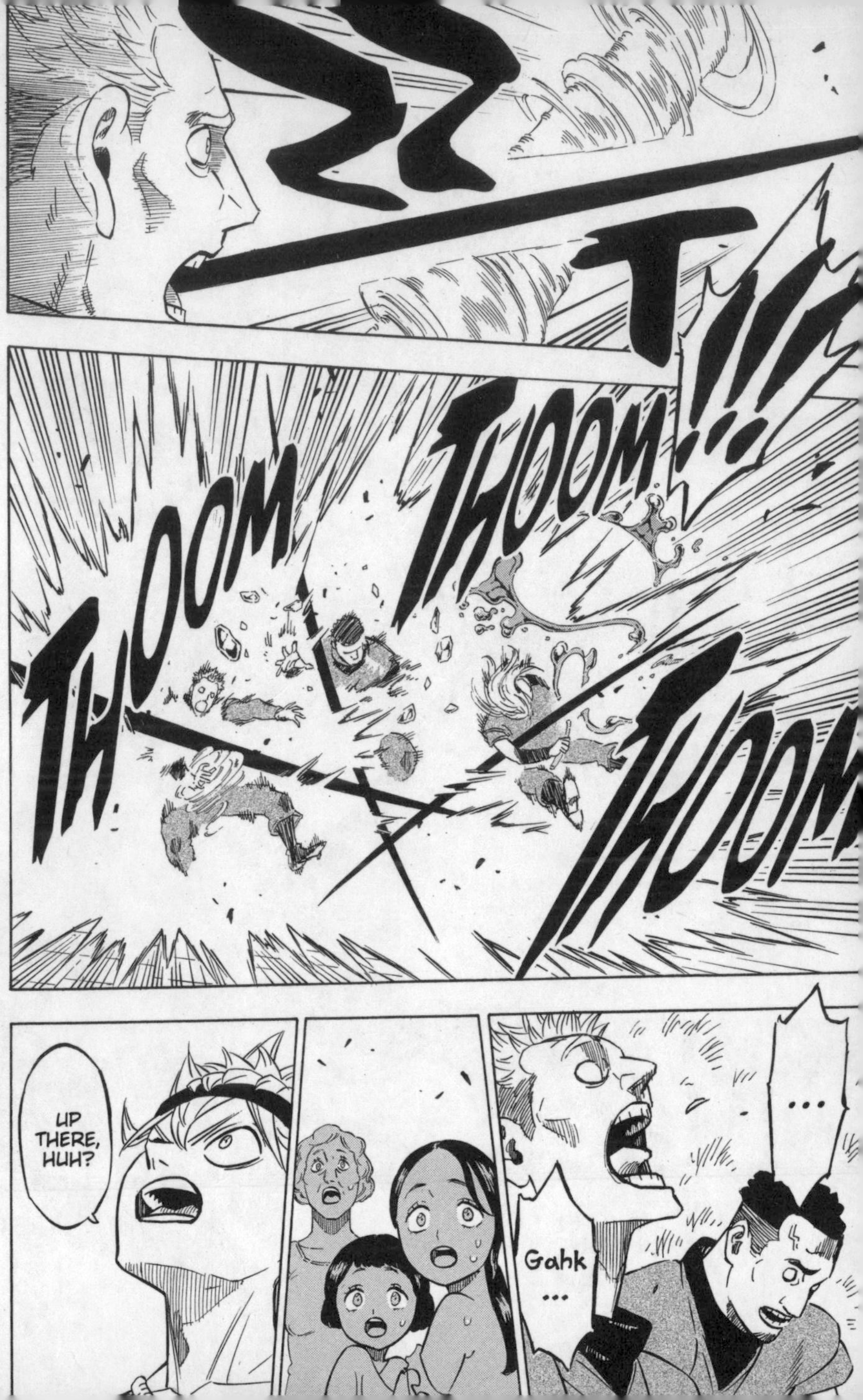
THOOM!!!
THOOM
THOOM
...
Gahk ...
UP THERE, HUH?

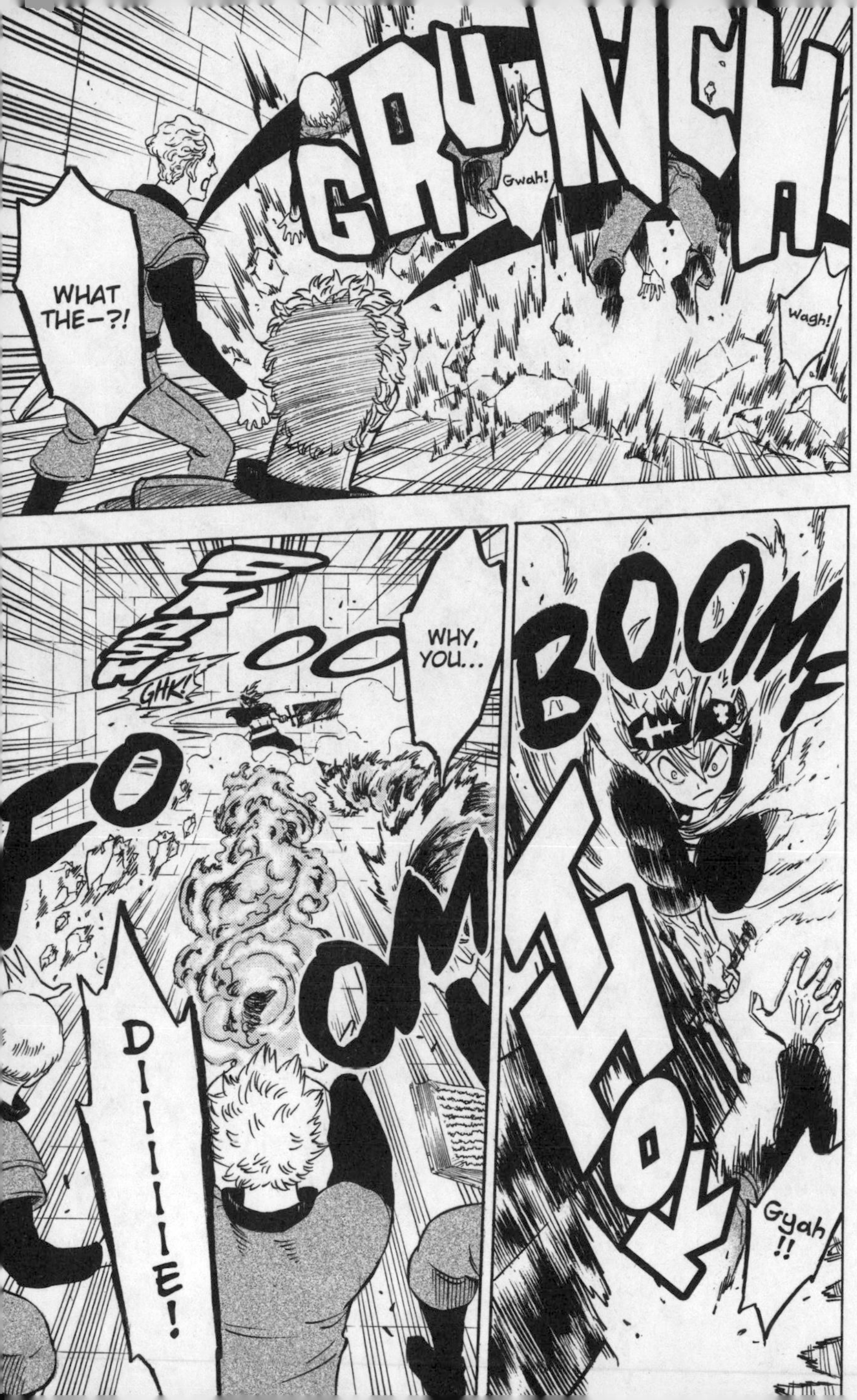
Wagh!
GRUNCH
Gwah!
WHAT THE–?!
BOOM
Gyah!!
WHY, YOU...
GHK!
DIIIIIE!

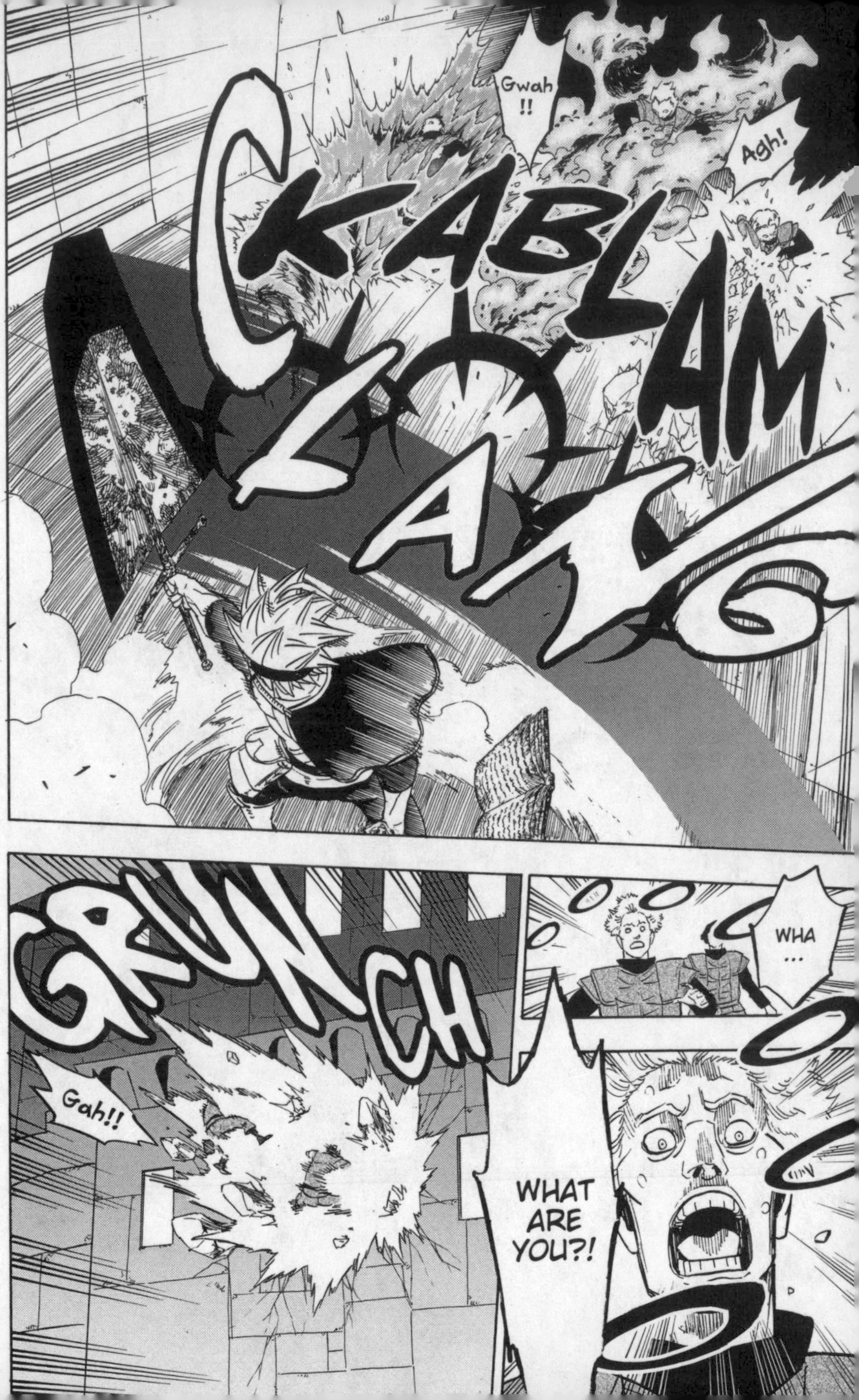
Gwah!!
Agh!
WHA ...
WHAT ARE YOU?!
CRUNCH
Gah!!

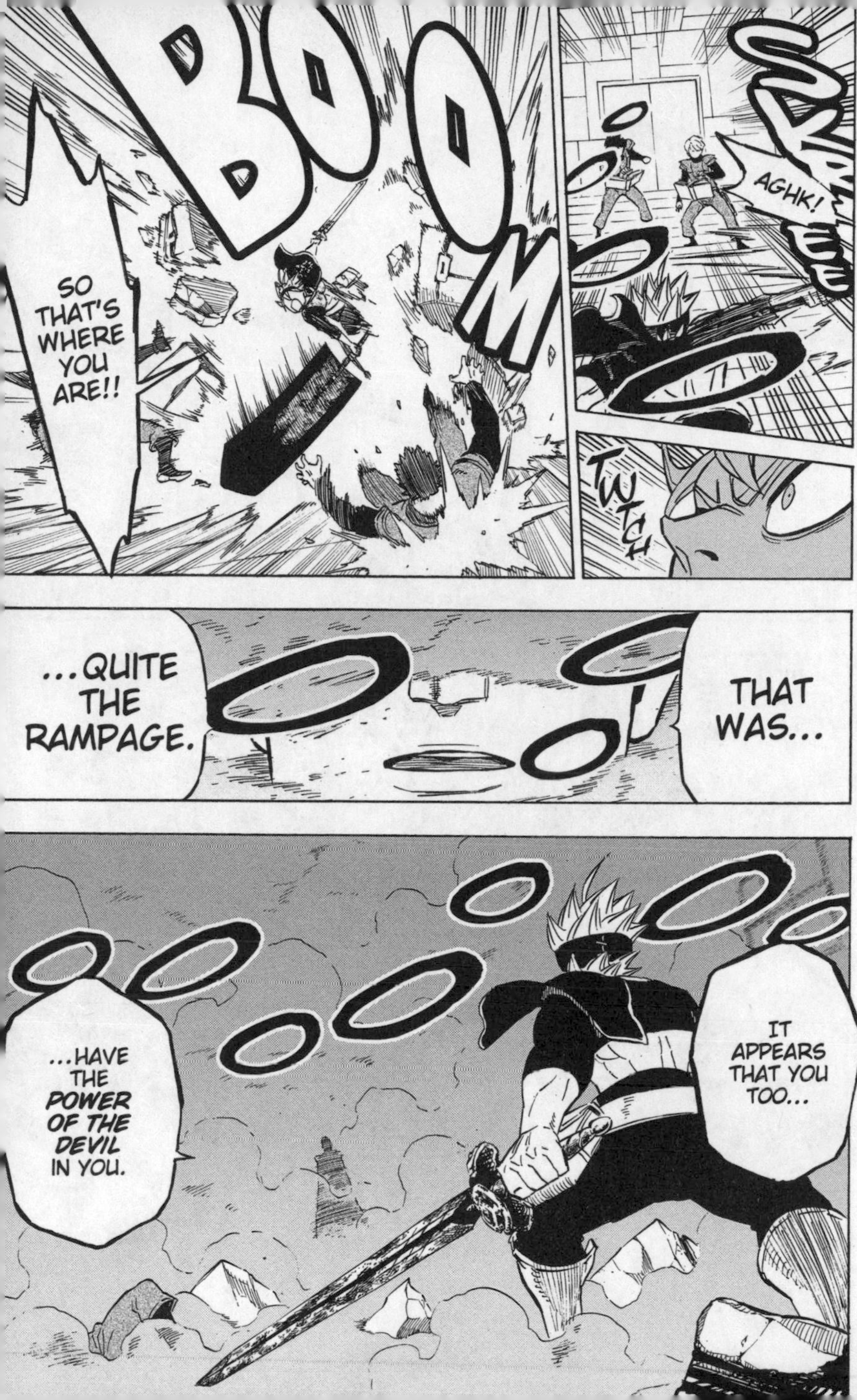
AGHK!
TWITCH
BOOM
SO THAT'S WHERE YOU ARE!!
THAT WAS...
...QUITE THE RAMPAGE.
IT APPEARS THAT YOU TOO...
...HAVE THE *POWER OF THE DEVIL* IN YOU.

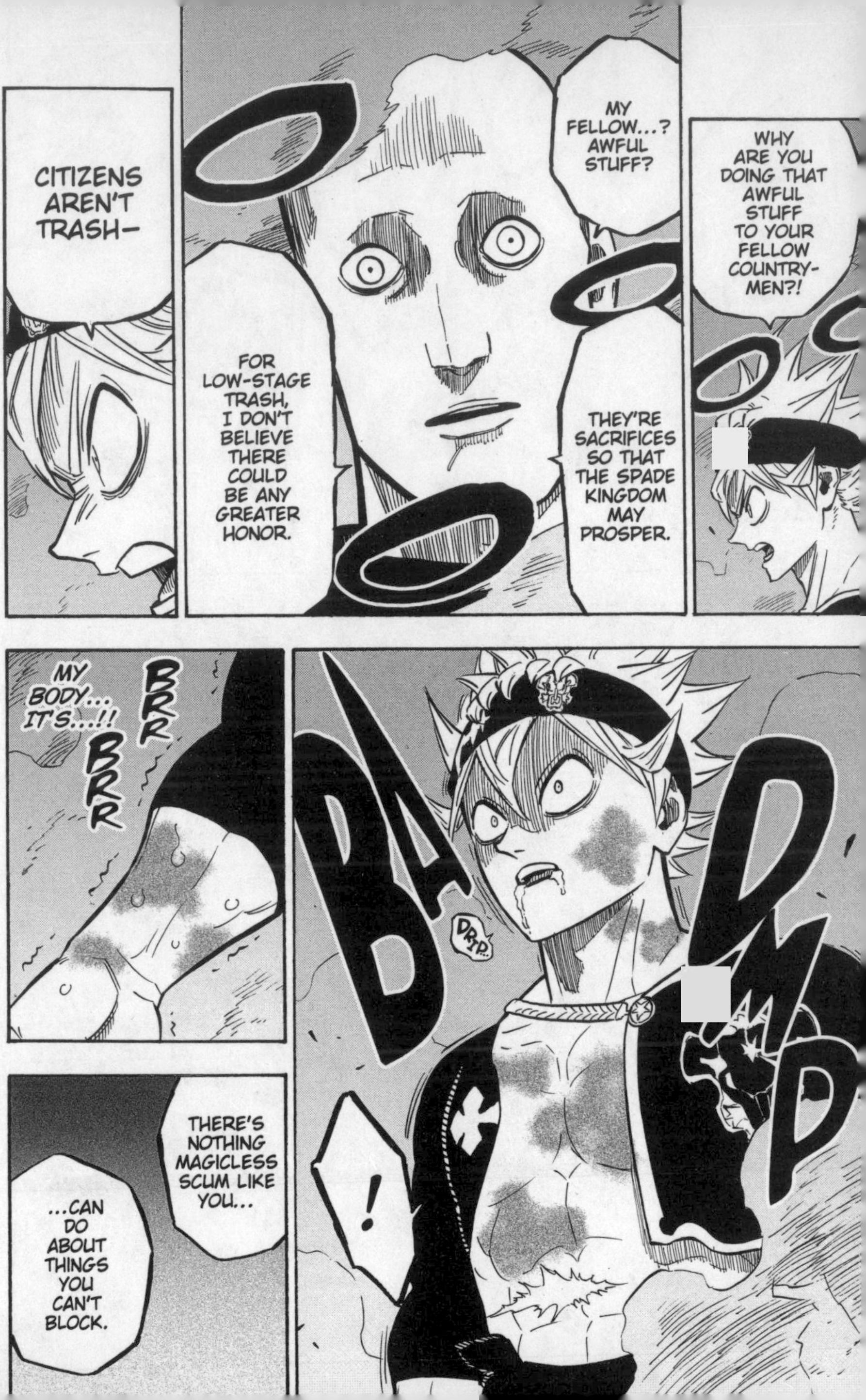
WHY ARE YOU DOING THAT AWFUL STUFF TO YOUR FELLOW COUNTRYMEN?!
MY FELLOW...? AWFUL STUFF?
THEY'RE SACRIFICES SO THAT THE SPADE KINGDOM MAY PROSPER.
FOR LOW-STAGE TRASH, I DON'T BELIEVE THERE COULD BE ANY GREATER HONOR.
CITIZENS AREN'T TRASH—
BA DMP
DRIP...
!
MY BODY... IT'S...!!
BRRR
BRRR
THERE'S NOTHING MAGICLESS SCUM LIKE YOU...
...CAN DO ABOUT THINGS YOU CAN'T BLOCK.

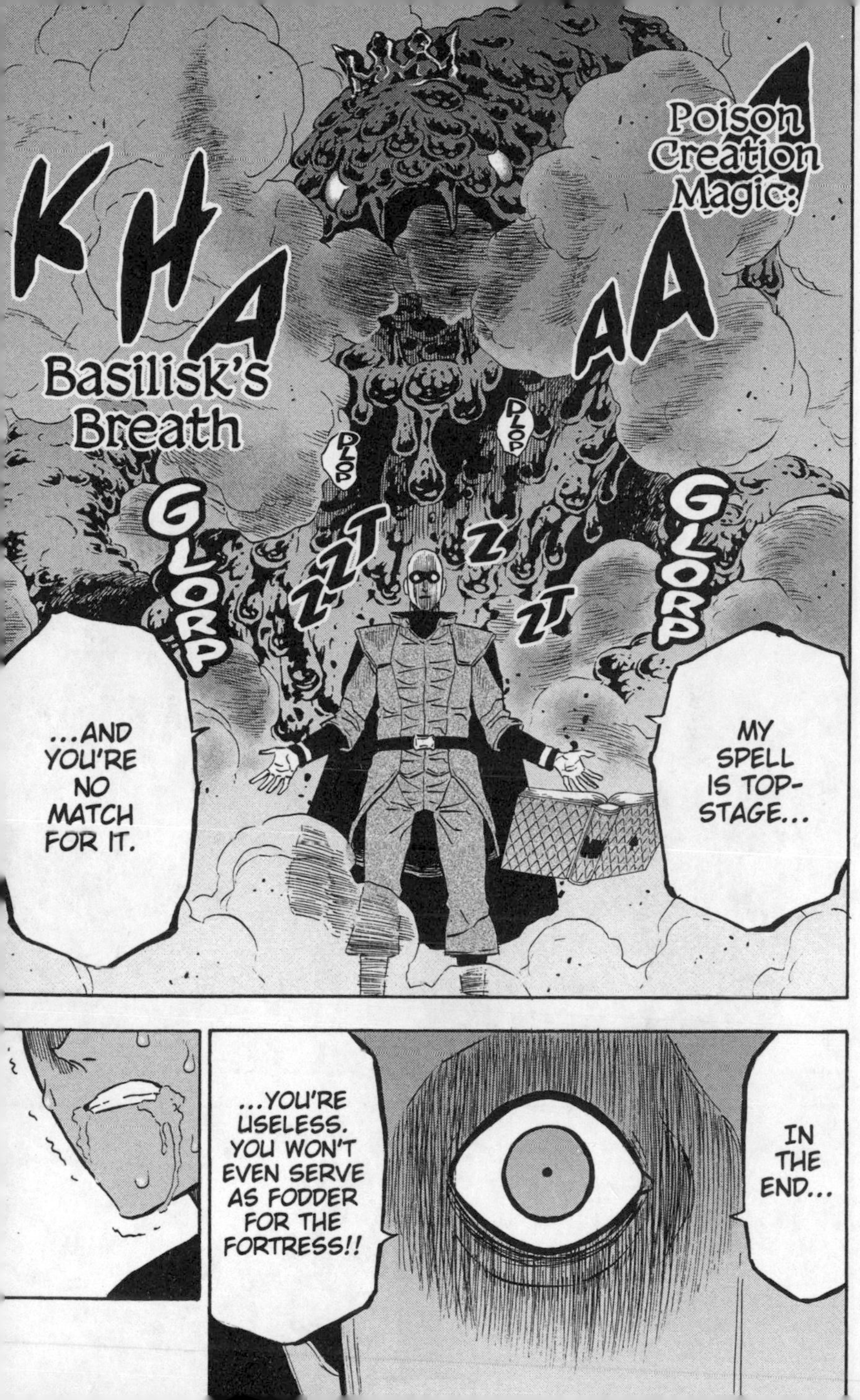
Poison Creation Magic:
KHAAA
Basilisk's Breath
DLOP
DLOP
GLORP
ZZZT
ZZT
GLORP
MY SPELL IS TOP-STAGE...
...AND YOU'RE NO MATCH FOR IT.
IN THE END...
...YOU'RE USELESS. YOU WON'T EVEN SERVE AS FODDER FOR THE FORTRESS!!

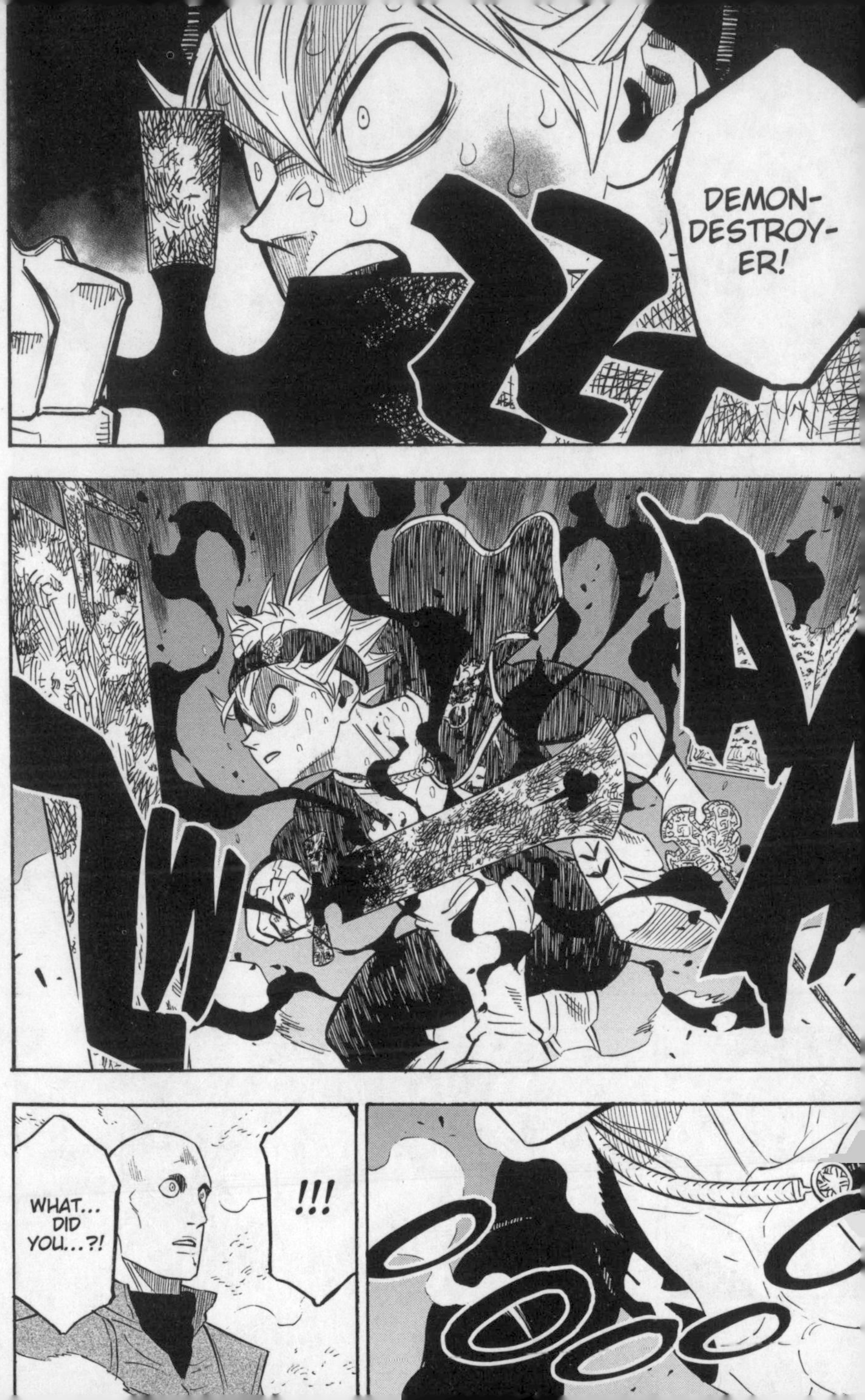
DEMON-
DESTROY-
ER!
!!!
WHAT...
DID
YOU...?!

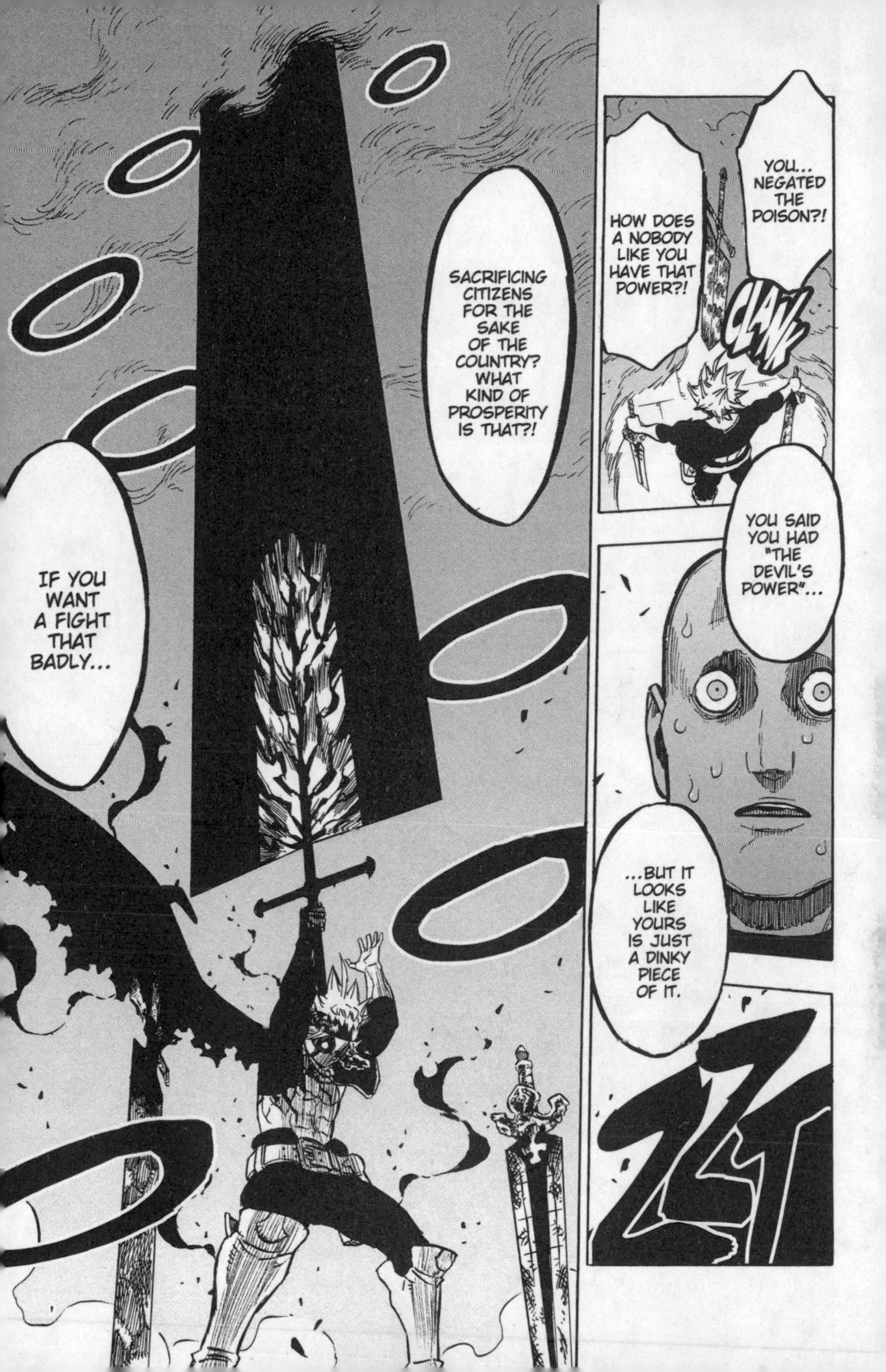
YOU... NEGATED THE POISON?!
HOW DOES A NOBODY LIKE YOU HAVE THAT POWER?!
CLANK
YOU SAID YOU HAD "THE DEVIL'S POWER"...
...BUT IT LOOKS LIKE YOURS IS JUST A DINKY PIECE OF IT.
ZZT
SACRIFICING CITIZENS FOR THE SAKE OF THE COUNTRY? WHAT KIND OF PROSPERITY IS THAT?!
IF YOU WANT A FIGHT THAT BADLY...

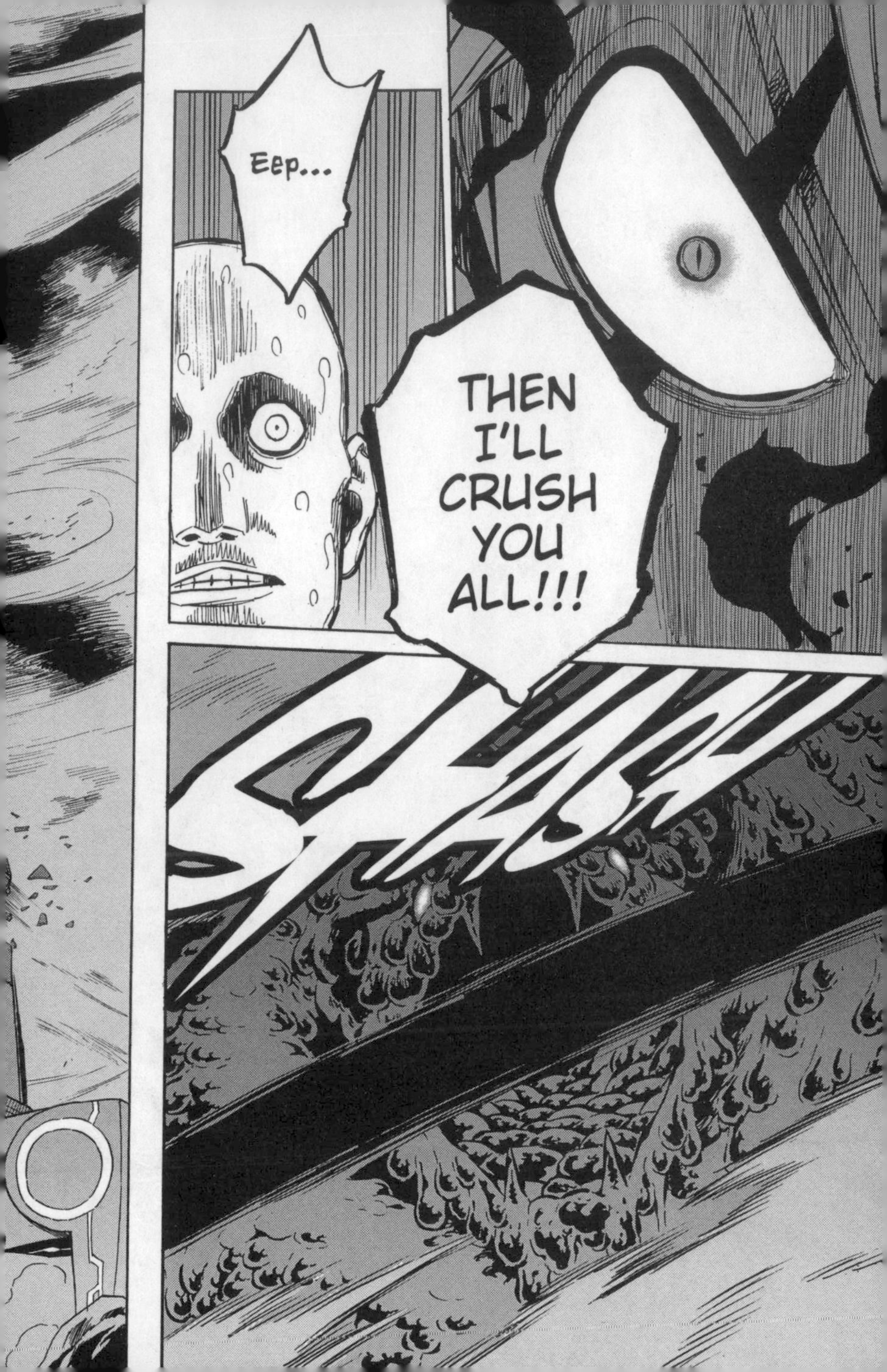
Eep...
THEN I'LL CRUSH YOU ALL!!!
SHAA

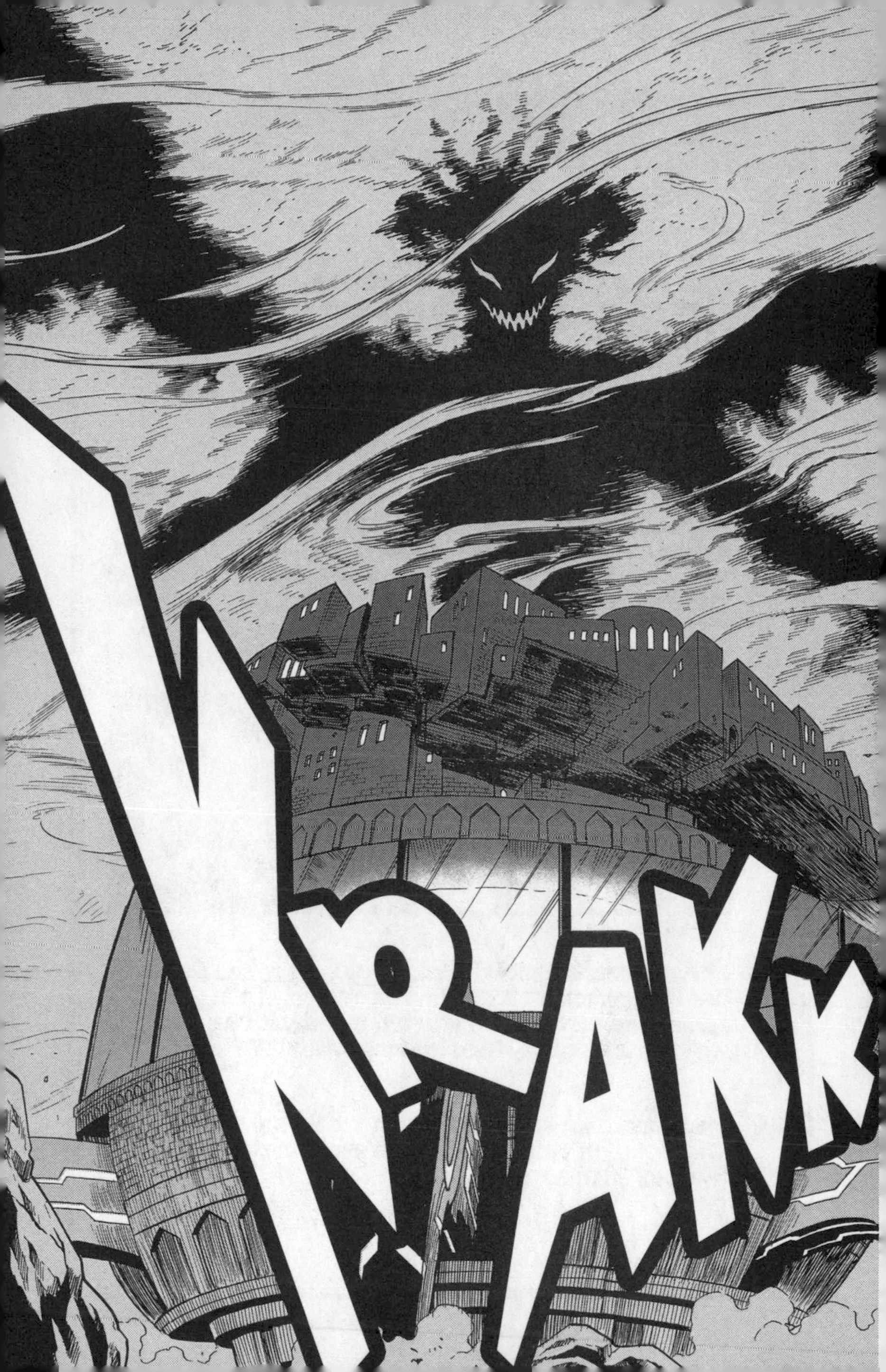
KRAKK

The Assorted Questions Brigade No. 2

Q: Kirsch said the amount of magic power a person has is determined from birth and doesn't change, but Theresa said that the power to work with the mana that dwells in nature can be increased at any age. What's the difference? (*Time Garden*, Tokyo)

A: What Kirsch is talking about is individuals' innate magic. When Theresa talked about the power to work with the mana that dwells in nature, she meant that, when casting a spell, in addition to their own magic, the caster takes magic from the natural world around them~like air, fire, water, earth, plants, etc.~and uses it to augment what they have. For an ordinary person, it doesn't make that big a difference, but for someone who's worked with natural mana for long years, the way Theresa has, it can be a pretty decent boost. The elves and the people of the Heart Kingdom are particularly good at this, and depending on the individual, the boost it provides can be enormous.

FWASH
KRAK DOOO

THEIR INTERNAL MANA WAS PHENOMENAL, AND THEIR CONTROL OF NATURAL MANA WAS IN A WHOLE DIFFERENT LEAGUE...
"LOVED BY MANA," HUH...? HAW HAW! THEY'LL BE WORTH SLICING UP!!

THAT'S ENOUGH OF THAT!
FOOOM
I WON'T GIVE YOU THIS BOY!!

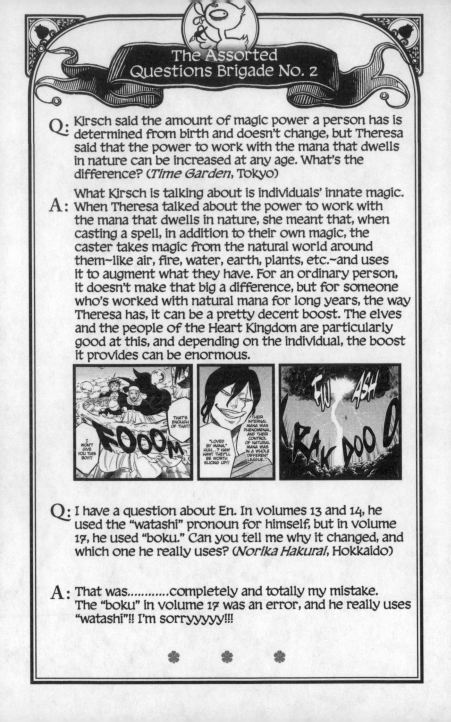

Q: I have a question about En. In volumes 13 and 14, he used the "watashi" pronoun for himself, but in volume 17, he used "boku." Can you tell me why it changed, and which one he really uses? (*Norika Hakurai*, Hokkaido)

A: That was............completely and totally my mistake. The "boku" in volume 17 was an error, and he really uses "watashi"!! I'm sorryyyyy!!!

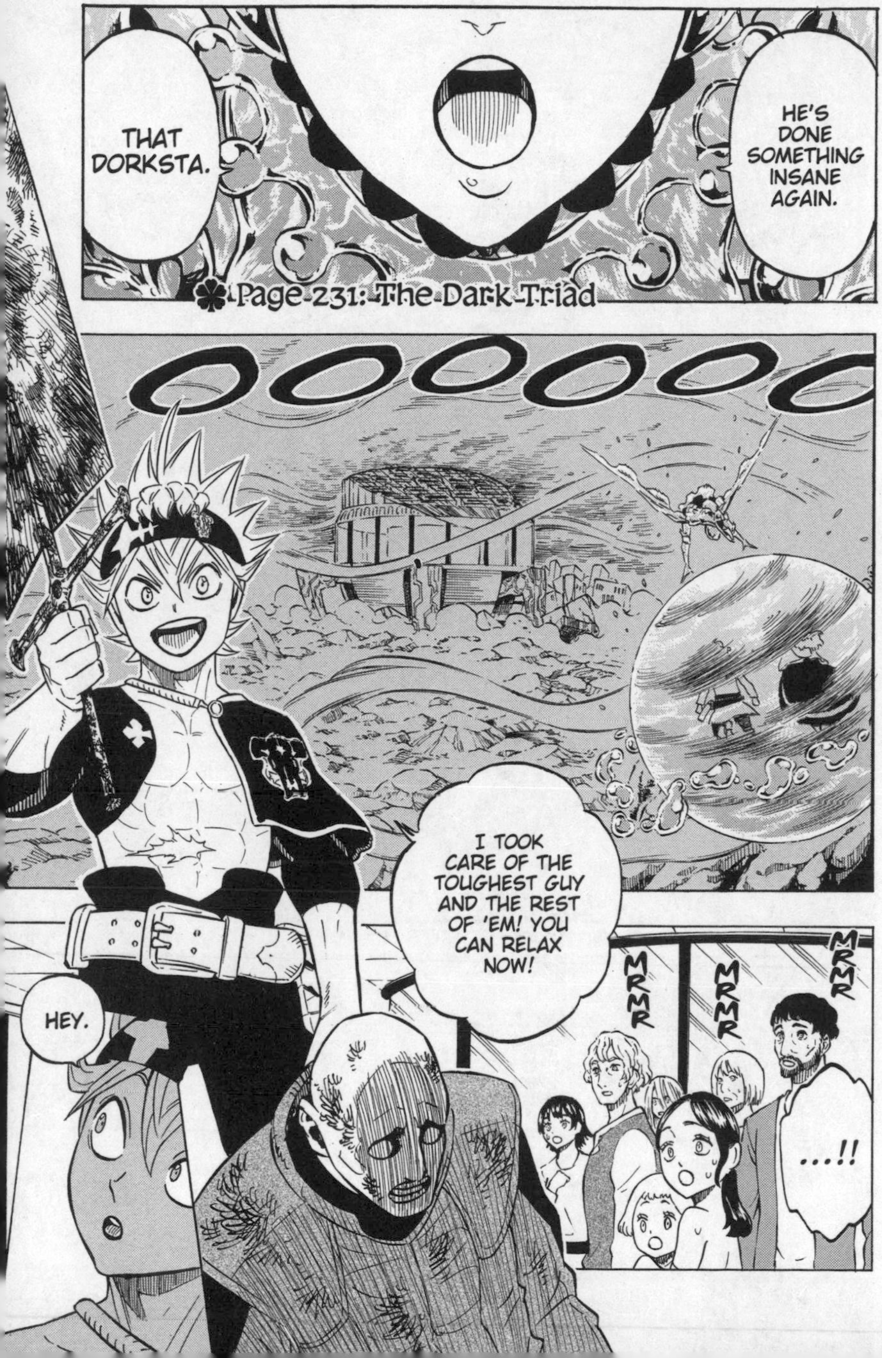
HE'S DONE SOMETHING INSANE AGAIN.
THAT DORKSTA.
Page 231: The Dark Triad
OOOOOO
MRMR
MRMR
MRMR
...!!
I TOOK CARE OF THE TOUGHEST GUY AND THE REST OF 'EM! YOU CAN RELAX NOW!
HEY.

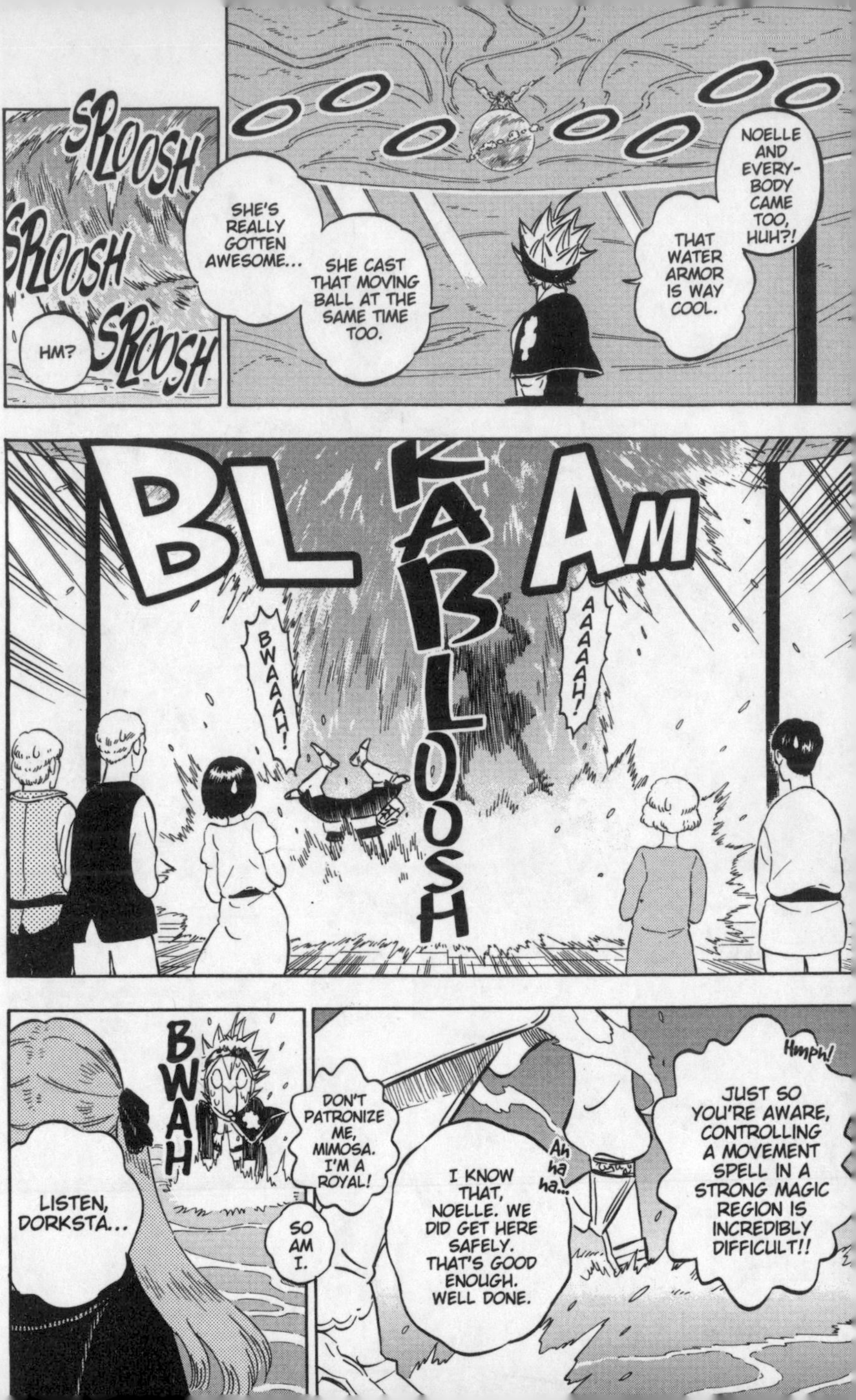
OOOOOOOOO
NOELLE AND EVERYBODY CAME TOO, HUH?!
THAT WATER ARMOR IS WAY COOL.
SHE CAST THAT MOVING BALL AT THE SAME TIME TOO.
SHE'S REALLY GOTTEN AWESOME...
SPLOOSH
SPLOOSH
SPLOOSH
HM?
BLAM
KABLOOOOSH
AAAAAH!
BWAAAAH!
Humph!
JUST SO YOU'RE AWARE, CONTROLLING A MOVEMENT SPELL IN A STRONG MAGIC REGION IS INCREDIBLY DIFFICULT!!
Ah ha ha...
I KNOW THAT, NOELLE. WE DID GET HERE SAFELY. THAT'S GOOD ENOUGH. WELL DONE.
DON'T PATRONIZE ME, MIMOSA. I'M A ROYAL!
SO AM I.
BWAH
LISTEN, DORKSTA...

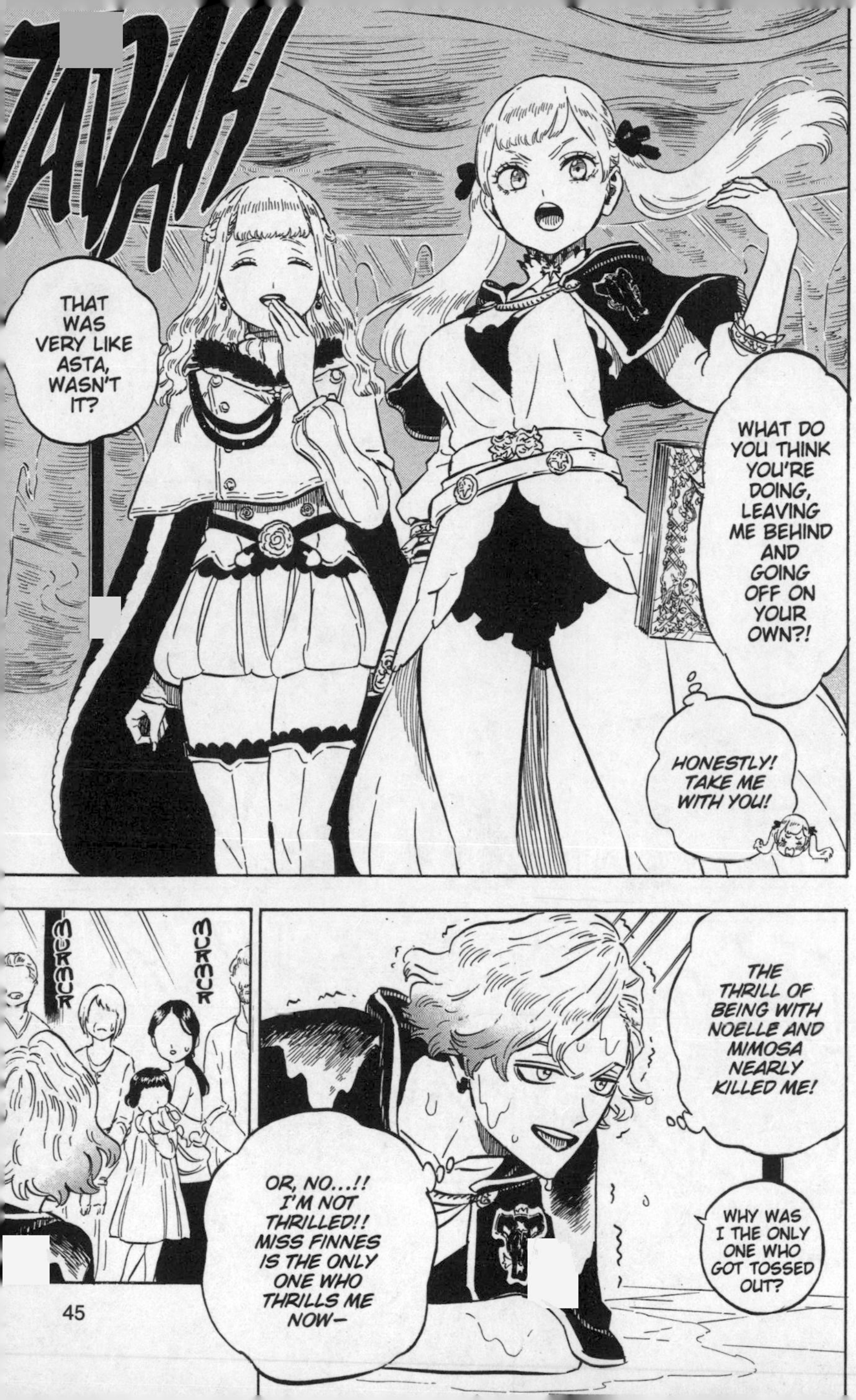
WHAT DO YOU THINK YOU'RE DOING, LEAVING ME BEHIND AND GOING OFF ON YOUR OWN?!
HONESTLY! TAKE ME WITH YOU!
THAT WAS VERY LIKE ASTA, WASN'T IT?
THE THRILL OF BEING WITH NOELLE AND MIMOSA NEARLY KILLED ME!
WHY WAS I THE ONLY ONE WHO GOT TOSSED OUT?
OR, NO...!! I'M NOT THRILLED!! MISS FINNES IS THE ONLY ONE WHO THRILLS ME NOW–
MURMUR
MURMUR

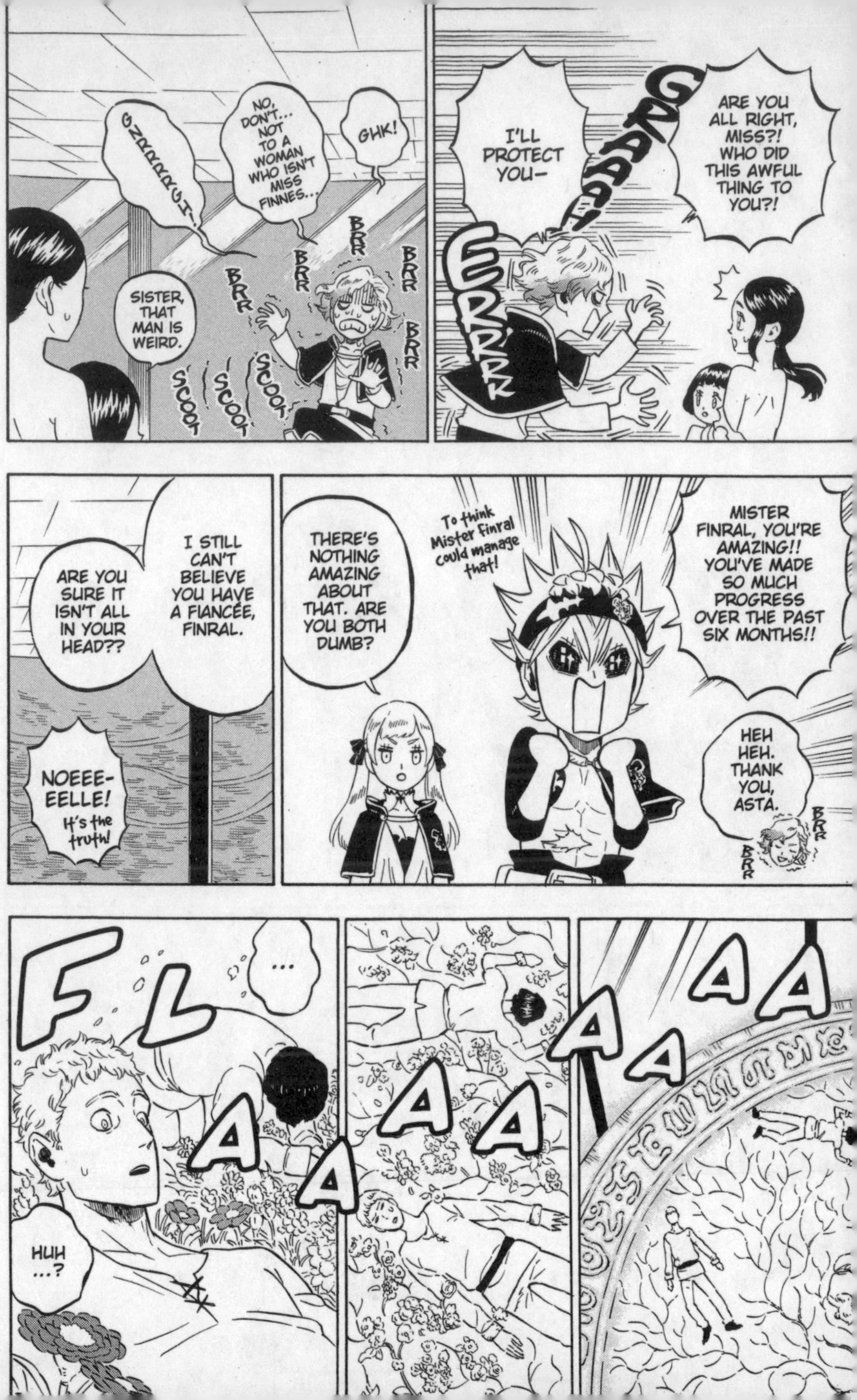
ARE YOU ALL RIGHT, MISS?! WHO DID THIS AWFUL THING TO YOU?!
GAAAAH!
I'LL PROTECT YOU-
ERRRR
GHK!
NO, DON'T... NOT TO A WOMAN WHO ISN'T MISS FINNES...
GNRRRRGI!!
BRR BRR BRR BRR BRR
SISTER, THAT MAN IS WEIRD.
SCOOT SCOOT SCOOT
MISTER FINRAL, YOU'RE AMAZING!! YOU'VE MADE SO MUCH PROGRESS OVER THE PAST SIX MONTHS!!
To think Mister Finral could manage that!
HEH HEH. THANK YOU, ASTA.
BRR BRR
THERE'S NOTHING AMAZING ABOUT THAT. ARE YOU BOTH DUMB?
I STILL CAN'T BELIEVE YOU HAVE A FIANCÉE, FINRAL.
ARE YOU SURE IT ISN'T ALL IN YOUR HEAD??
NOEEE-EELLE! It's the truth!
AAAAAA
FLAAAA
...
HUH ...?

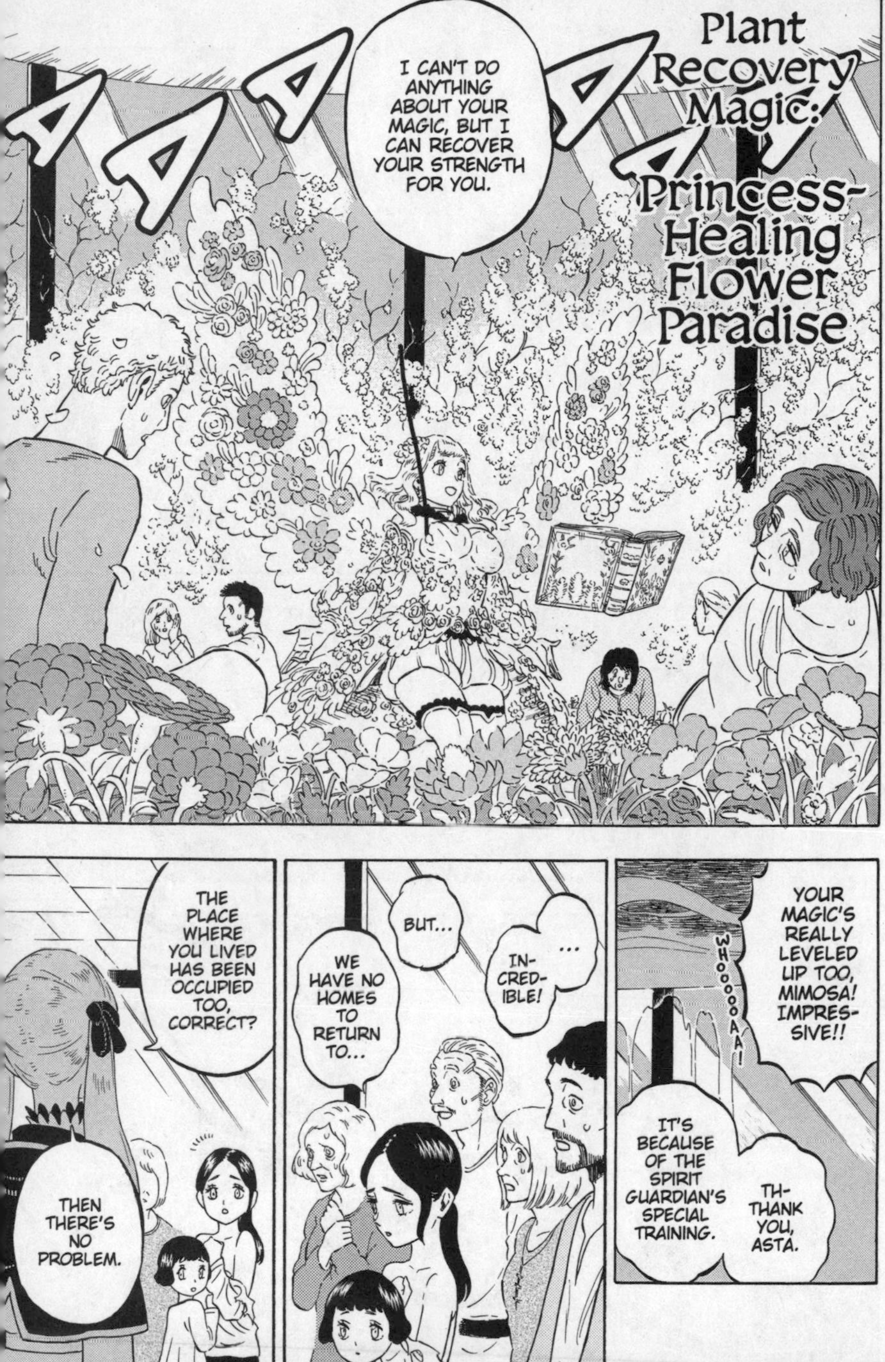
AAAAAA
I CAN'T DO ANYTHING ABOUT YOUR MAGIC, BUT I CAN RECOVER YOUR STRENGTH FOR YOU.
Plant Recovery Magic: Princess-Healing Flower Paradise
YOUR MAGIC'S REALLY LEVELED UP TOO, MIMOSA! IMPRESSIVE!!
WHOOOOOAA!
TH-THANK YOU, ASTA.
IT'S BECAUSE OF THE SPIRIT GUARDIAN'S SPECIAL TRAINING.
...
IN-CREDIBLE!
BUT...
WE HAVE NO HOMES TO RETURN TO...
THE PLACE WHERE YOU LIVED HAS BEEN OCCUPIED TOO, CORRECT?
THEN THERE'S NO PROBLEM.

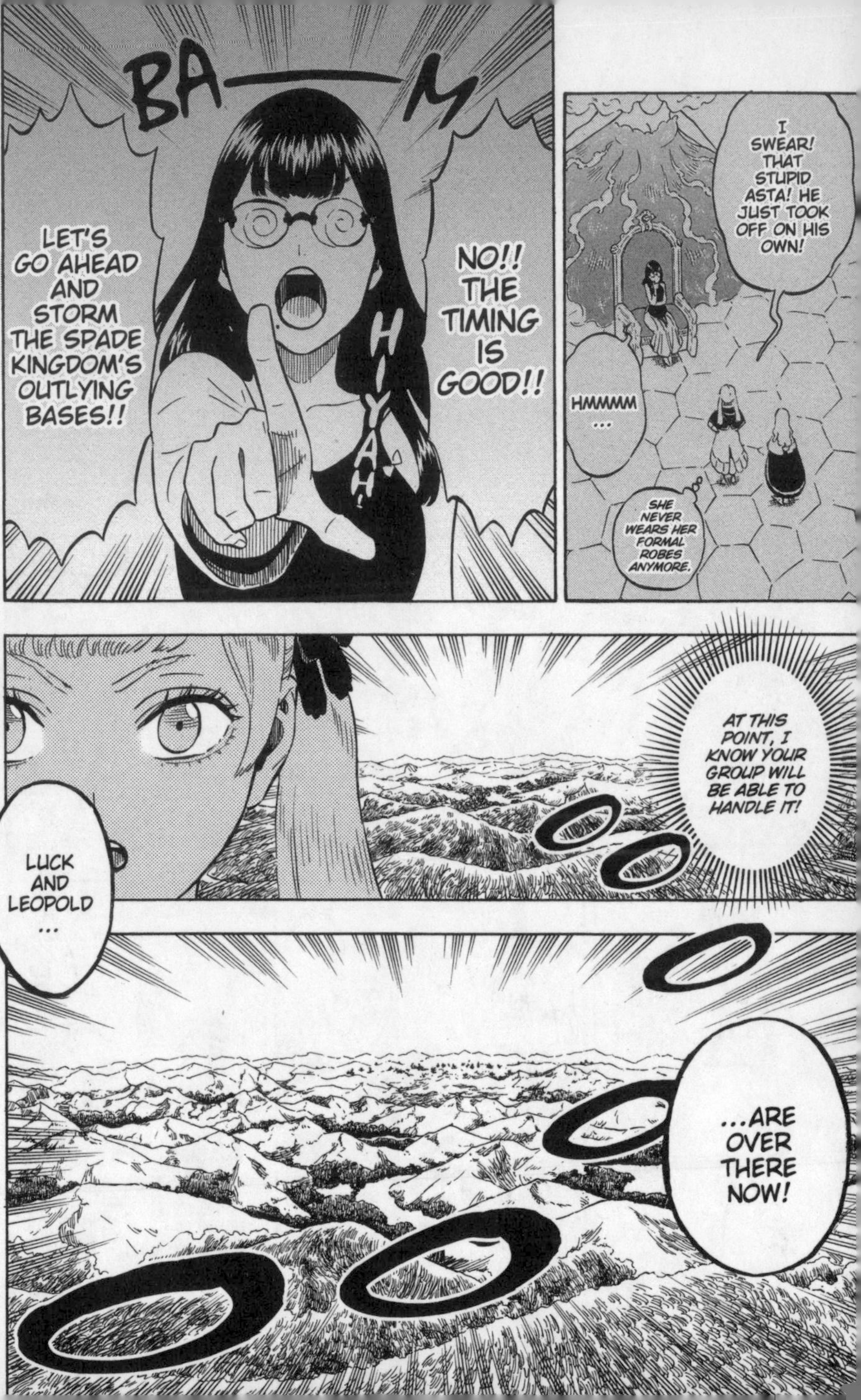
I SWEAR! THAT STUPID ASTA! HE JUST TOOK OFF ON HIS OWN!
HMMMM ...
SHE NEVER WEARS HER FORMAL ROBES ANYMORE.
BA——M
NO!! THE TIMING IS GOOD!!
HIYAH!
LET'S GO AHEAD AND STORM THE SPADE KINGDOM'S OUTLYING BASES!!
AT THIS POINT, I KNOW YOUR GROUP WILL BE ABLE TO HANDLE IT!
LUCK AND LEOPOLD ...
...ARE OVER THERE NOW!

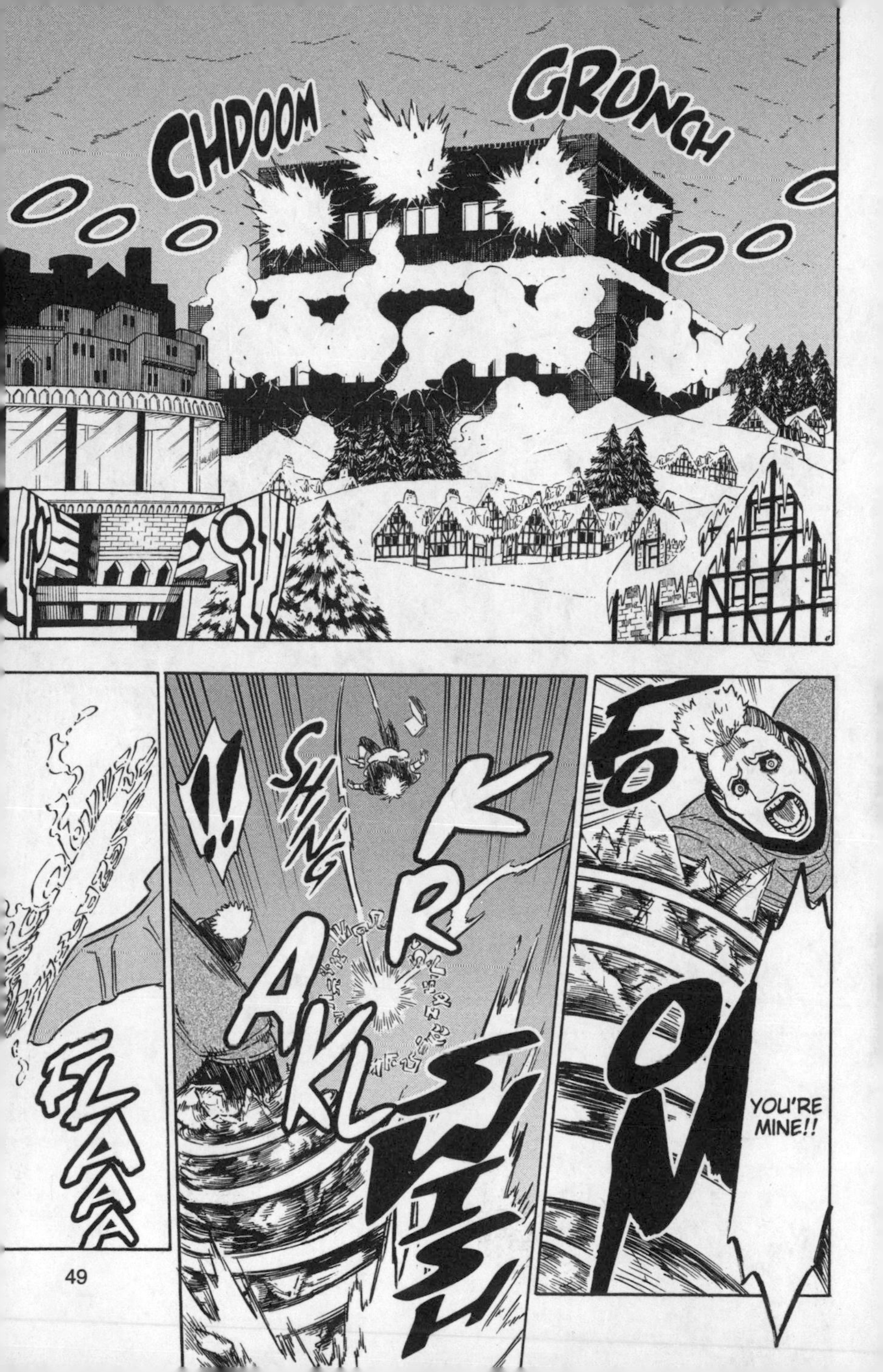
GRUNCH
CHDOOM
YOU'RE MINE!!
!!
SHING
KRAKL
SWISH

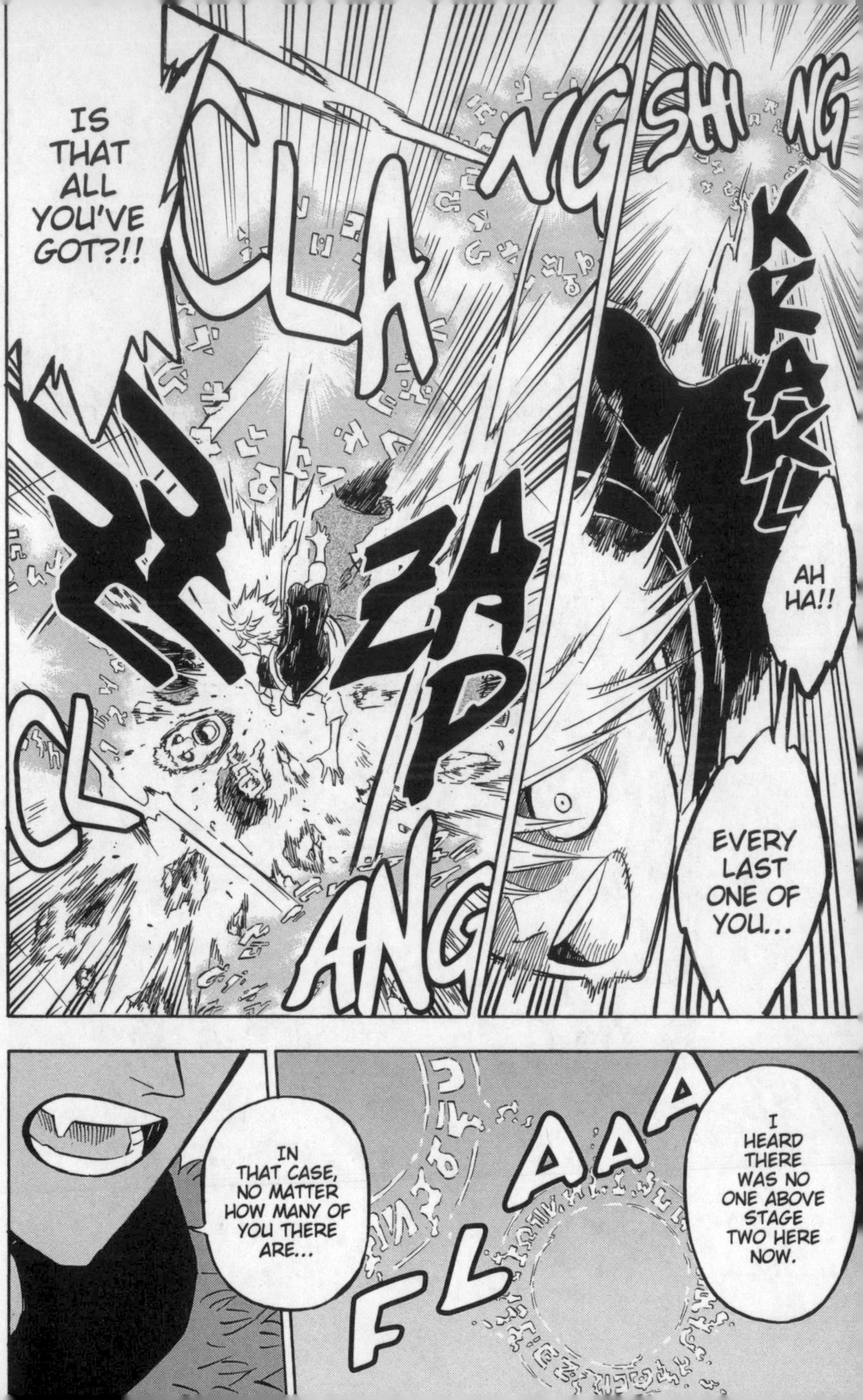
SHIING
KRAKL
AH HA!!
EVERY LAST ONE OF YOU...
CLANG
IS THAT ALL YOU'VE GOT?!!
ZAP
CL
ANG
I HEARD THERE WAS NO ONE ABOVE STAGE TWO HERE NOW.
FLAAAA
IN THAT CASE, NO MATTER HOW MANY OF YOU THERE ARE...

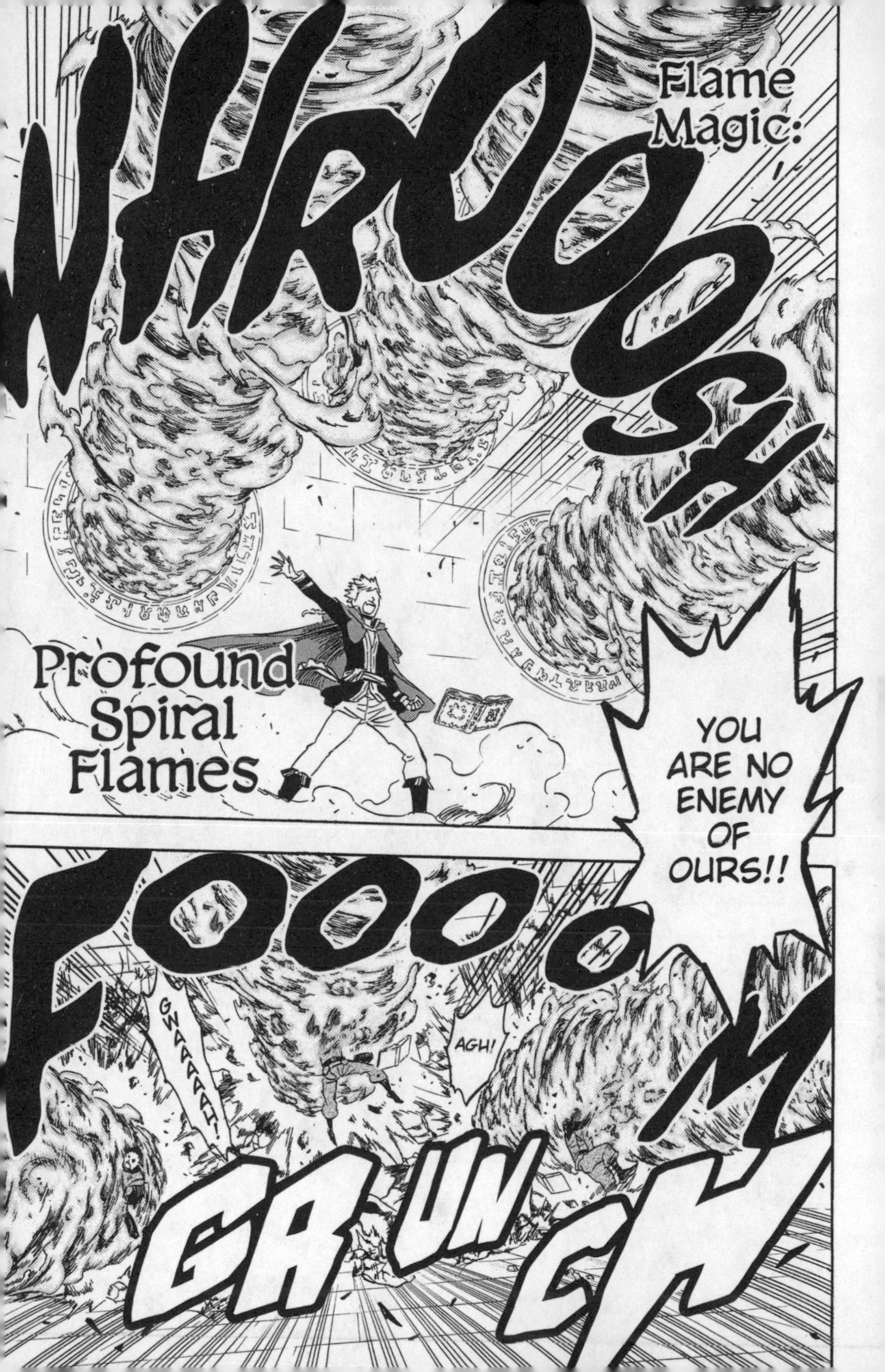
Flame Magic:
WHOOOSH
Profound Spiral Flames
YOU ARE NO ENEMY OF OURS!!
FOOOOM
AGH!
GWAAAAAH!
CRUNCH

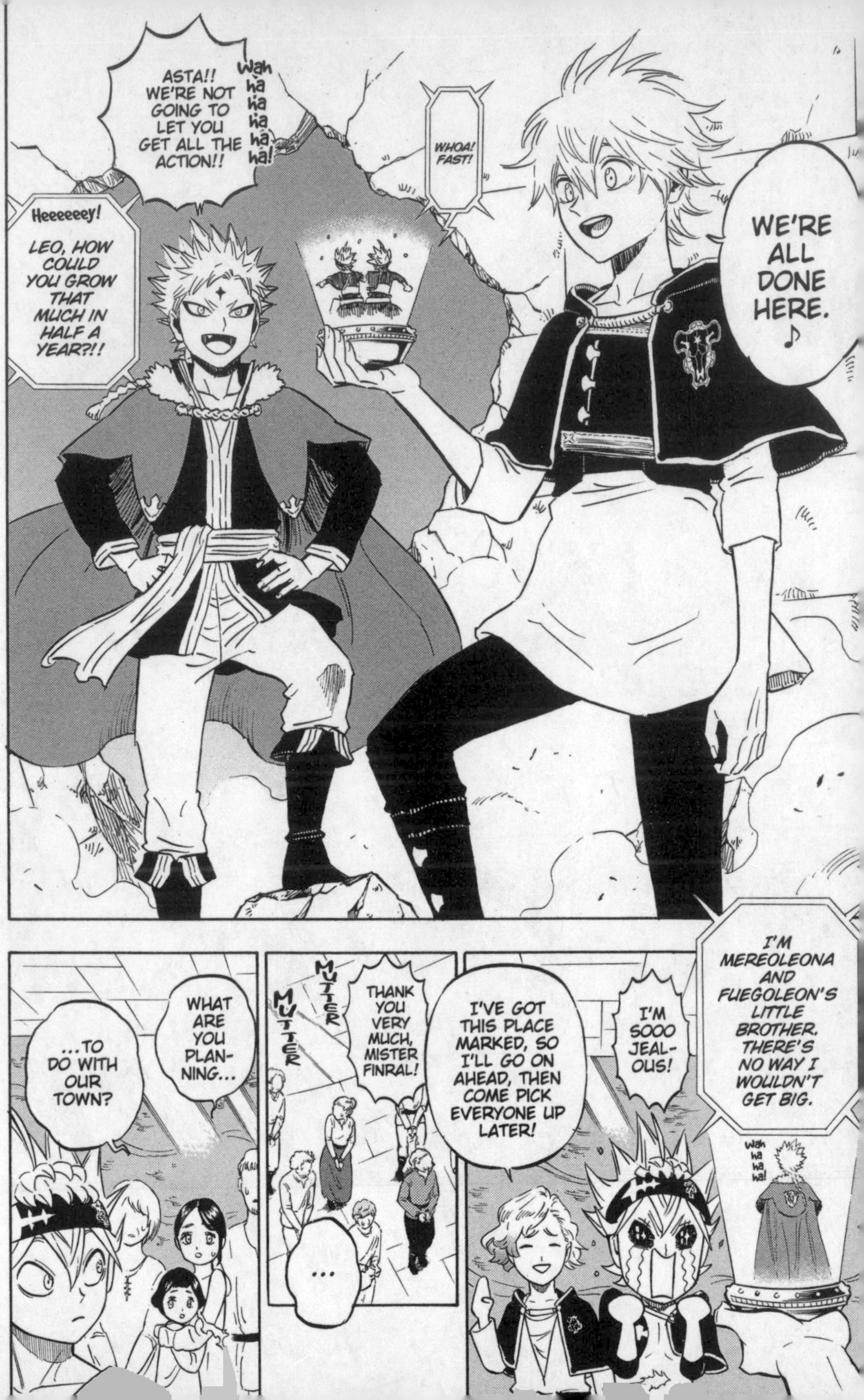
WE'RE ALL DONE HERE. ♪
WHOA! FAST!
ASTA!! WE'RE NOT GOING TO LET YOU GET ALL THE ACTION!!
Wah ha ha ha ha ha!
Heeeeeey!
LEO, HOW COULD YOU GROW THAT MUCH IN HALF A YEAR?!!
I'M MEREOLEONA AND FUEGOLEON'S LITTLE BROTHER. THERE'S NO WAY I WOULDN'T GET BIG.
Wah ha ha ha
I'M SOOO JEAL-OUS!
I'VE GOT THIS PLACE MARKED, SO I'LL GO ON AHEAD, THEN COME PICK EVERYONE UP LATER!
MUTTER
MUTTER
THANK YOU VERY MUCH, MISTER FINRAL!
...
WHAT ARE YOU PLAN-NING...
...TO DO WITH OUR TOWN?

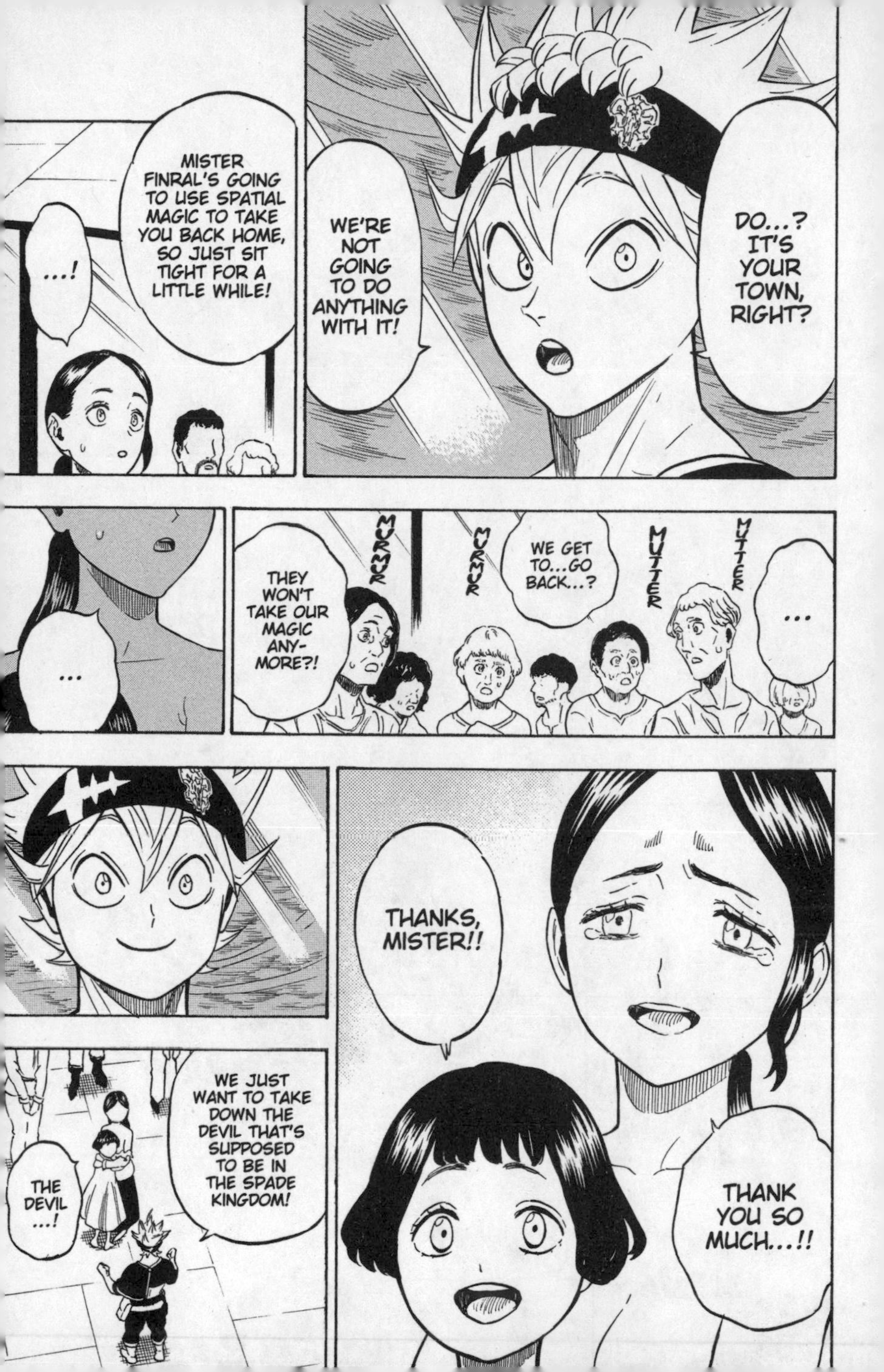
DO...? IT'S YOUR TOWN, RIGHT?
WE'RE NOT GOING TO DO ANYTHING WITH IT!
MISTER FINRAL'S GOING TO USE SPATIAL MAGIC TO TAKE YOU BACK HOME, SO JUST SIT TIGHT FOR A LITTLE WHILE!
...!
...
MUTTER
MUTTER
WE GET TO...GO BACK...?
MURMUR
MURMUR
THEY WON'T TAKE OUR MAGIC ANY-MORE?!
...
THANKS, MISTER!!
THANK YOU SO MUCH...!!
WE JUST WANT TO TAKE DOWN THE DEVIL THAT'S SUPPOSED TO BE IN THE SPADE KINGDOM!
THE DEVIL ...!

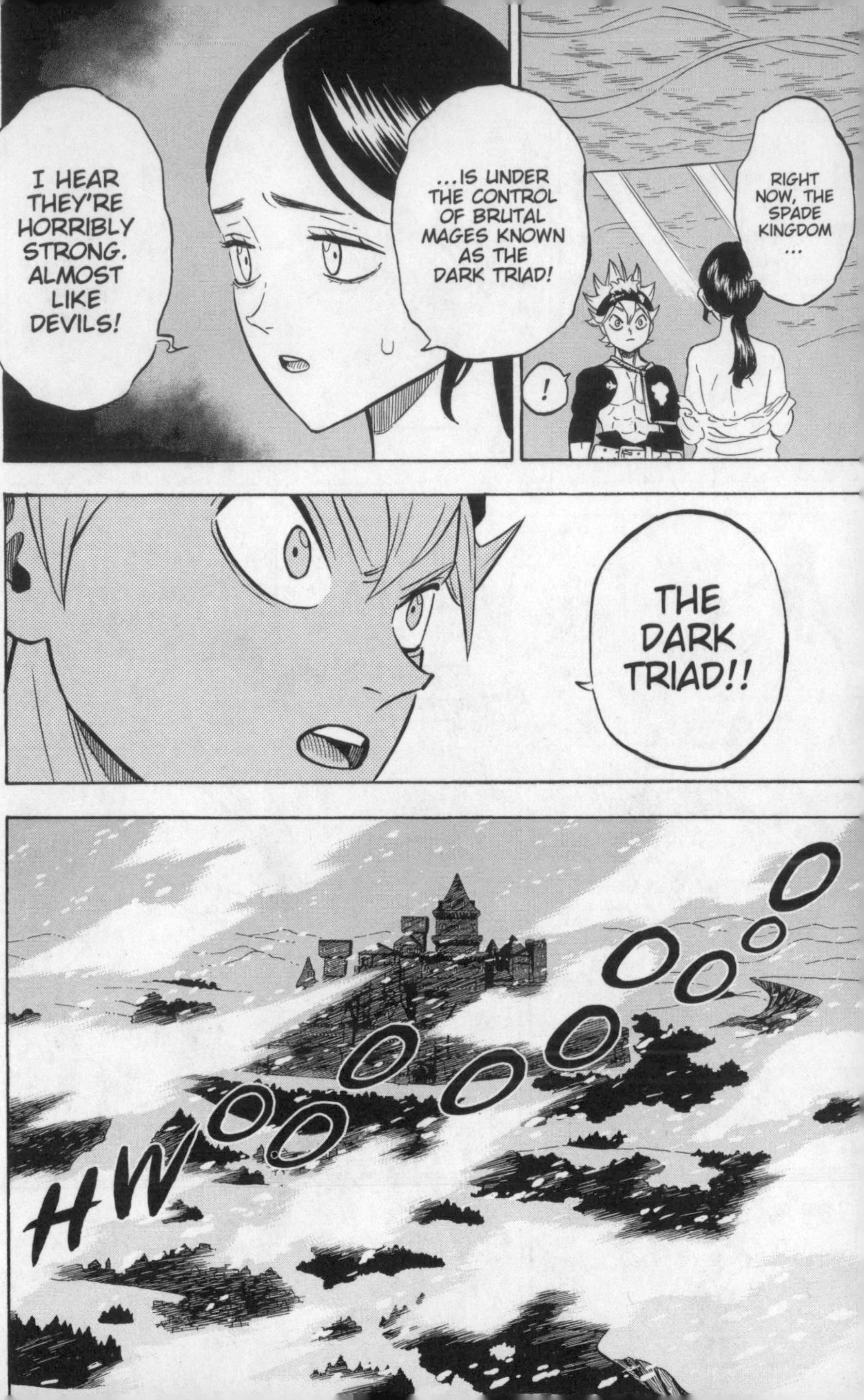
RIGHT NOW, THE SPADE KINGDOM ...
!
...IS UNDER THE CONTROL OF BRUTAL MAGES KNOWN AS THE DARK TRIAD!
I HEAR THEY'RE HORRIBLY STRONG. ALMOST LIKE DEVILS!
THE DARK TRIAD!!
HWOOOOOOOOOO

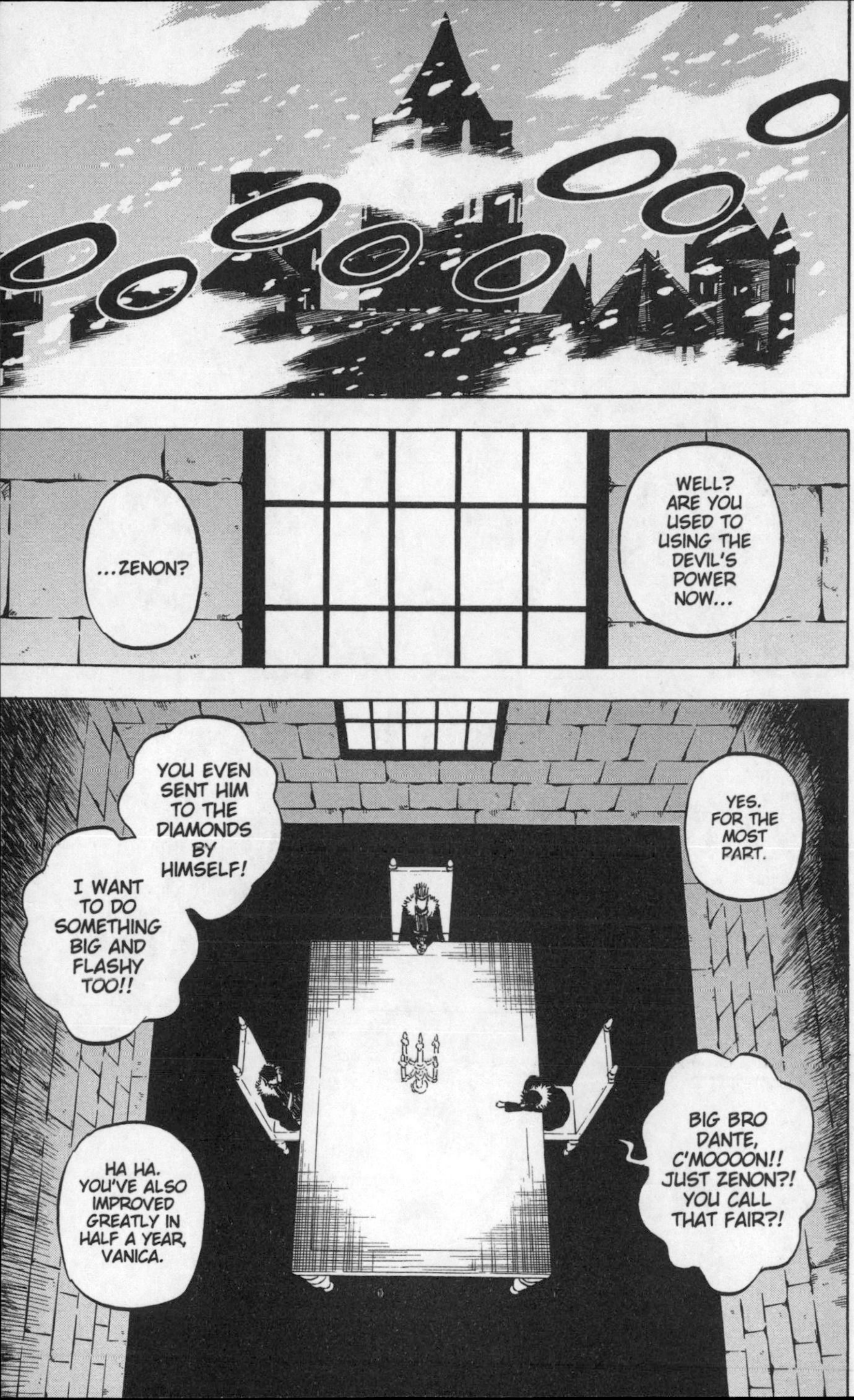
WELL? ARE YOU USED TO USING THE DEVIL'S POWER NOW...
...ZENON?
YES. FOR THE MOST PART.
YOU EVEN SENT HIM TO THE DIAMONDS BY HIMSELF!
I WANT TO DO SOMETHING BIG AND FLASHY TOO!!
BIG BRO DANTE, C'MOOOON!! JUST ZENON?! YOU CALL THAT FAIR?!
HA HA. YOU'VE ALSO IMPROVED GREATLY IN HALF A YEAR, VANICA.

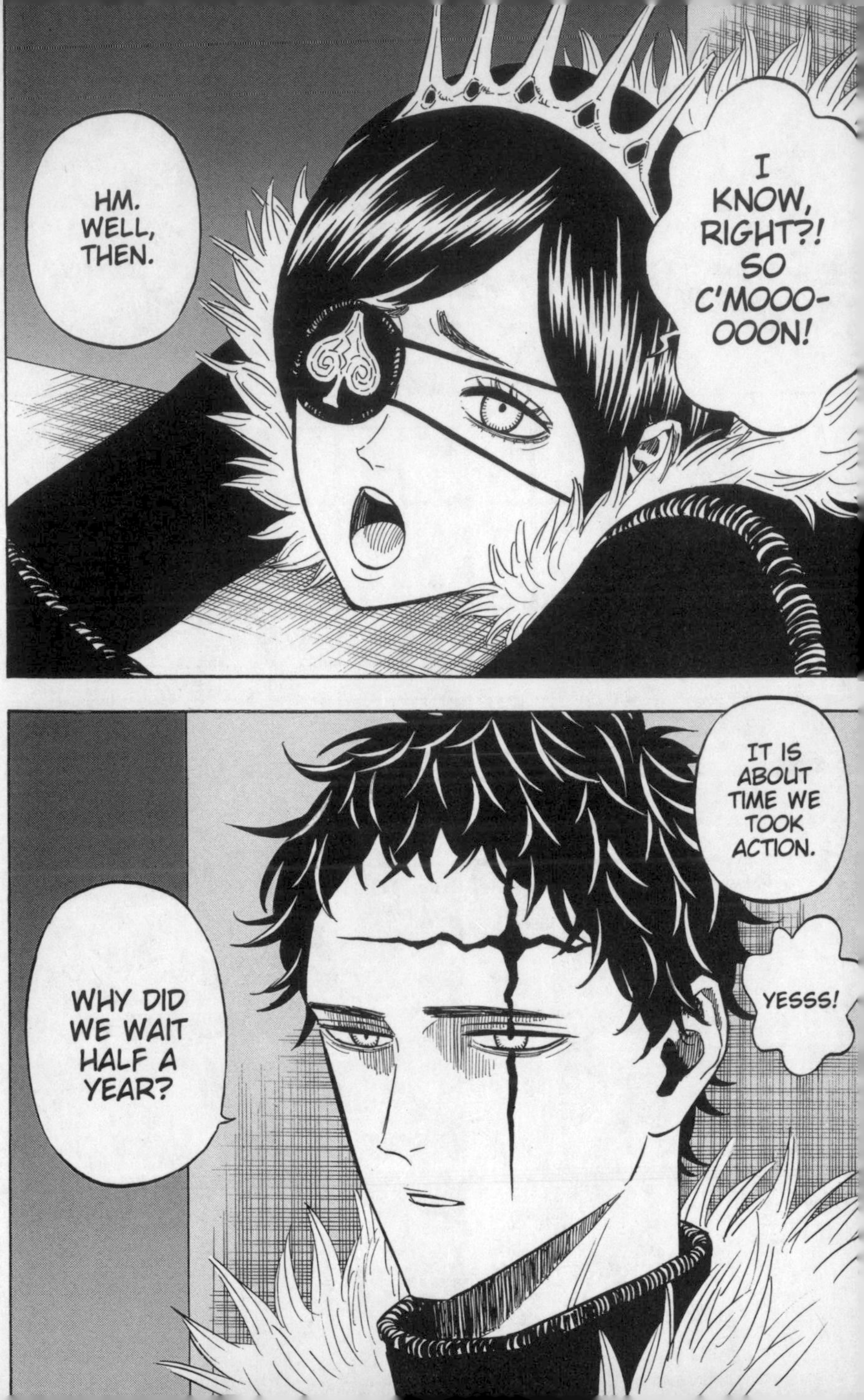
I KNOW, RIGHT?! SO C'MOOOO-OOON!
HM. WELL, THEN.
IT IS ABOUT TIME WE TOOK ACTION.
YESSS!
WHY DID WE WAIT HALF A YEAR?

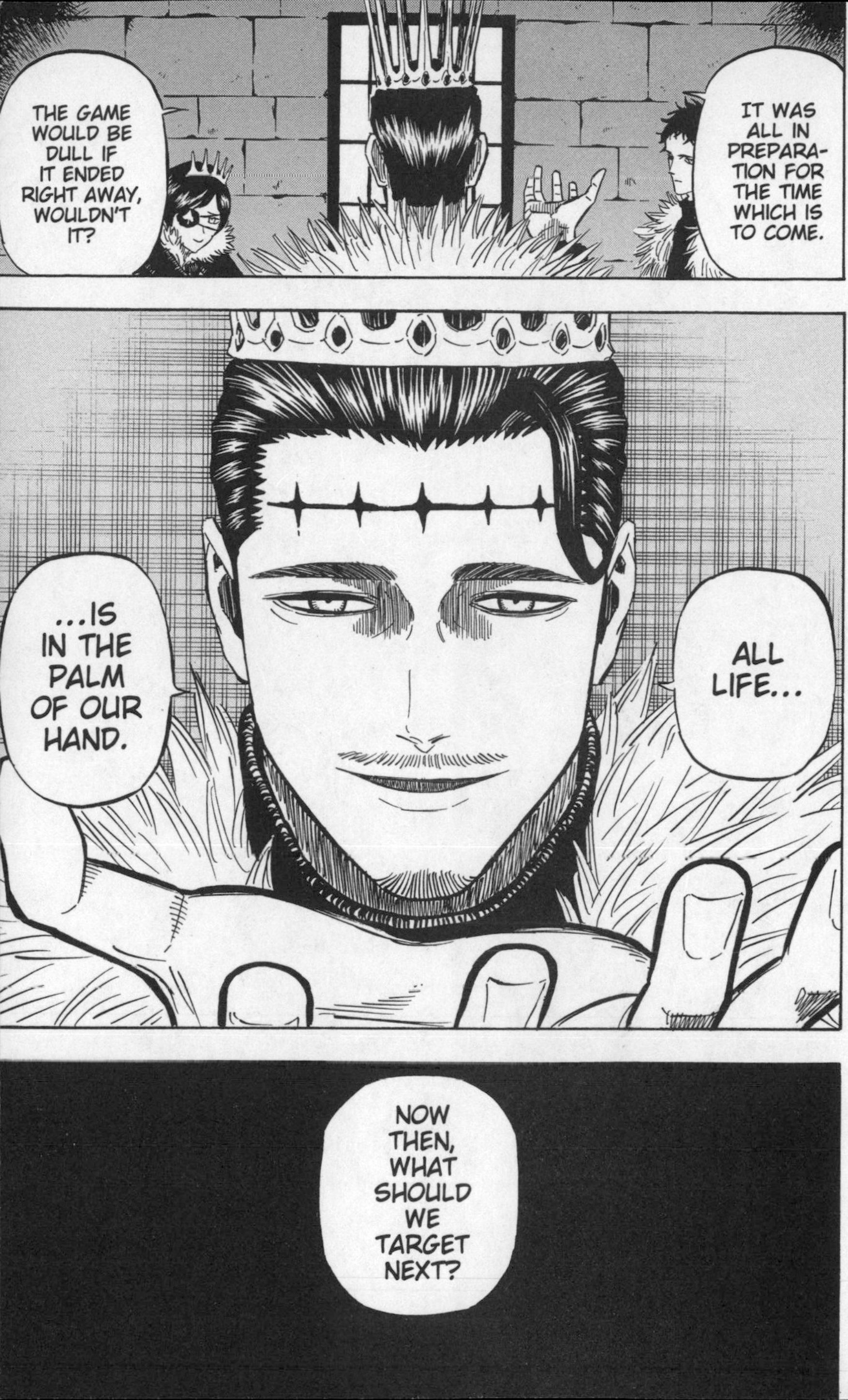
IT WAS ALL IN PREPARATION FOR THE TIME WHICH IS TO COME.
THE GAME WOULD BE DULL IF IT ENDED RIGHT AWAY, WOULDN'T IT?
ALL LIFE...
...IS IN THE PALM OF OUR HAND.
NOW THEN, WHAT SHOULD WE TARGET NEXT?

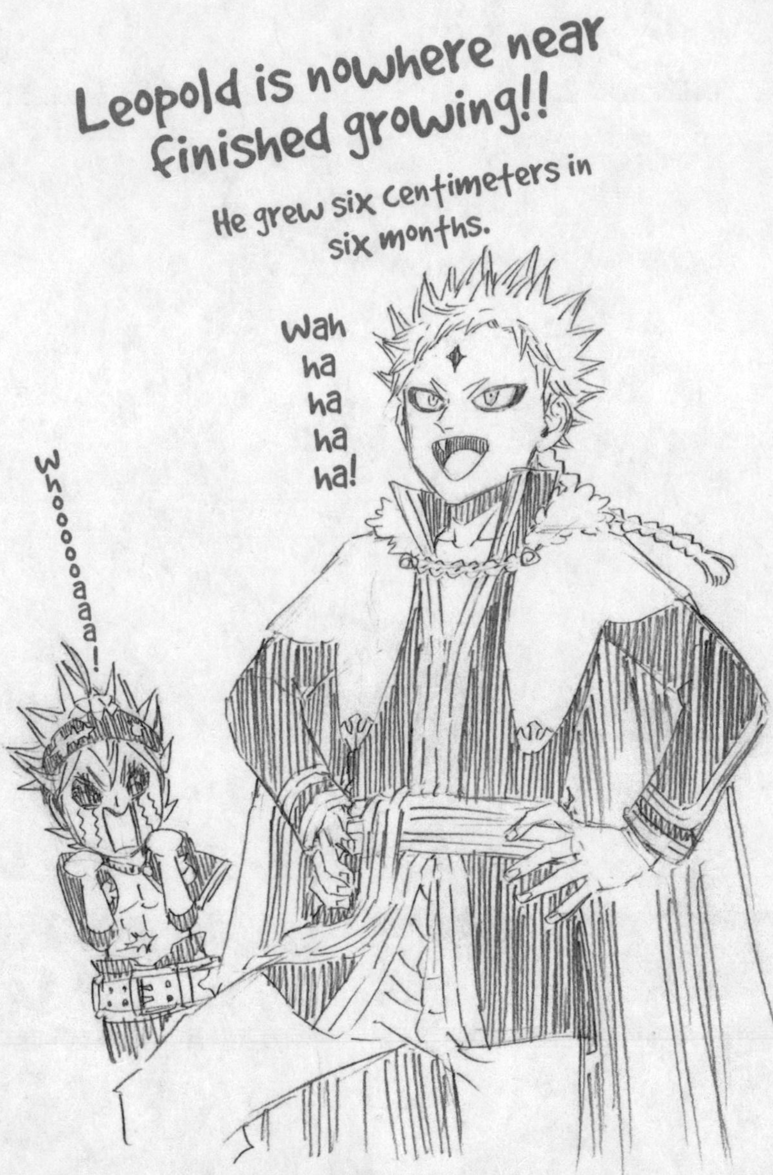
Leopold is nowhere near finished growing!!
He grew six centimeters in six months.
Wah ha ha ha ha!
Whooooaaa!

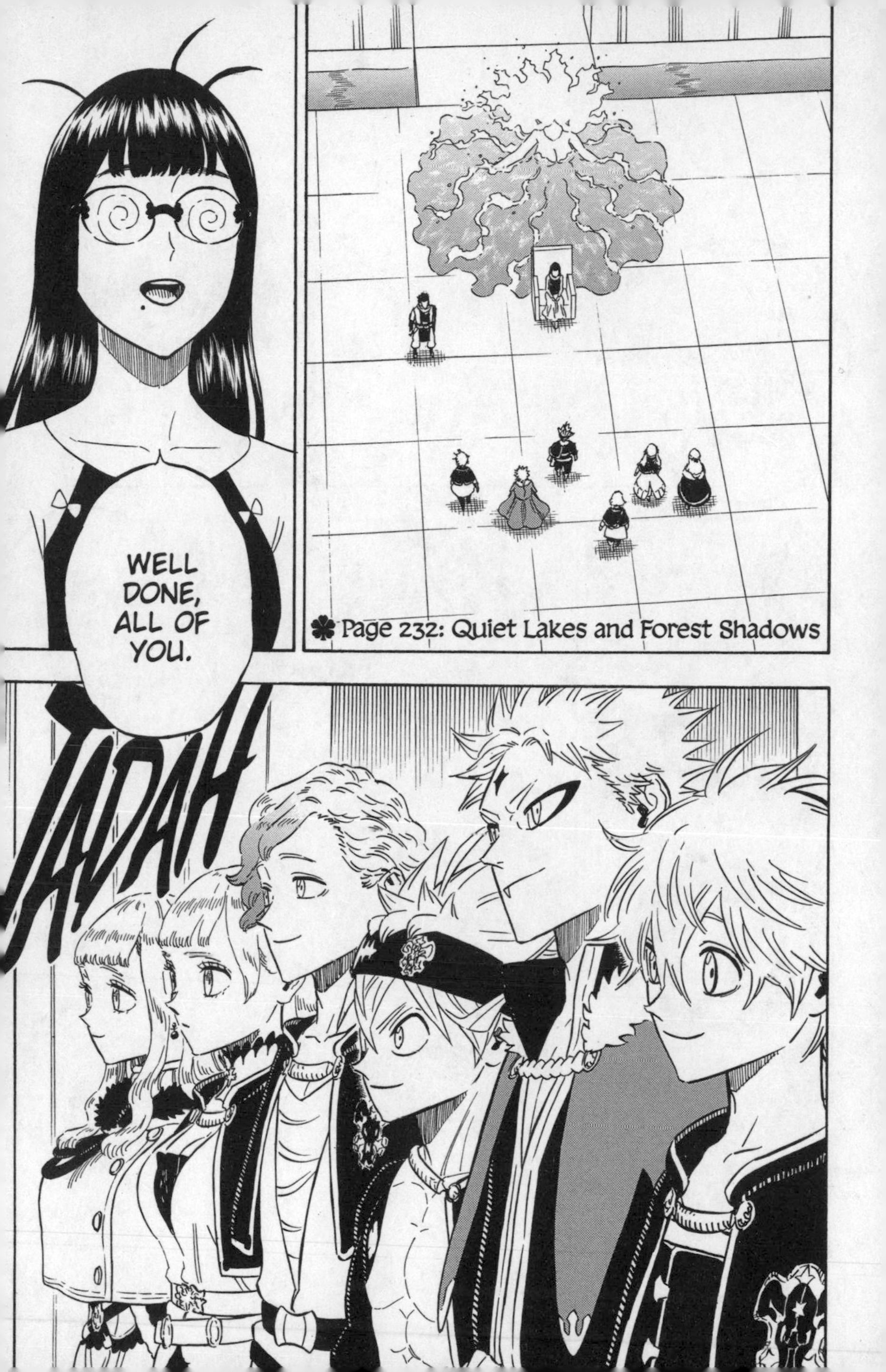
Page 232: Quiet Lakes and Forest Shadows
WELL DONE, ALL OF YOU.

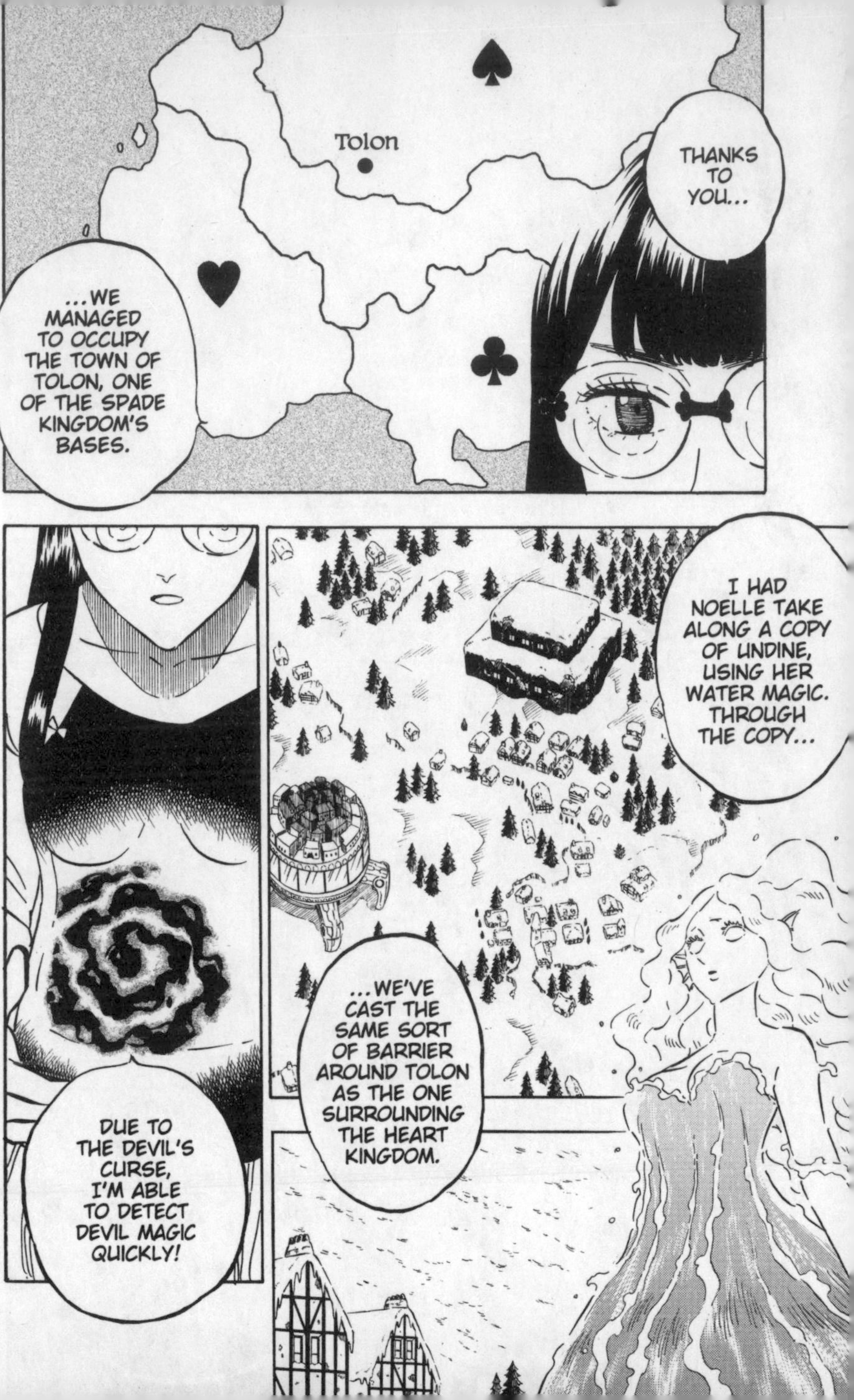
Tolon
THANKS TO YOU...
...WE MANAGED TO OCCUPY THE TOWN OF TOLON, ONE OF THE SPADE KINGDOM'S BASES.
I HAD NOELLE TAKE ALONG A COPY OF UNDINE, USING HER WATER MAGIC. THROUGH THE COPY...
...WE'VE CAST THE SAME SORT OF BARRIER AROUND TOLON AS THE ONE SURROUNDING THE HEART KINGDOM.
DUE TO THE DEVIL'S CURSE, I'M ABLE TO DETECT DEVIL MAGIC QUICKLY!

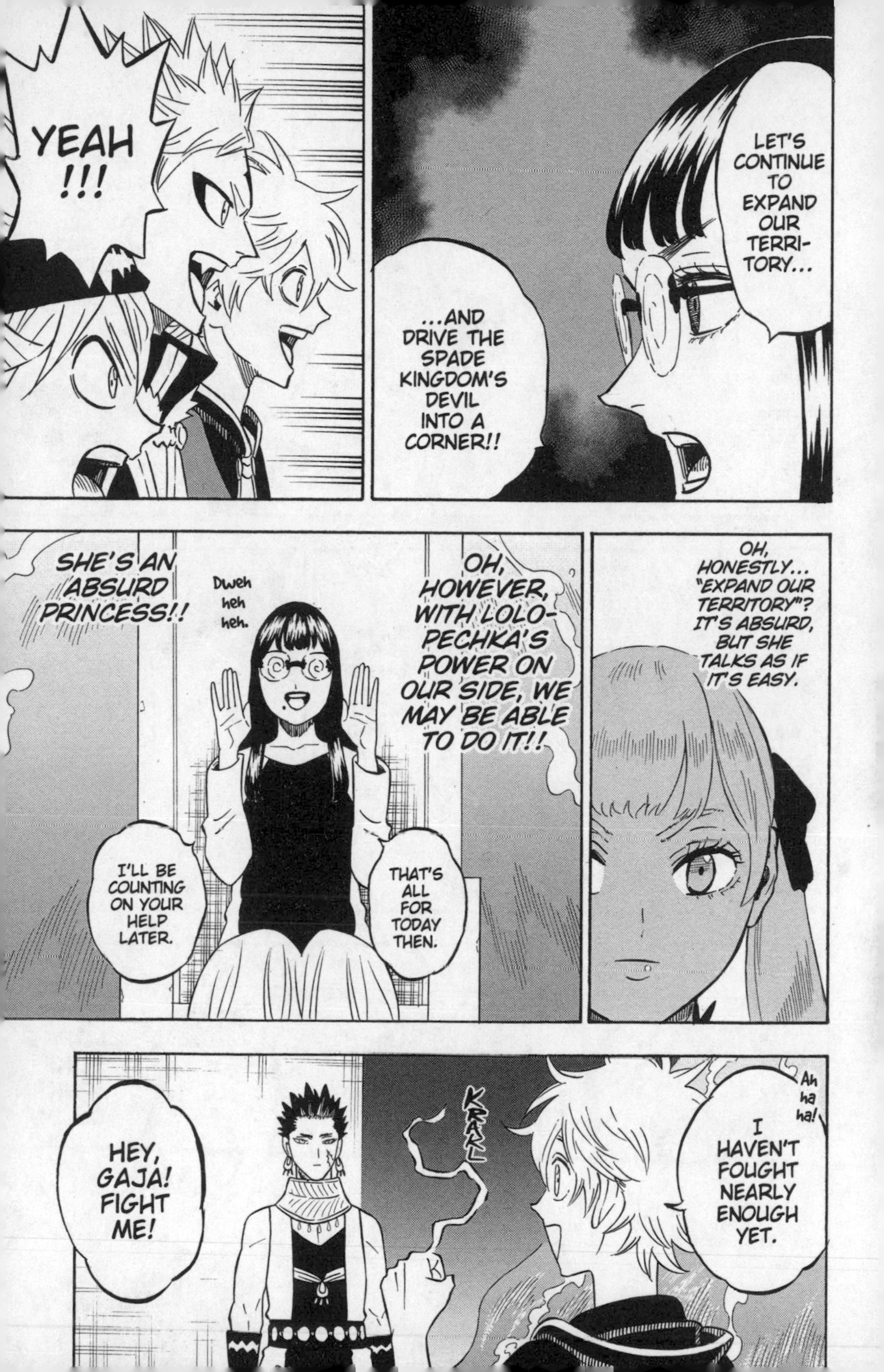
LET'S CONTINUE TO EXPAND OUR TERRITORY...
...AND DRIVE THE SPADE KINGDOM'S DEVIL INTO A CORNER!!
YEAH !!!
OH, HONESTLY... "EXPAND OUR TERRITORY"? IT'S ABSURD, BUT SHE TALKS AS IF IT'S EASY.
OH, HOWEVER, WITH LOLO-PECHKA'S POWER ON OUR SIDE, WE MAY BE ABLE TO DO IT!!
SHE'S AN ABSURD PRINCESS!!
Dweh heh heh.
THAT'S ALL FOR TODAY THEN.
I'LL BE COUNTING ON YOUR HELP LATER.
Ah ha ha!
I HAVEN'T FOUGHT NEARLY ENOUGH YET.
KRAK
HEY, GAJA! FIGHT ME!

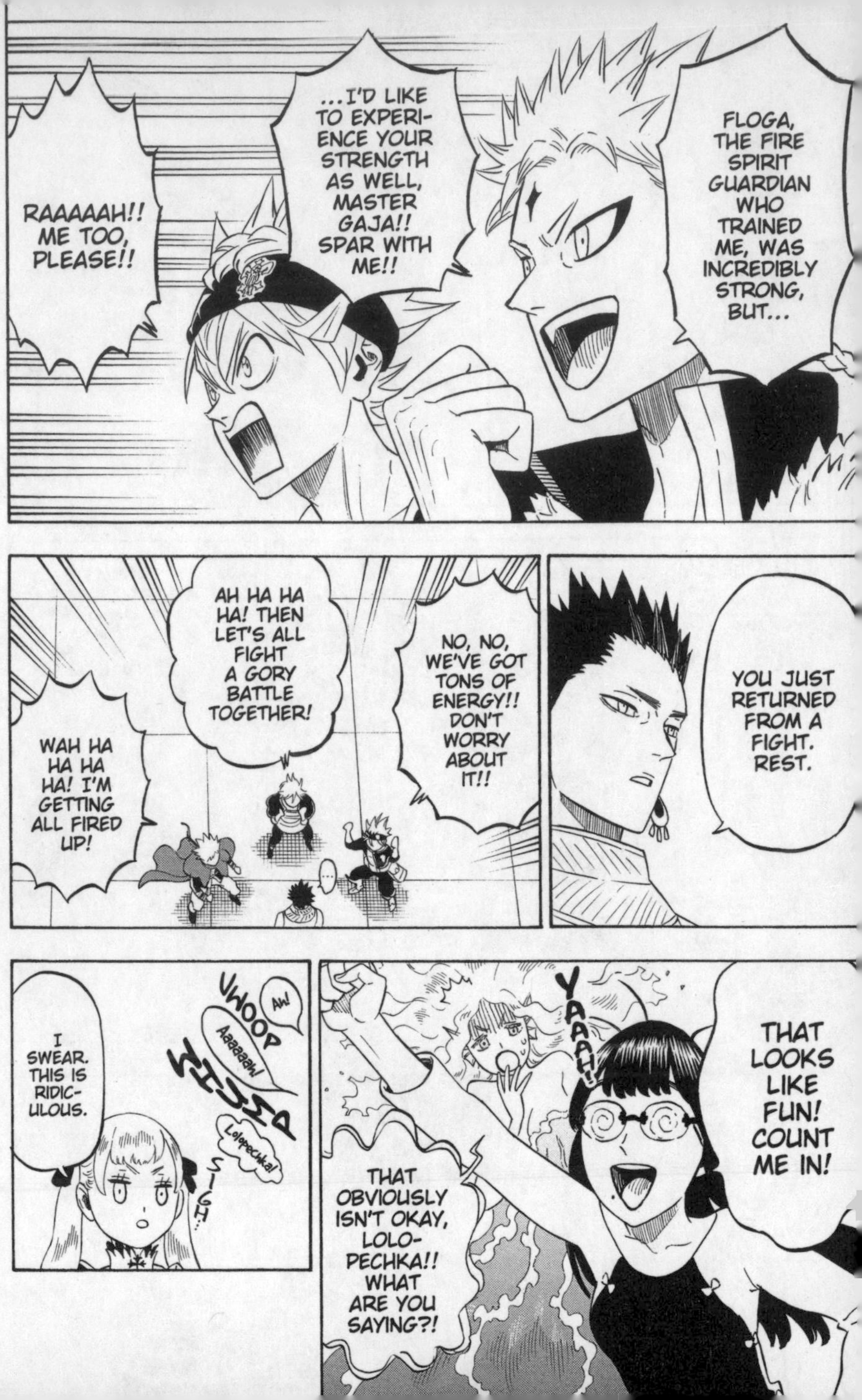
FLOGA, THE FIRE SPIRIT GUARDIAN WHO TRAINED ME, WAS INCREDIBLY STRONG, BUT...
...I'D LIKE TO EXPERIENCE YOUR STRENGTH AS WELL, MASTER GAJA!! SPAR WITH ME!!
RAAAAAH!! ME TOO, PLEASE!!
YOU JUST RETURNED FROM A FIGHT. REST.
NO, NO, WE'VE GOT TONS OF ENERGY!! DON'T WORRY ABOUT IT!!
AH HA HA HA! THEN LET'S ALL FIGHT A GORY BATTLE TOGETHER!
WAH HA HA HA HA! I'M GETTING ALL FIRED UP!
...
THAT LOOKS LIKE FUN! COUNT ME IN!
YAAAH!
THAT OBVIOUSLY ISN'T OKAY, LOLOPECHKA!! WHAT ARE YOU SAYING?!
Ah!
Aaaaaaah!
Lolopechka!
SIGH...
I SWEAR. THIS IS RIDICULOUS.

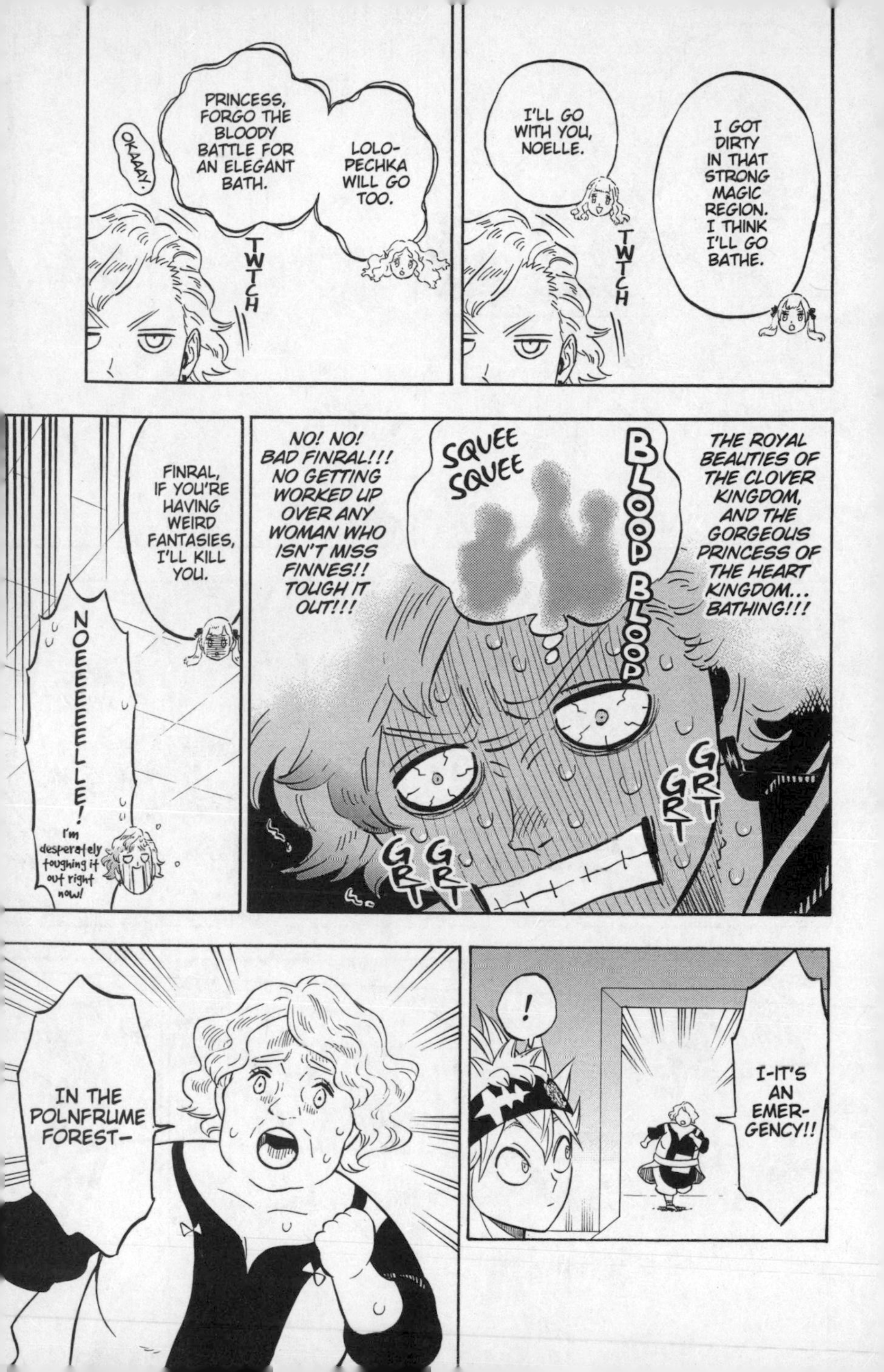
I GOT DIRTY IN THAT STRONG MAGIC REGION. I THINK I'LL GO BATHE.
I'LL GO WITH YOU, NOELLE.
TWTCH
PRINCESS, FORGO THE BLOODY BATTLE FOR AN ELEGANT BATH. LOLO-PECHKA WILL GO TOO.
TWTCH
OKAAAY.
THE ROYAL BEAUTIES OF THE CLOVER KINGDOM, AND THE GORGEOUS PRINCESS OF THE HEART KINGDOM... BATHING!!!
BLOOP BLOOP
SQUEE SQUEE
NO! NO! BAD FINRAL!!! NO GETTING WORKED UP OVER ANY WOMAN WHO ISN'T MISS FINNES!! TOUGH IT OUT!!!
GRT GRT
GRT GRT
FINRAL, IF YOU'RE HAVING WEIRD FANTASIES, I'LL KILL YOU.
NOEEEEEELLE!
I'm desperately toughing it out right now!
!
I-IT'S AN EMERGENCY!!
IN THE POLNFRUME FOREST—

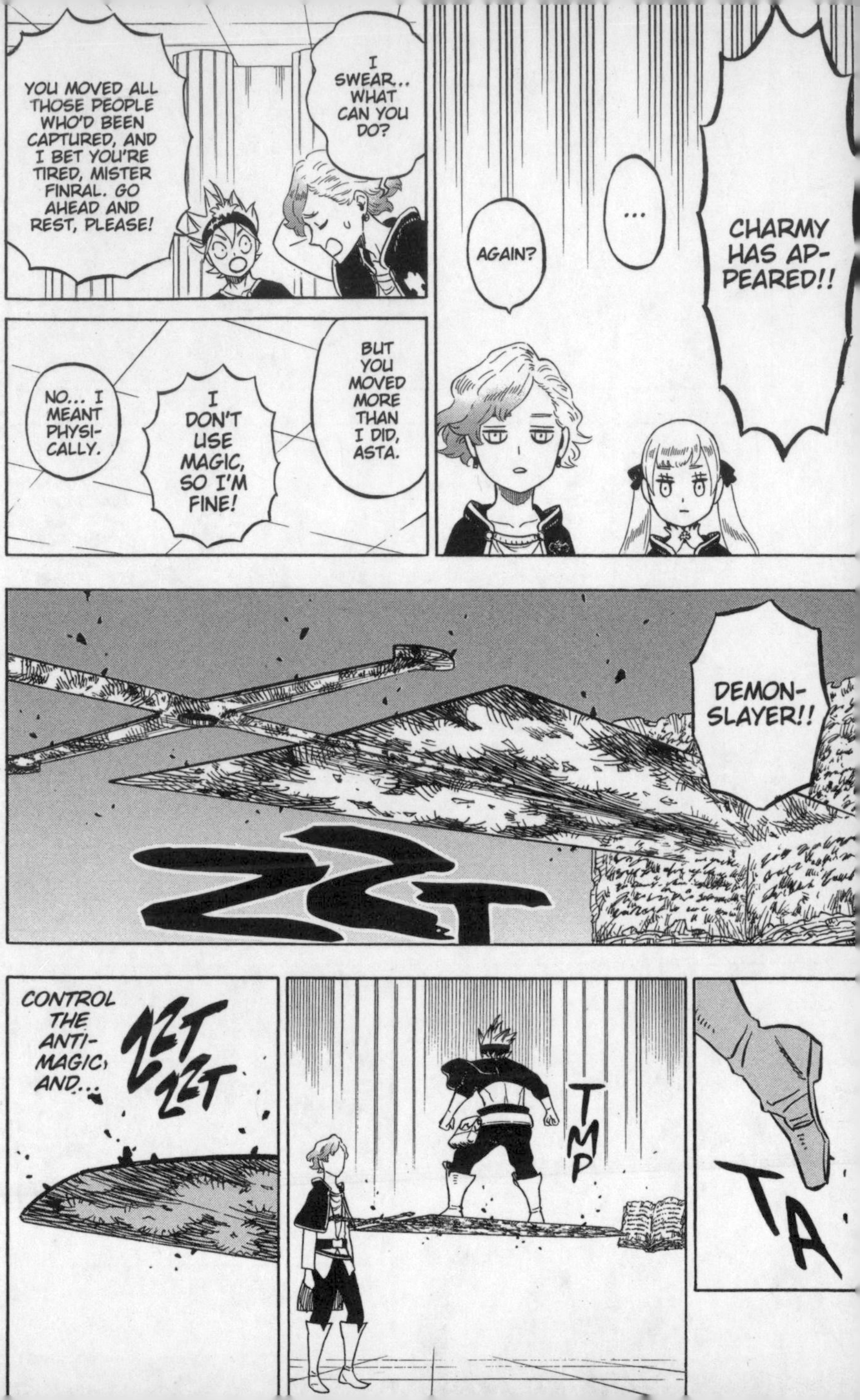
CHARMY HAS APPEARED!!
...
AGAIN?
I SWEAR... WHAT CAN YOU DO?
YOU MOVED ALL THOSE PEOPLE WHO'D BEEN CAPTURED, AND I BET YOU'RE TIRED, MISTER FINRAL. GO AHEAD AND REST, PLEASE!
BUT YOU MOVED MORE THAN I DID, ASTA.
I DON'T USE MAGIC, SO I'M FINE!
NO... I MEANT PHYSICALLY.
DEMON-SLAYER!!
ZZT
TA
TMP
ZZT ZZT
CONTROL THE ANTI-MAGIC, AND...

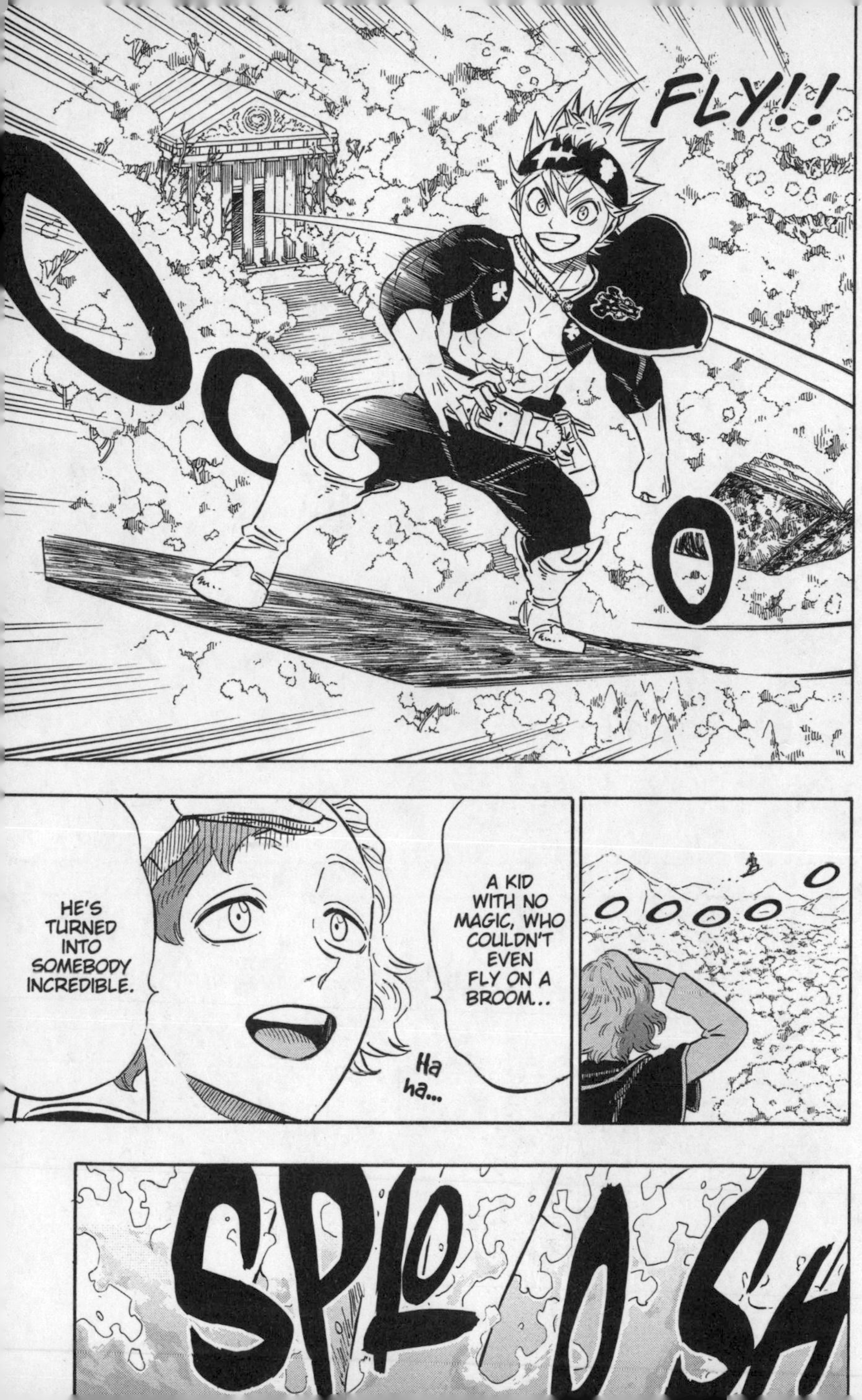
FLY!!
A KID WITH NO MAGIC, WHO COULDN'T EVEN FLY ON A BROOM...
Ha ha...
HE'S TURNED INTO SOMEBODY INCREDIBLE.
SPLOOSH

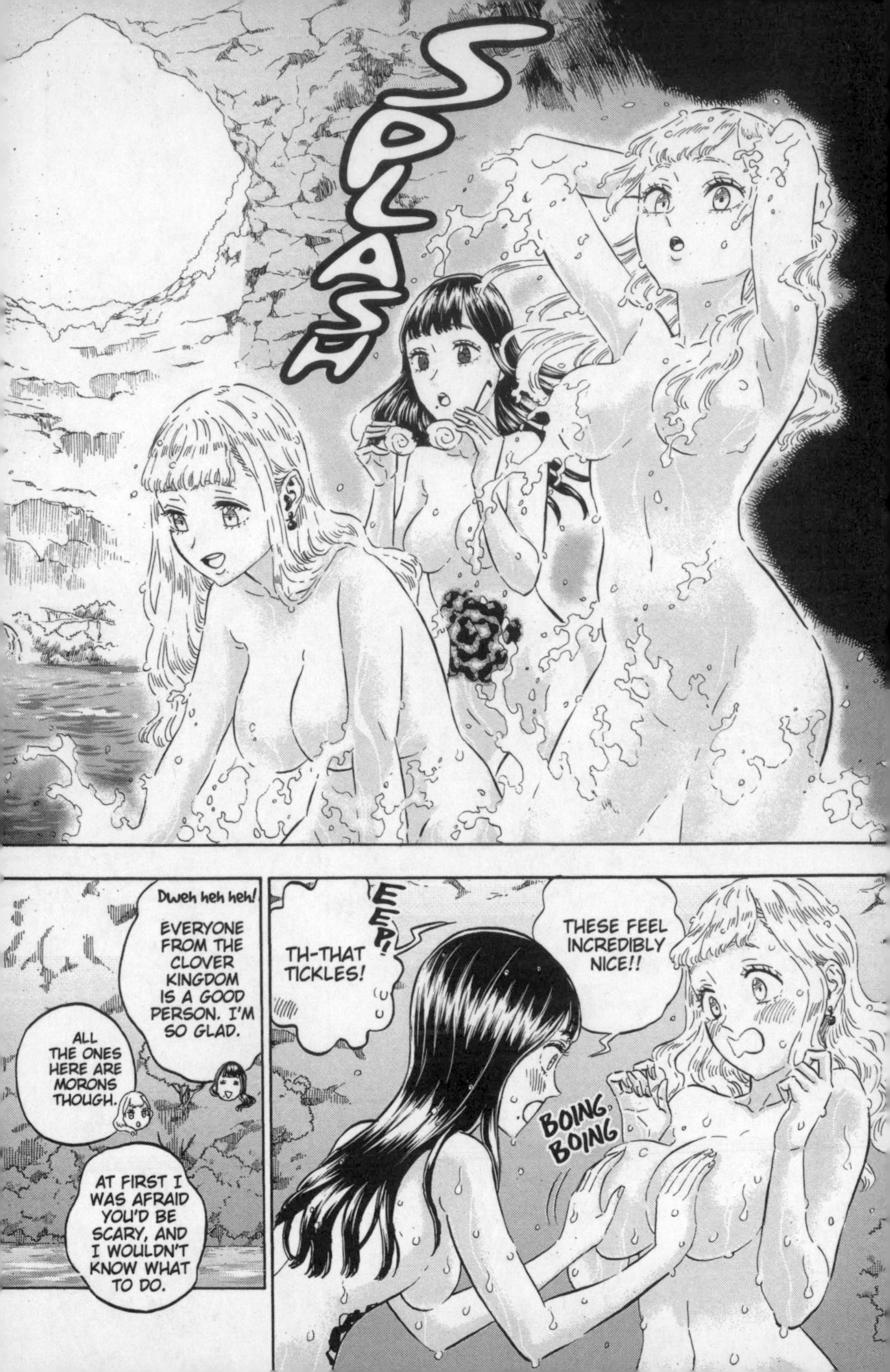
SPLASH
THESE FEEL INCREDIBLY NICE!!
EEP!
TH-THAT TICKLES!
BOING BOING
Dweh heh heh!
EVERYONE FROM THE CLOVER KINGDOM IS A GOOD PERSON. I'M SO GLAD.
ALL THE ONES HERE ARE MORONS THOUGH.
AT FIRST I WAS AFRAID YOU'D BE SCARY, AND I WOULDN'T KNOW WHAT TO DO.

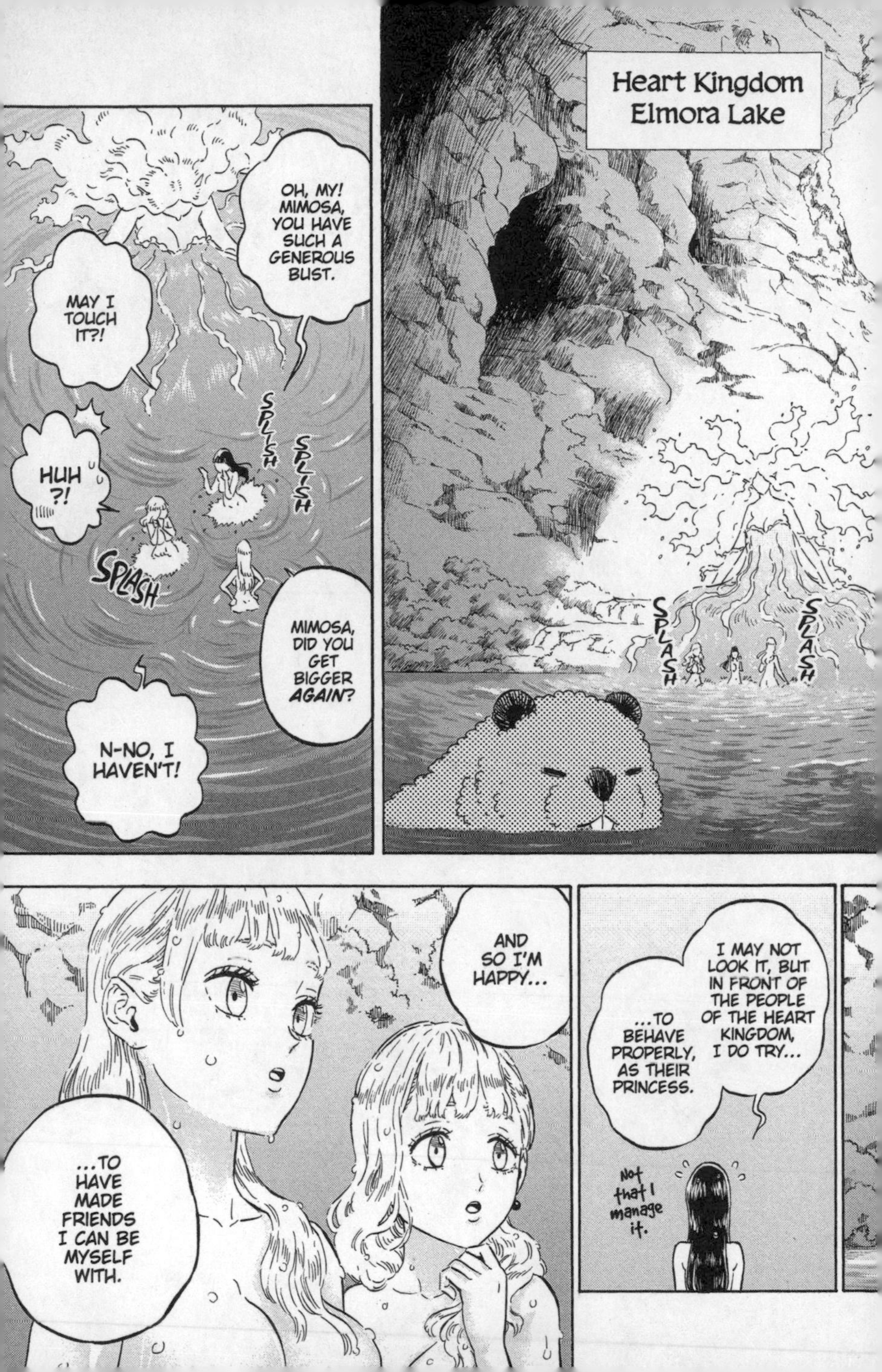
Heart Kingdom
Elmora Lake
SPLASH
SPLASH
OH, MY! MIMOSA, YOU HAVE SUCH A GENEROUS BUST.
MAY I TOUCH IT?!
SPLISH
SPLISH
HUH ?!
MIMOSA, DID YOU GET BIGGER *AGAIN*?
SPLASH
N-NO, I HAVEN'T!
I MAY NOT LOOK IT, BUT IN FRONT OF THE PEOPLE OF THE HEART KINGDOM, I DO TRY...
...TO BEHAVE PROPERLY, AS THEIR PRINCESS.
Not that I manage it.
AND SO I'M HAPPY...
...TO HAVE MADE FRIENDS I CAN BE MYSELF WITH.

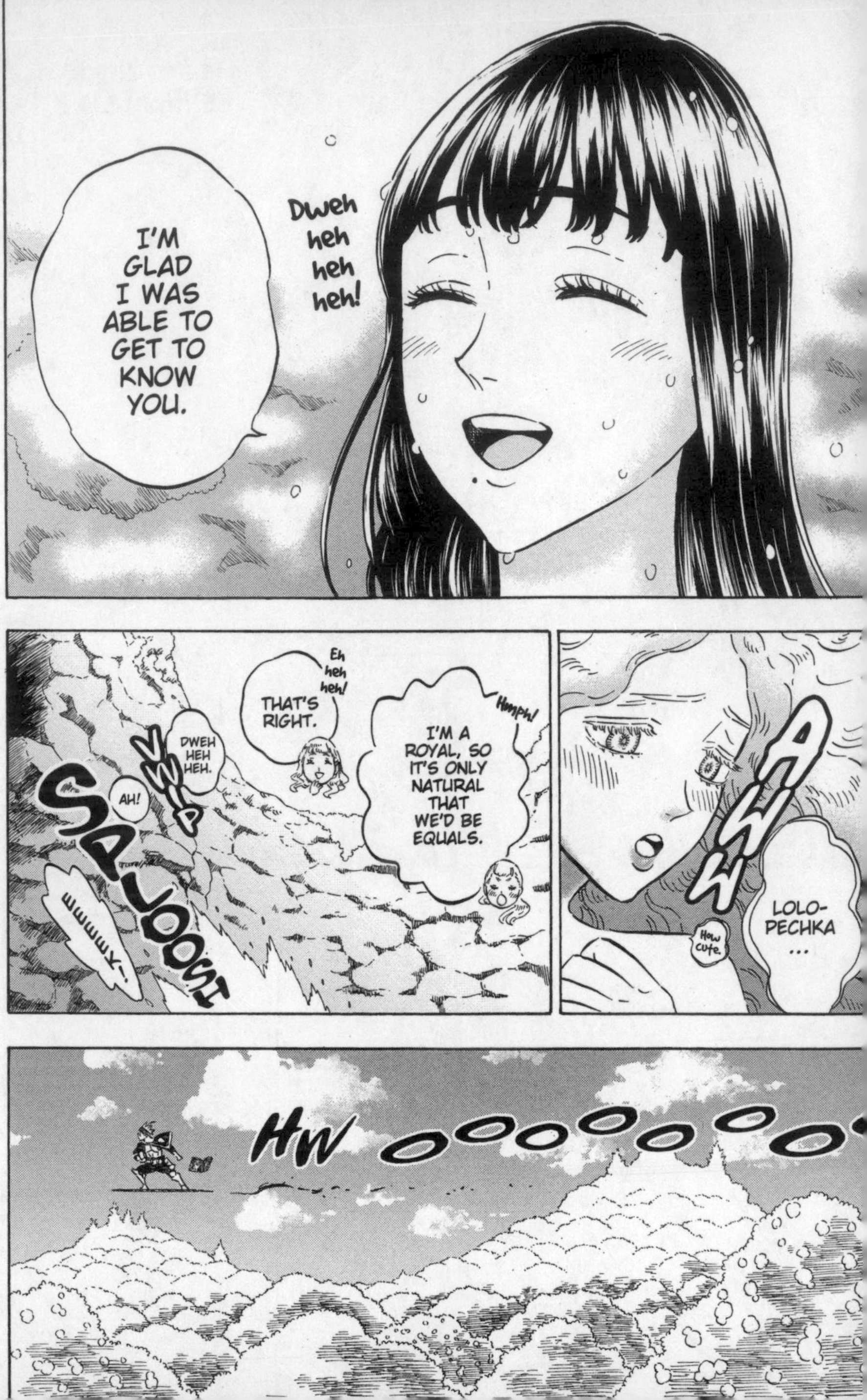
Dweh heh heh heh!
I'M GLAD I WAS ABLE TO GET TO KNOW YOU.
AWWW
LOLO-PECHKA ...
How cute.
Hmph!
I'M A ROYAL, SO IT'S ONLY NATURAL THAT WE'D BE EQUALS.
Eh heh heh!
THAT'S RIGHT.
DWEH HEH HEH.
VWIP
AH!
SPLOOSH!
HWOOOOOOOO

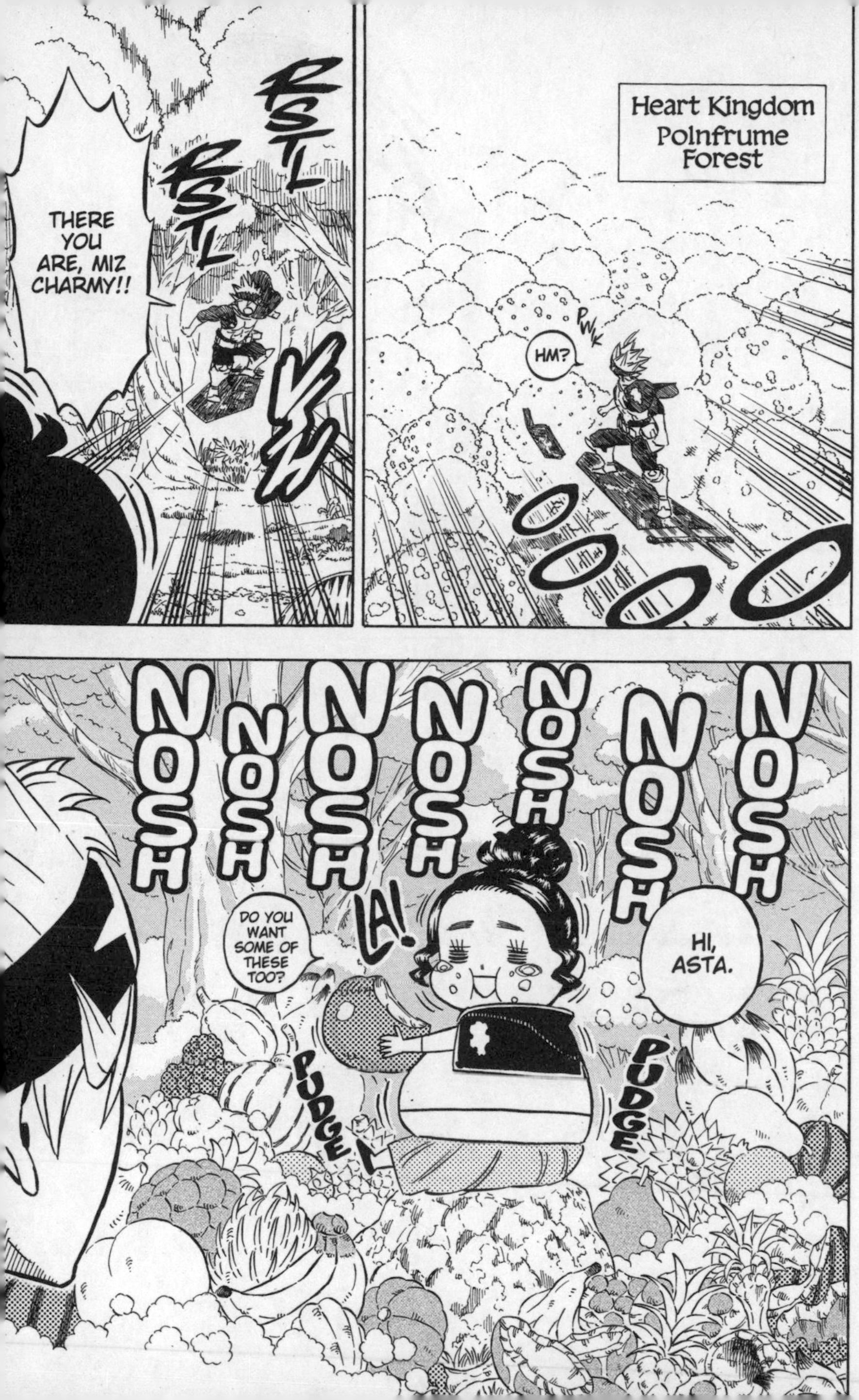
Heart Kingdom Poinfrume Forest
PWK
HM?
RSTL
RSTL
THERE YOU ARE, MIZ CHARMY!!
NOSH NOSH NOSH NOSH NOSH NOSH NOSH
HI, ASTA.
PUDGE
LA!
DO YOU WANT SOME OF THESE TOO?
PUDGE

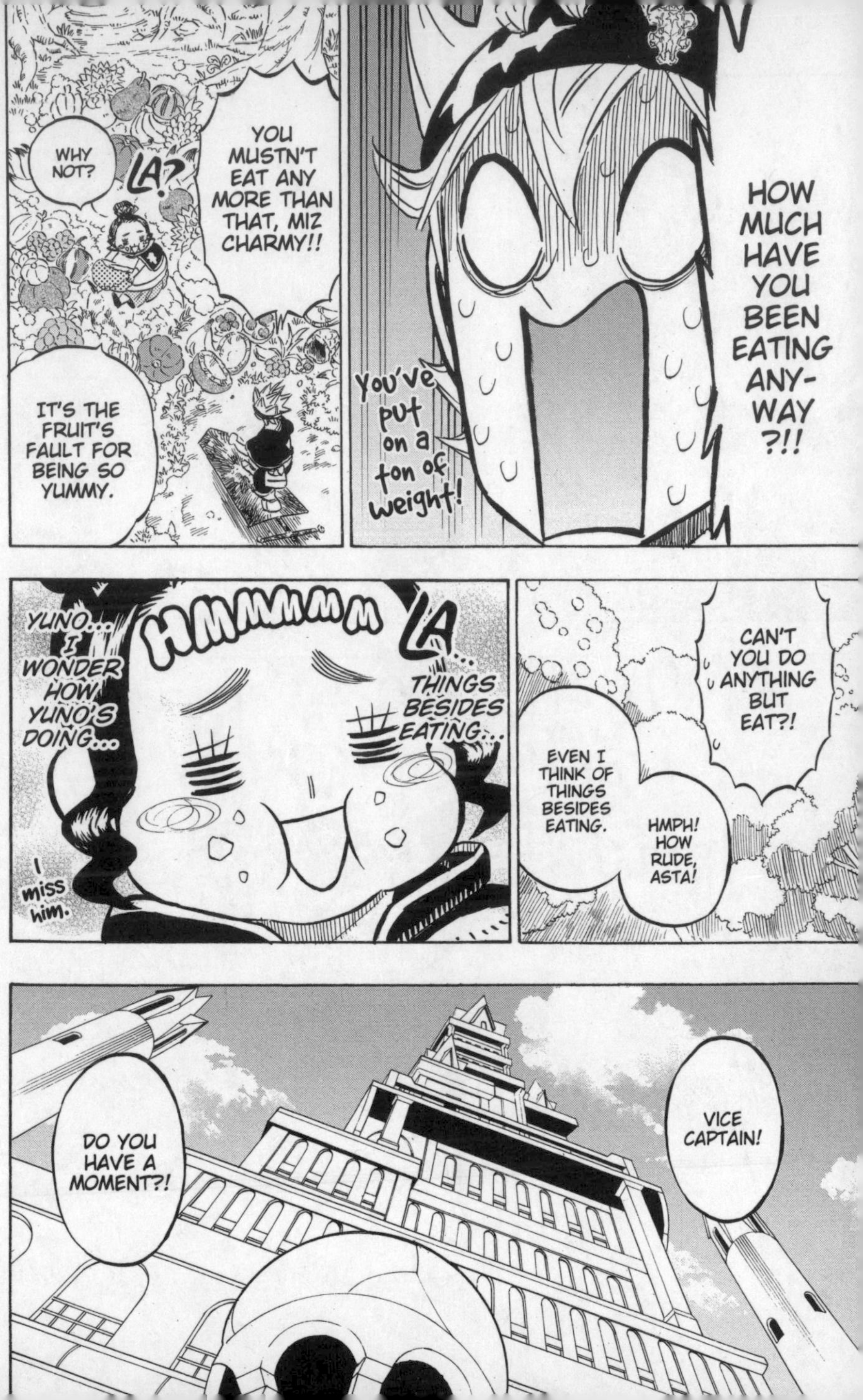
HOW MUCH HAVE YOU BEEN EATING ANY-WAY?!!
You've put on a ton of weight!
YOU MUSTN'T EAT ANY MORE THAN THAT, MIZ CHARMY!!
LA?
WHY NOT?
IT'S THE FRUIT'S FAULT FOR BEING SO YUMMY.
CAN'T YOU DO ANYTHING BUT EAT?!
HMPH! HOW RUDE, ASTA!
EVEN I THINK OF THINGS BESIDES EATING.
THINGS BESIDES EATING...
HMMMMMM LA...
YUNO... I WONDER HOW YUNO'S DOING...
I miss him.
VICE CAPTAIN!
DO YOU HAVE A MOMENT?!

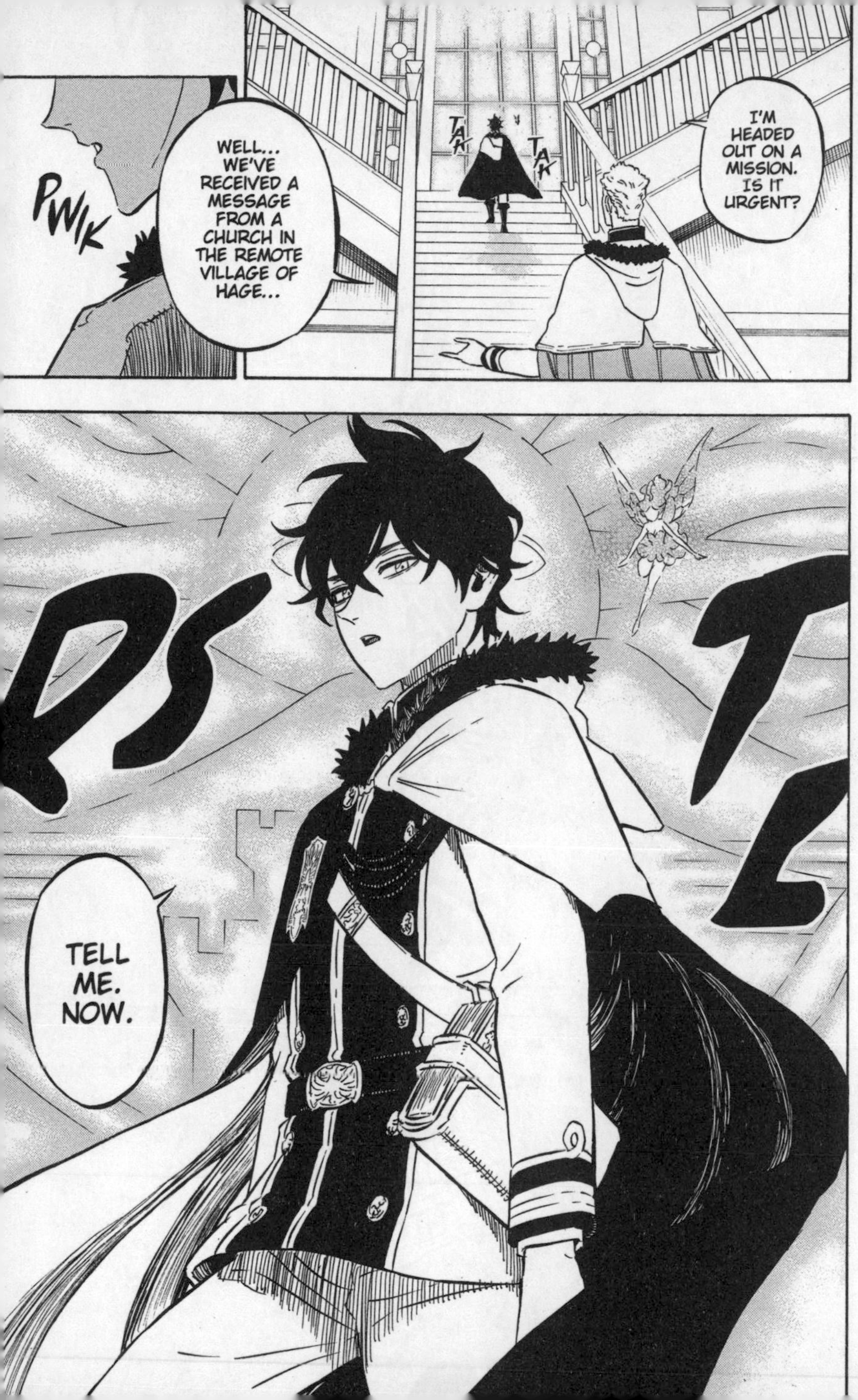
TAK
TAK
I'M HEADED OUT ON A MISSION. IS IT URGENT?
PWIK
WELL... WE'VE RECEIVED A MESSAGE FROM A CHURCH IN THE REMOTE VILLAGE OF HAGE...
TELL ME. NOW.

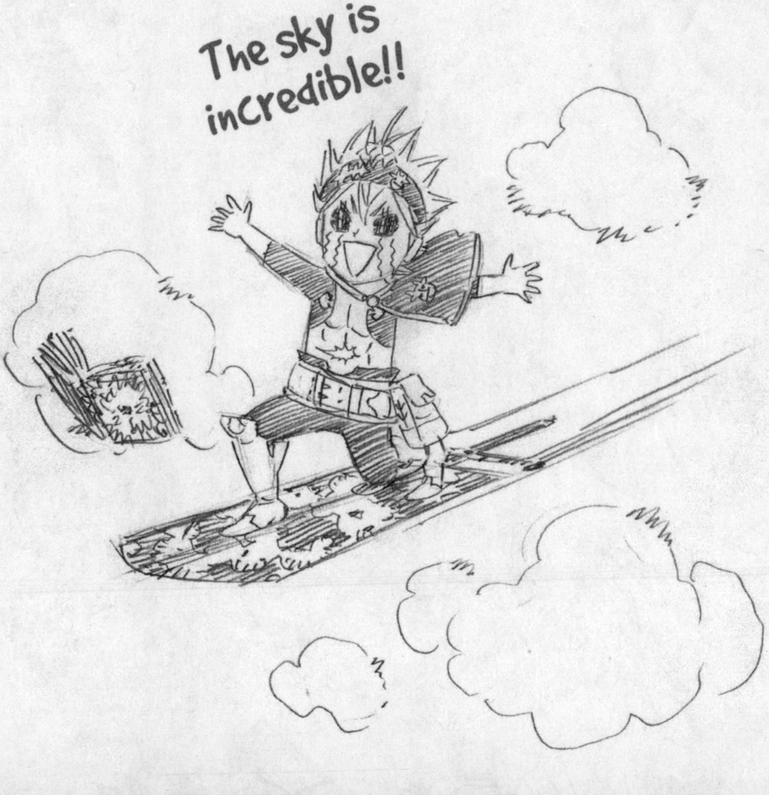
The sky is incredible!!

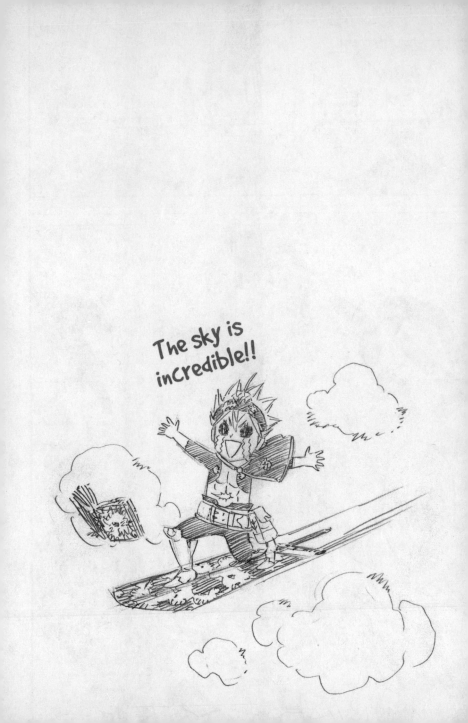

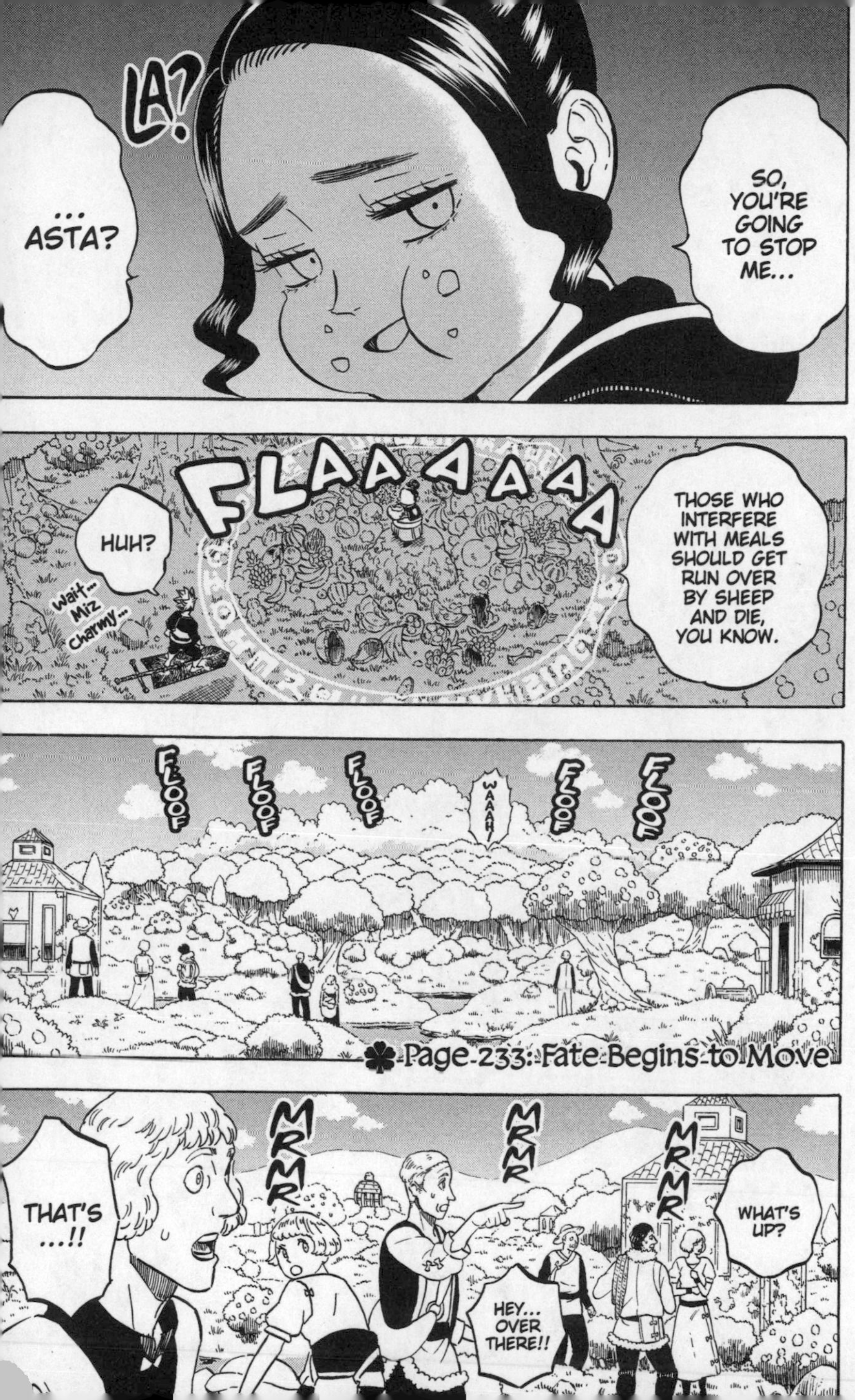
SO, YOU'RE GOING TO STOP ME...
LA?
... ASTA?
THOSE WHO INTERFERE WITH MEALS SHOULD GET RUN OVER BY SHEEP AND DIE, YOU KNOW.
FLAAAAAA
HUH?
Wait... Miz Charmy...
FLOOF
FLOOF
WAAAH!
FLOOF
FLOOF
FLOOF
Page 233: Fate Begins to Move
WHAT'S UP?
MRMR
MRMR
HEY... OVER THERE!!
MRMR
THAT'S ...!!

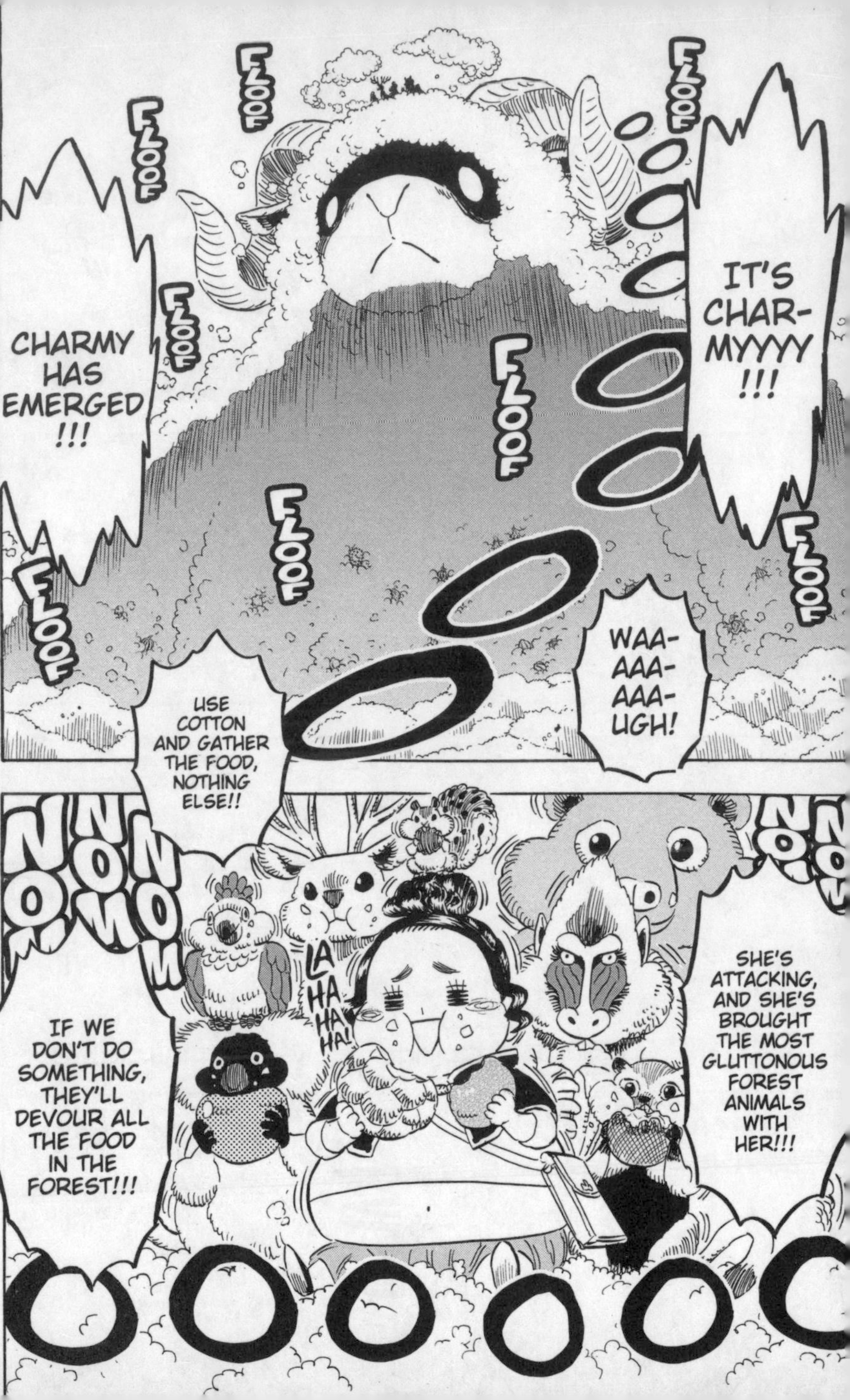
FLOOF
IT'S CHARMYYYY!!!
FLOOF
FLOOF
CHARMY HAS EMERGED!!!
FLOOF
FLOOF
FLOOF
FLOOF
WAAAAAAAAAUGH!
USE COTTON AND GATHER THE FOOD, NOTHING ELSE!!
NOM
SHE'S ATTACKING, AND SHE'S BROUGHT THE MOST GLUTTONOUS FOREST ANIMALS WITH HER!!!
LAHAHAHA!
NOM NOM NOM
IF WE DON'T DO SOMETHING, THEY'LL DEVOUR ALL THE FOOD IN THE FOREST!!!
OOOOOOC

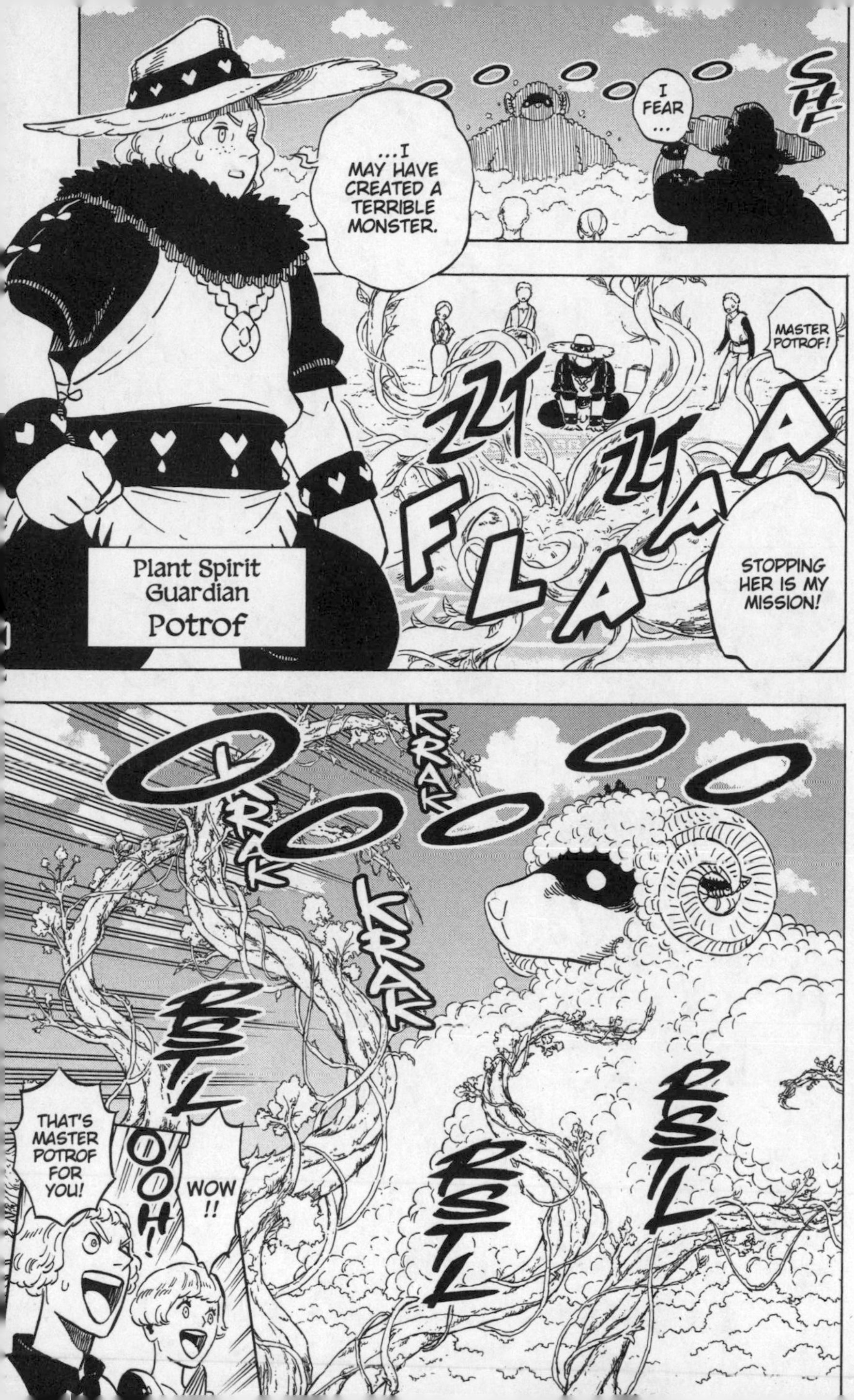
SHF
I FEAR ...
...I MAY HAVE CREATED A TERRIBLE MONSTER.
Plant Spirit Guardian Potrof
MASTER POTROF!
STOPPING HER IS MY MISSION!
FLAAA
KRAK KRAK KRAK
RSTL RSTL RSTL
THAT'S MASTER POTROF FOR YOU!
WOW!!
OOH!

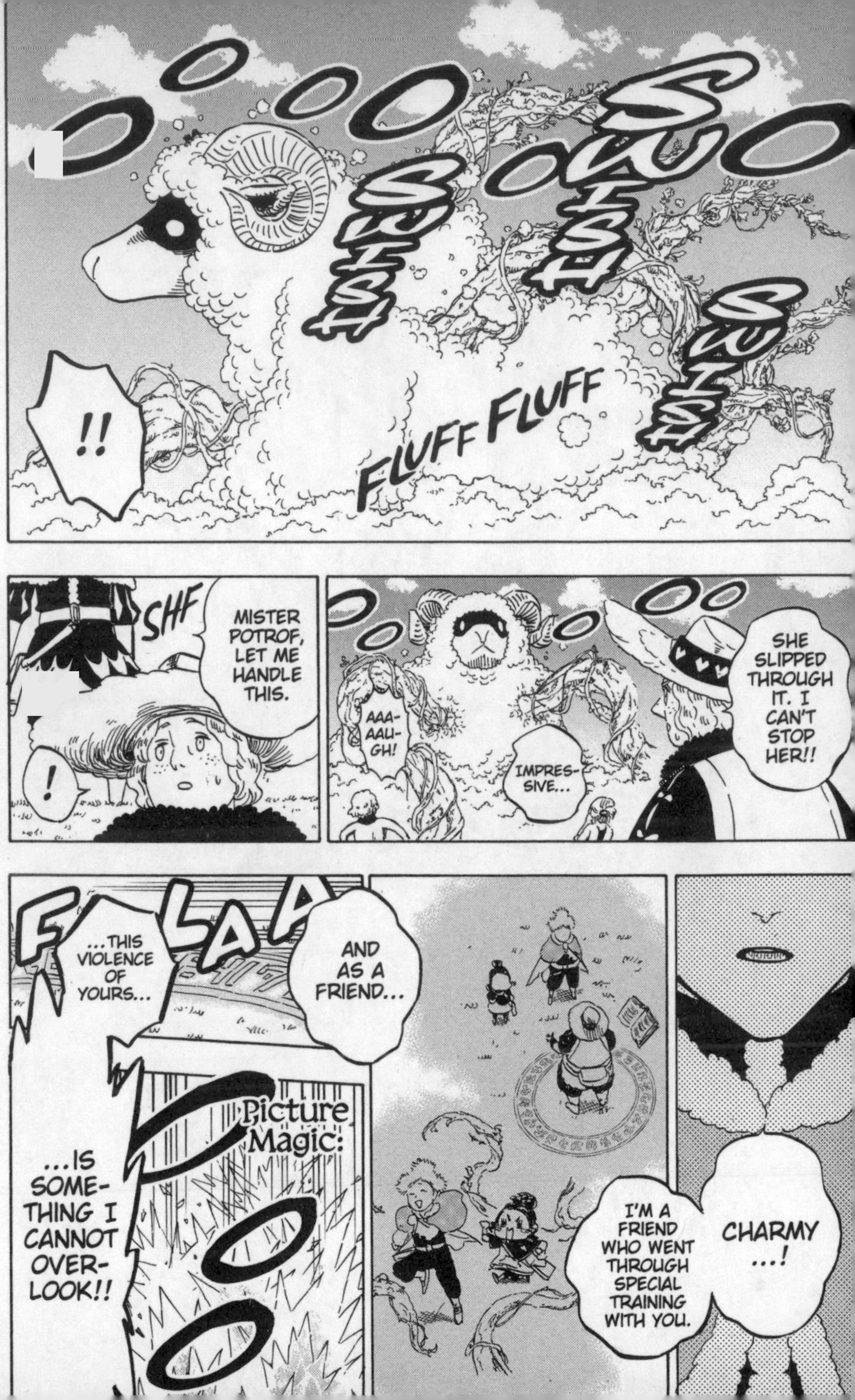
SWISH
SWISH
SWISH
FLUFF FLUFF
!!
SHE SLIPPED THROUGH IT. I CAN'T STOP HER!!
IMPRESSIVE...
AAAAAUGH!
MISTER POTROF, LET ME HANDLE THIS.
SHF
!
CHARMY ...!
I'M A FRIEND WHO WENT THROUGH SPECIAL TRAINING WITH YOU.
AND AS A FRIEND...
...THIS VIOLENCE OF YOURS...
...IS SOMETHING I CANNOT OVERLOOK!!
Picture Magic:

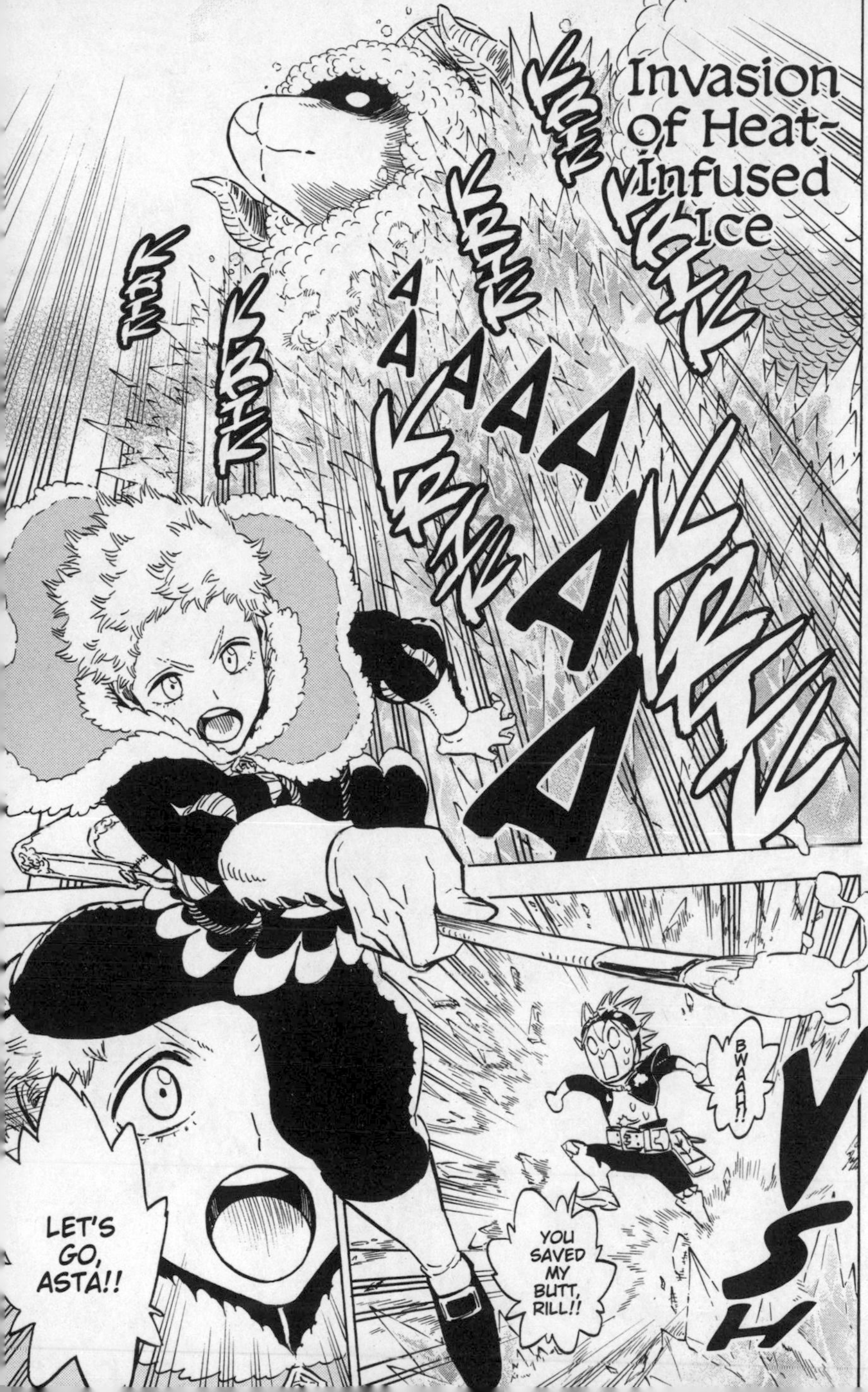
Invasion of Heat-Infused Ice
BWAAAH!!
YOU SAVED MY BUTT, RILL!!
LET'S GO, ASTA!!

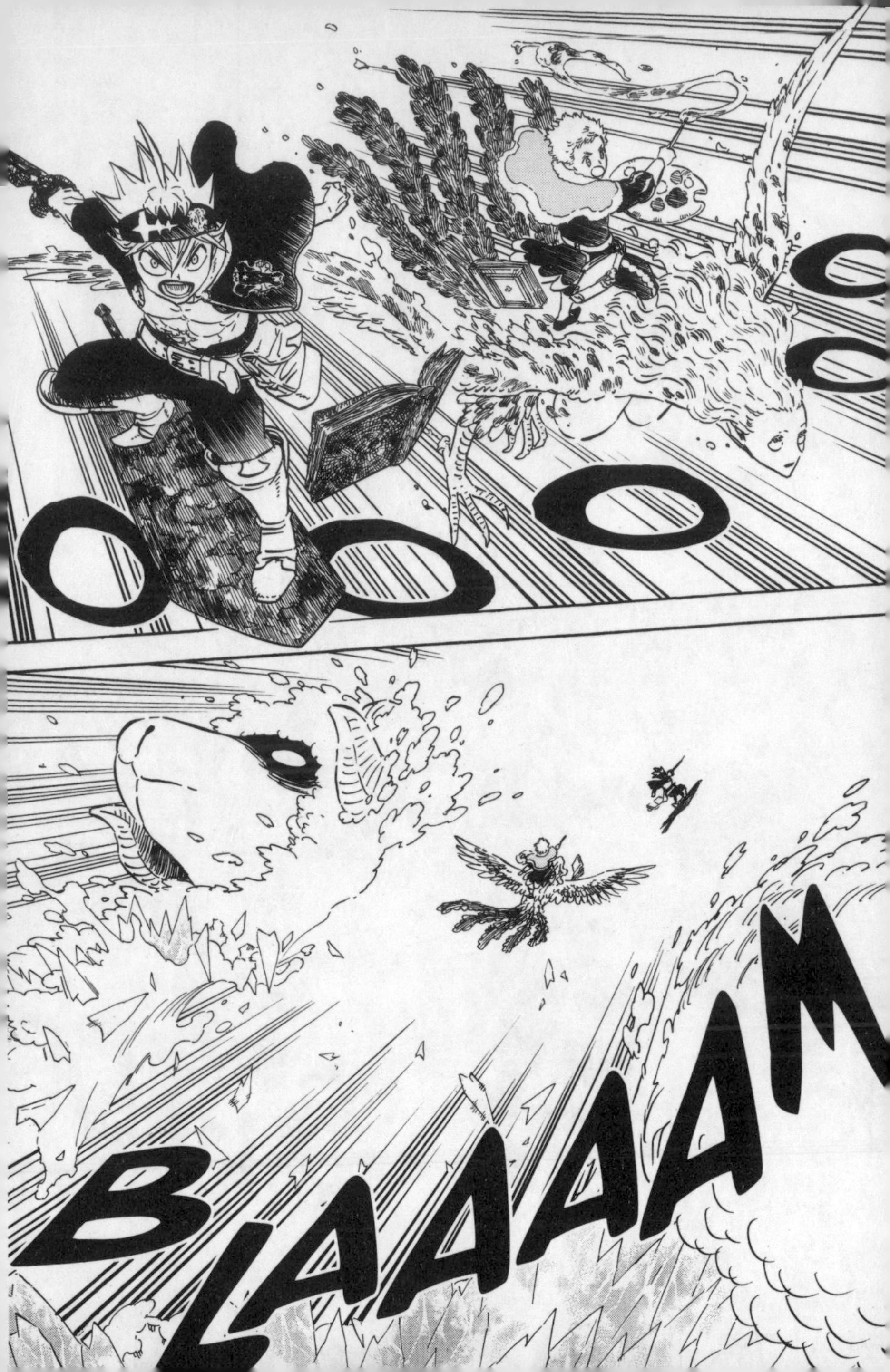
OOOOO
BLAAAAM

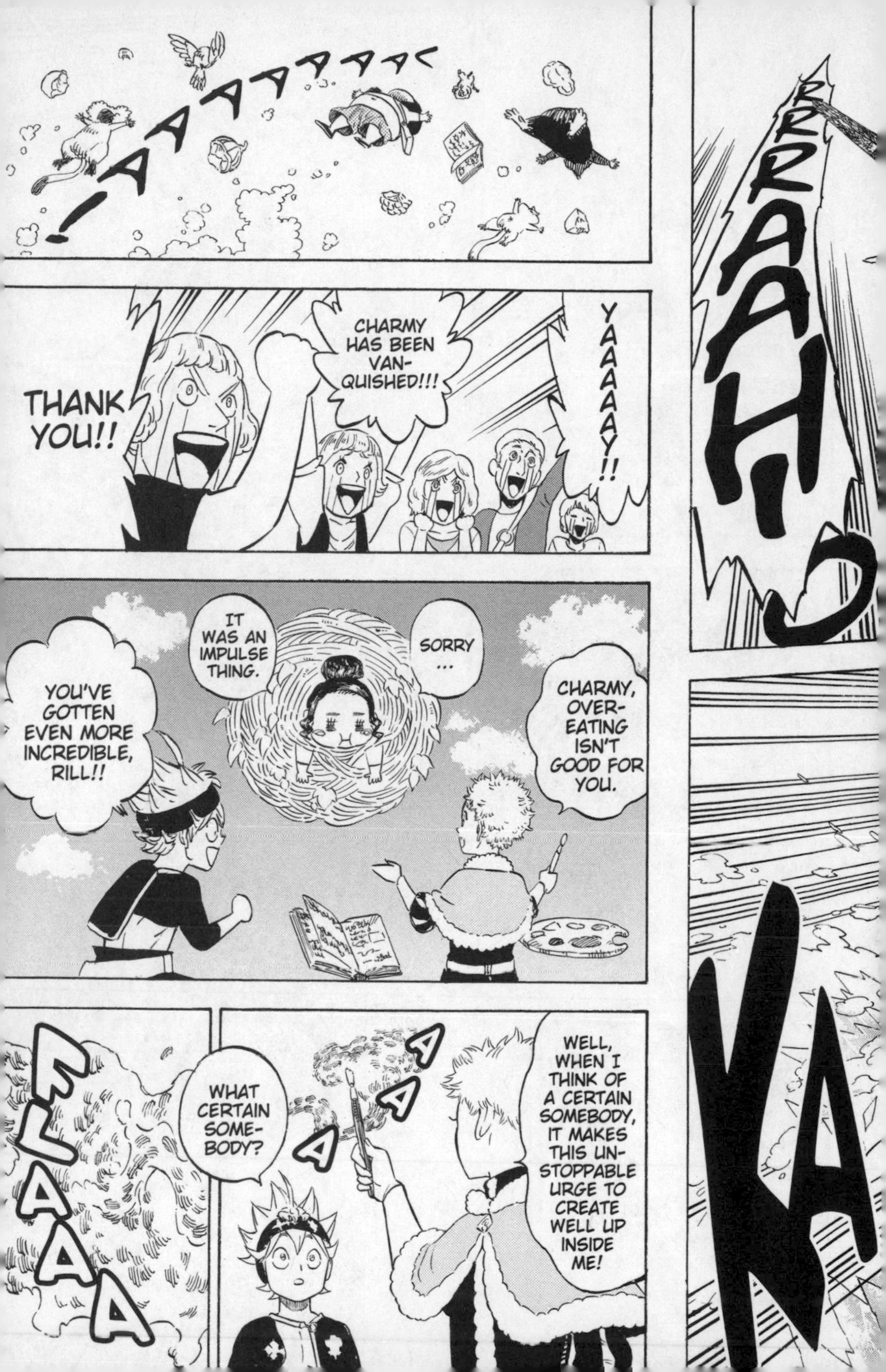
RRRAAAHH
KA
AAAAAAAAA!
YAAAAAAY!!
CHARMY HAS BEEN VAN-QUISHED!!!
THANK YOU!!
CHARMY, OVER-EATING ISN'T GOOD FOR YOU.
SORRY...
IT WAS AN IMPULSE THING.
YOU'VE GOTTEN EVEN MORE INCREDIBLE, RILL!!
WELL, WHEN I THINK OF A CERTAIN SOMEBODY, IT MAKES THIS UN-STOPPABLE URGE TO CREATE WELL UP INSIDE ME!
AAA
WHAT CERTAIN SOME-BODY?
FLAAAAA

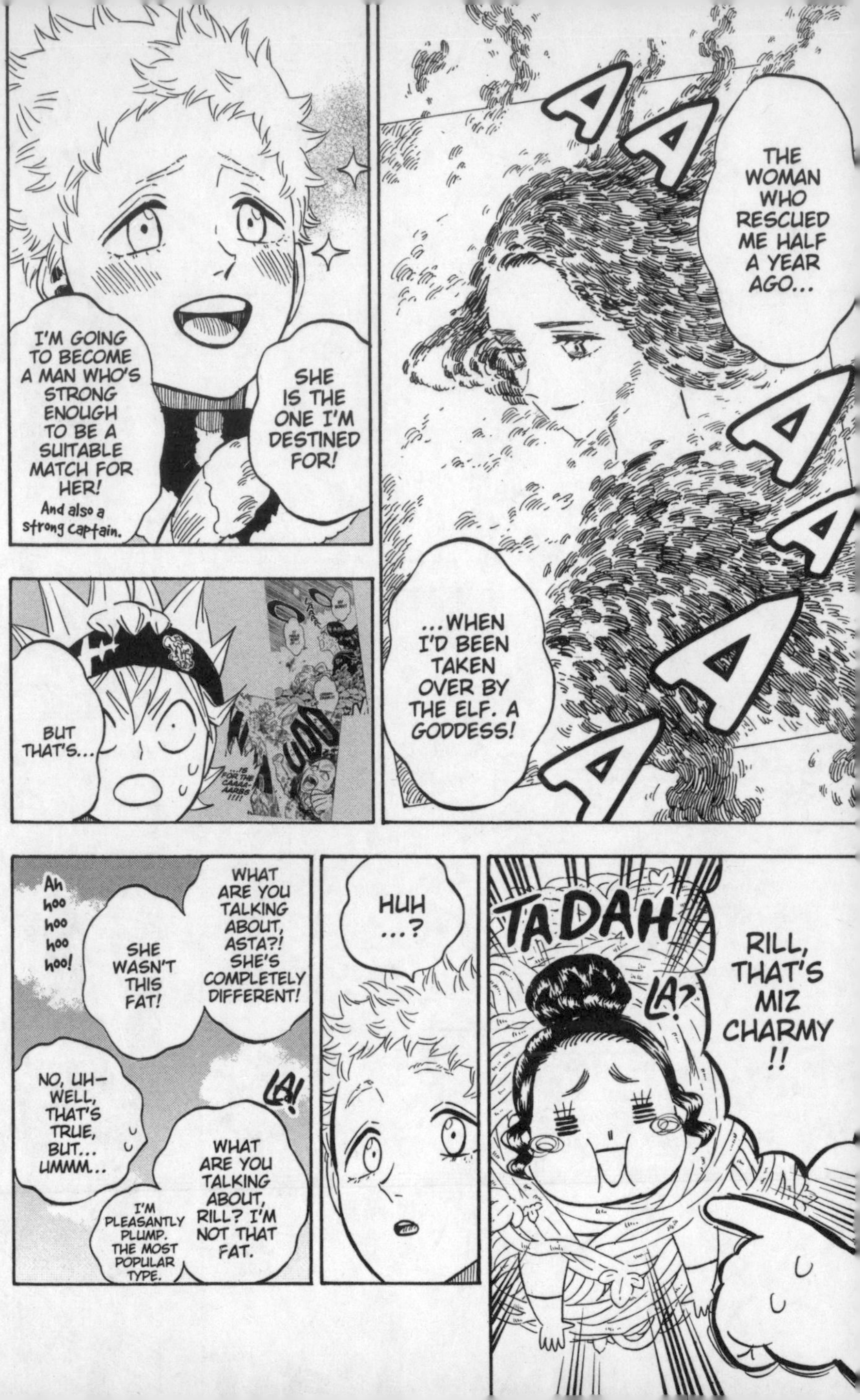
THE WOMAN WHO RESCUED ME HALF A YEAR AGO...
AAAAA
...WHEN I'D BEEN TAKEN OVER BY THE ELF. A GODDESS!
SHE IS THE ONE I'M DESTINED FOR!
I'M GOING TO BECOME A MAN WHO'S STRONG ENOUGH TO BE A SUITABLE MATCH FOR HER!
And also a strong captain.
BUT THAT'S...
TADAH
LA?
RILL, THAT'S MIZ CHARMY!!
HUH ...?
LA!
WHAT ARE YOU TALKING ABOUT, ASTA?! SHE'S COMPLETELY DIFFERENT!
SHE WASN'T THIS FAT!
Ah hoo hoo hoo hoo!
NO, UH— WELL, THAT'S TRUE, BUT... UMMM...
WHAT ARE YOU TALKING ABOUT, RILL? I'M NOT THAT FAT.
I'M PLEASANTLY PLUMP. THE MOST POPULAR TYPE.

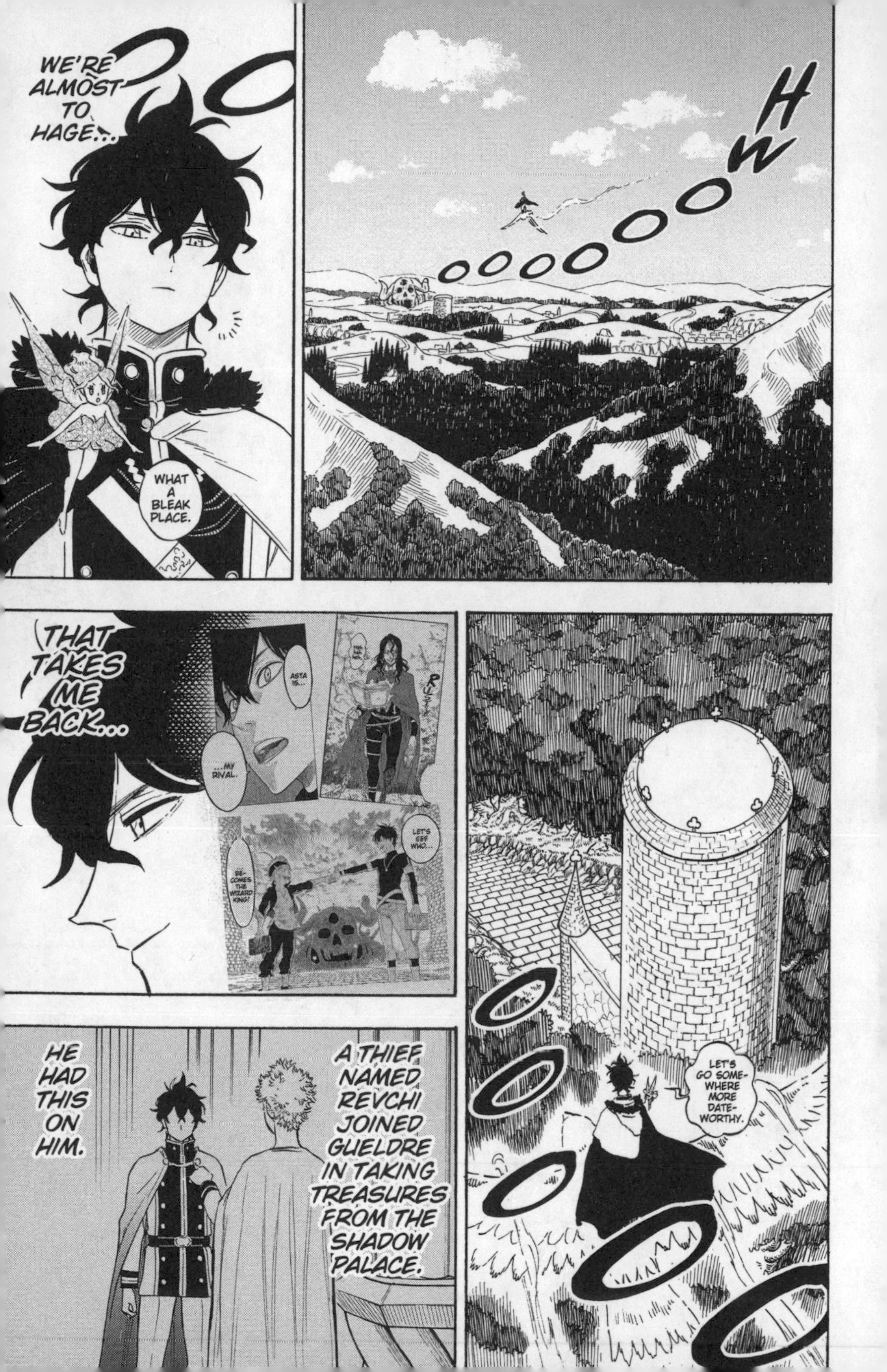
HWOOOOOOOO
WE'RE ALMOST TO HAGE...
WHAT A BLEAK PLACE.
LET'S GO SOME-WHERE MORE DATE-WORTHY.
THAT TAKES ME BACK...
RUSTLE
ASTA IS...
...MY RIVAL.
LET'S SEE WHO...
...BE-COMES THE WIZARD KING!
A THIEF NAMED REVCHI JOINED GUELDRE IN TAKING TREASURES FROM THE SHADOW PALACE.
HE HAD THIS ON HIM.

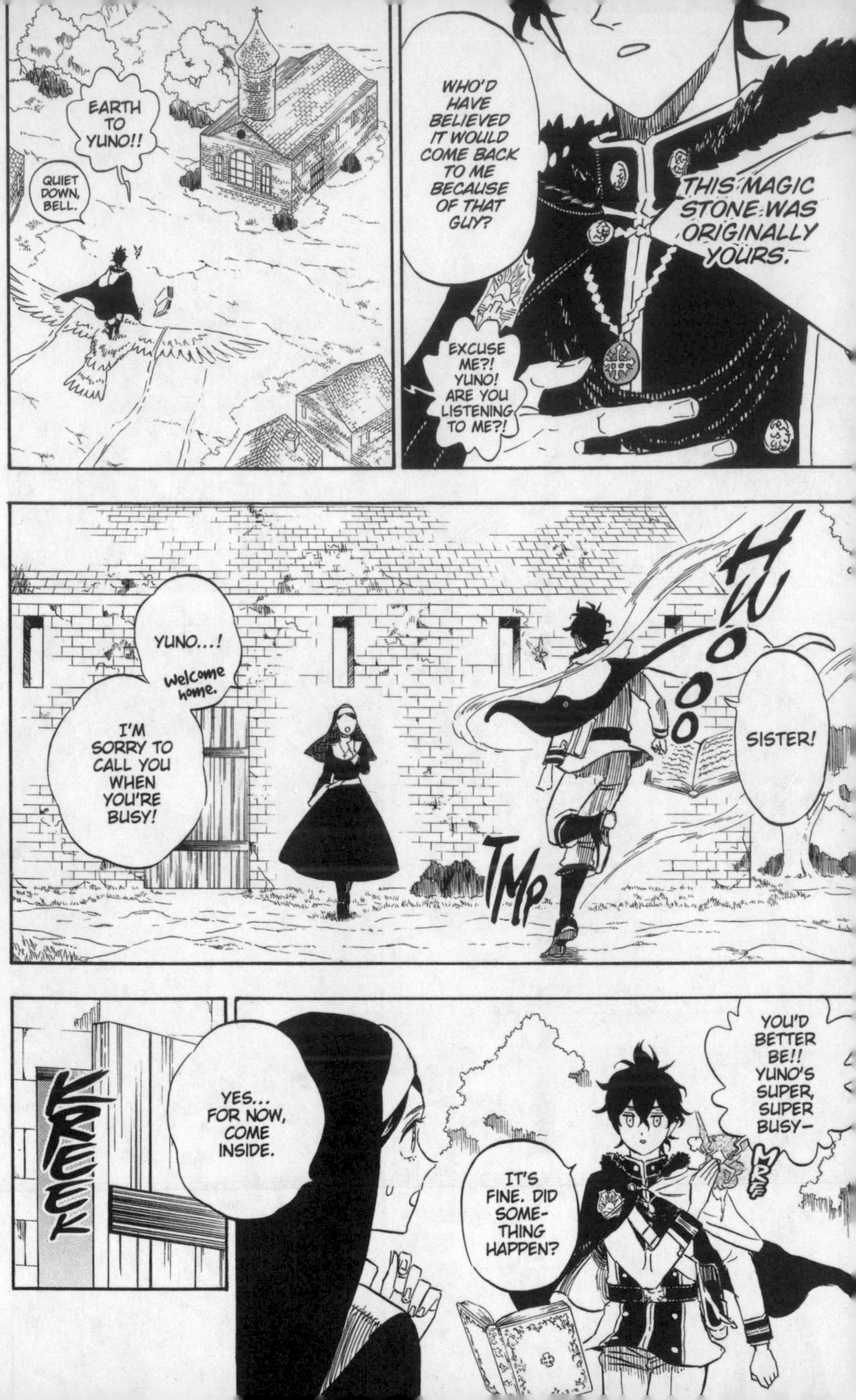
THIS MAGIC STONE WAS ORIGINALLY YOURS.
WHO'D HAVE BELIEVED IT WOULD COME BACK TO ME BECAUSE OF THAT GUY?
EXCUSE ME?! YUNO! ARE YOU LISTENING TO ME?!
EARTH TO YUNO!!
QUIET DOWN, BELL.
HWOOOO
SISTER!
TMP
YUNO...!
welcome home.
I'M SORRY TO CALL YOU WHEN YOU'RE BUSY!
YOU'D BETTER BE!! YUNO'S SUPER, SUPER BUSY—
MRF
IT'S FINE. DID SOMETHING HAPPEN?
YES... FOR NOW, COME INSIDE.
KREEK

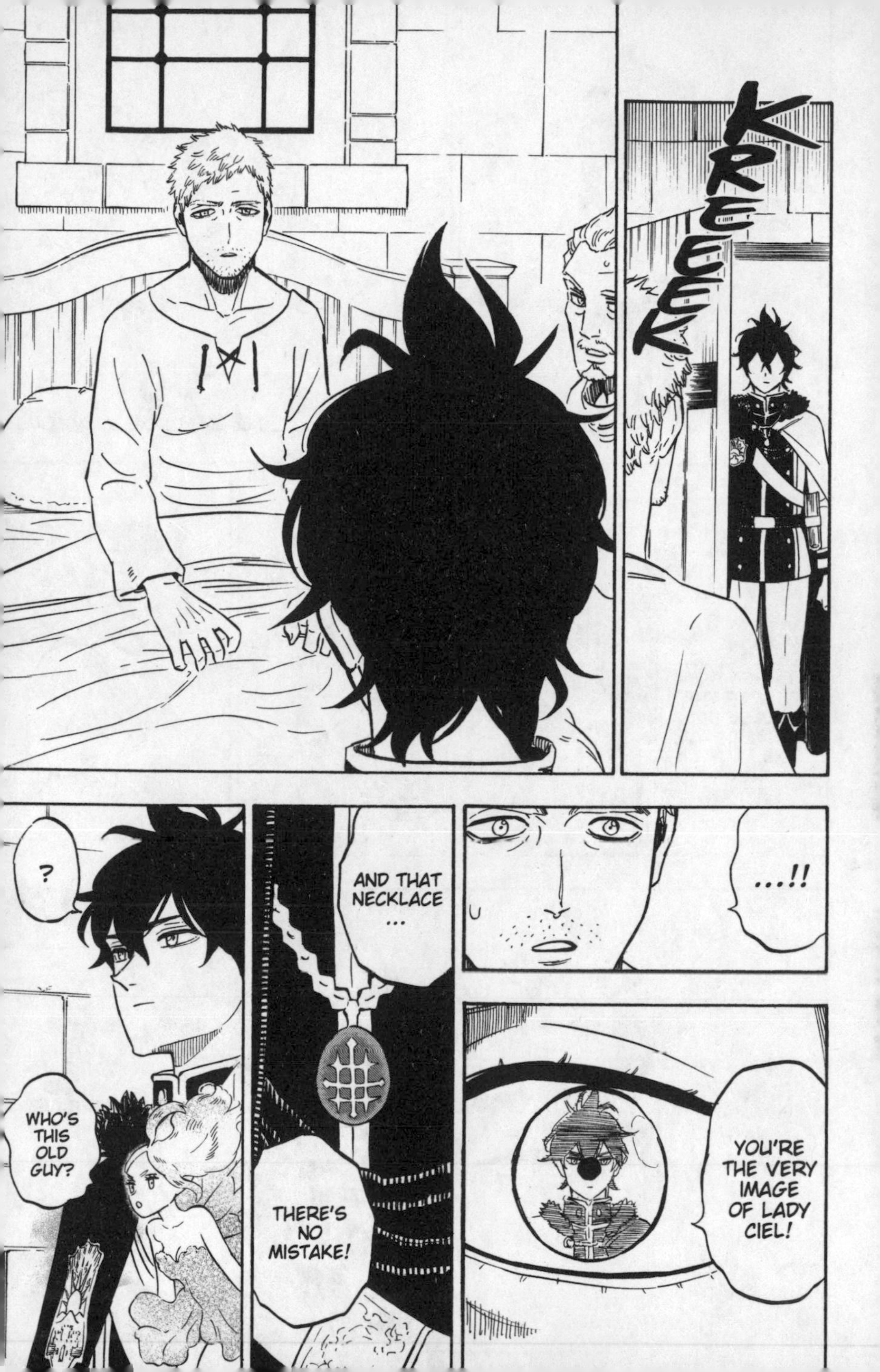
KREEEK
...!!
YOU'RE THE VERY IMAGE OF LADY CIEL!
AND THAT NECKLACE ...
THERE'S NO MISTAKE!
?
WHO'S THIS OLD GUY?

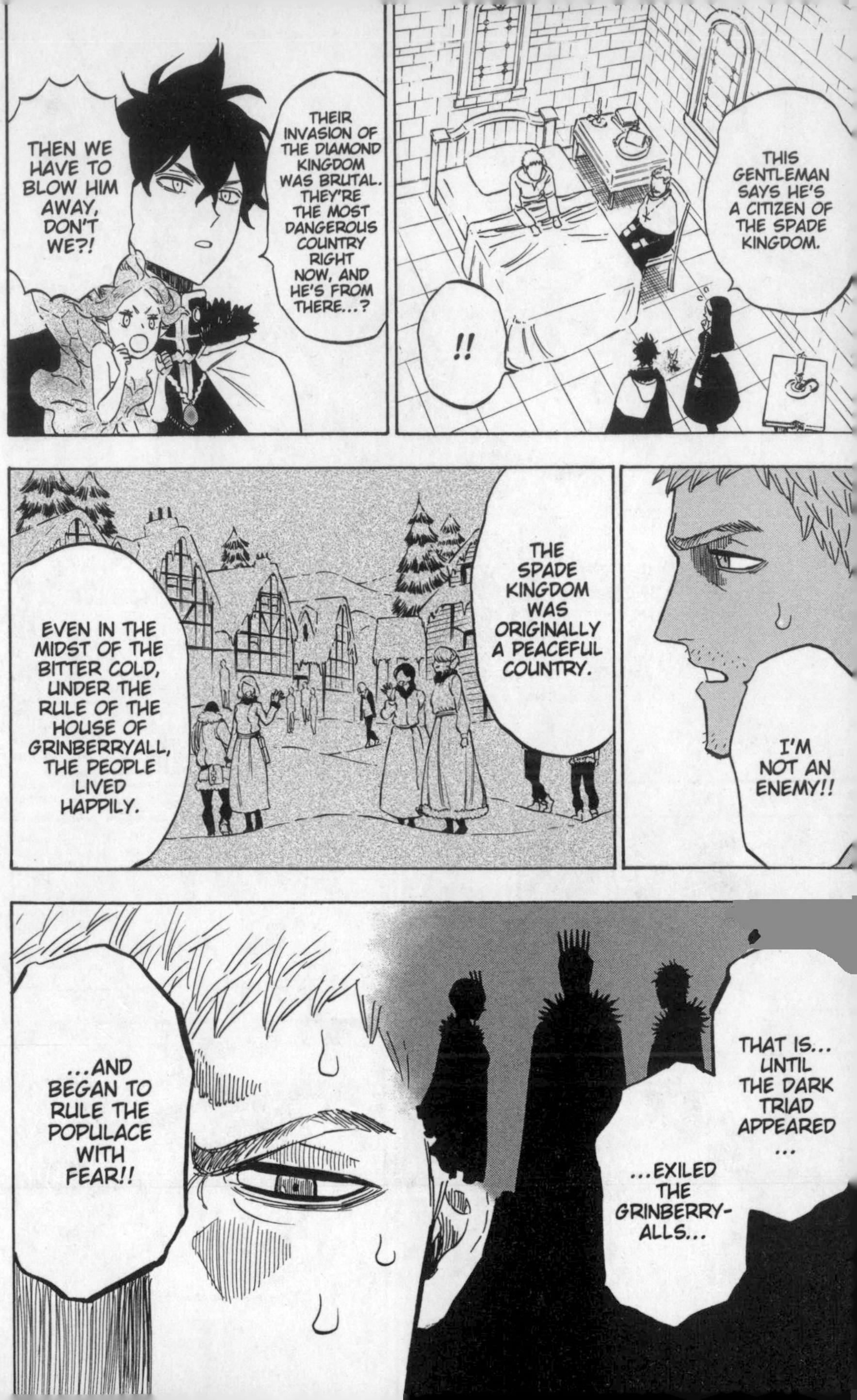
THIS GENTLEMAN SAYS HE'S A CITIZEN OF THE SPADE KINGDOM.
!!
THEIR INVASION OF THE DIAMOND KINGDOM WAS BRUTAL. THEY'RE THE MOST DANGEROUS COUNTRY RIGHT NOW, AND HE'S FROM THERE...?
THEN WE HAVE TO BLOW HIM AWAY, DON'T WE?!
I'M NOT AN ENEMY!!
THE SPADE KINGDOM WAS ORIGINALLY A PEACEFUL COUNTRY.
EVEN IN THE MIDST OF THE BITTER COLD, UNDER THE RULE OF THE HOUSE OF GRINBERRYALL, THE PEOPLE LIVED HAPPILY.
THAT IS... UNTIL THE DARK TRIAD APPEARED ...
...EXILED THE GRINBERRY-ALLS...
...AND BEGAN TO RULE THE POPULACE WITH FEAR!!

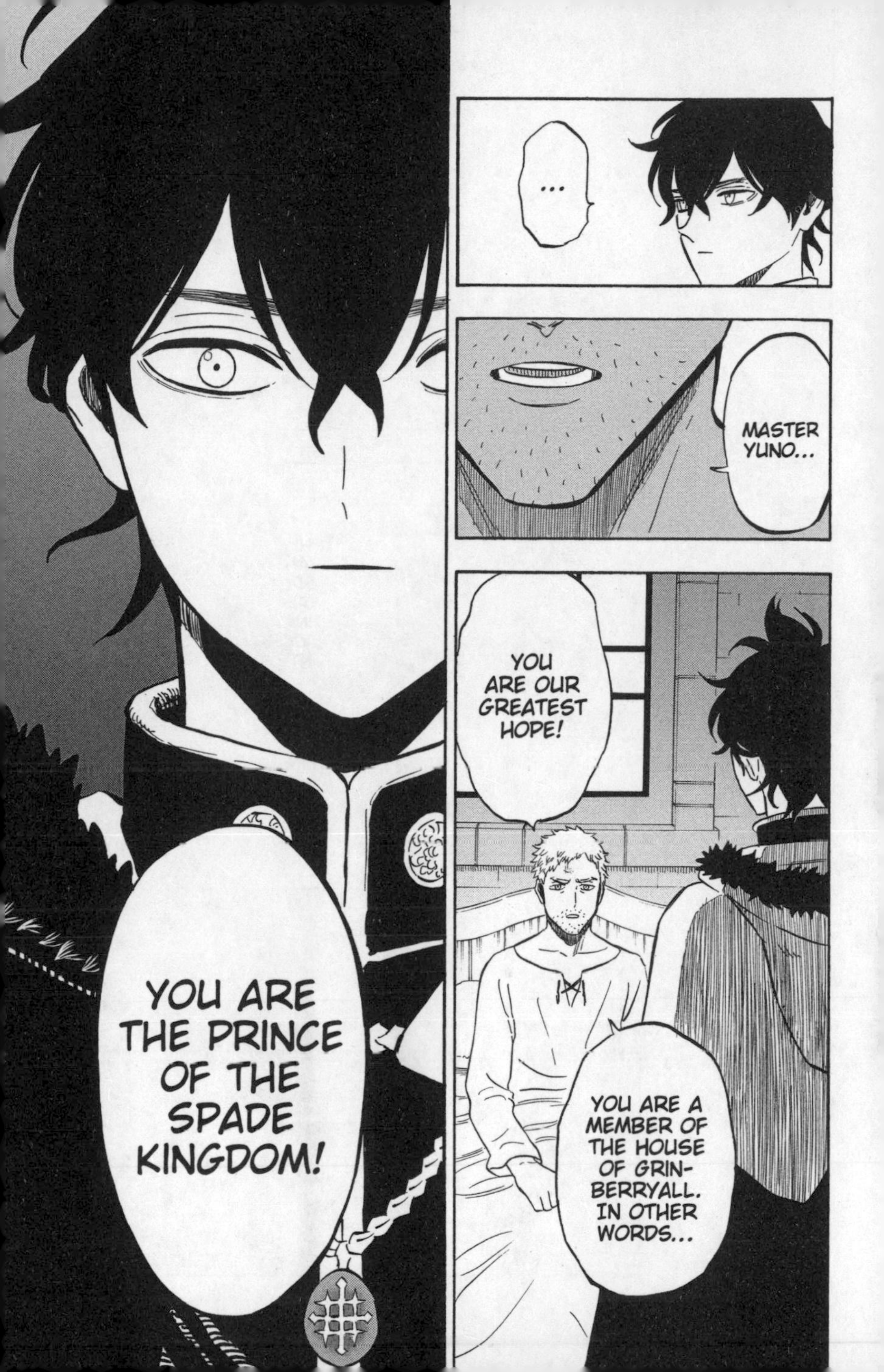
...
MASTER YUNO...
YOU ARE OUR GREATEST HOPE!
YOU ARE A MEMBER OF THE HOUSE OF GRIN-BERRYALL. IN OTHER WORDS...
YOU ARE THE PRINCE OF THE SPADE KINGDOM!

YAAAAAY!!
CHARMY HAS BEEN VAN-QUISHED!!!
THANK YOU!!

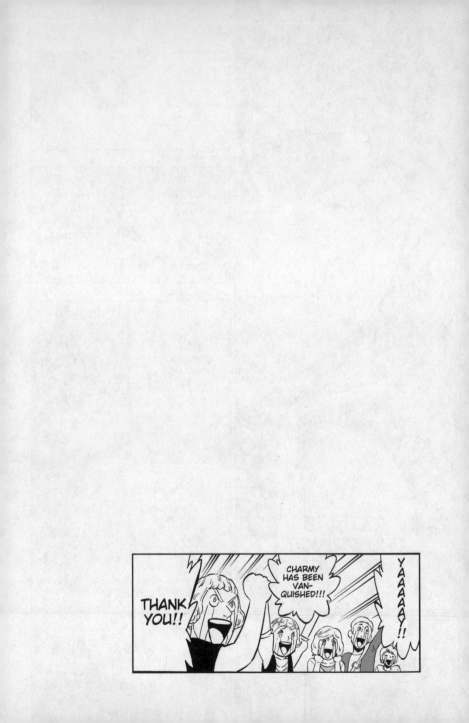

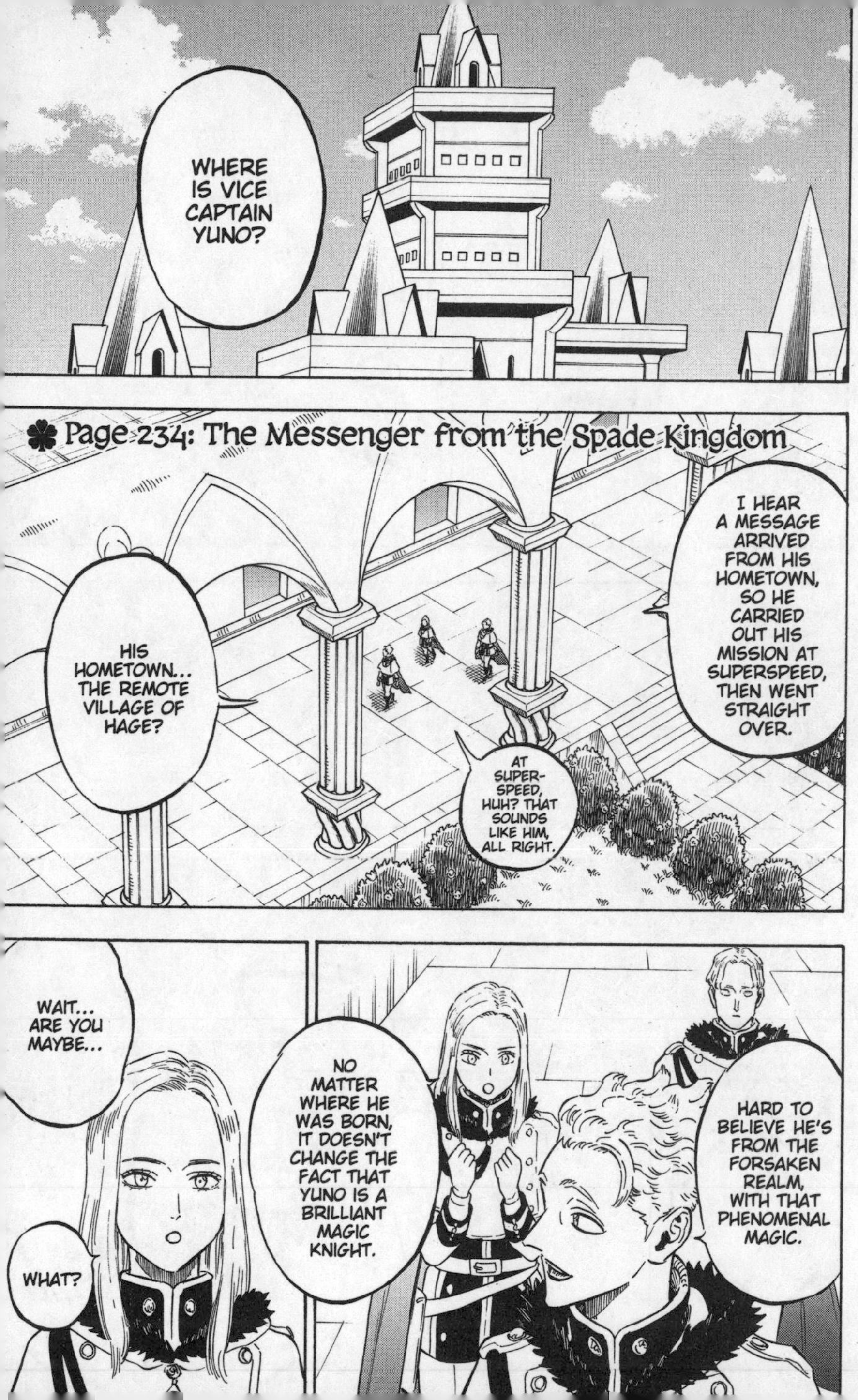
WHERE IS VICE CAPTAIN YUNO?
Page 234: The Messenger from the Spade Kingdom
I HEAR A MESSAGE ARRIVED FROM HIS HOMETOWN, SO HE CARRIED OUT HIS MISSION AT SUPERSPEED, THEN WENT STRAIGHT OVER.
HIS HOMETOWN... THE REMOTE VILLAGE OF HAGE?
AT SUPER-SPEED, HUH? THAT SOUNDS LIKE HIM, ALL RIGHT.
HARD TO BELIEVE HE'S FROM THE FORSAKEN REALM, WITH THAT PHENOMENAL MAGIC.
NO MATTER WHERE HE WAS BORN, IT DOESN'T CHANGE THE FACT THAT YUNO IS A BRILLIANT MAGIC KNIGHT.
WAIT... ARE YOU MAYBE...
WHAT?

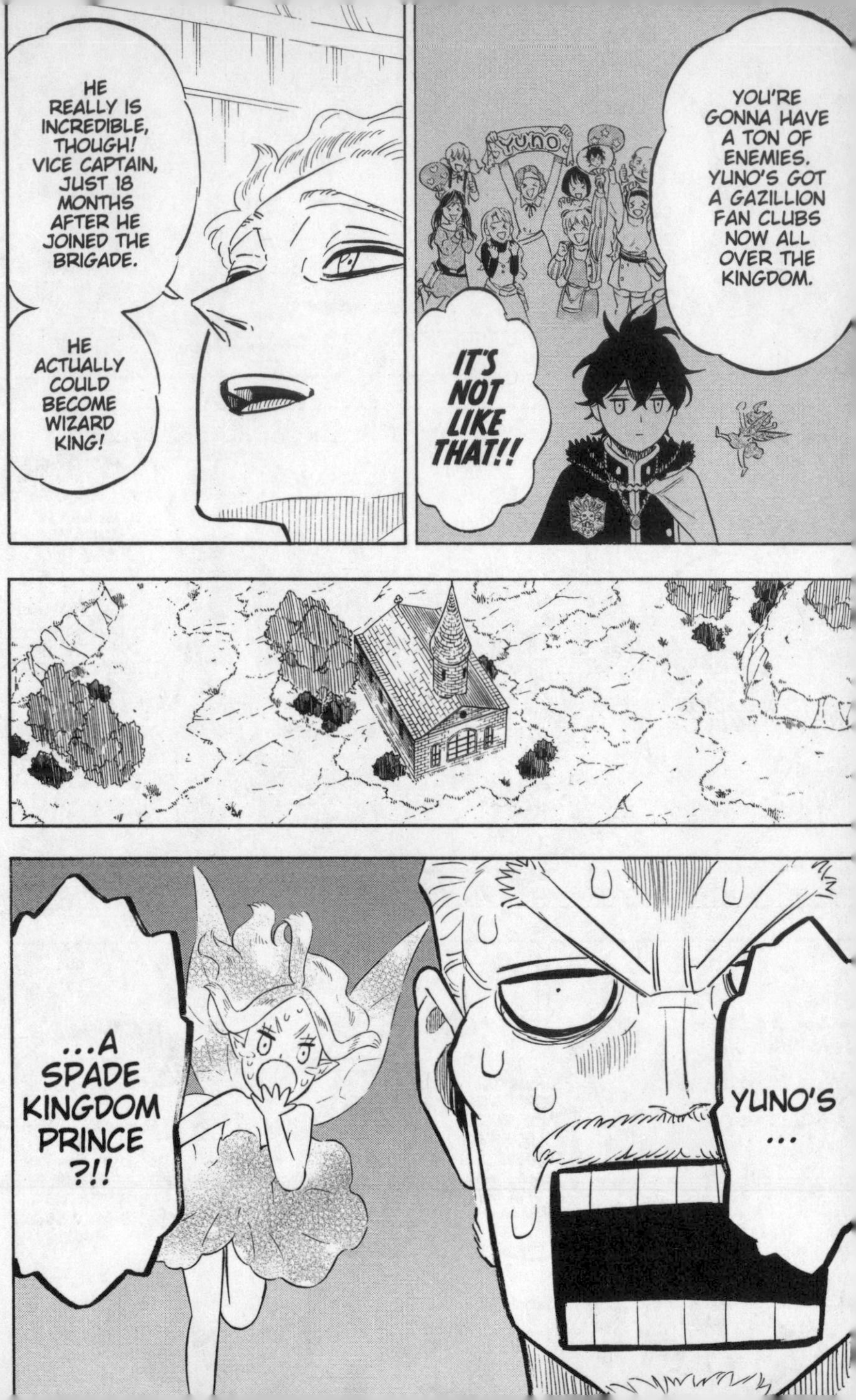
YOU'RE GONNA HAVE A TON OF ENEMIES. YUNO'S GOT A GAZILLION FAN CLUBS NOW ALL OVER THE KINGDOM.
YUNO
IT'S NOT LIKE THAT!!
HE REALLY IS INCREDIBLE, THOUGH! VICE CAPTAIN, JUST 18 MONTHS AFTER HE JOINED THE BRIGADE.
HE ACTUALLY COULD BECOME WIZARD KING!
YUNO'S ...
...A SPADE KINGDOM PRINCE ?!!

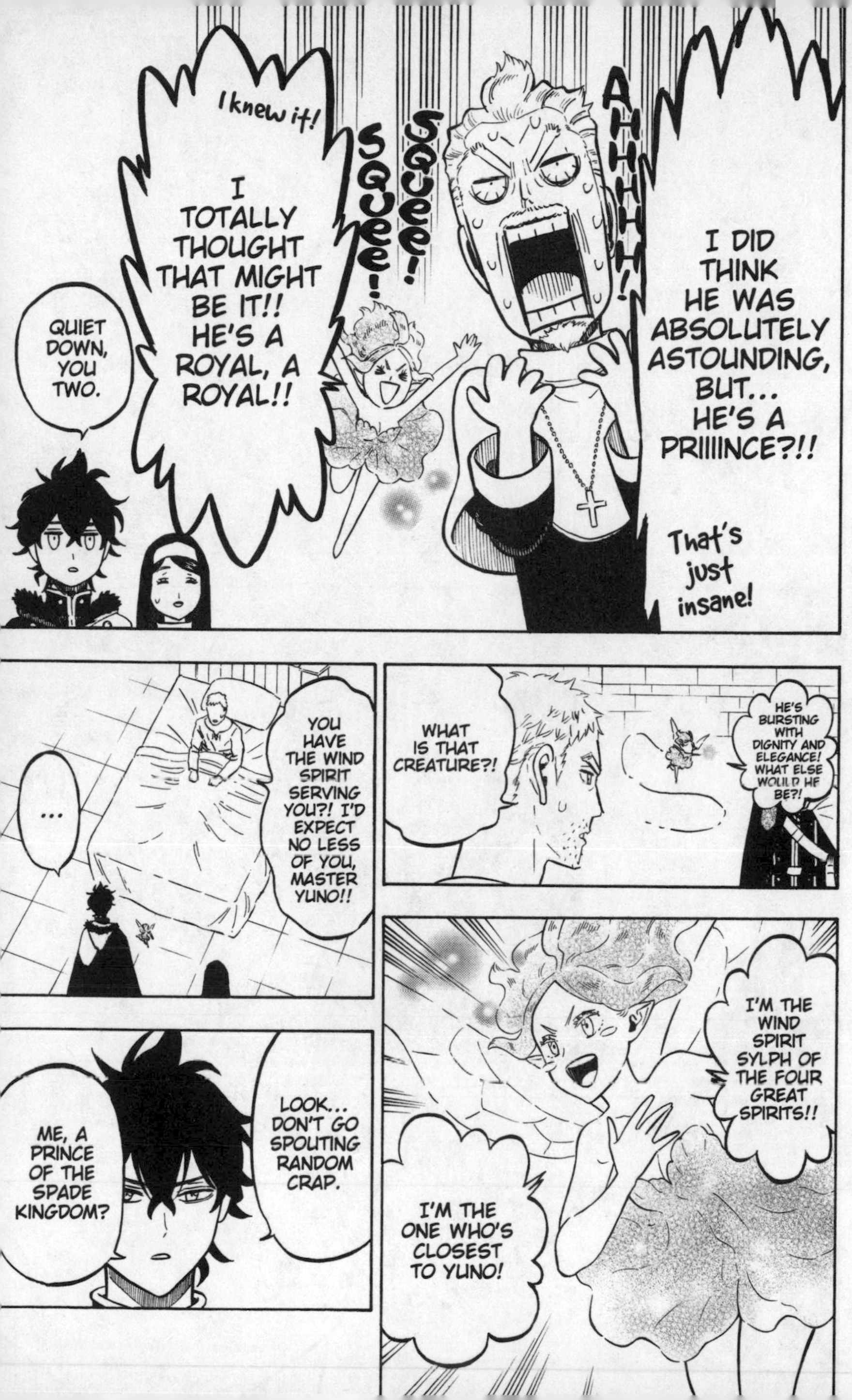
AHHHHHH!
I DID THINK HE WAS ABSOLUTELY ASTOUNDING, BUT... HE'S A PRIIIINCE?!!
That's just insane!
SQUEEE! SQUEEE!
I knew it!
I TOTALLY THOUGHT THAT MIGHT BE IT!! HE'S A ROYAL, A ROYAL!!
QUIET DOWN, YOU TWO.
HE'S BURSTING WITH DIGNITY AND ELEGANCE! WHAT ELSE WOULD HE BE?!
WHAT IS THAT CREATURE?!
YOU HAVE THE WIND SPIRIT SERVING YOU?! I'D EXPECT NO LESS OF YOU, MASTER YUNO!!
...
I'M THE WIND SPIRIT SYLPH OF THE FOUR GREAT SPIRITS!!
I'M THE ONE WHO'S CLOSEST TO YUNO!
LOOK... DON'T GO SPOUTING RANDOM CRAP.
ME, A PRINCE OF THE SPADE KINGDOM?

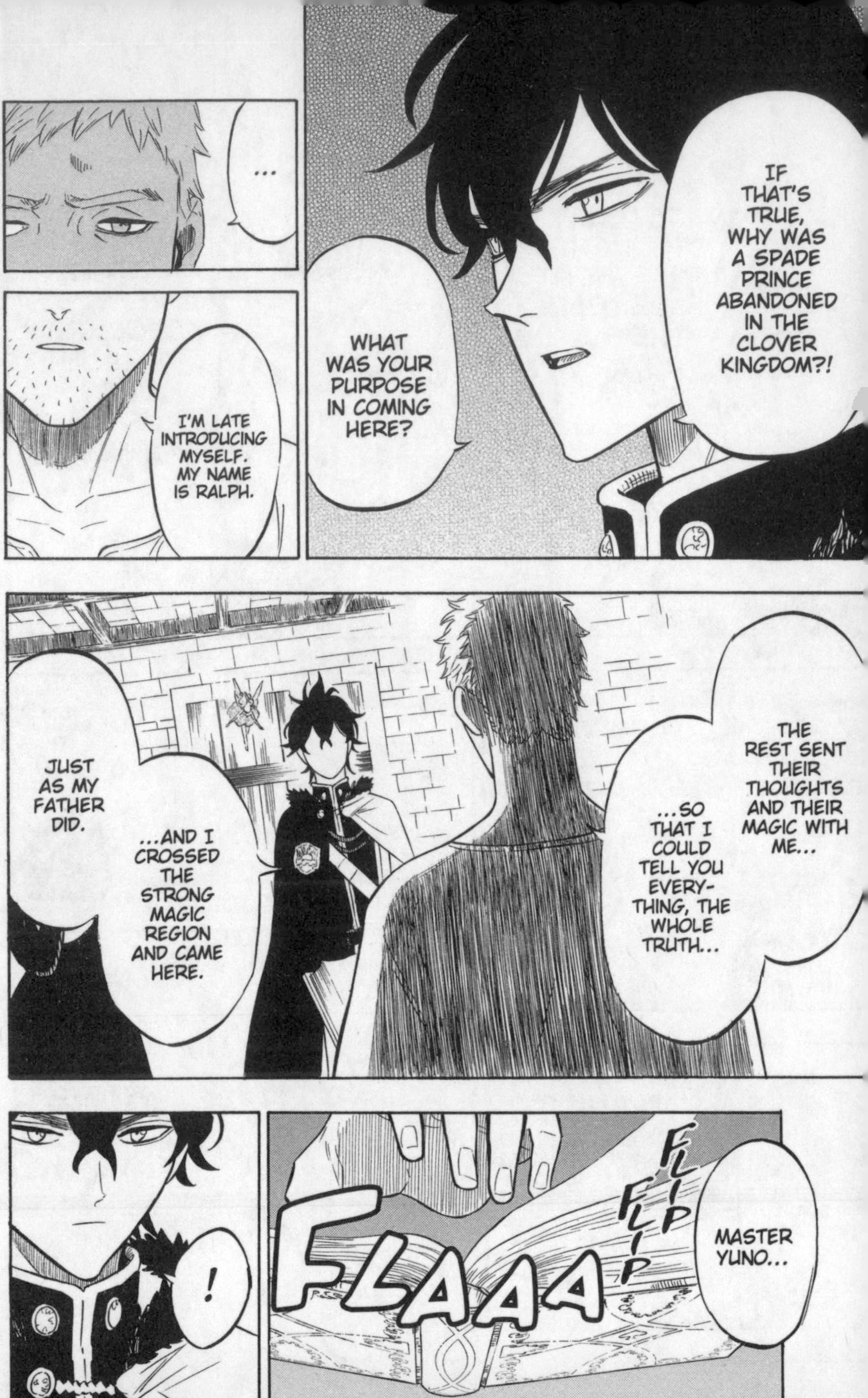
IF THAT'S TRUE, WHY WAS A SPADE PRINCE ABANDONED IN THE CLOVER KINGDOM?!
WHAT WAS YOUR PURPOSE IN COMING HERE?
...
I'M LATE INTRODUCING MYSELF. MY NAME IS RALPH.
THE REST SENT THEIR THOUGHTS AND THEIR MAGIC WITH ME...
...SO THAT I COULD TELL YOU EVERY-THING, THE WHOLE TRUTH...
...AND I CROSSED THE STRONG MAGIC REGION AND CAME HERE.
JUST AS MY FATHER DID.
MASTER YUNO...
FLIP FLIP
FLAAA
!

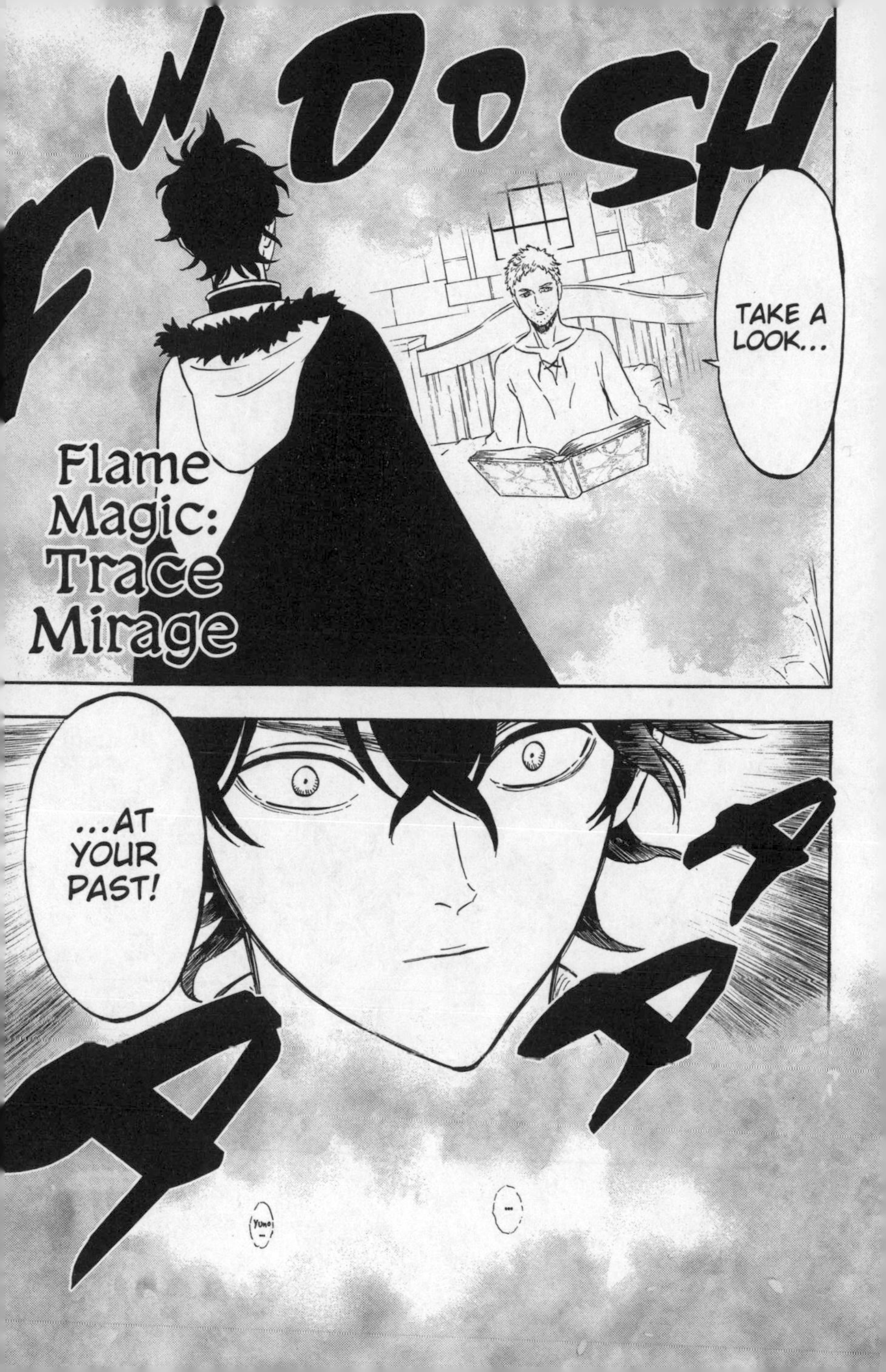
SWOOSH
TAKE A LOOK...
Flame Magic: Trace Mirage
...AT YOUR PAST!
...
Yuno...

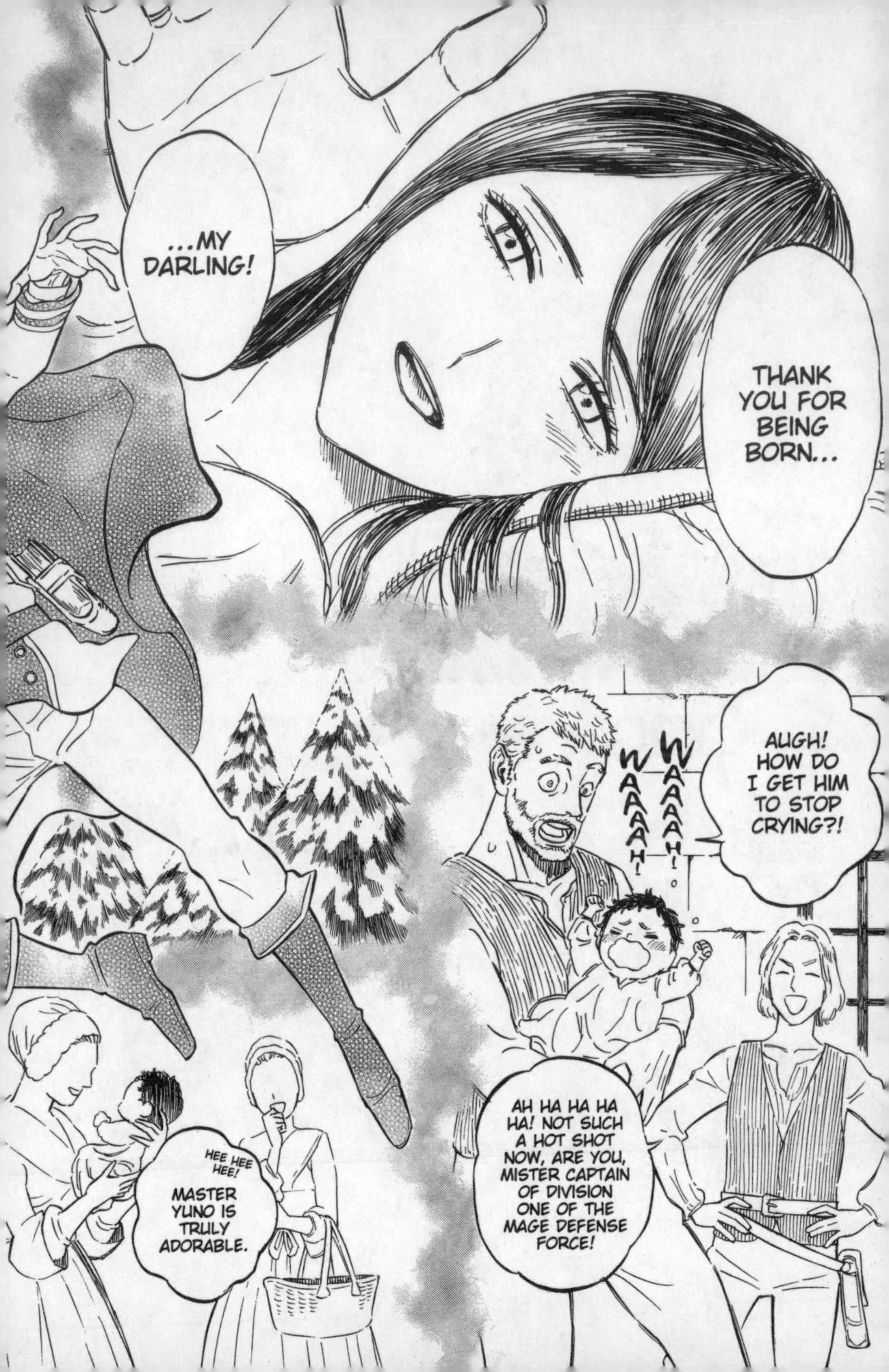
THANK YOU FOR BEING BORN...
...MY DARLING!
AUGH! HOW DO I GET HIM TO STOP CRYING?!
WAAAAAH!
WAAAAH!
AH HA HA HA HA! NOT SUCH A HOT SHOT NOW, ARE YOU, MISTER CAPTAIN OF DIVISION ONE OF THE MAGE DEFENSE FORCE!
HEE HEE HEE!
MASTER YUNO IS TRULY ADORABLE.

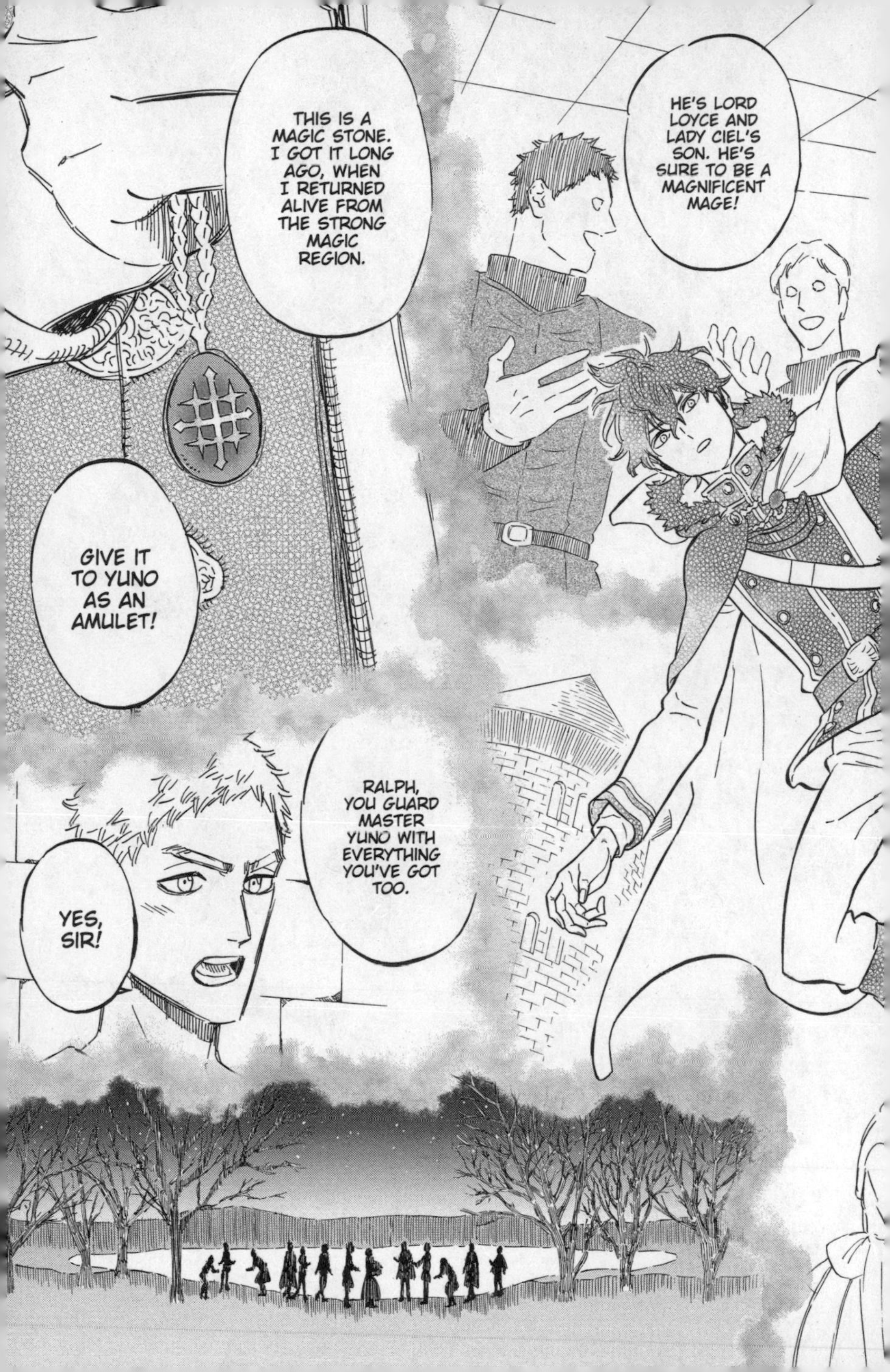
HE'S LORD LOYCE AND LADY CIEL'S SON. HE'S SURE TO BE A MAGNIFICENT MAGE!
THIS IS A MAGIC STONE. I GOT IT LONG AGO, WHEN I RETURNED ALIVE FROM THE STRONG MAGIC REGION.
GIVE IT TO YUNO AS AN AMULET!
RALPH, YOU GUARD MASTER YUNO WITH EVERYTHING YOU'VE GOT TOO.
YES, SIR!

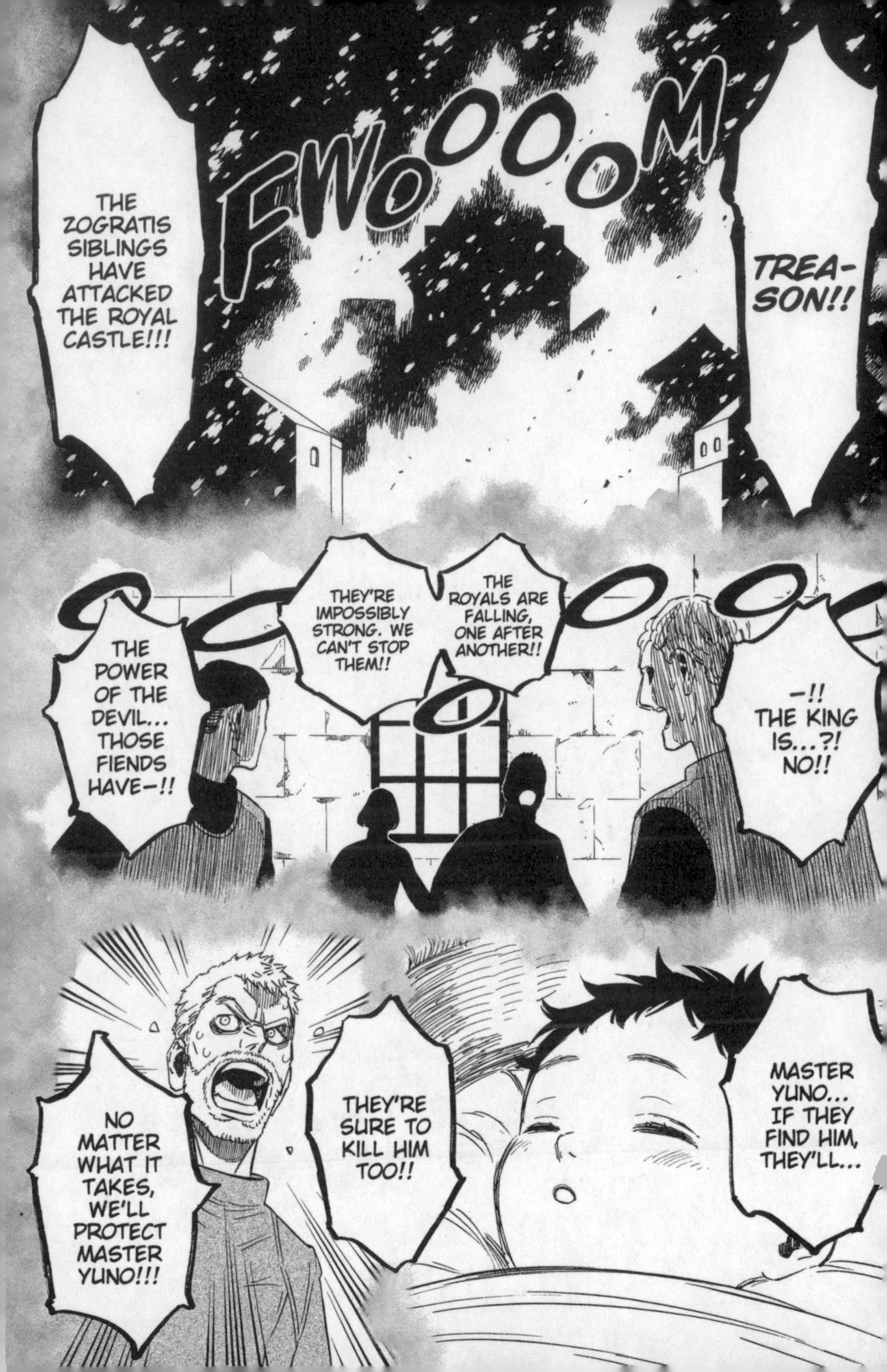
TREA-SON!!
FWOOOOM
THE ZOGRATIS SIBLINGS HAVE ATTACKED THE ROYAL CASTLE!!!
OOOOOOO
–!! THE KING IS...?! NO!!
THE ROYALS ARE FALLING, ONE AFTER ANOTHER!!
THEY'RE IMPOSSIBLY STRONG. WE CAN'T STOP THEM!!
THE POWER OF THE DEVIL... THOSE FIENDS HAVE–!!
MASTER YUNO... IF THEY FIND HIM, THEY'LL...
THEY'RE SURE TO KILL HIM TOO!!
NO MATTER WHAT IT TAKES, WE'LL PROTECT MASTER YUNO!!!

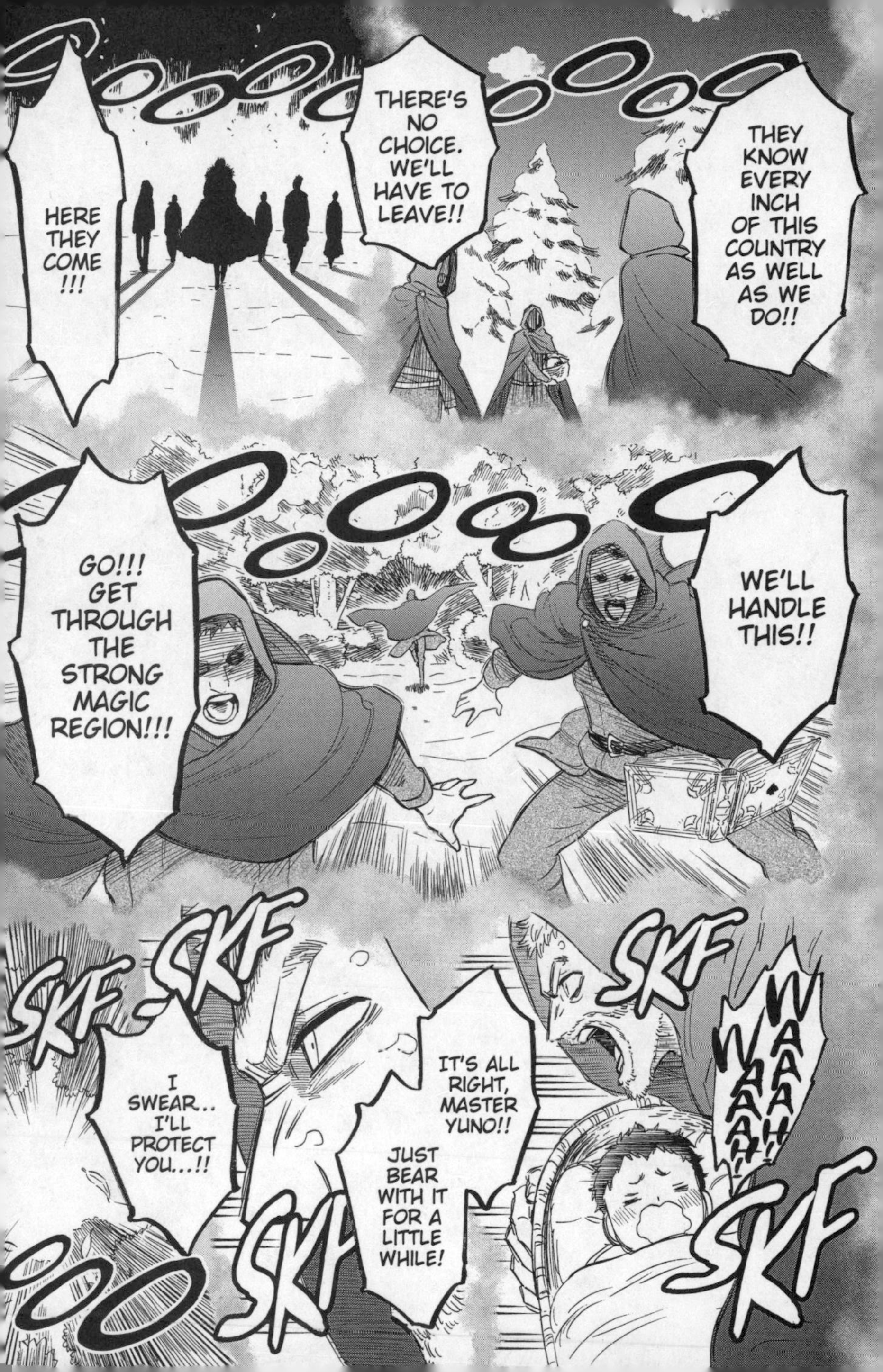
THEY KNOW EVERY INCH OF THIS COUNTRY AS WELL AS WE DO!!
THERE'S NO CHOICE. WE'LL HAVE TO LEAVE!!
HERE THEY COME!!!
WE'LL HANDLE THIS!!
GO!!! GET THROUGH THE STRONG MAGIC REGION!!!
SKF
WAAAAH!!
WAAAH!!
SKF
IT'S ALL RIGHT, MASTER YUNO!!
JUST BEAR WITH IT FOR A LITTLE WHILE!
SKF
SKF SKF
I SWEAR... I'LL PROTECT YOU...!!
SKF

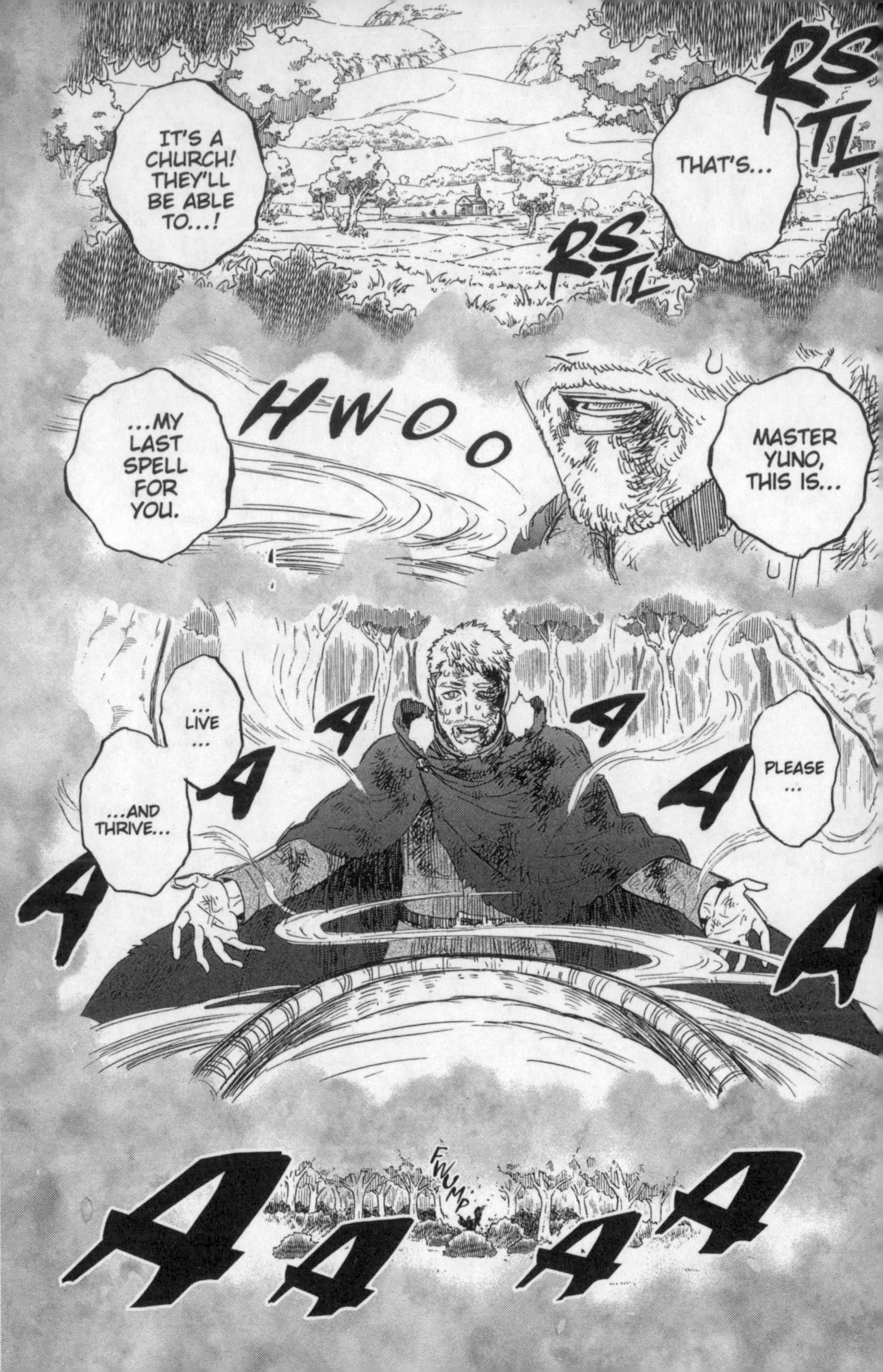
RSTL
THAT'S...
RSTL
IT'S A CHURCH! THEY'LL BE ABLE TO...!
MASTER YUNO, THIS IS...
HWOOO
...MY LAST SPELL FOR YOU.
PLEASE...
...LIVE...
...AND THRIVE...
AAAAAAAA
AAAAA
FWUMP

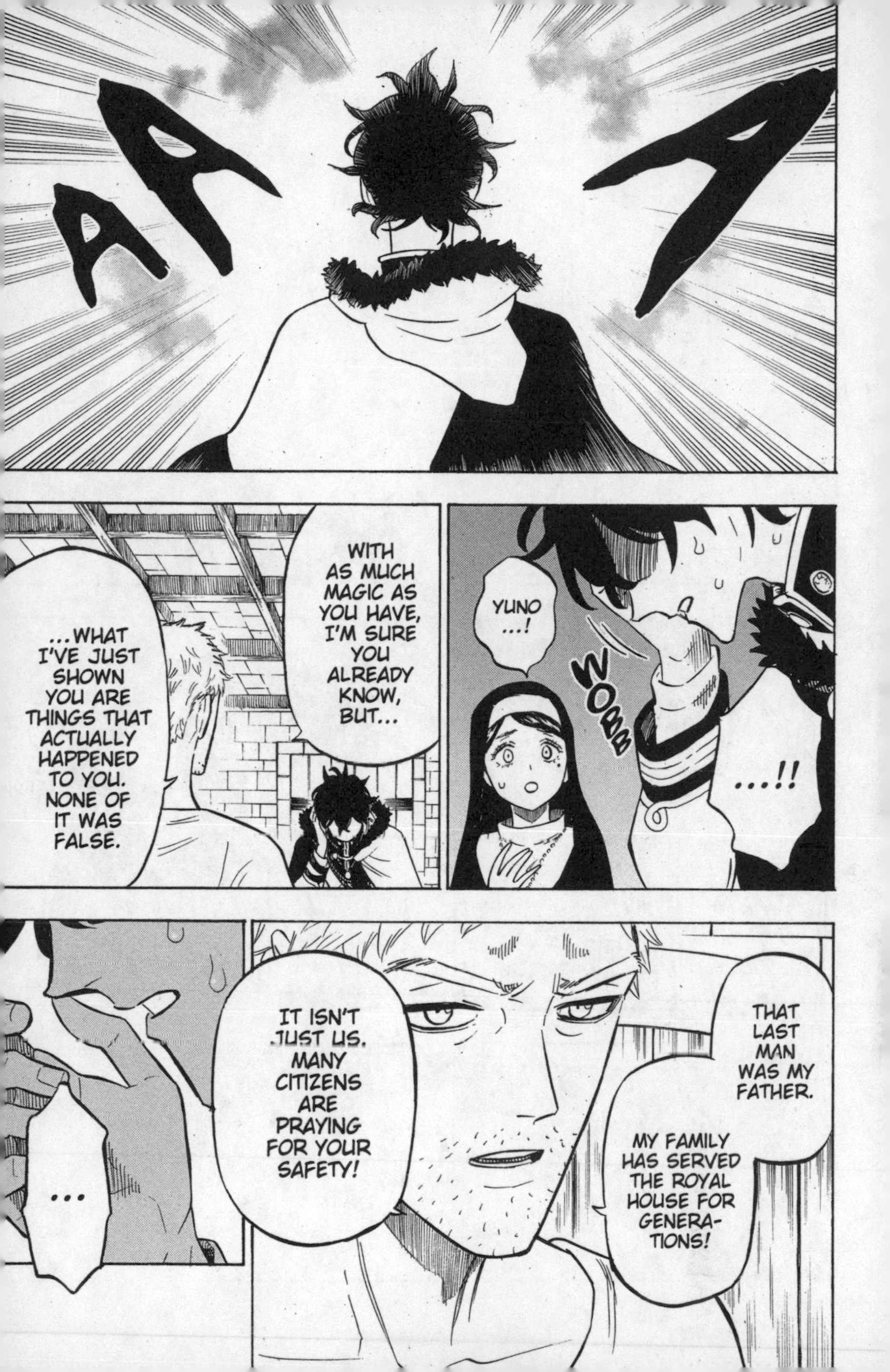
AAA
YUNO ...!
WOMM
...!!
WITH AS MUCH MAGIC AS YOU HAVE, I'M SURE YOU ALREADY KNOW, BUT...
...WHAT I'VE JUST SHOWN YOU ARE THINGS THAT ACTUALLY HAPPENED TO YOU. NONE OF IT WAS FALSE.
THAT LAST MAN WAS MY FATHER.
MY FAMILY HAS SERVED THE ROYAL HOUSE FOR GENERA-TIONS!
IT ISN'T JUST US. MANY CITIZENS ARE PRAYING FOR YOUR SAFETY!
...

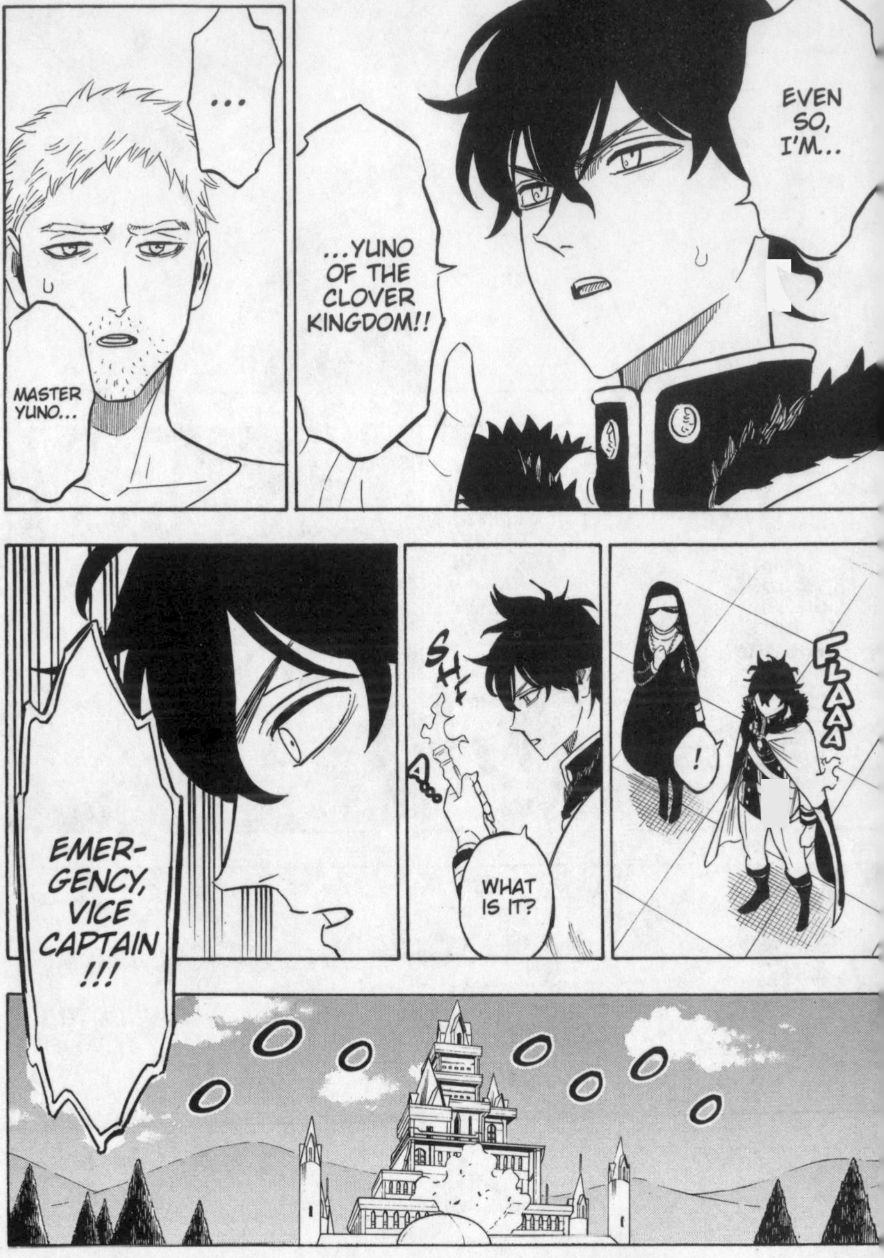
EVEN SO, I'M...
...YUNO OF THE CLOVER KINGDOM!!
...
MASTER YUNO...
FLAAA
!
SHI
WHAT IS IT?
EMERGENCY, VICE CAPTAIN!!!

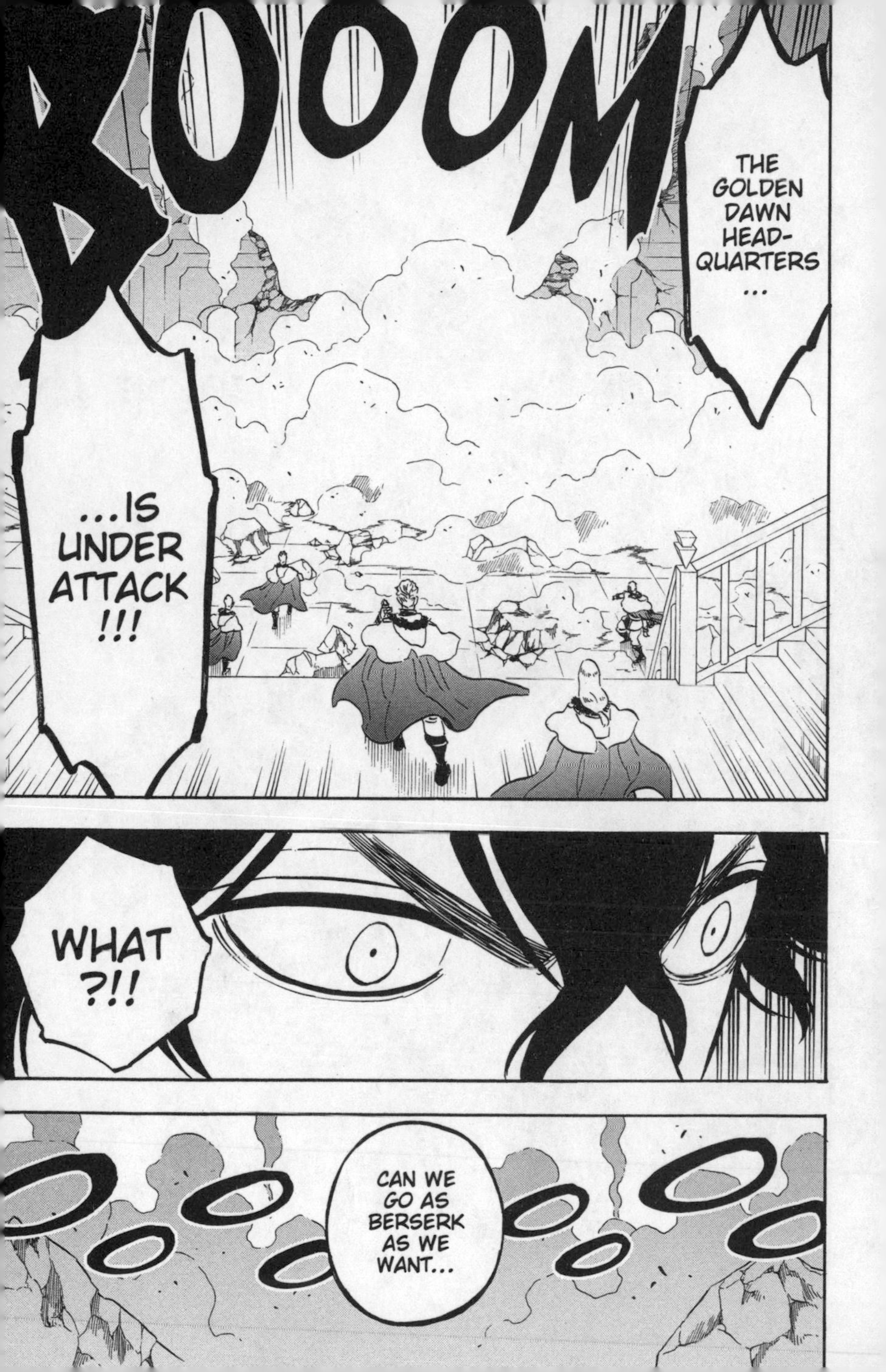
BOOOM
THE GOLDEN DAWN HEAD-QUARTERS...
...IS UNDER ATTACK!!!
WHAT?!!
CAN WE GO AS BERSERK AS WE WANT...

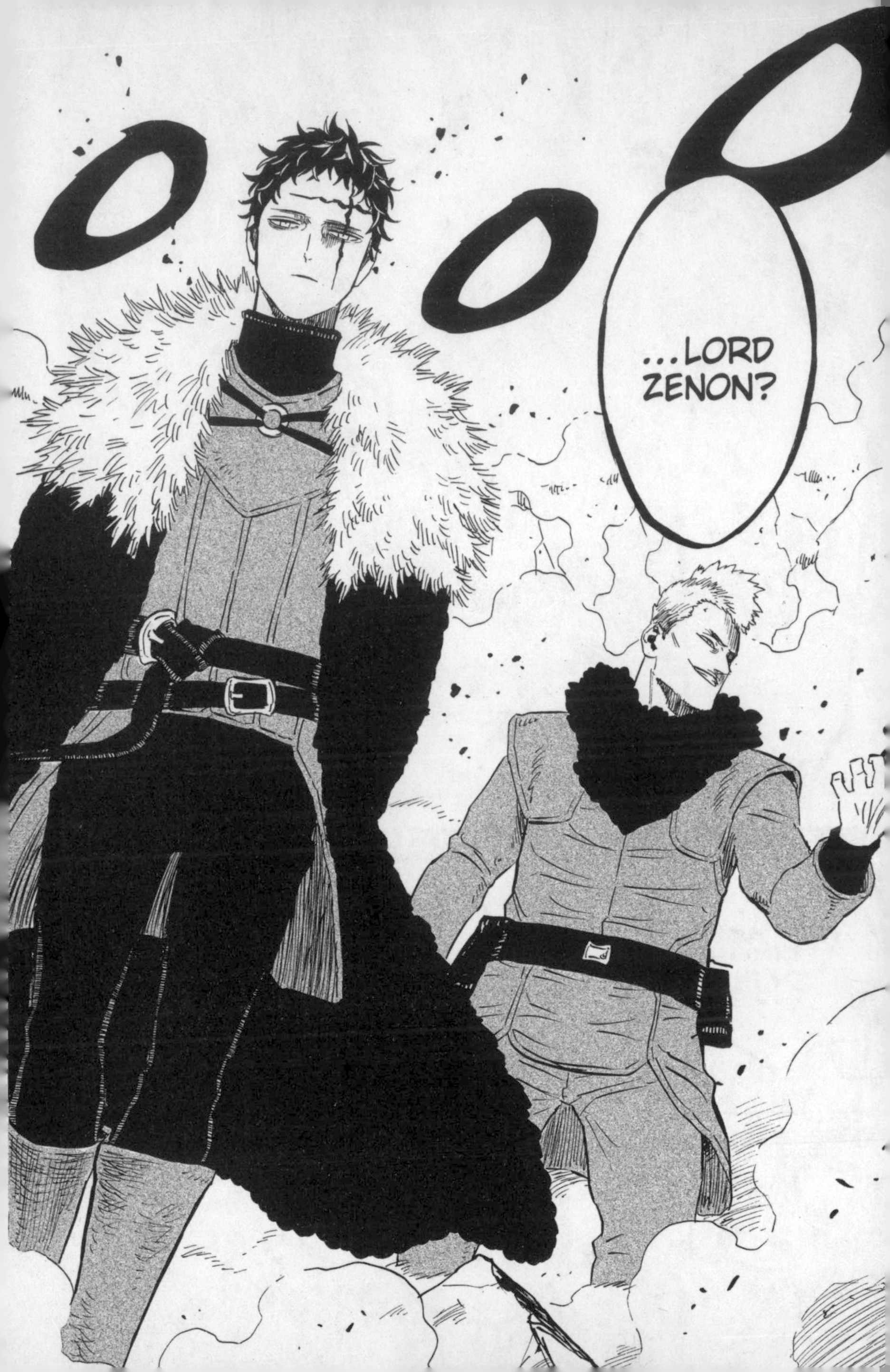
...LORD ZENON?

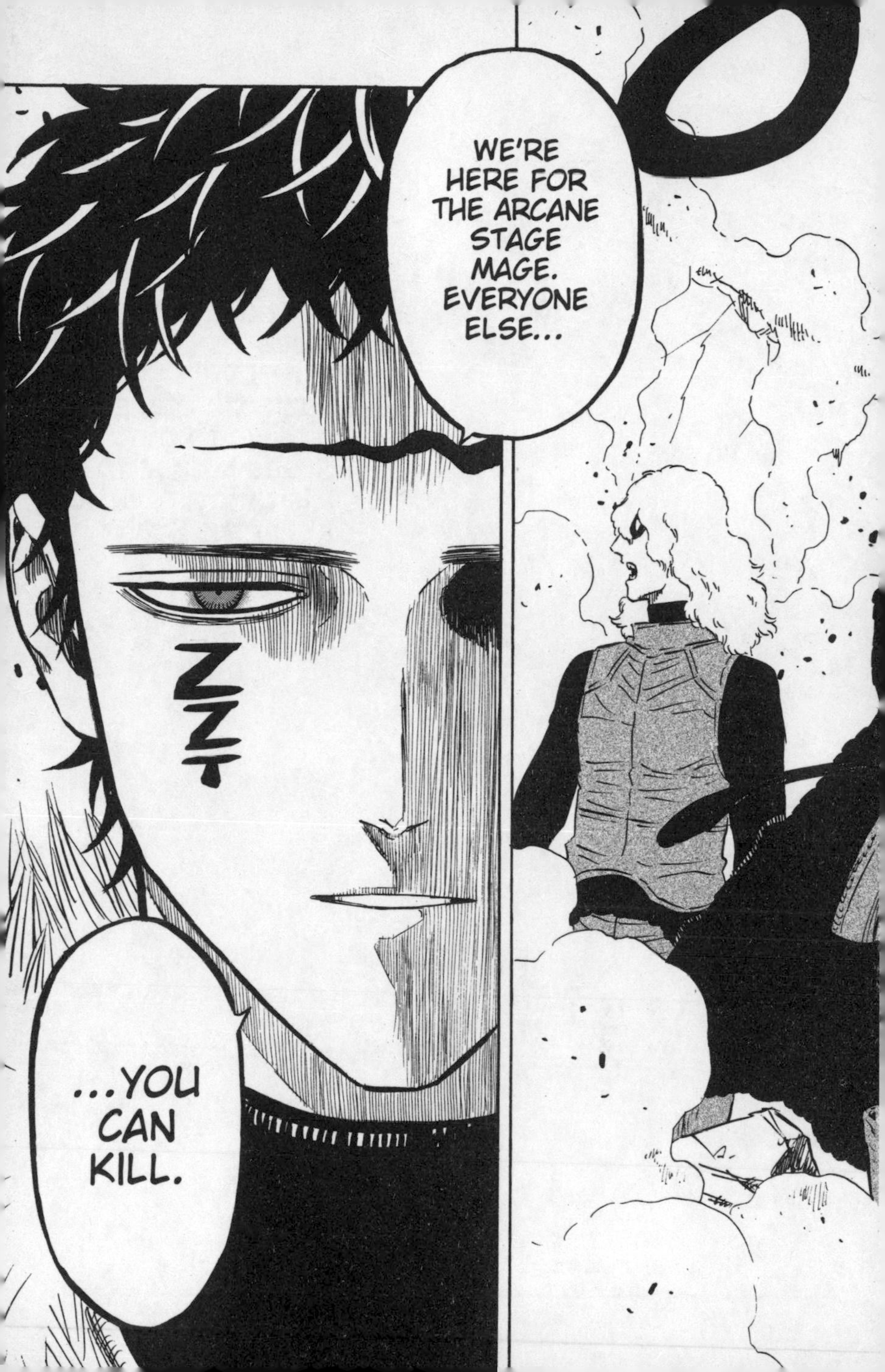
WE'RE HERE FOR THE ARCANE STAGE MAGE. EVERYONE ELSE...
...YOU CAN KILL.

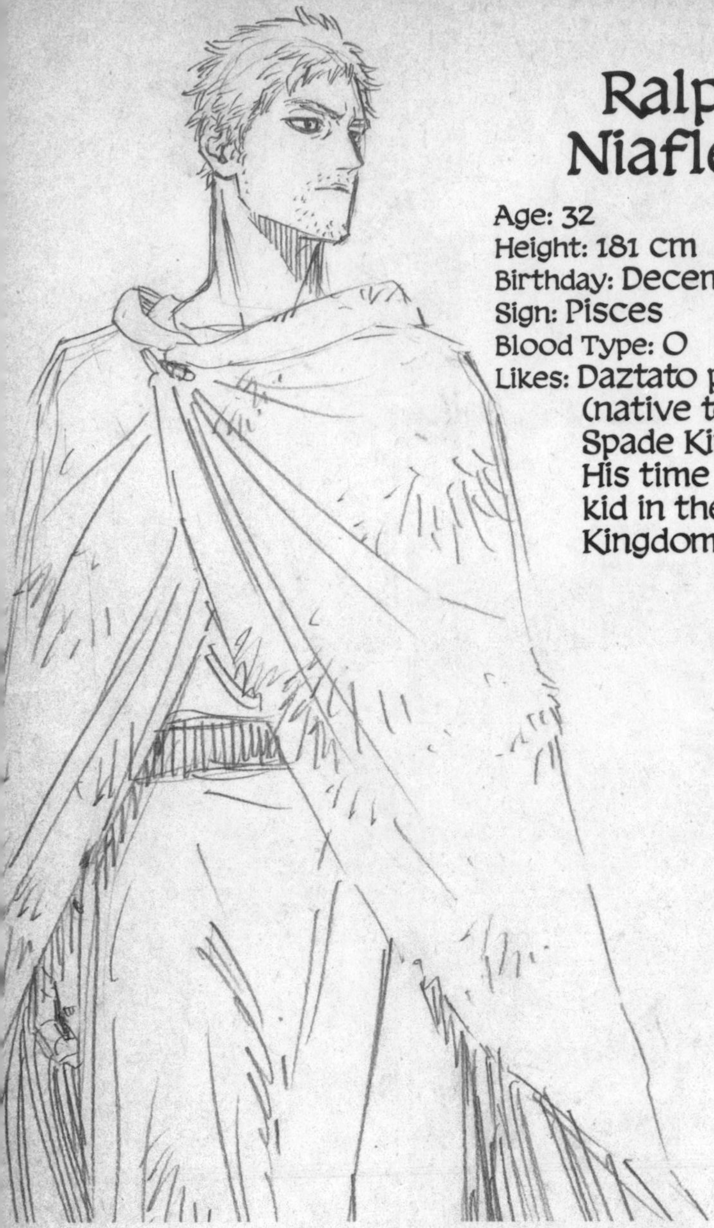

Ralph Niaflem

Age: 32
Height: 181 cm
Birthday: December 4
Sign: Pisces
Blood Type: O
Likes: Daztato potage soup (native to the Spade Kingdom)
His time as a little kid in the Spade Kingdom

Character Profile

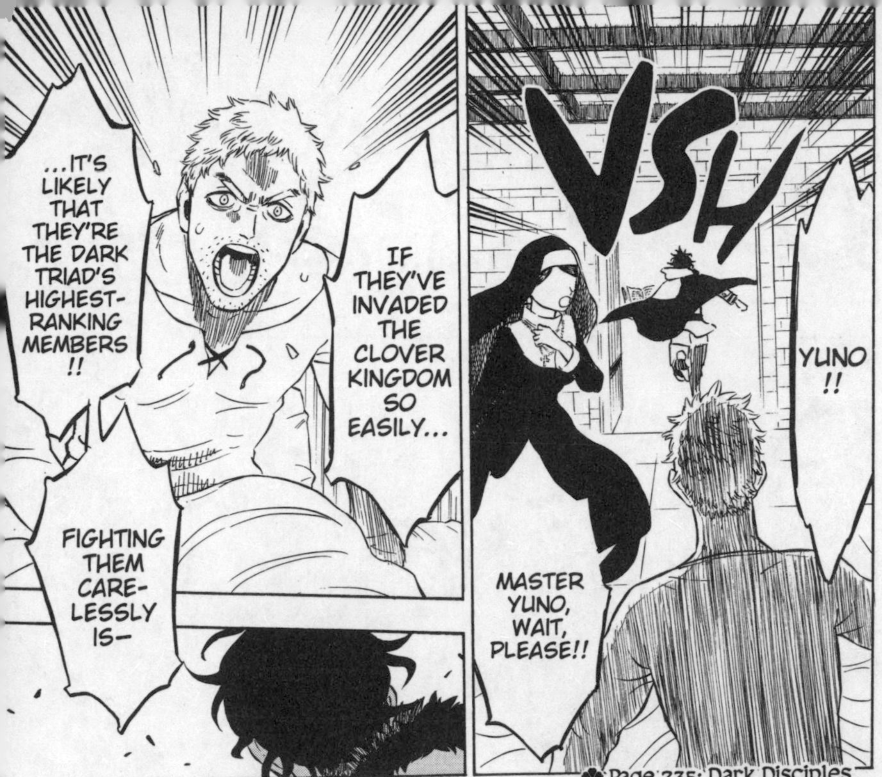
VSH
YUNO!!
MASTER YUNO, WAIT, PLEASE!!
IF THEY'VE INVADED THE CLOVER KINGDOM SO EASILY...
...IT'S LIKELY THAT THEY'RE THE DARK TRIAD'S HIGHEST-RANKING MEMBERS!!
FIGHTING THEM CARE-LESSLY IS—

Page 235: Dark Disciples

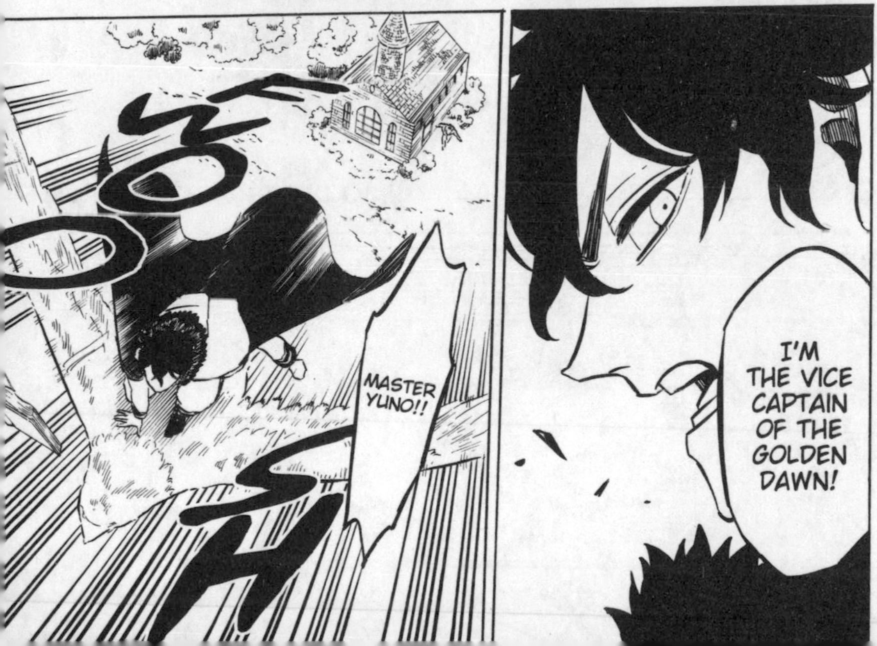
I'M THE VICE CAPTAIN OF THE GOLDEN DAWN!
MASTER YUNO!!

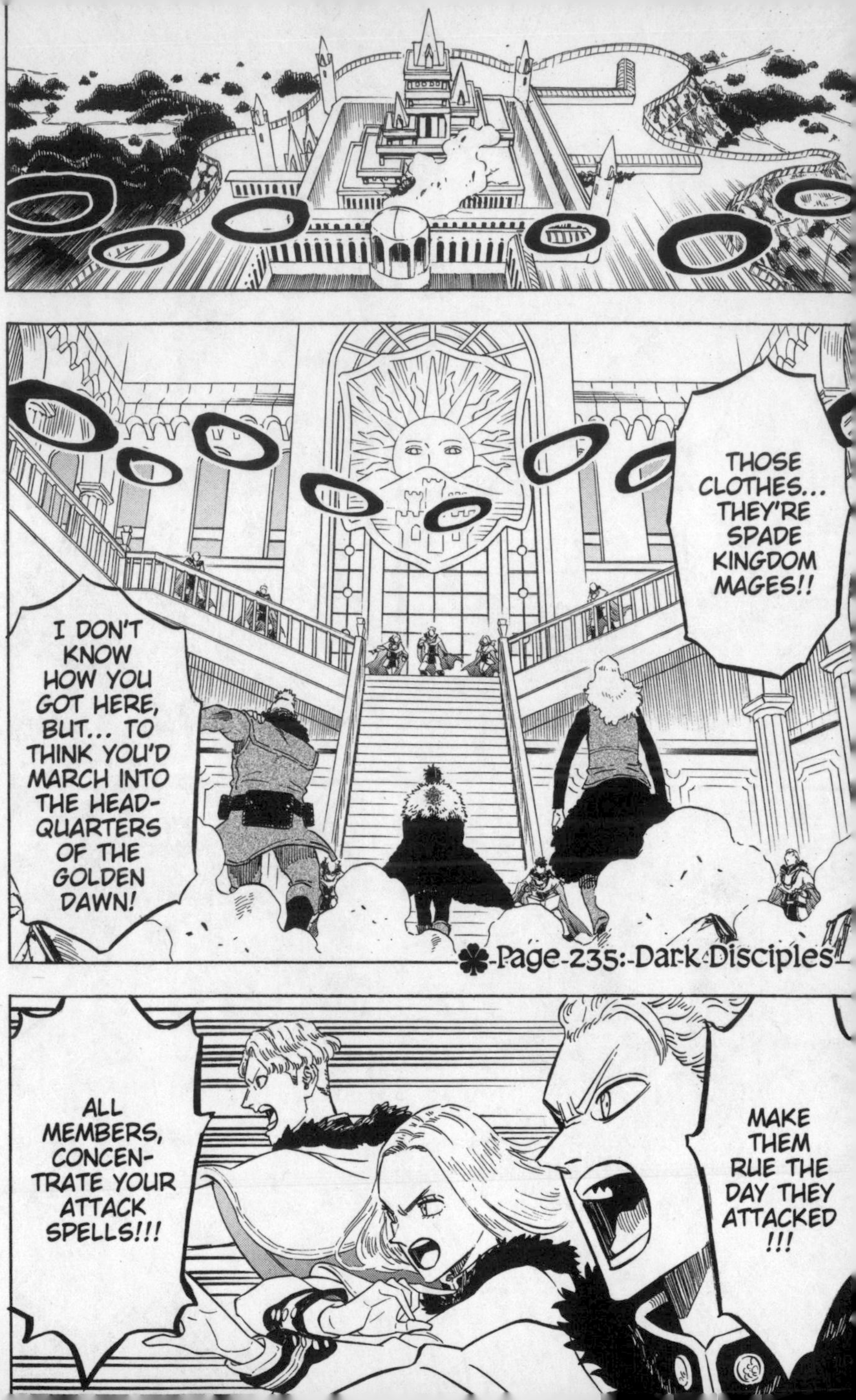
THOSE CLOTHES... THEY'RE SPADE KINGDOM MAGES!!
I DON'T KNOW HOW YOU GOT HERE, BUT... TO THINK YOU'D MARCH INTO THE HEAD-QUARTERS OF THE GOLDEN DAWN!
Page 235: Dark Disciples
MAKE THEM RUE THE DAY THEY ATTACKED!!!
ALL MEMBERS, CONCEN-TRATE YOUR ATTACK SPELLS!!!

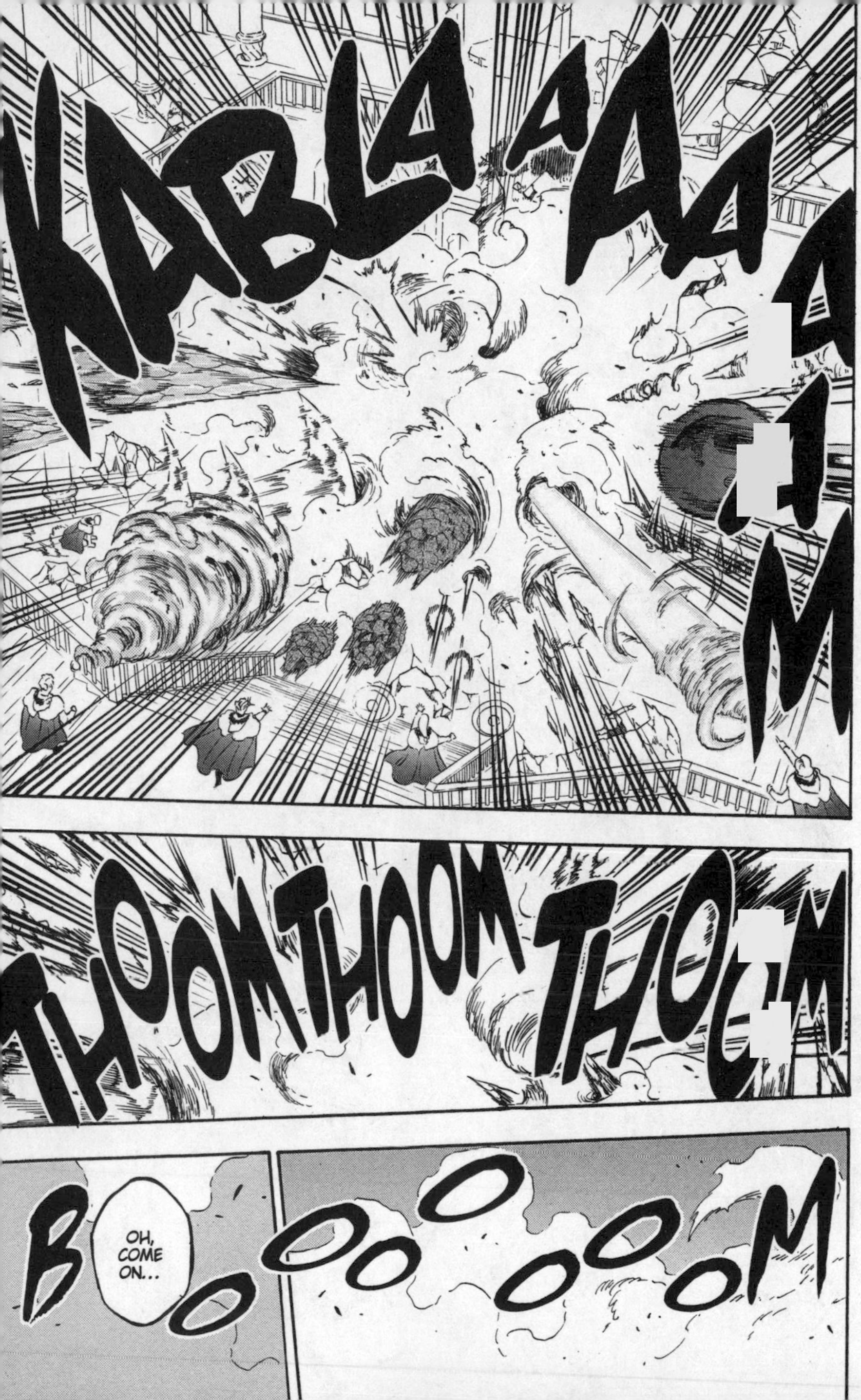
KABLAAAAAM
THOOM THOOM THOOM
BOOOOOOOOOM
OH, COME ON...

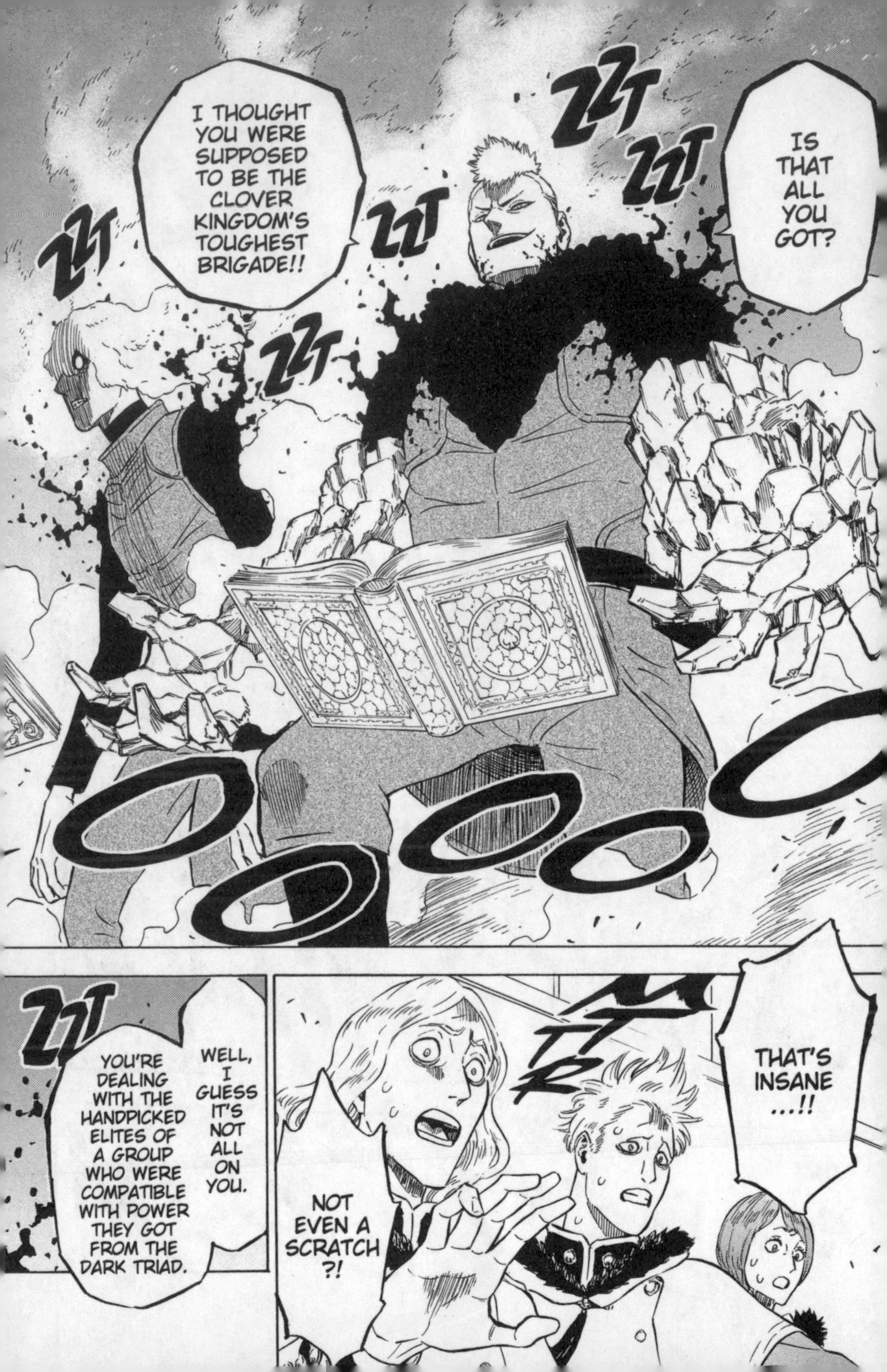
ZZT
IS THAT ALL YOU GOT?
I THOUGHT YOU WERE SUPPOSED TO BE THE CLOVER KINGDOM'S TOUGHEST BRIGADE!!
THAT'S INSANE ...!!
NOT EVEN A SCRATCH ?!
WELL, I GUESS IT'S NOT ALL ON YOU.
YOU'RE DEALING WITH THE HANDPICKED ELITES OF A GROUP WHO WERE COMPATIBLE WITH POWER THEY GOT FROM THE DARK TRIAD.
ZZT

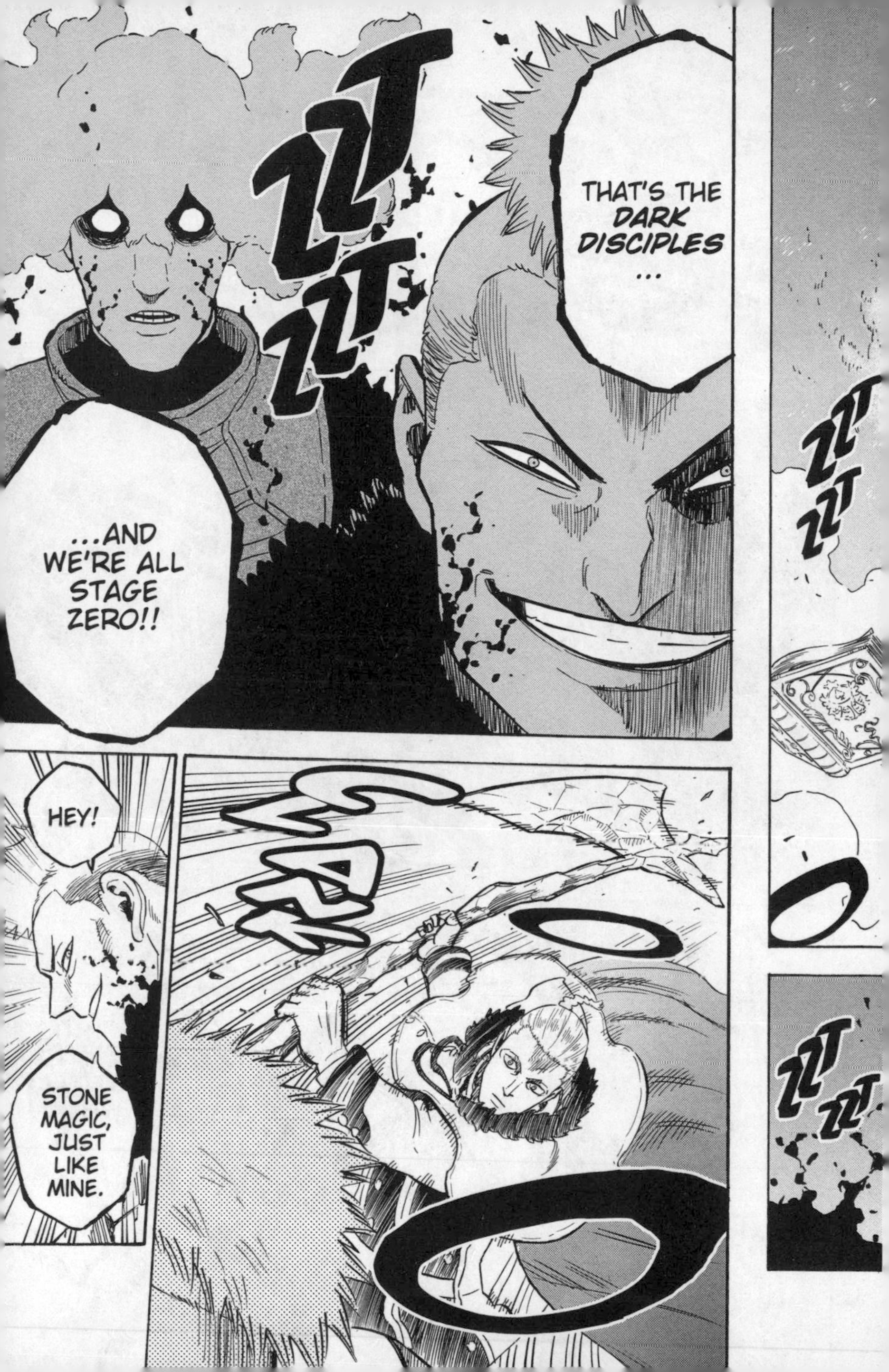

THAT'S THE DARK DISCIPLES...
...AND WE'RE ALL STAGE ZERO!!
ZZZT ZZZT
HEY!
STONE MAGIC, JUST LIKE MINE.

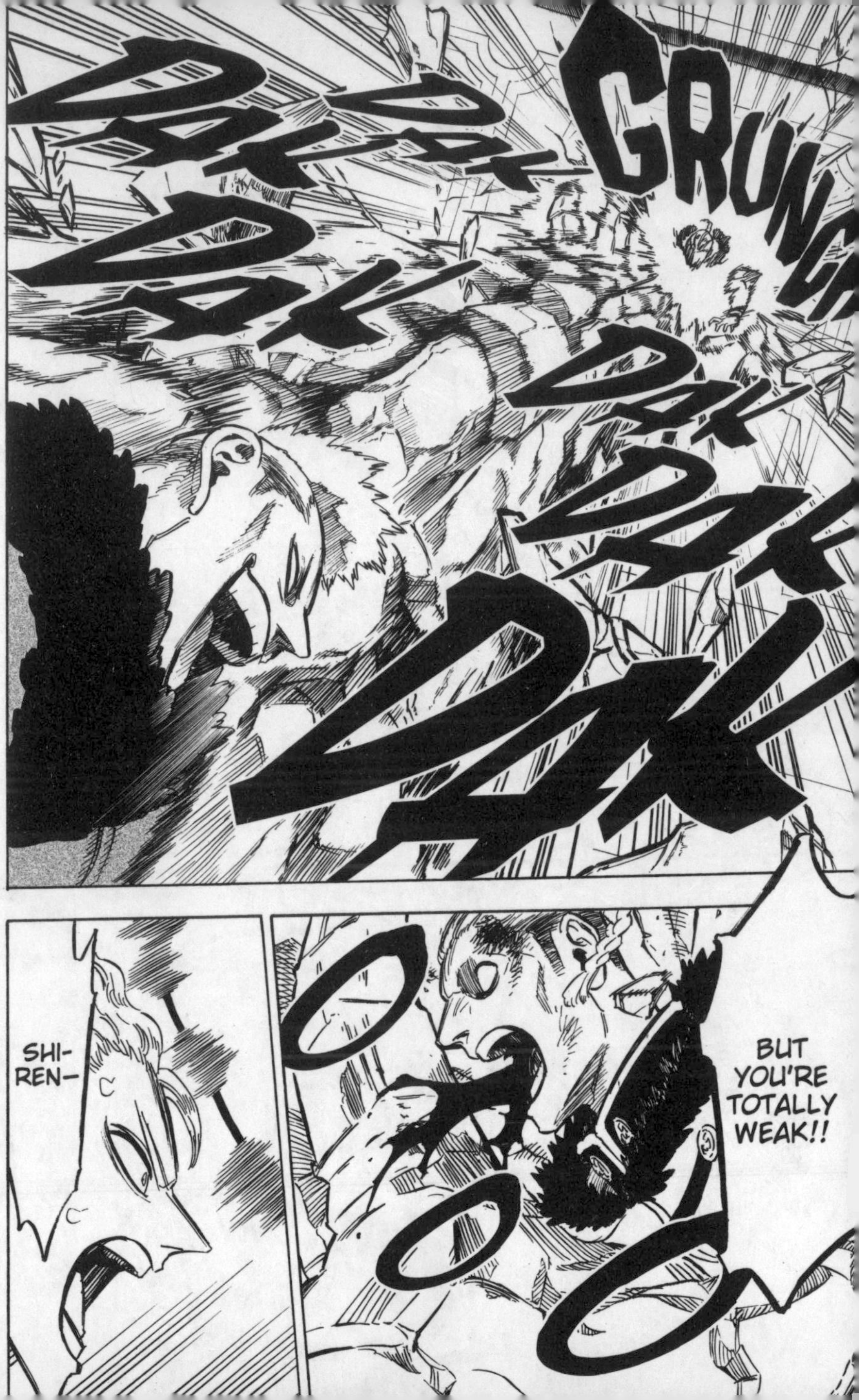
GRUNC
DAK
DAK
DAK
DAK
DAK
BUT YOU'RE TOTALLY WEAK!!
SHI-
REN-

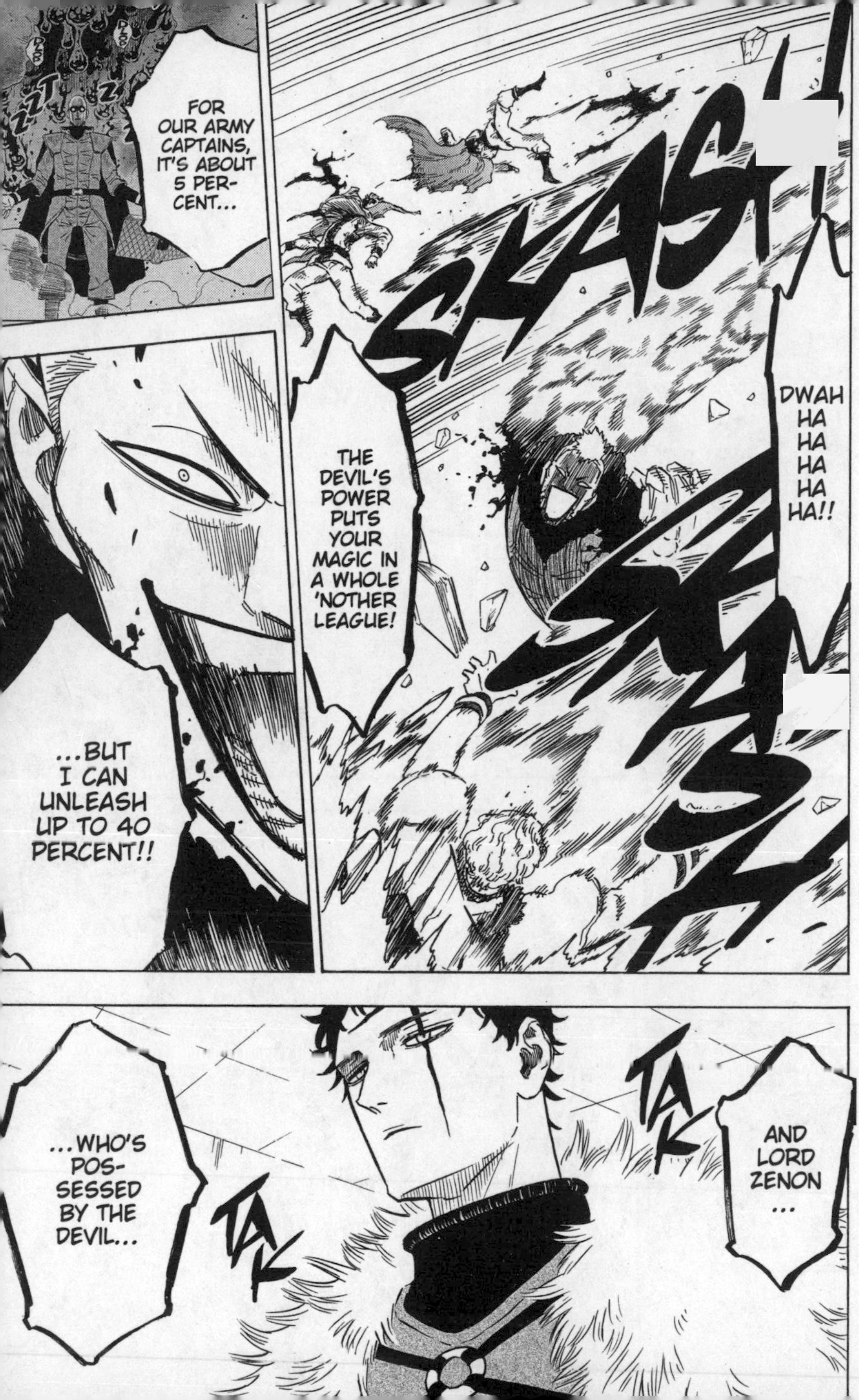
SKASH
DWAH HA HA HA HA HA!!
SKASH
THE DEVIL'S POWER PUTS YOUR MAGIC IN A WHOLE 'NOTHER LEAGUE!
FOR OUR ARMY CAPTAINS, IT'S ABOUT 5 PER-CENT...
...BUT I CAN UNLEASH UP TO 40 PERCENT!!
AND LORD ZENON...
TAK
TAK
...WHO'S POS-SESSED BY THE DEVIL...

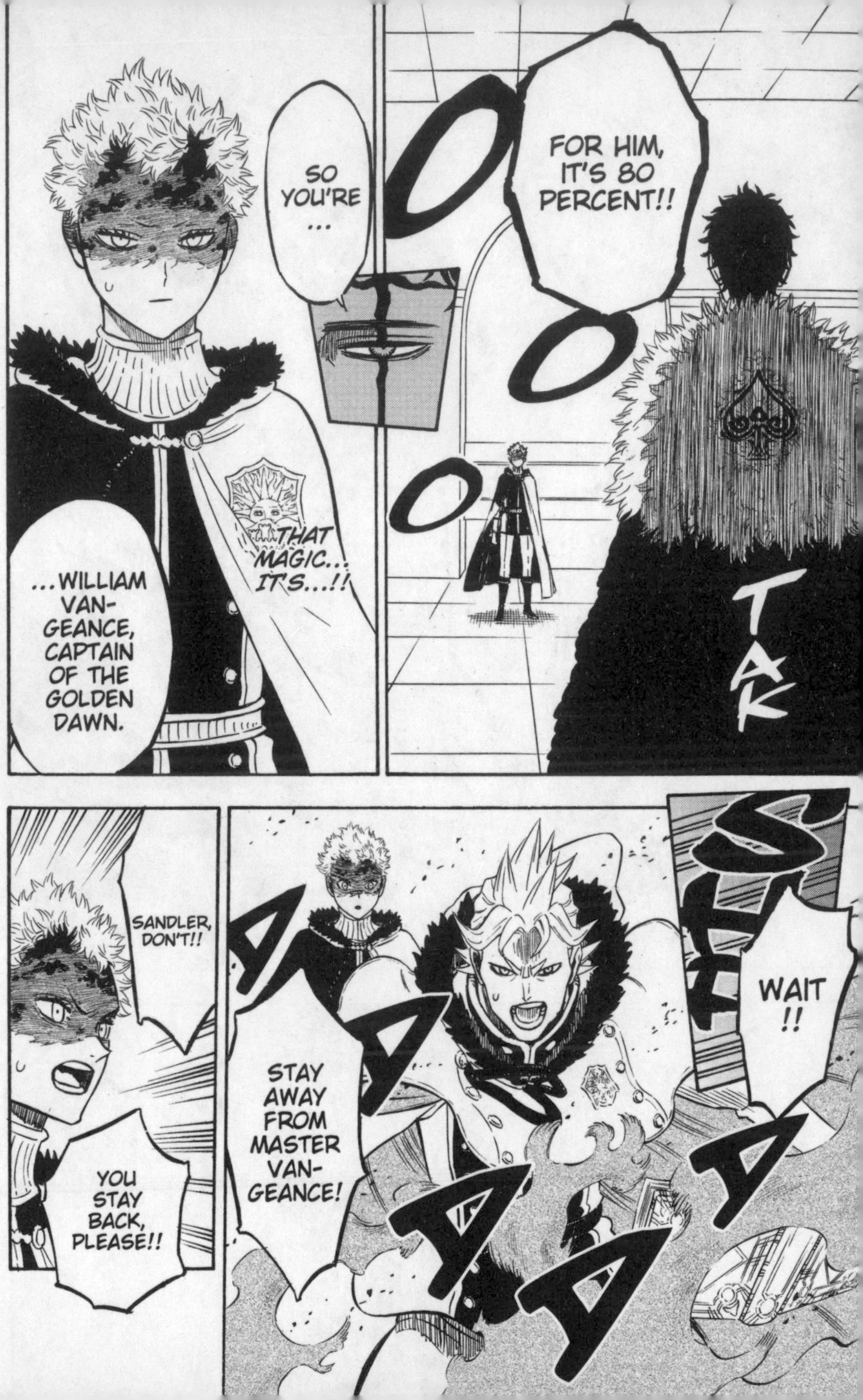
OOOO
FOR HIM, IT'S 80 PERCENT!!
TAK
SO YOU'RE ...
THAT MAGIC... IT'S...!!
...WILLIAM VAN-GEANCE, CAPTAIN OF THE GOLDEN DAWN.
SHH
WAIT !!
AAAAAAA
STAY AWAY FROM MASTER VAN-GEANCE!
SANDLER, DON'T!!
YOU STAY BACK, PLEASE!!

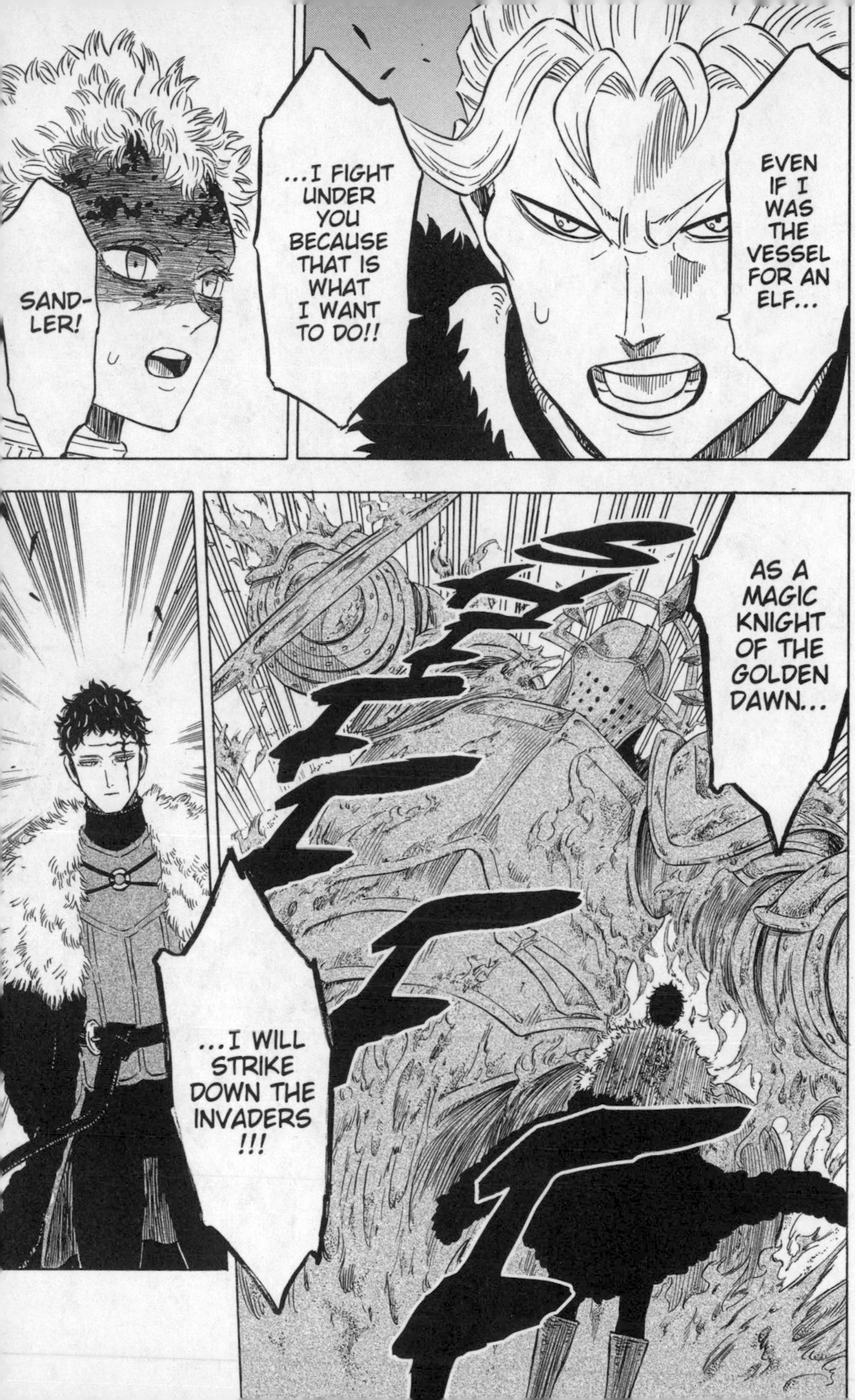
EVEN IF I WAS THE VESSEL FOR AN ELF...
...I FIGHT UNDER YOU BECAUSE THAT IS WHAT I WANT TO DO!!
SANDLER!
AS A MAGIC KNIGHT OF THE GOLDEN DAWN...
...I WILL STRIKE DOWN THE INVADERS!!!

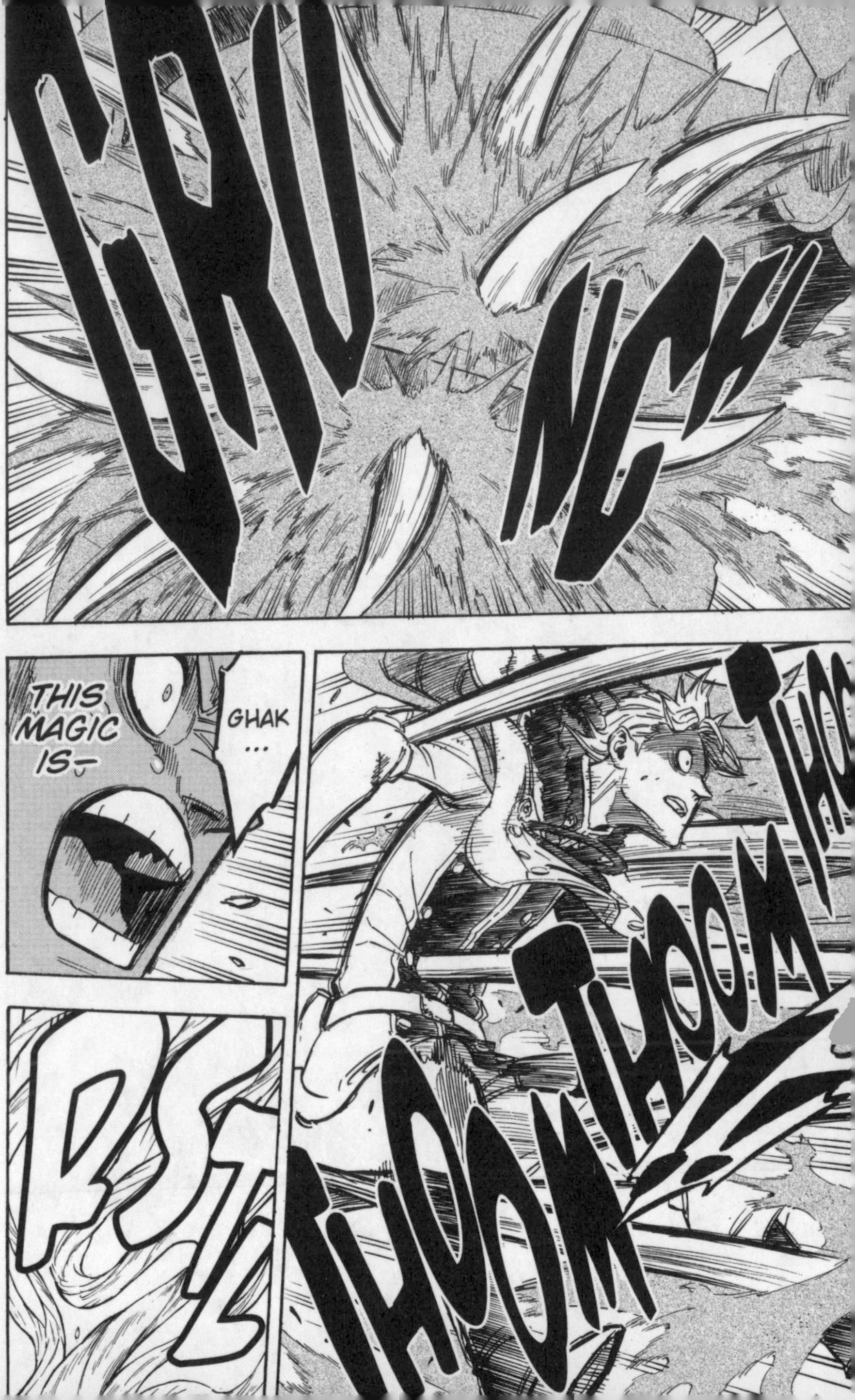
CRUNCH
THOOM THOOM THOOM
GHAK...
THIS MAGIC IS—
PST

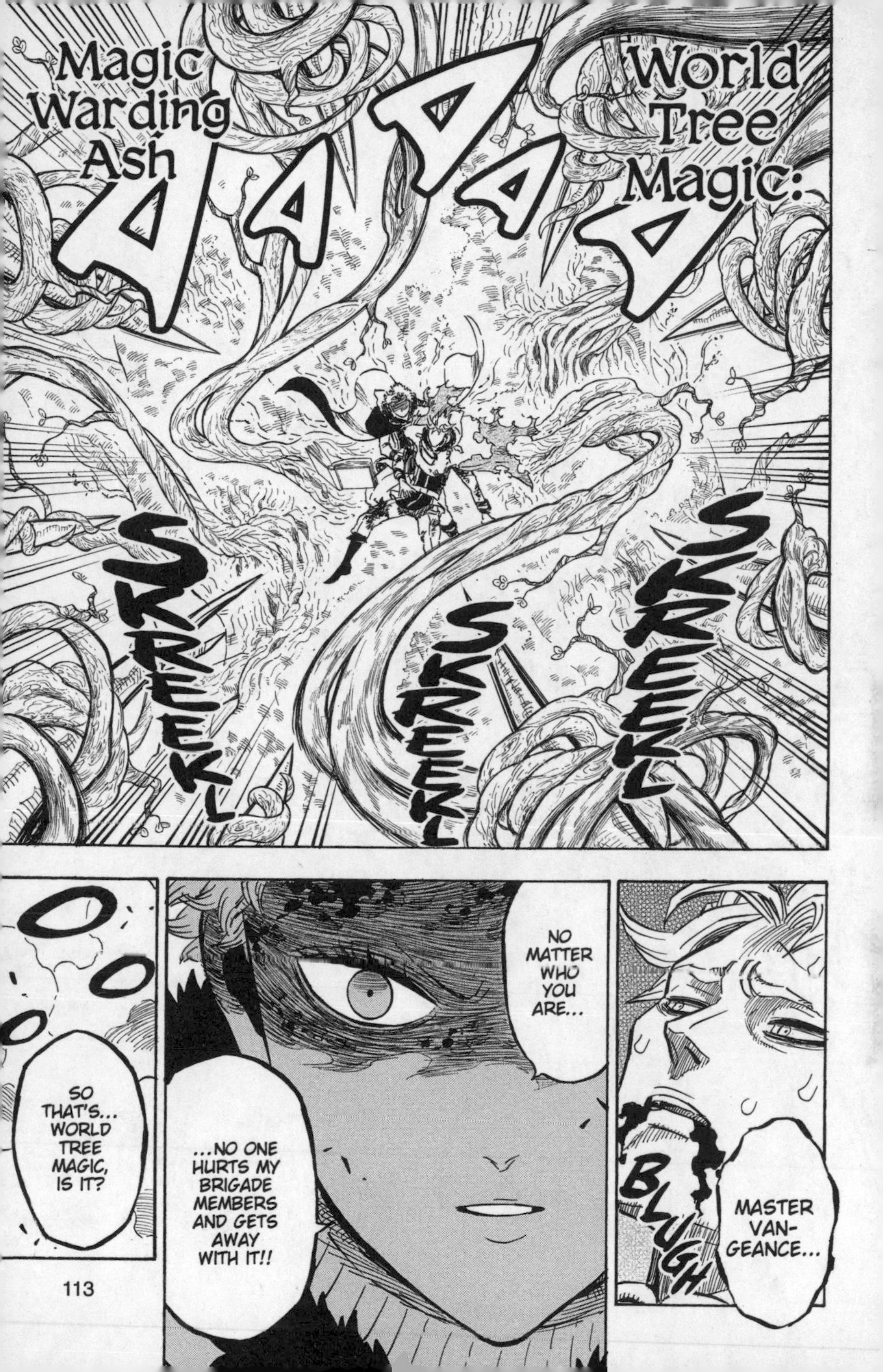
World Tree Magic:
Magic Warding Ash
AAAAA
SKREEKL
SKREEKL
SKREEKL
BLUGH
MASTER VANGEANCE...
NO MATTER WHO YOU ARE...
...NO ONE HURTS MY BRIGADE MEMBERS AND GETS AWAY WITH IT!!
OOO
SO THAT'S... WORLD TREE MAGIC, IS IT?

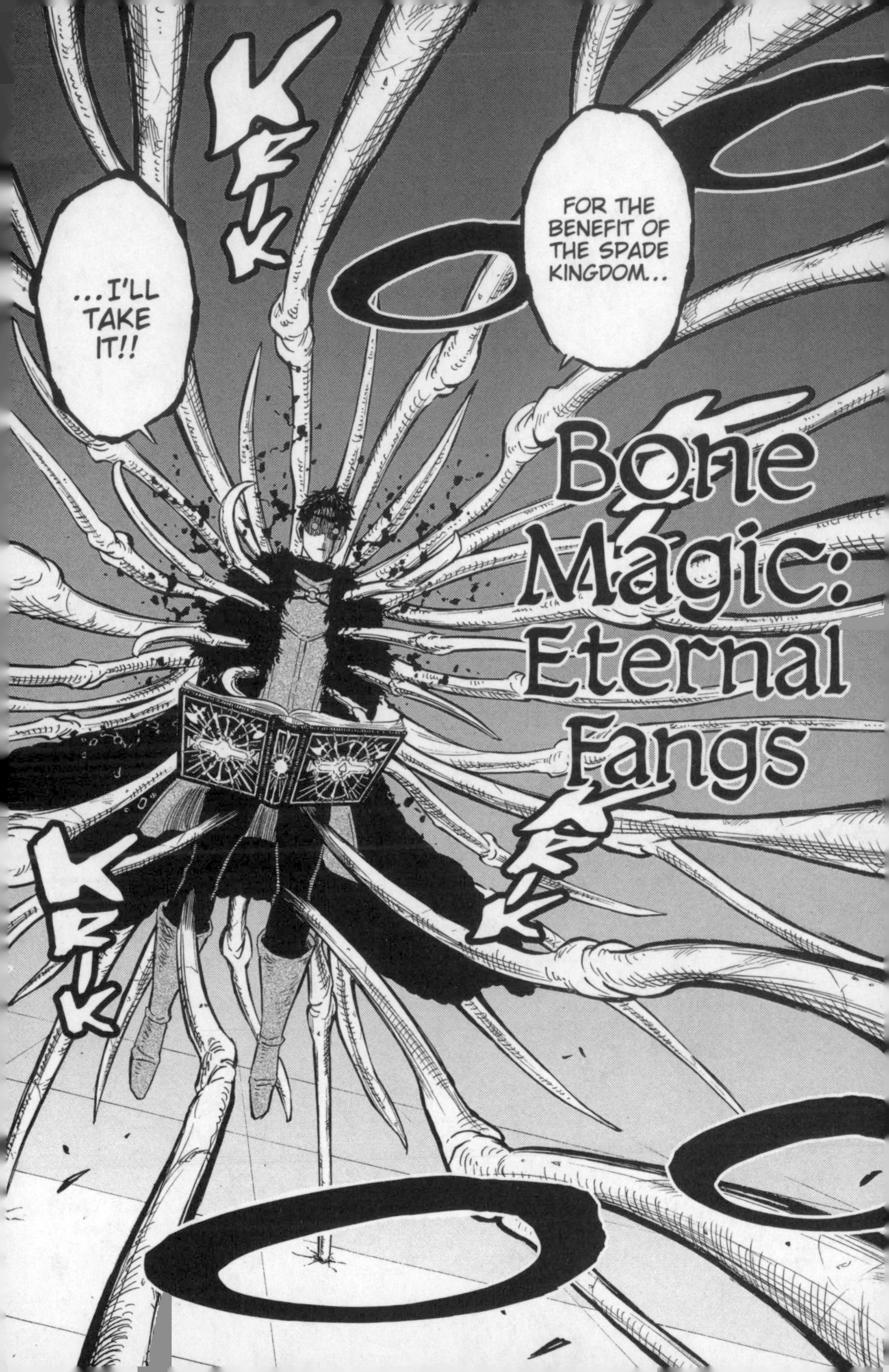
KRIK
FOR THE BENEFIT OF THE SPADE KINGDOM...
...I'LL TAKE IT!!
Bone Magic: Eternal Fangs
KRIK
KRIK

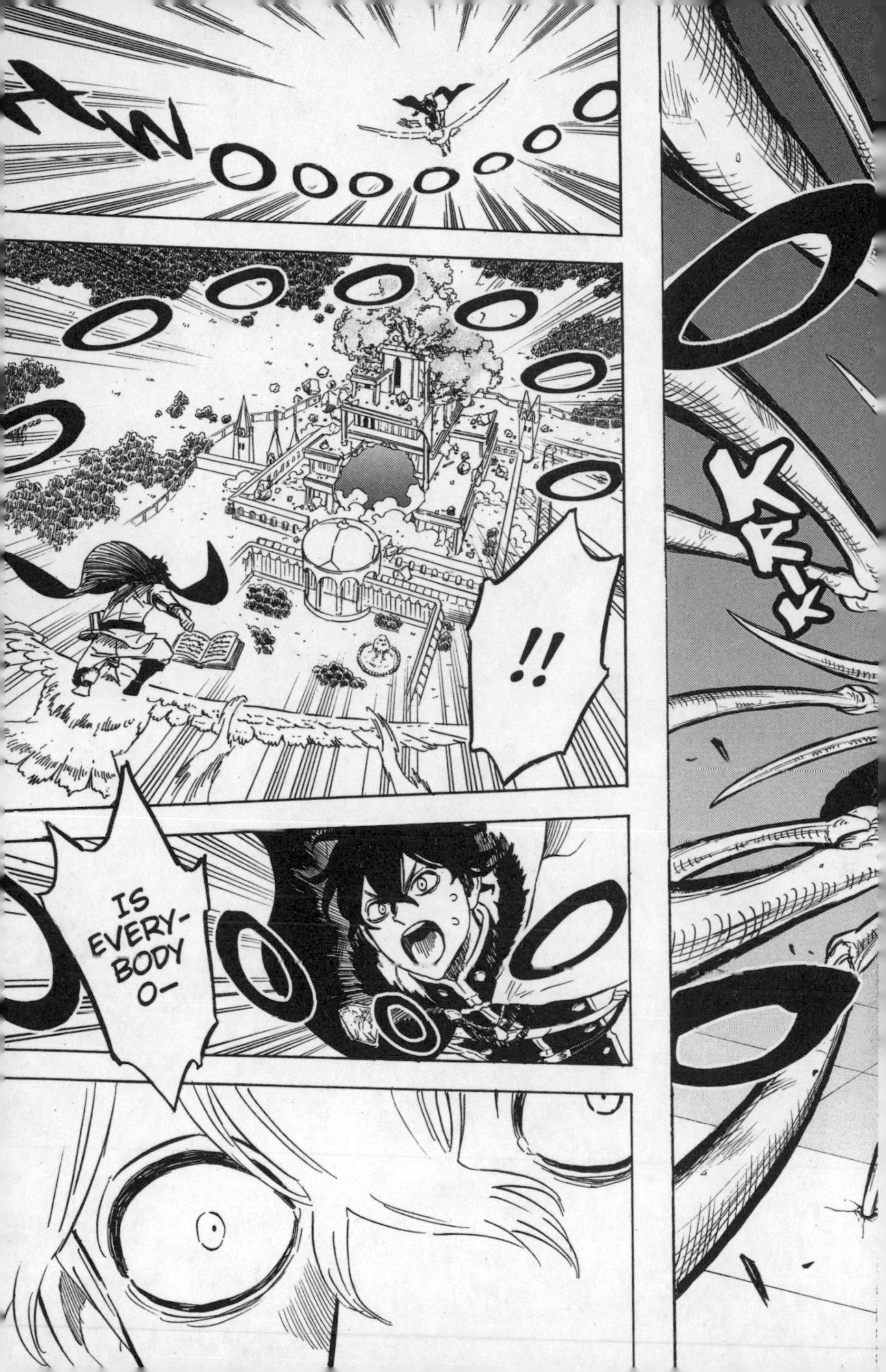
KRAK
ZWOOOOOOO
!!
IS EVERY-BODY O-

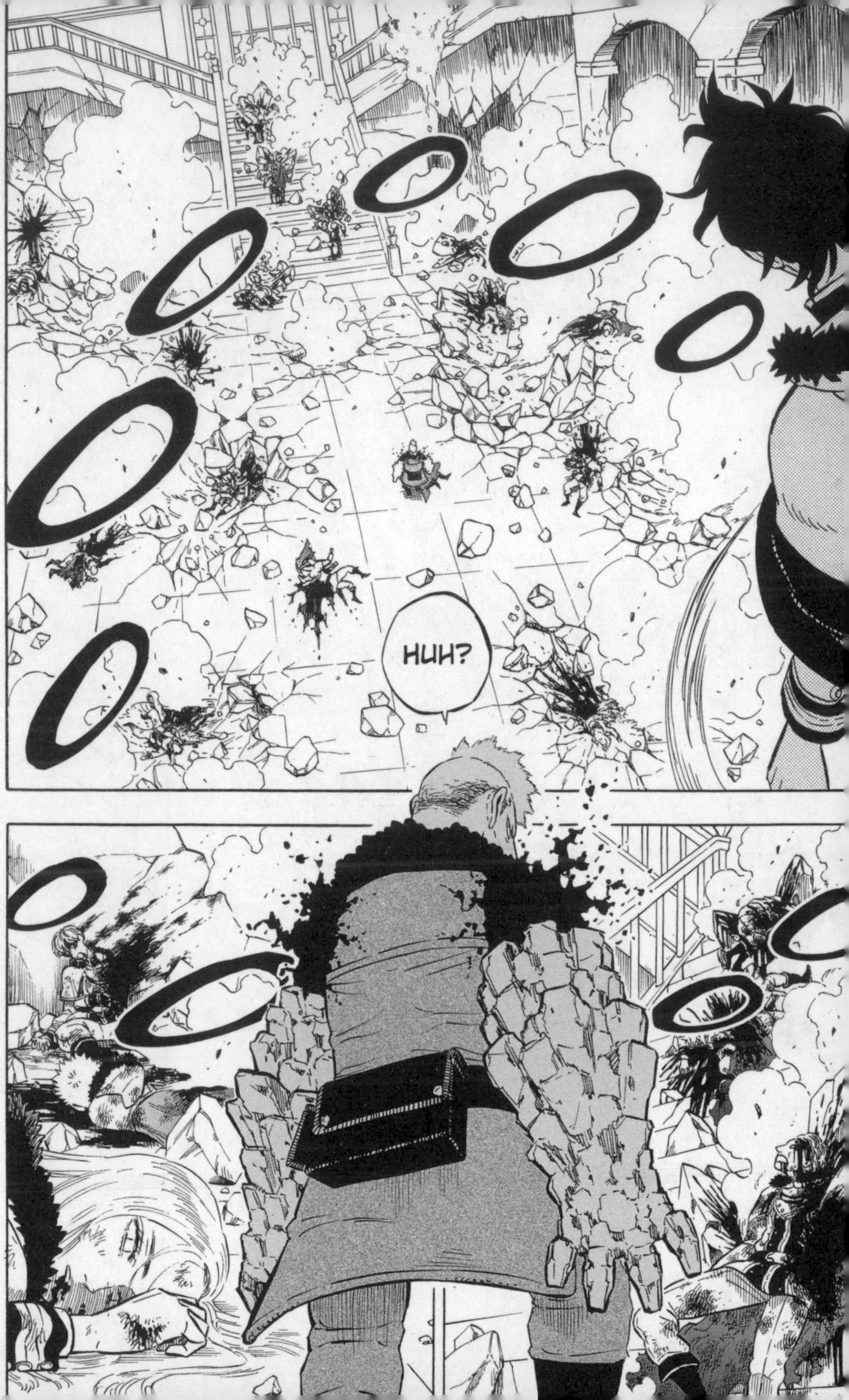
HUH?

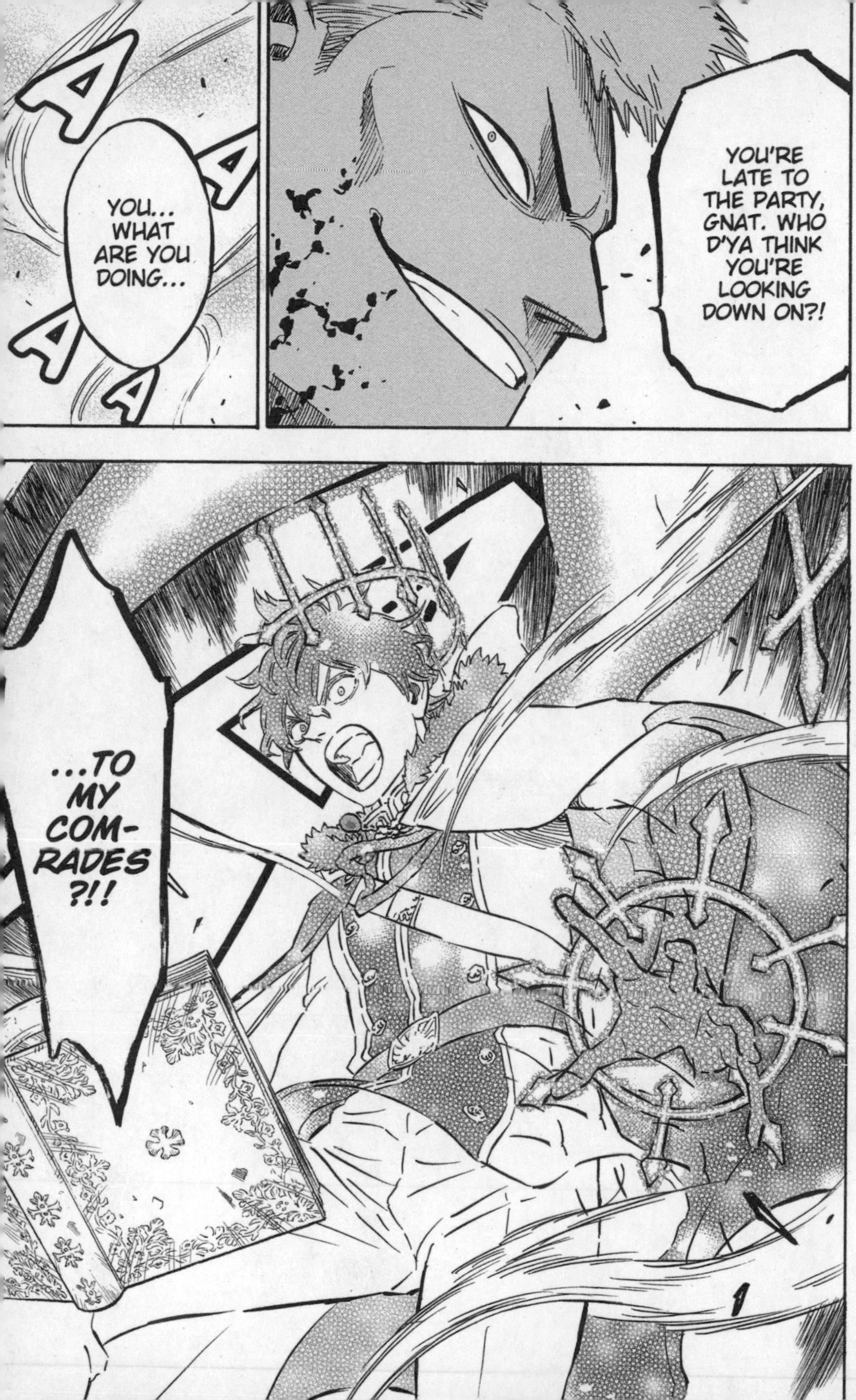
YOU'RE LATE TO THE PARTY, GNAT. WHO D'YA THINK YOU'RE LOOKING DOWN ON?!
AAAAA
YOU... WHAT ARE YOU DOING...
...TO MY COM-RADES?!!

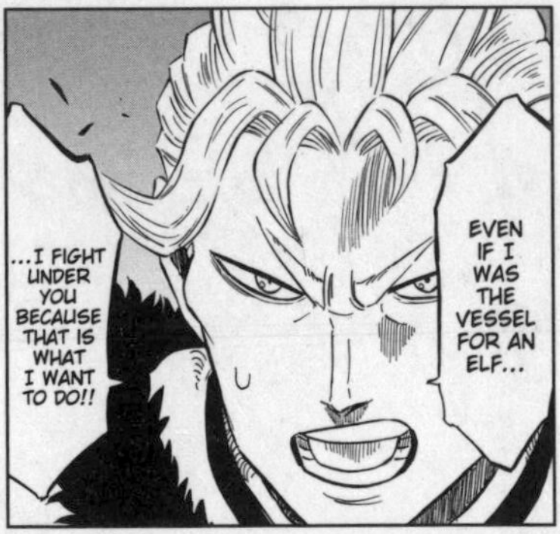
EVEN IF I WAS THE VESSEL FOR AN ELF...
...I FIGHT UNDER YOU BECAUSE THAT IS WHAT I WANT TO DO!!

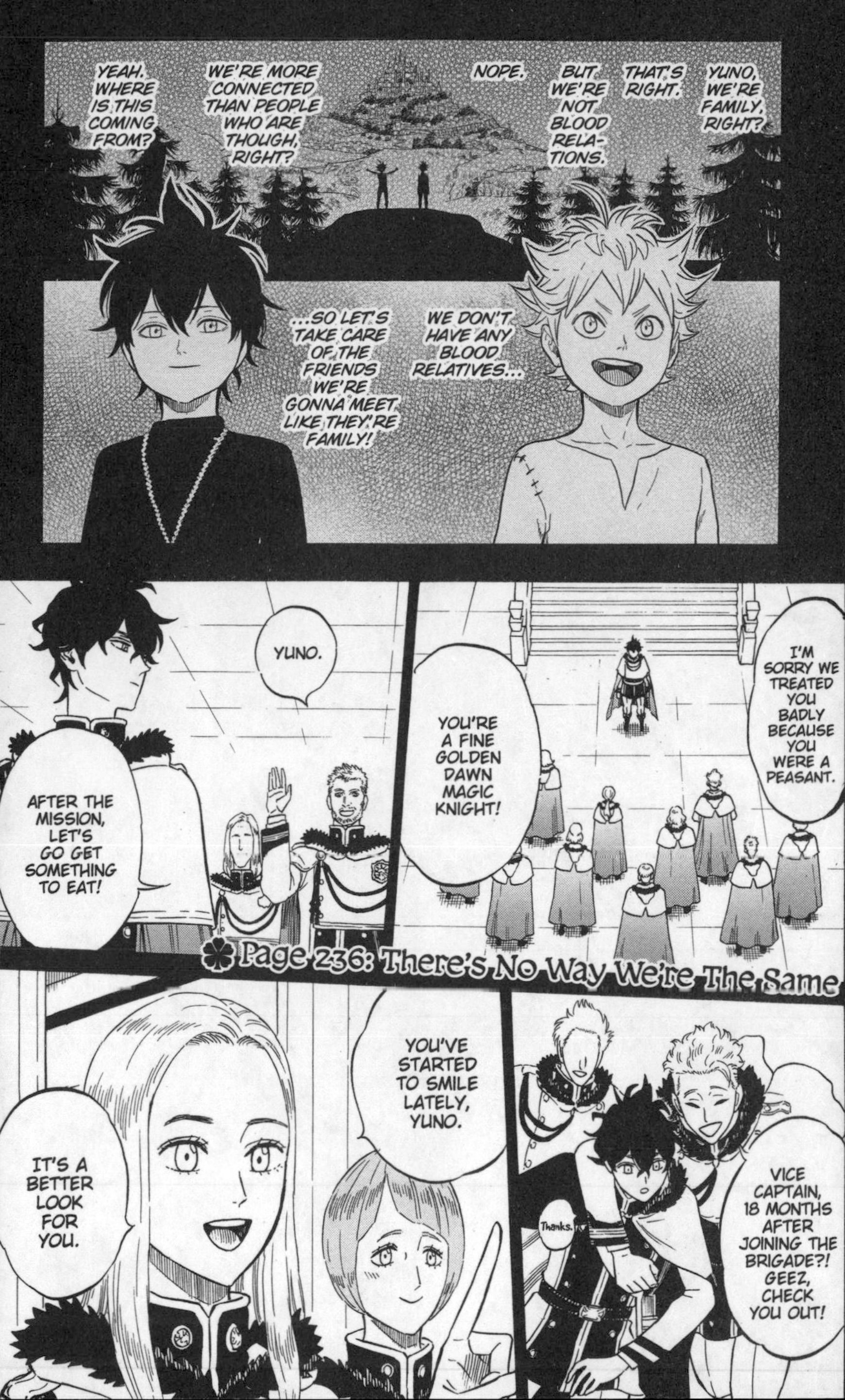
YUNO, WE'RE FAMILY, RIGHT?
THAT'S RIGHT.
BUT WE'RE NOT BLOOD RELATIONS.
NOPE.
WE'RE MORE CONNECTED THAN PEOPLE WHO ARE THOUGH, RIGHT?
YEAH. WHERE IS THIS COMING FROM?
WE DON'T HAVE ANY BLOOD RELATIVES...
...SO LET'S TAKE CARE OF THE FRIENDS WE'RE GONNA MEET LIKE THEY'RE FAMILY!
I'M SORRY WE TREATED YOU BADLY BECAUSE YOU WERE A PEASANT.
YOU'RE A FINE GOLDEN DAWN MAGIC KNIGHT!
YUNO.
AFTER THE MISSION, LET'S GO GET SOMETHING TO EAT!
Page 236: There's No Way We're The Same
VICE CAPTAIN, 18 MONTHS AFTER JOINING THE BRIGADE?! GEEZ, CHECK YOU OUT!
Thanks.
YOU'VE STARTED TO SMILE LATELY, YUNO.
IT'S A BETTER LOOK FOR YOU.

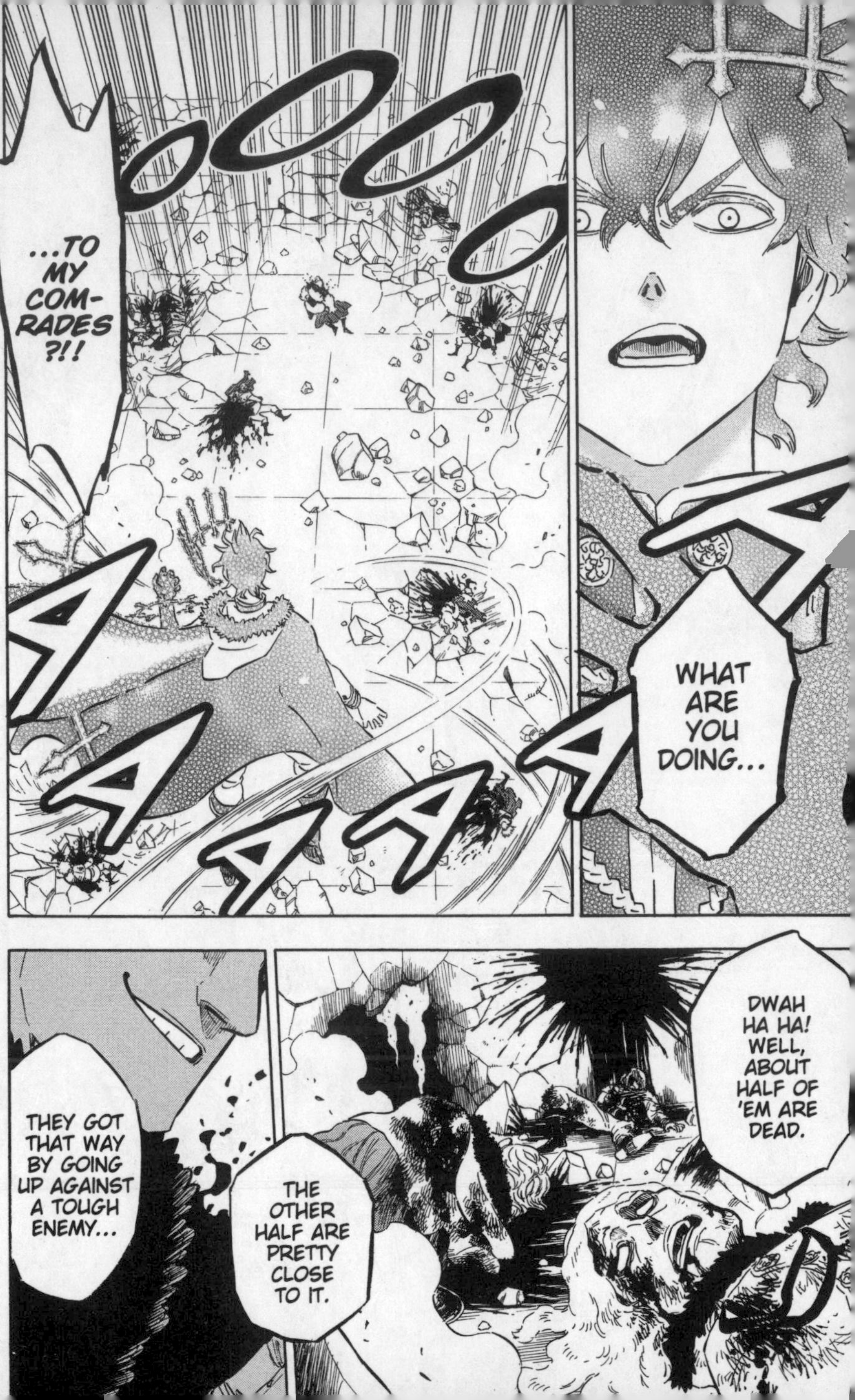
WHAT ARE YOU DOING...
...TO MY COM-RADES ?!!
DWAH HA HA! WELL, ABOUT HALF OF 'EM ARE DEAD.
THE OTHER HALF ARE PRETTY CLOSE TO IT.
THEY GOT THAT WAY BY GOING UP AGAINST A TOUGH ENEMY...

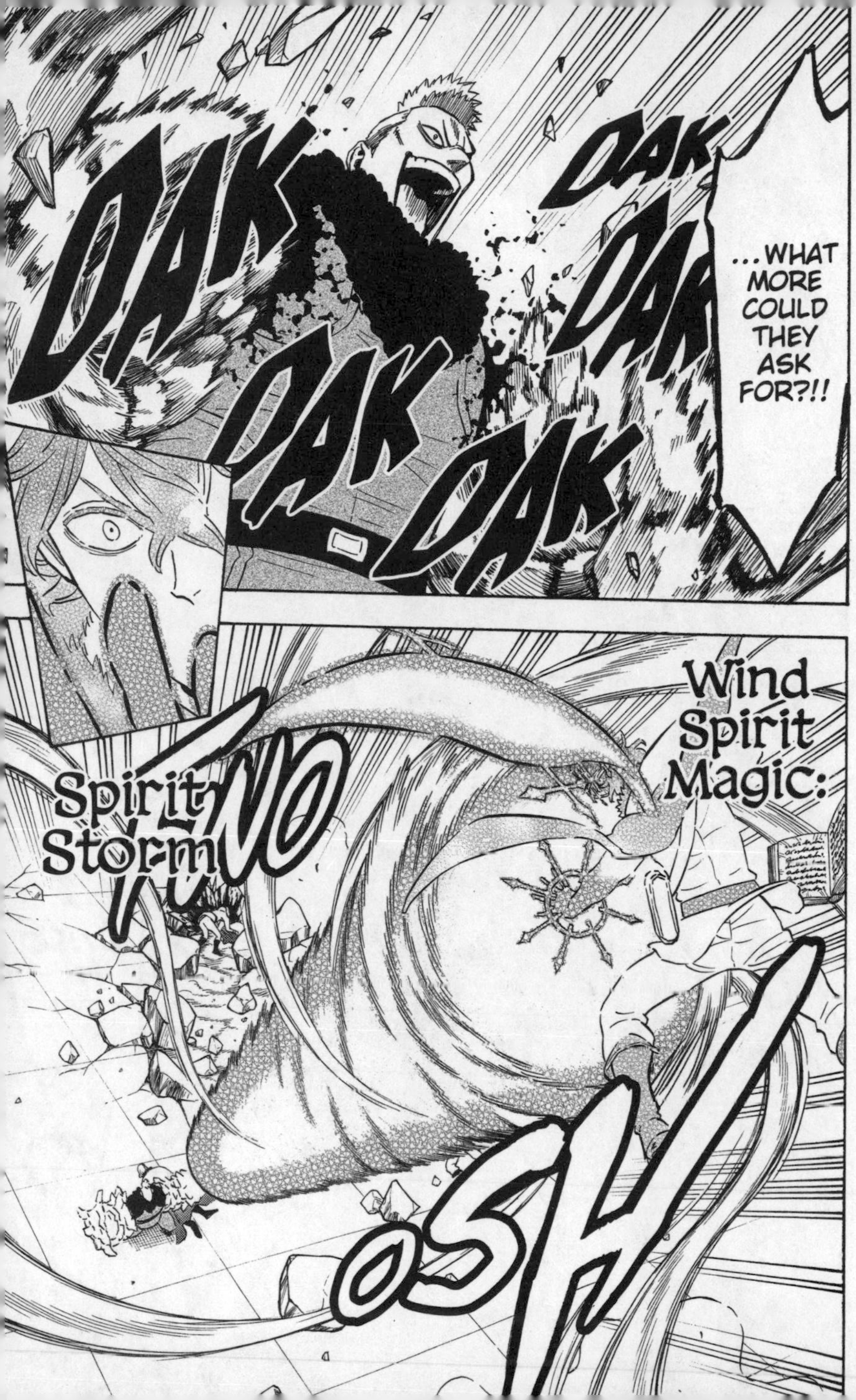
DAK
DAK
DAK
DAK
DAK
DAK
...WHAT MORE COULD THEY ASK FOR?!!
Wind Spirit Magic:
Spirit Storm

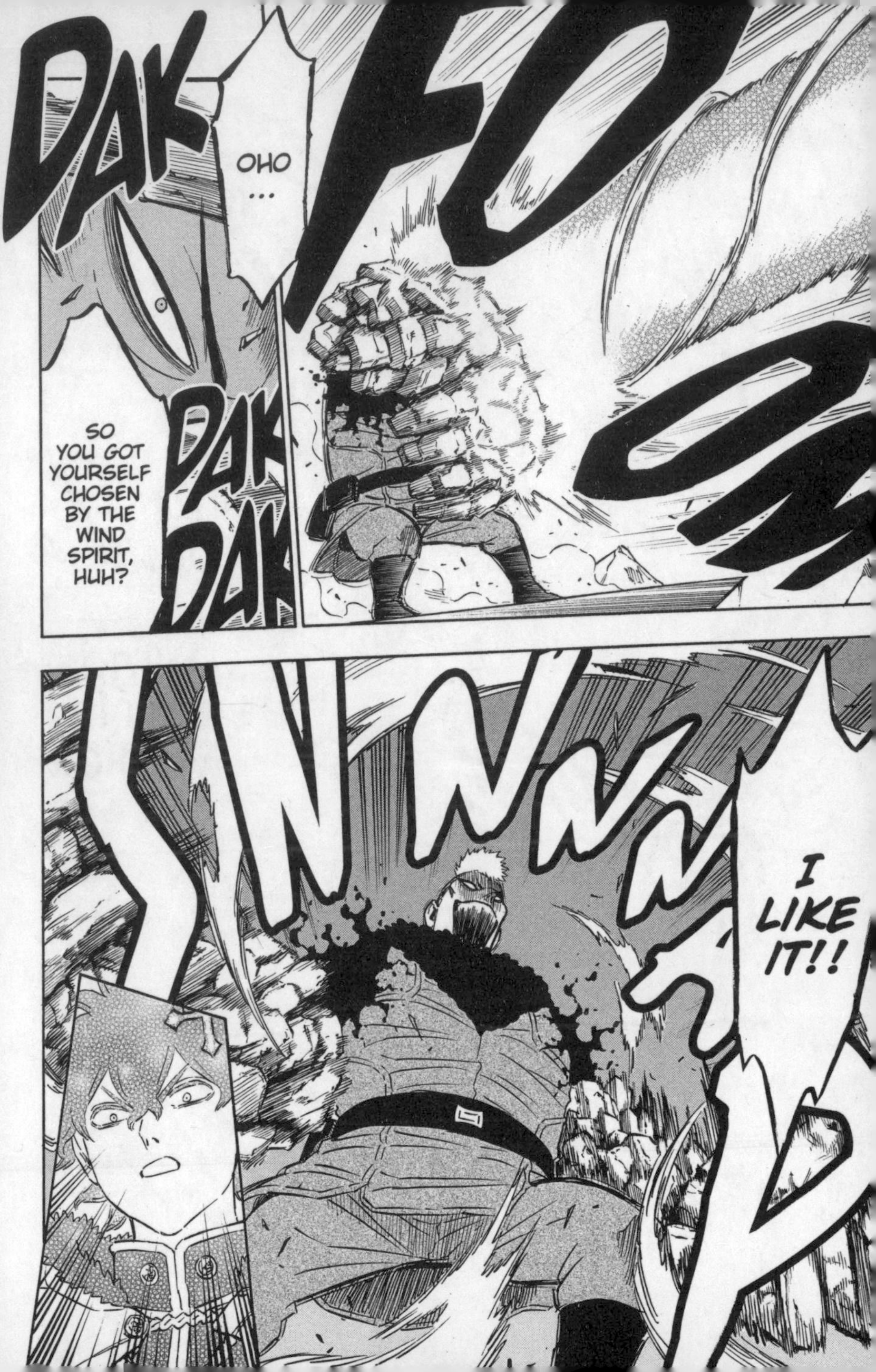
DAK
OHO ...
DAK DAK
SO YOU GOT YOURSELF CHOSEN BY THE WIND SPIRIT, HUH?
I LIKE IT!!

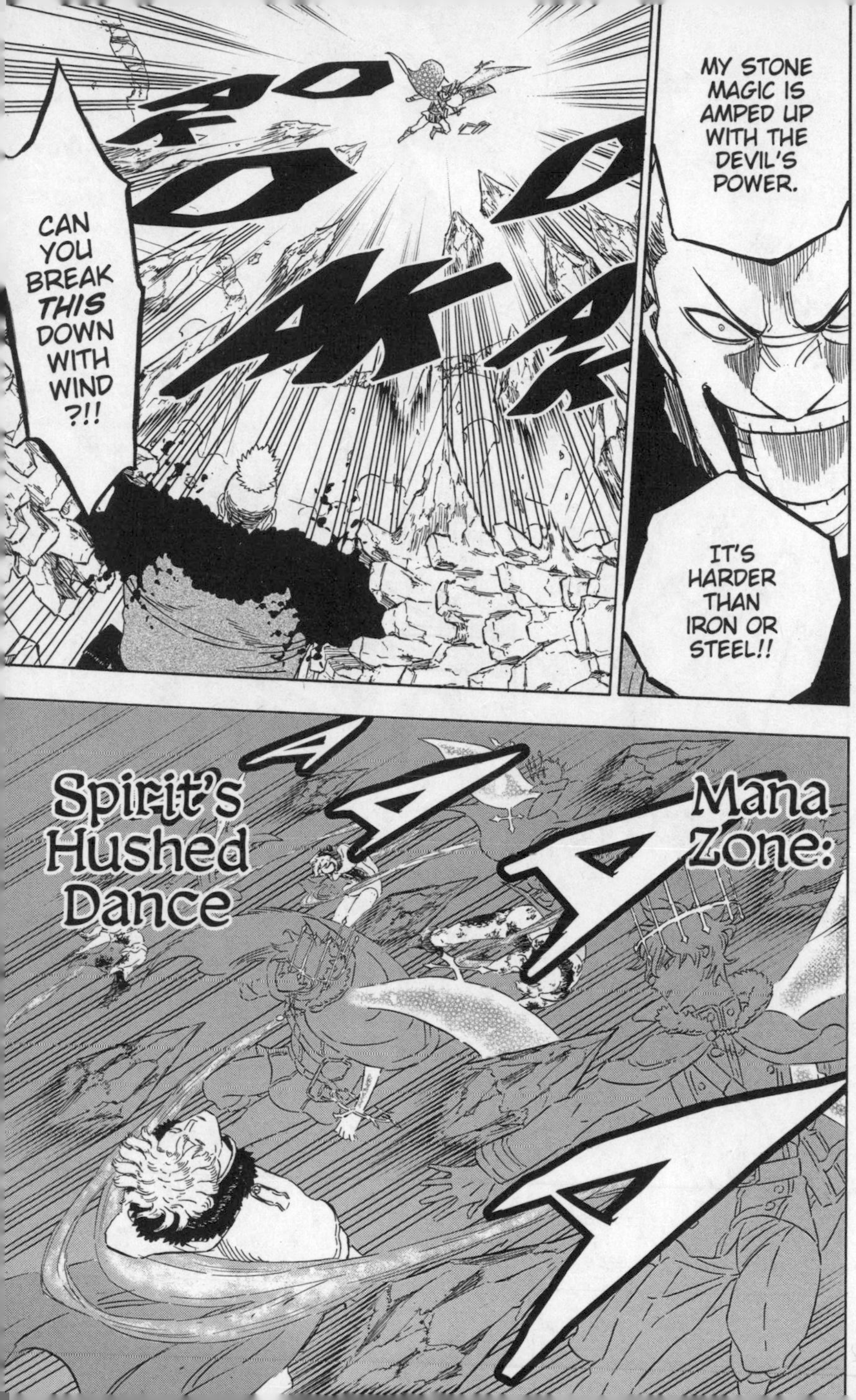
MY STONE MAGIC IS AMPED UP WITH THE DEVIL'S POWER.
IT'S HARDER THAN IRON OR STEEL!!
CAN YOU BREAK *THIS* DOWN WITH WIND?!!
Mana Zone:
Spirit's Hushed Dance

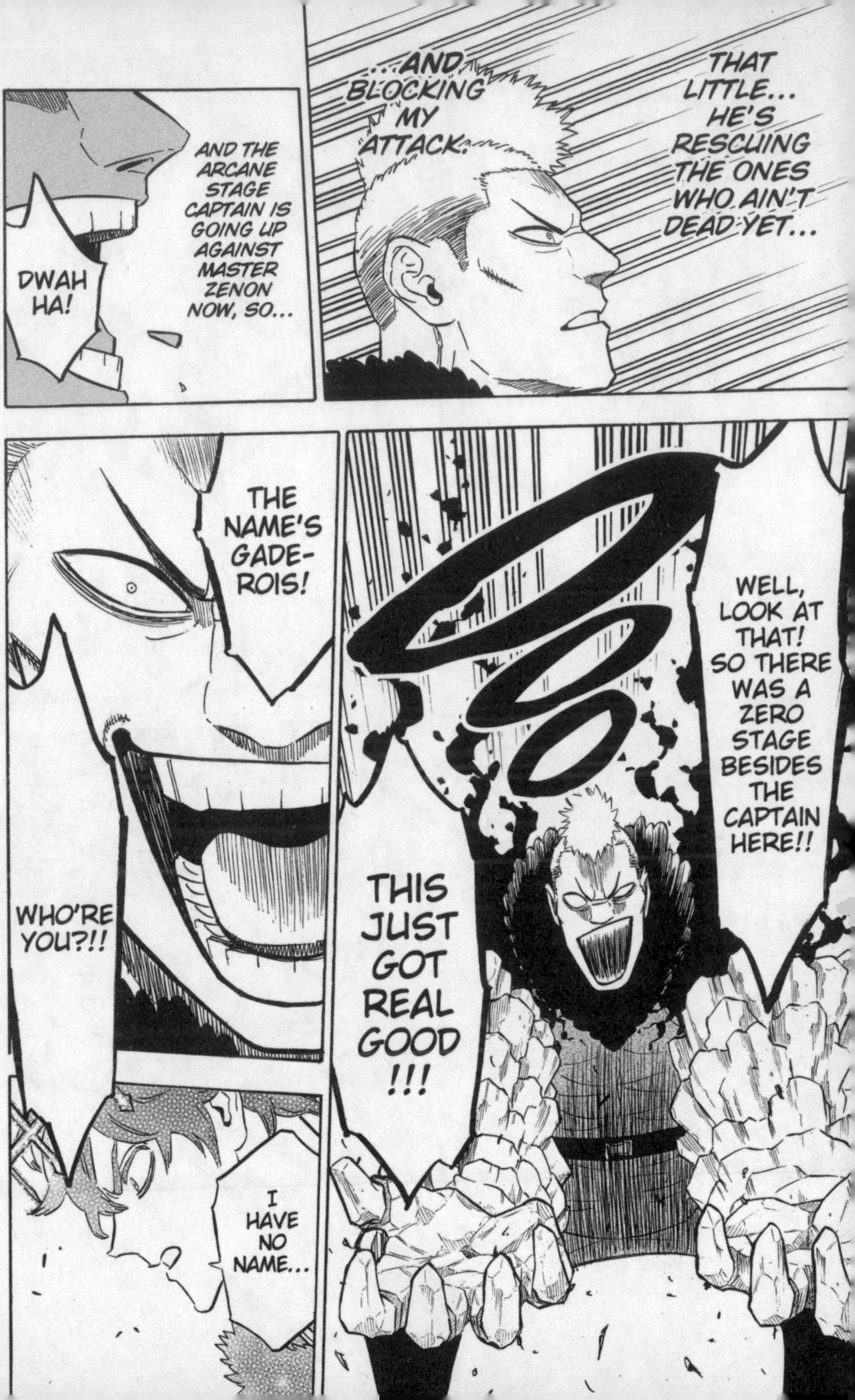
THAT LITTLE... HE'S RESCUING THE ONES WHO AIN'T DEAD YET...
...AND BLOCKING MY ATTACK.
AND THE ARCANE STAGE CAPTAIN IS GOING UP AGAINST MASTER ZENON NOW, SO...
DWAH HA!
WELL, LOOK AT THAT! SO THERE WAS A ZERO STAGE BESIDES THE CAPTAIN HERE!!
THIS JUST GOT REAL GOOD!!!
THE NAME'S GADEROIS!
WHO'RE YOU?!!
I HAVE NO NAME...

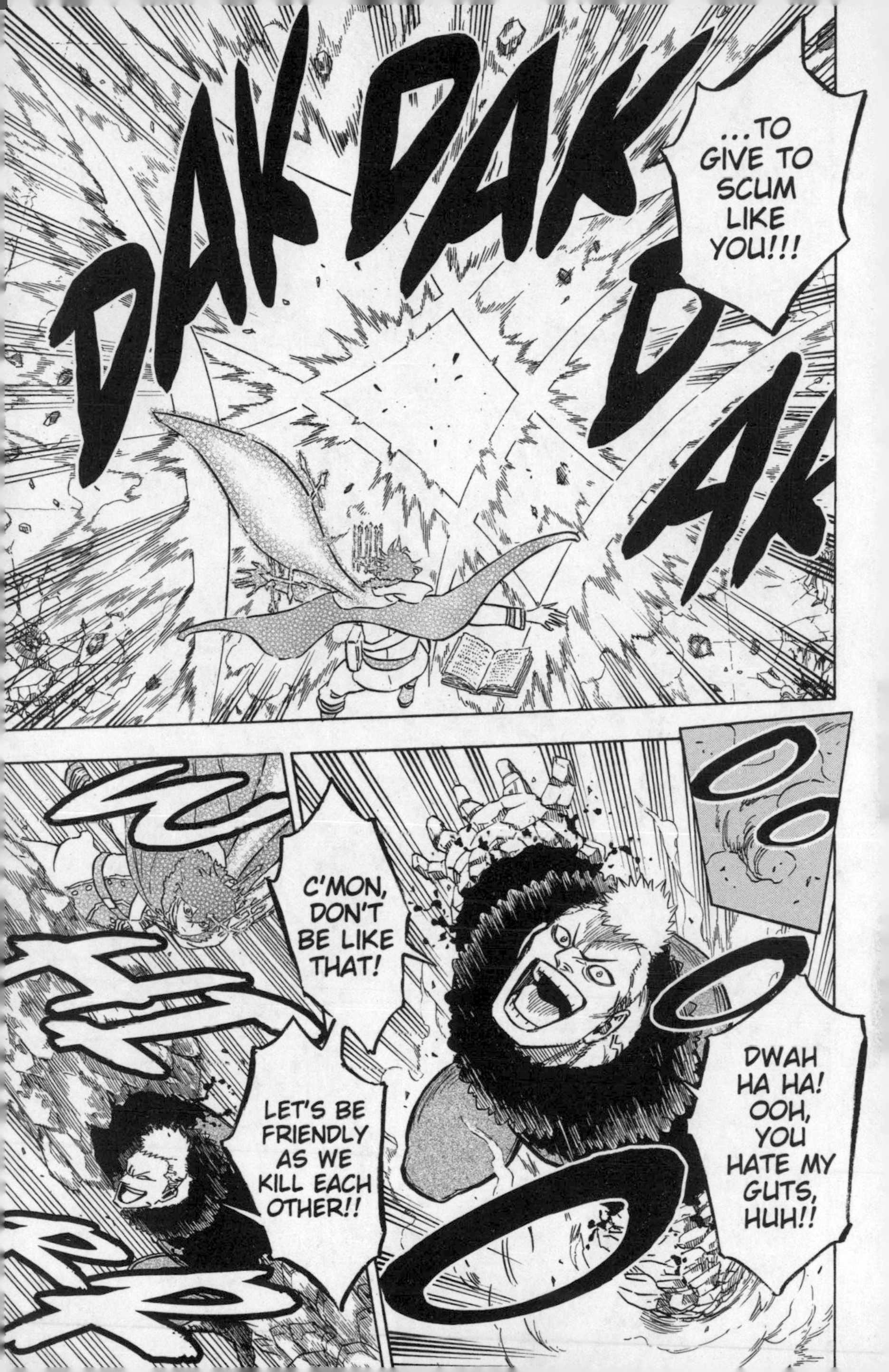
...TO GIVE TO SCUM LIKE YOU!!!
DAK DAK DAK DAK
DWAH HA HA! OOH, YOU HATE MY GUTS, HUH!!
C'MON, DON'T BE LIKE THAT!
LET'S BE FRIENDLY AS WE KILL EACH OTHER!!

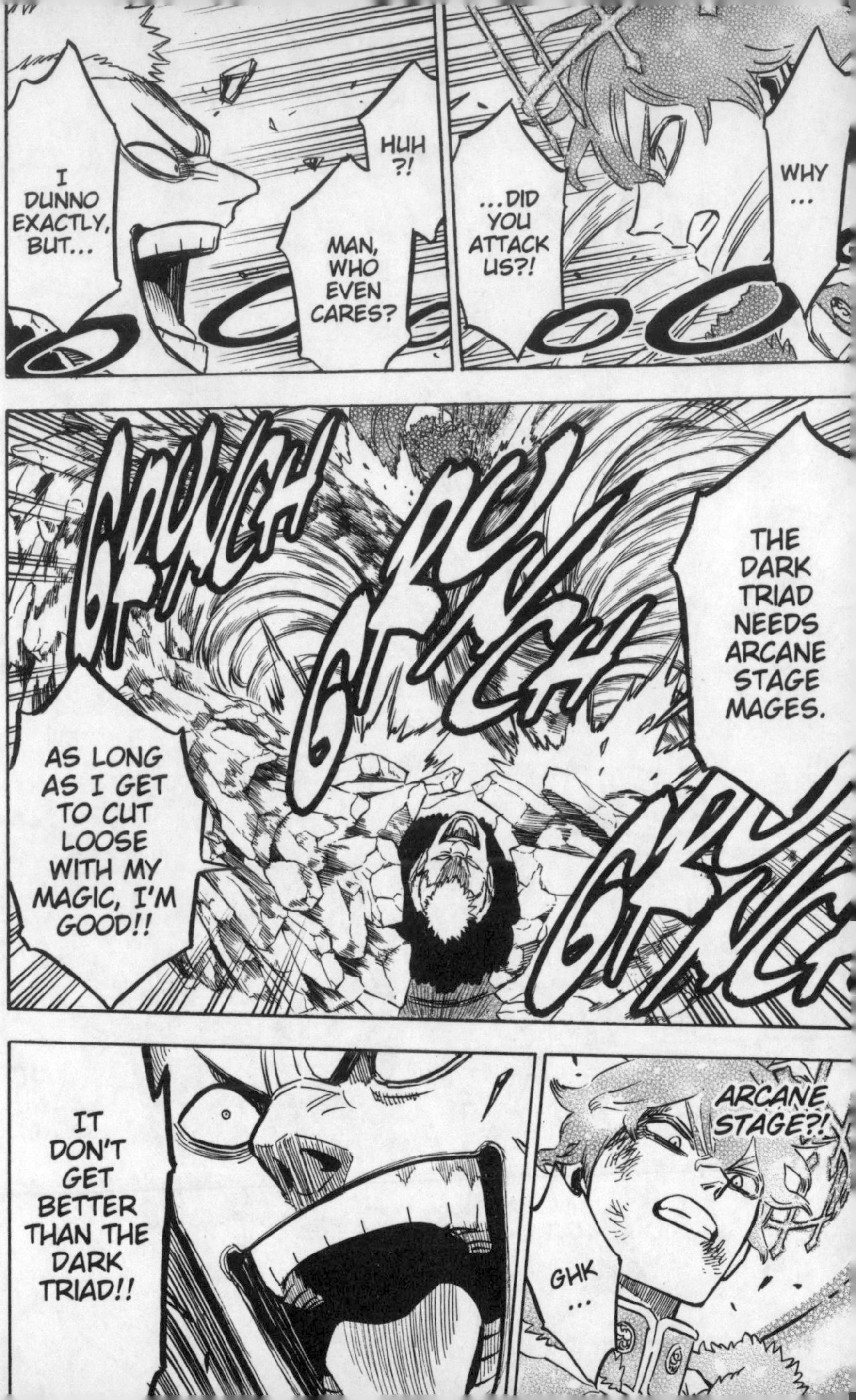
WHY...
...DID YOU ATTACK US?!
HUH ?!
MAN, WHO EVEN CARES?
I DUNNO EXACTLY, BUT...
THE DARK TRIAD NEEDS ARCANE STAGE MAGES.
AS LONG AS I GET TO CUT LOOSE WITH MY MAGIC, I'M GOOD!!
ARCANE STAGE?!
GHK...
IT DON'T GET BETTER THAN THE DARK TRIAD!!

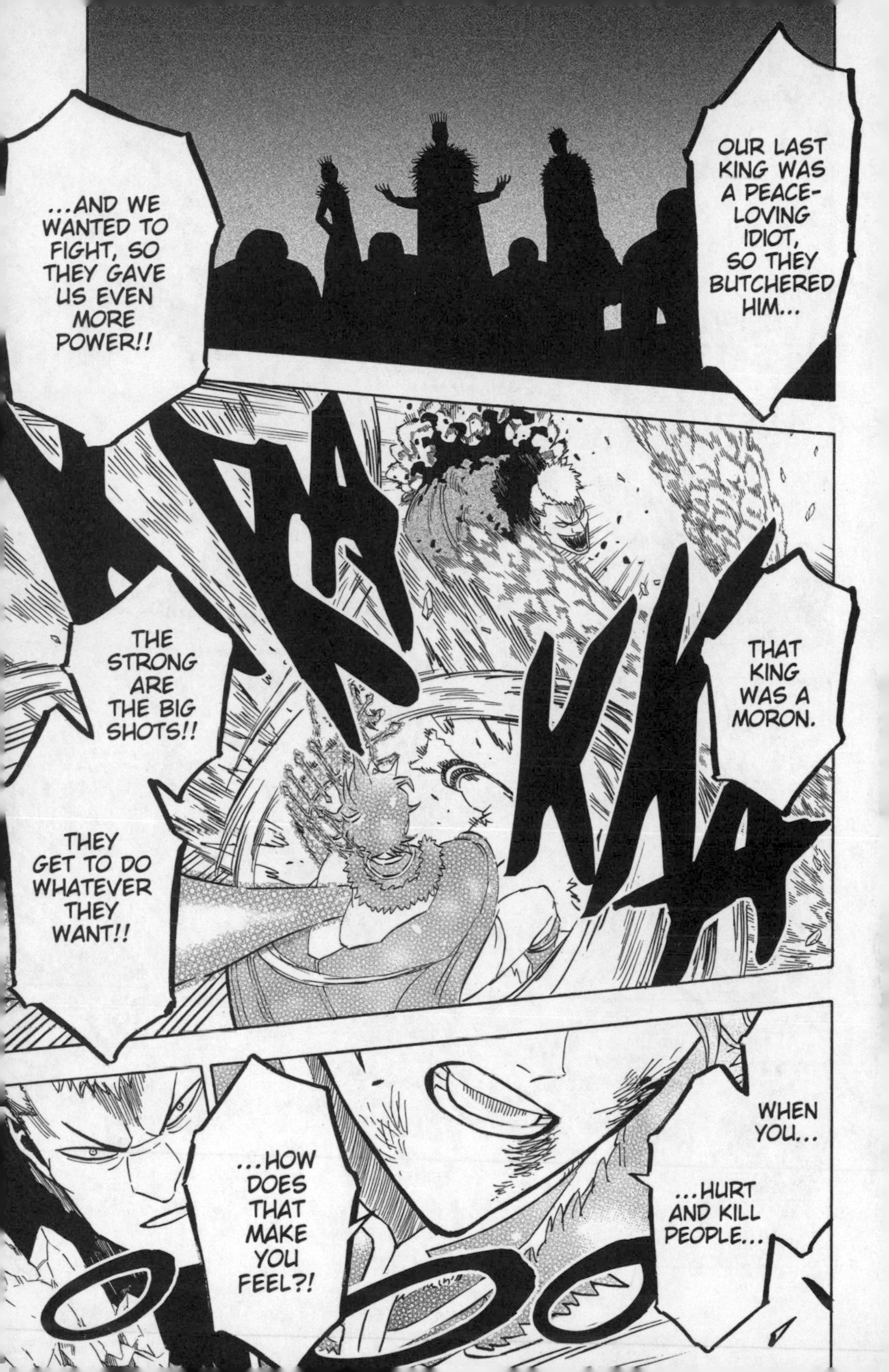
OUR LAST KING WAS A PEACE-LOVING IDIOT, SO THEY BUTCHERED HIM...
...AND WE WANTED TO FIGHT, SO THEY GAVE US EVEN MORE POWER!!
THAT KING WAS A MORON.
THE STRONG ARE THE BIG SHOTS!!
THEY GET TO DO WHATEVER THEY WANT!!
WHEN YOU...
...HURT AND KILL PEOPLE...
...HOW DOES THAT MAKE YOU FEEL?!

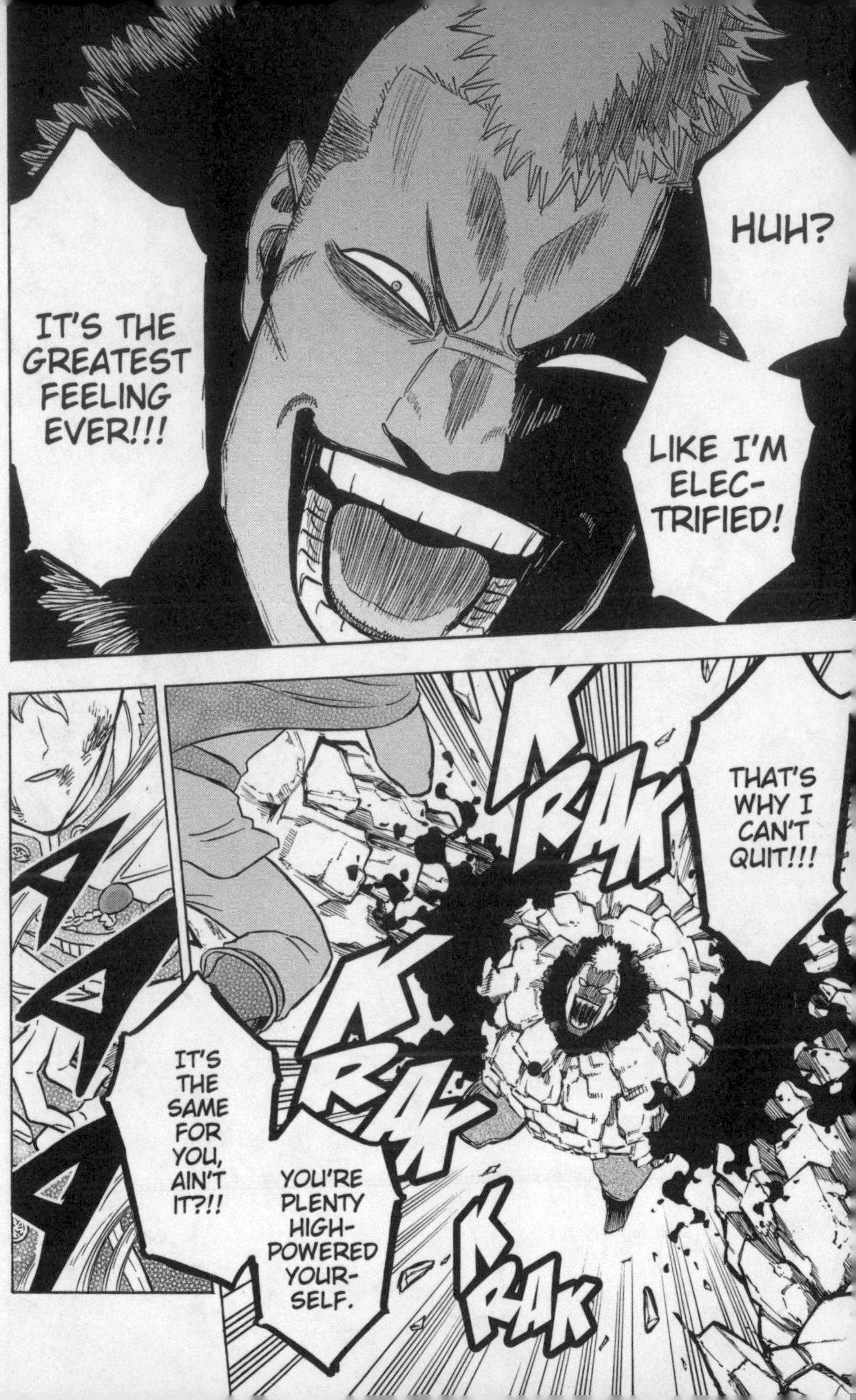
HUH?
LIKE I'M ELEC-TRIFIED!
IT'S THE GREATEST FEELING EVER!!!
THAT'S WHY I CAN'T QUIT!!!
KRAK
KRAK
IT'S THE SAME FOR YOU, AIN'T IT?!!
YOU'RE PLENTY HIGH-POWERED YOUR-SELF.
KRAK

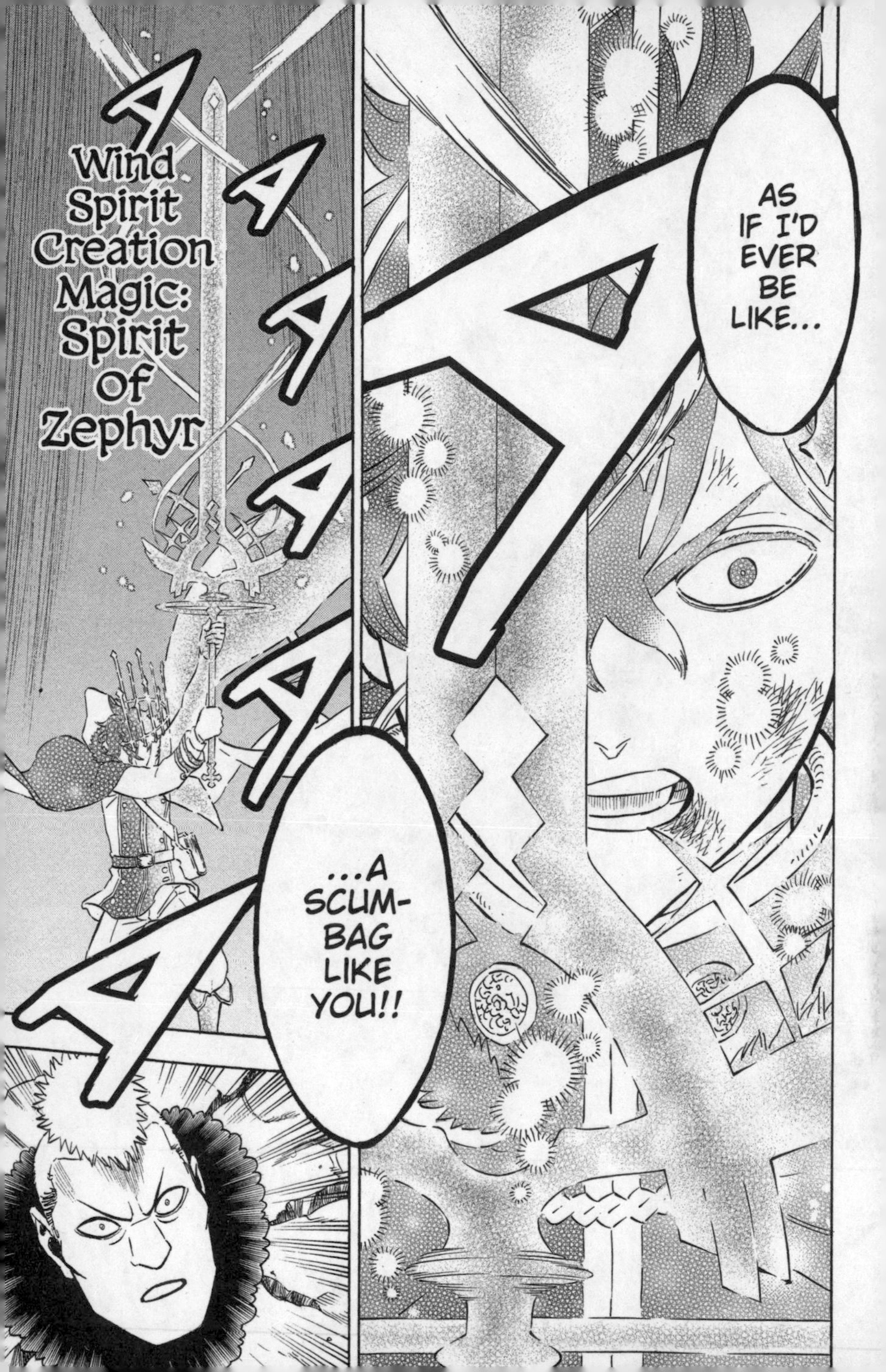
AS IF I'D EVER BE LIKE...
...A SCUM-BAG LIKE YOU!!
Wind Spirit Creation Magic: Spirit of Zephyr

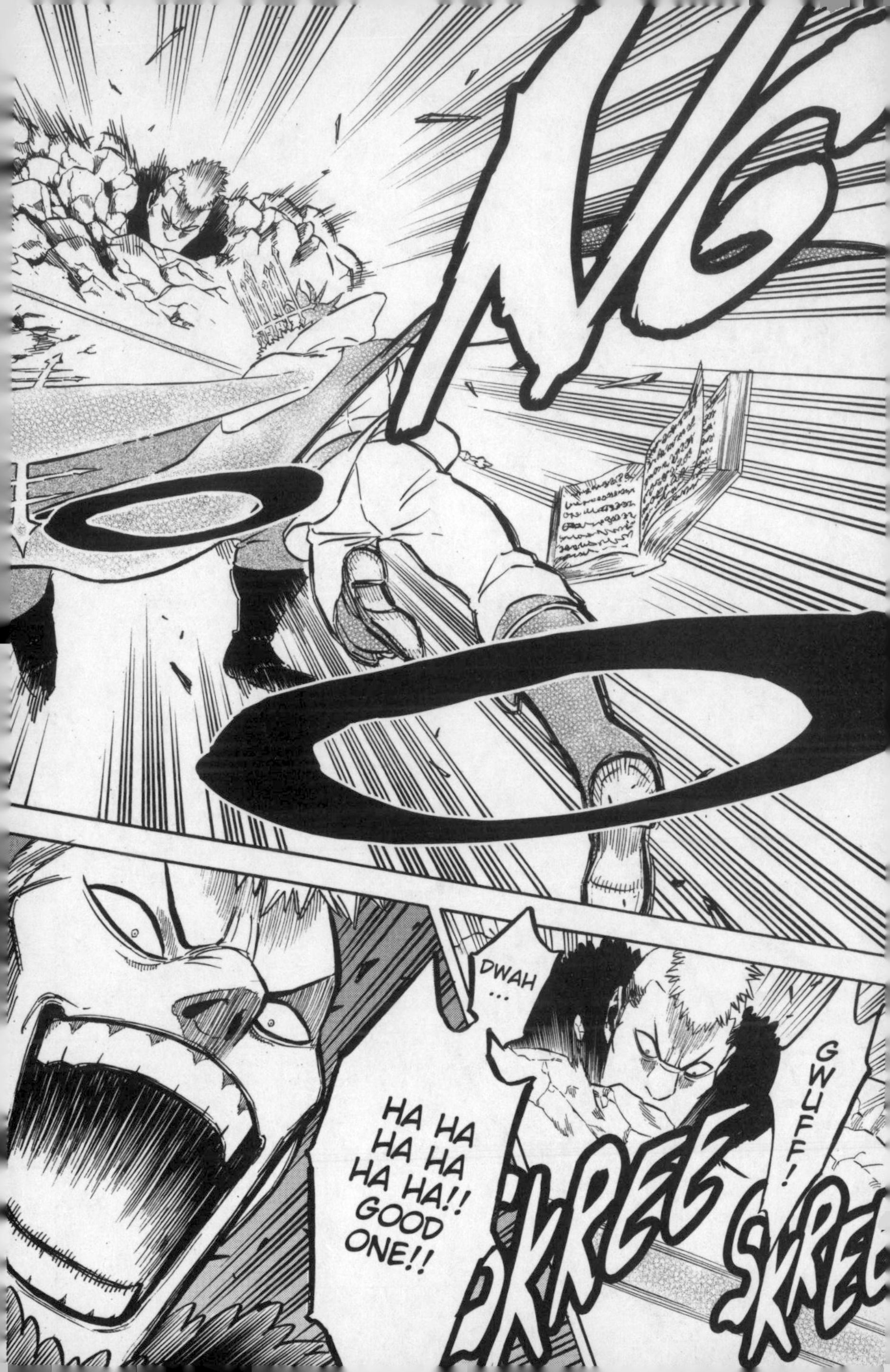
NOOO
GWUFF!
DWAH...
SKREE
SKREE
HA HA HA HA HA HA!! GOOD ONE!!

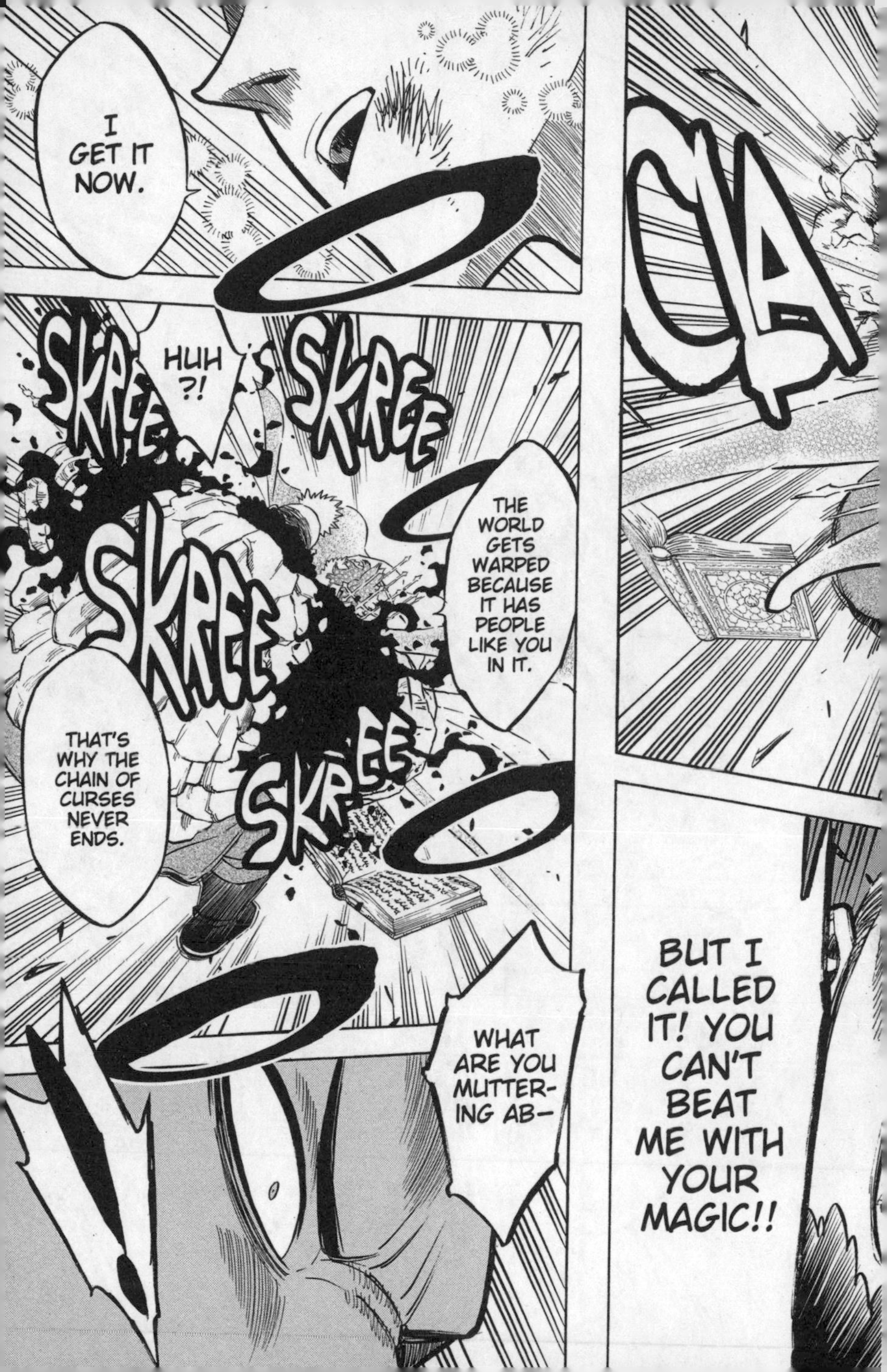
CLA
BUT I CALLED IT! YOU CAN'T BEAT ME WITH YOUR MAGIC!!
I GET IT NOW.
SKREE
HUH ?!
SKREE
THE WORLD GETS WARPED BECAUSE IT HAS PEOPLE LIKE YOU IN IT.
SKREE
SKREE
THAT'S WHY THE CHAIN OF CURSES NEVER ENDS.
WHAT ARE YOU MUTTER-ING AB—

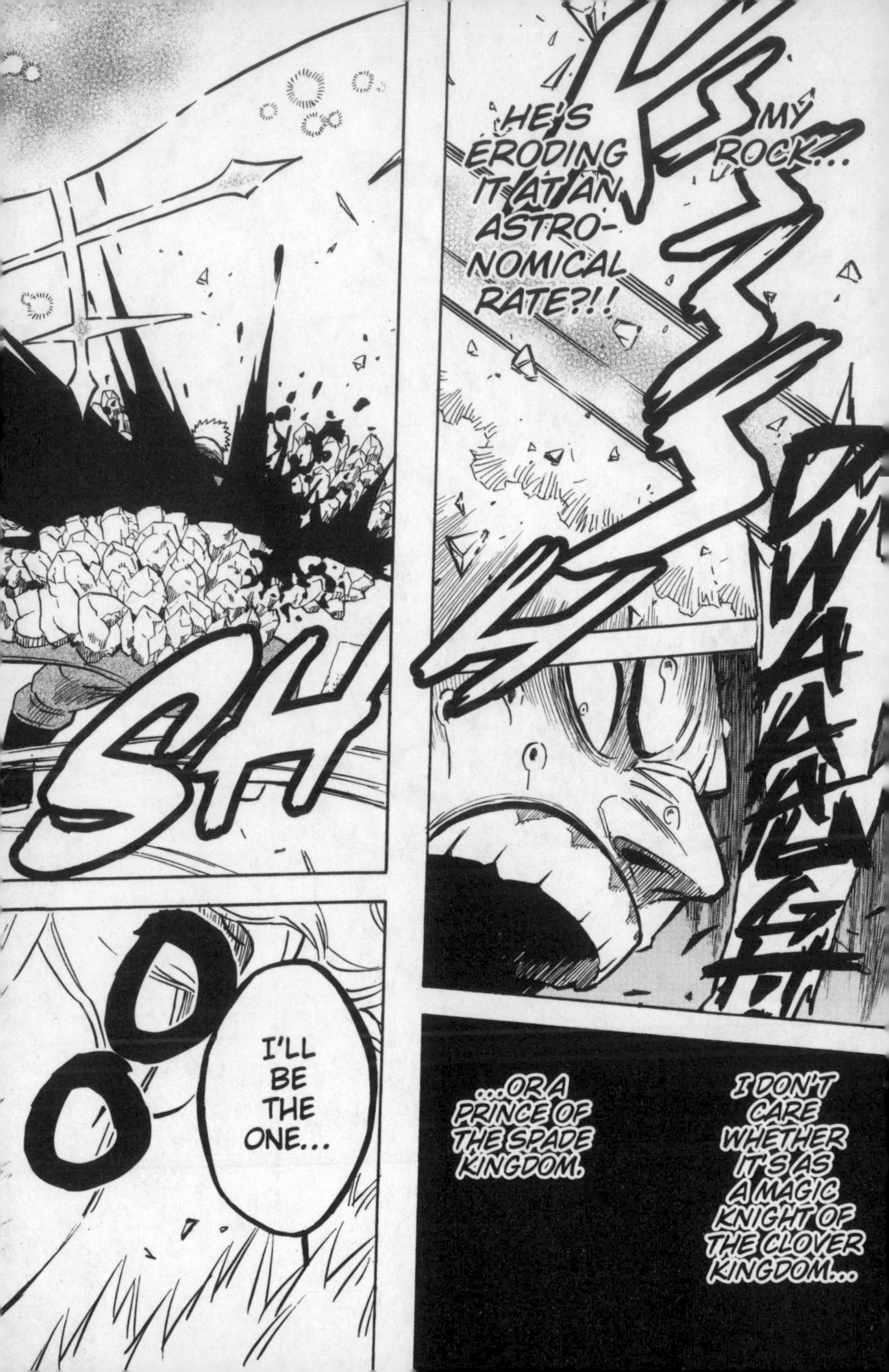
MY ROCK...
HE'S ERODING IT AT AN ASTRONOMICAL RATE?!!
SH
I DON'T CARE WHETHER IT'S AS A MAGIC KNIGHT OF THE CLOVER KINGDOM...
...OR A PRINCE OF THE SPADE KINGDOM.
I'LL BE THE ONE...

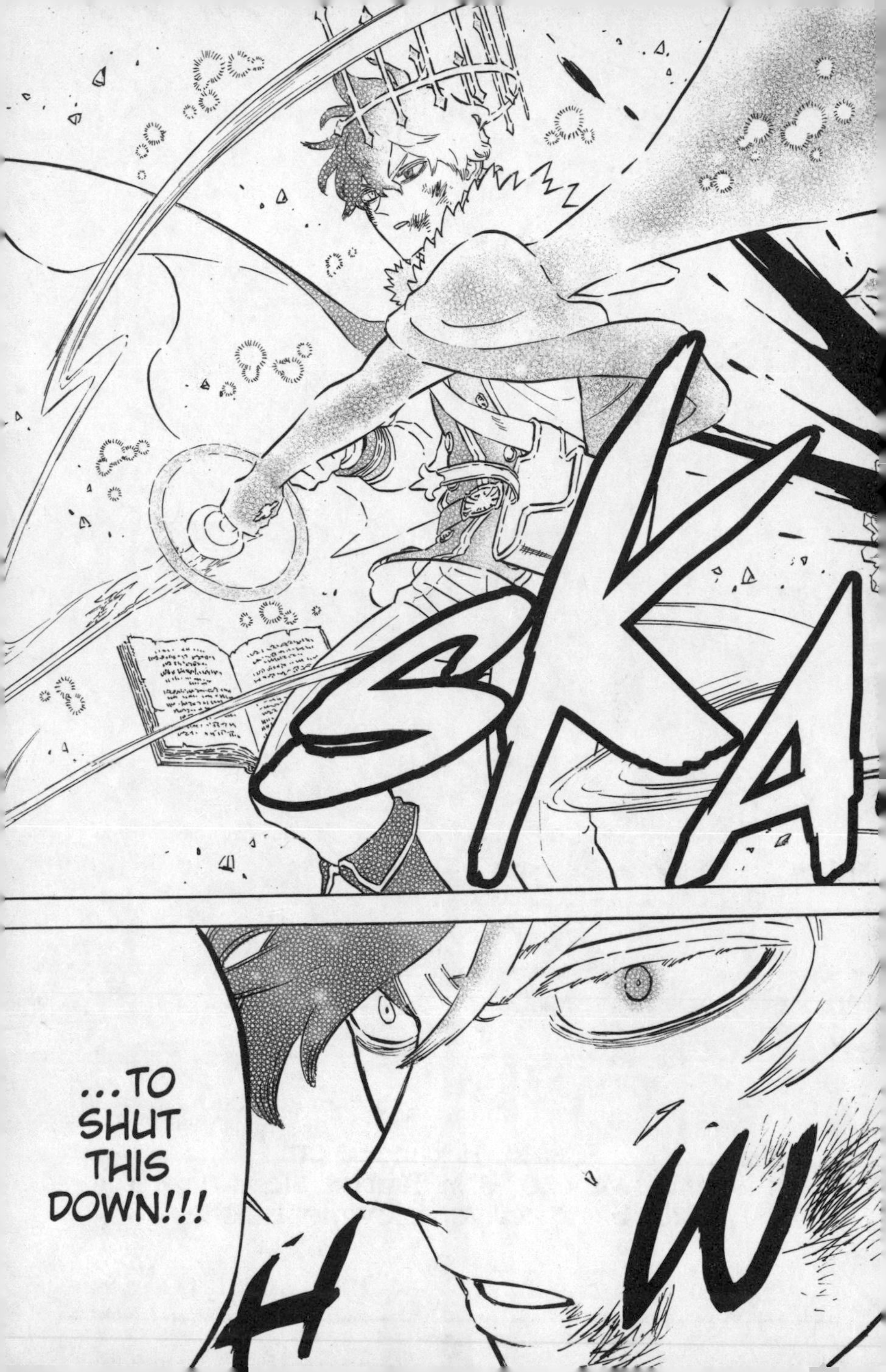
SKA
...TO SHUT THIS DOWN!!!

Gaderois Godroc

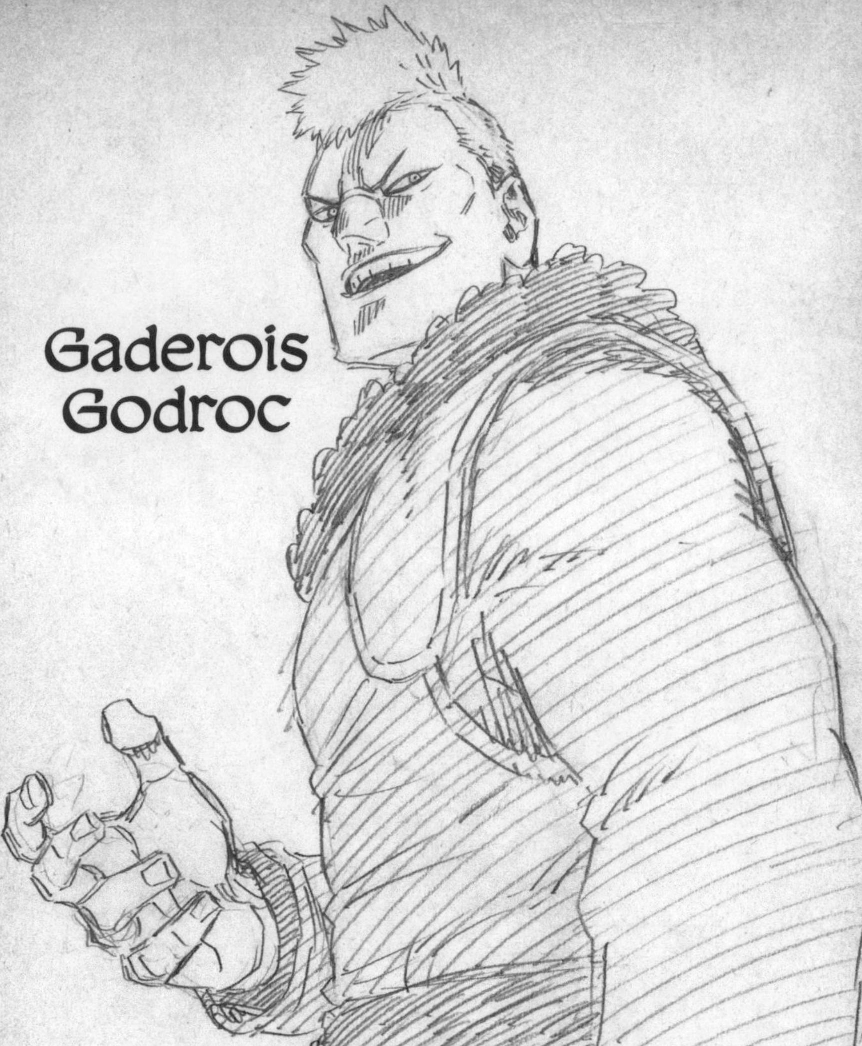

Age: 26 Height: 180 cm
Birthday: May 20 Sign: Taurus Blood Type: B
Likes: Being active, spicy meat dishes

Character Profile

Page 237: Sheer Obstinacy

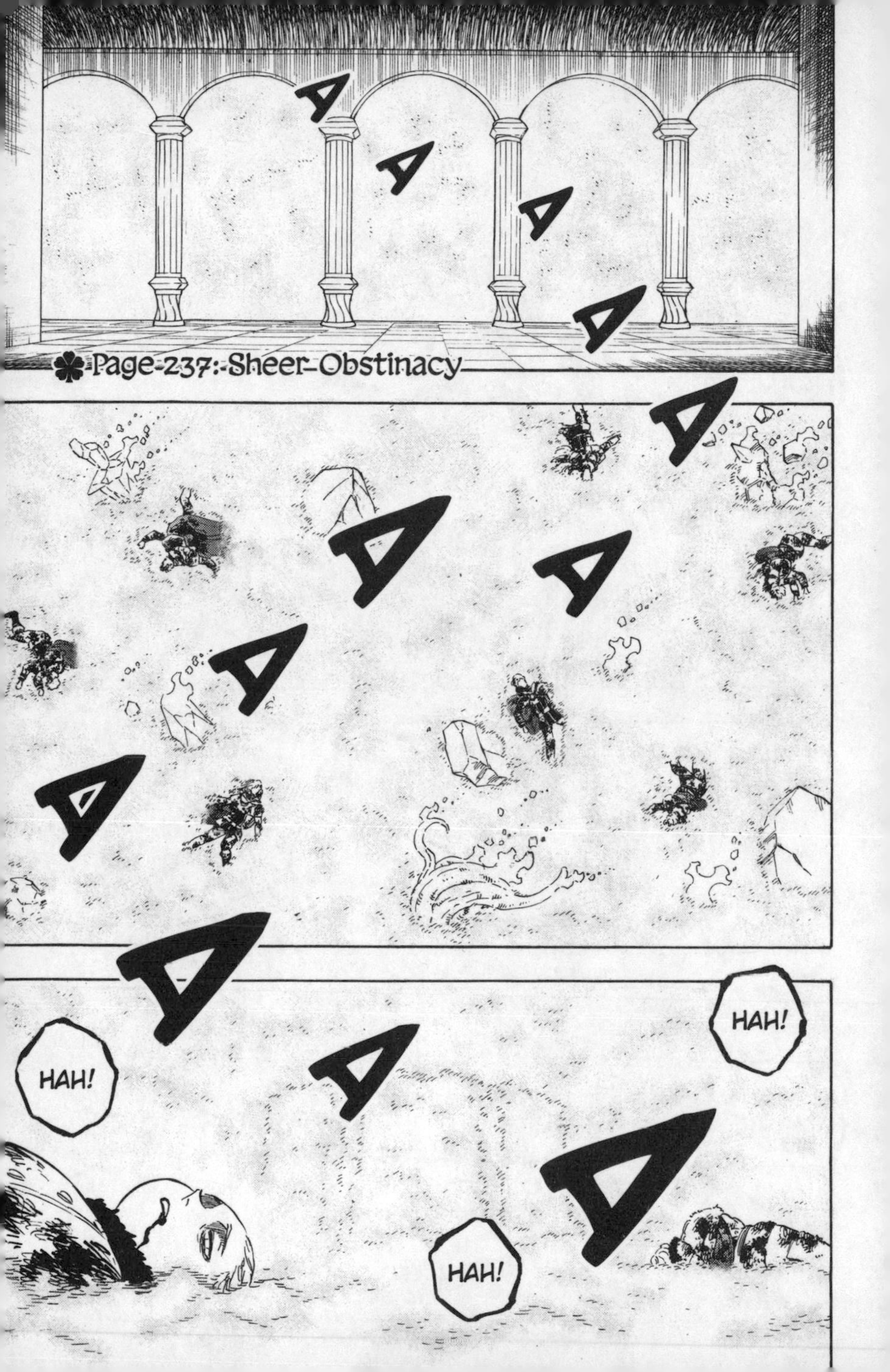
AAAAAAAAAAAA
HAH!
HAH!
HAH!

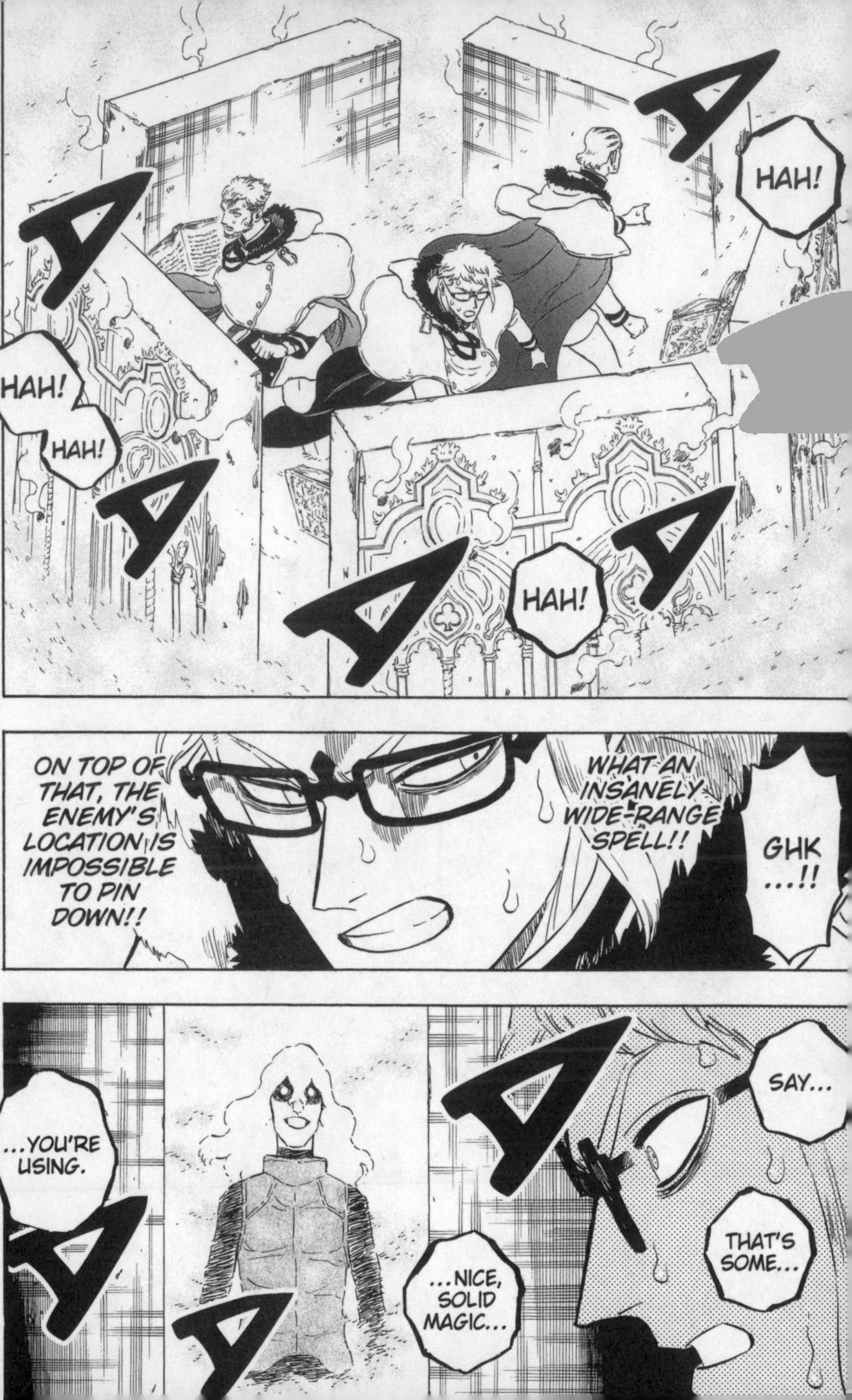
HAH!
HAH!
HAH!
HAH!
GHK ...!!
WHAT AN INSANELY WIDE-RANGE SPELL!!
ON TOP OF THAT, THE ENEMY'S LOCATION IS IMPOSSIBLE TO PIN DOWN!!
SAY...
THAT'S SOME...
...NICE, SOLID MAGIC...
...YOU'RE USING.

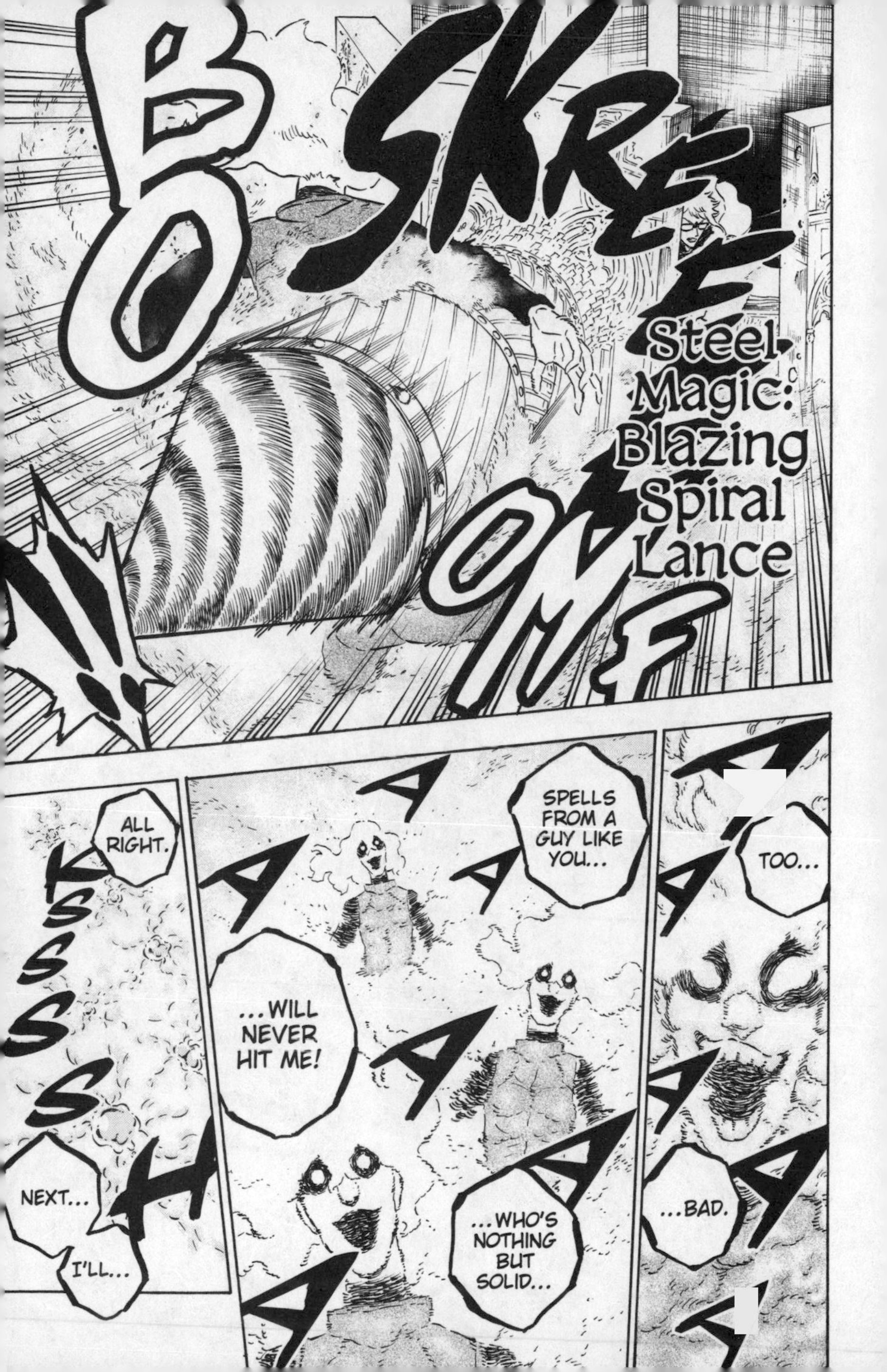
Steel Magic: Blazing Spiral Lance
TOO...
...BAD.
SPELLS FROM A GUY LIKE YOU...
...WHO'S NOTHING BUT SOLID...
...WILL NEVER HIT ME!
ALL RIGHT.
KSSSSH
NEXT...
I'LL...

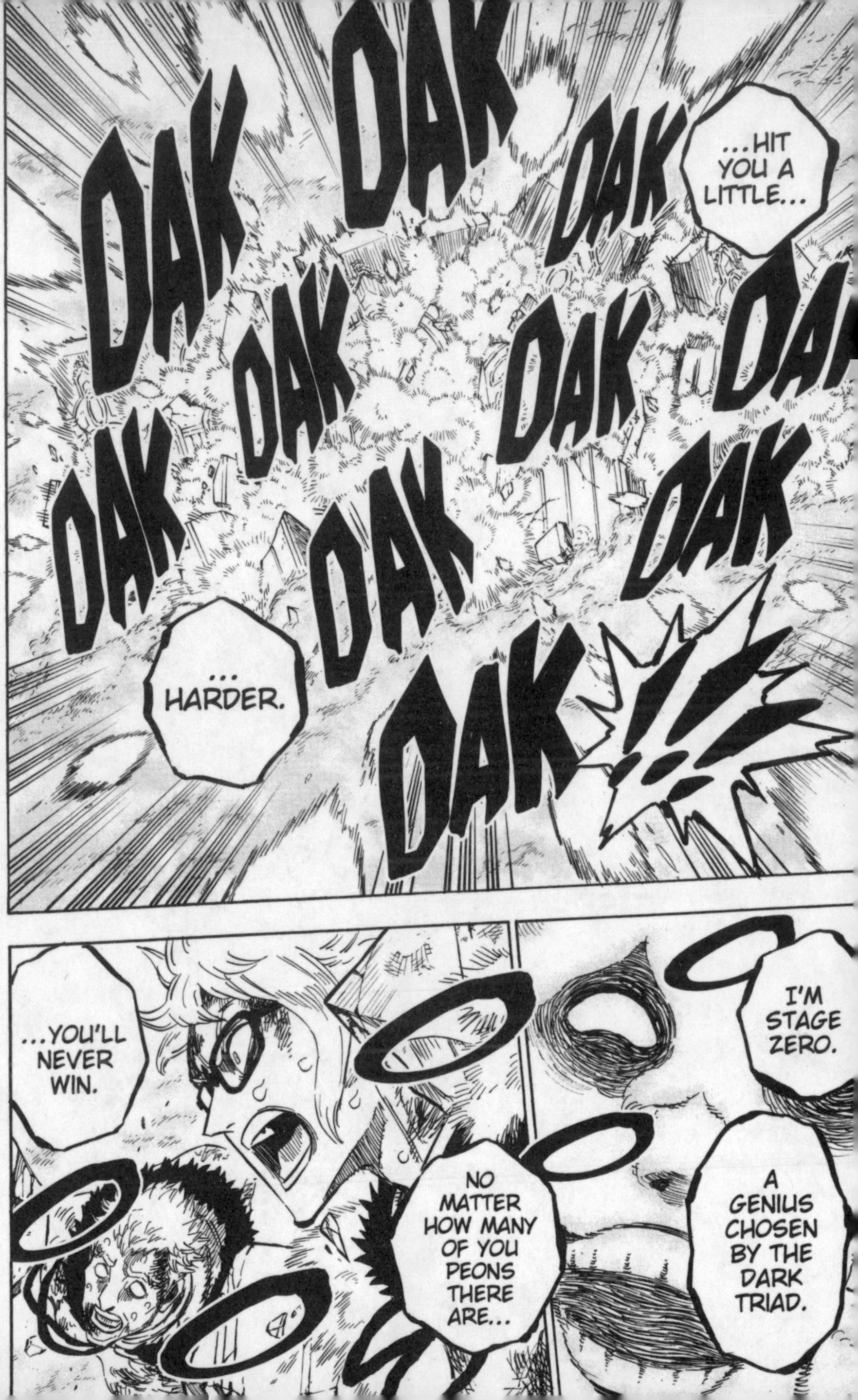
DAK DAK DAK
...HIT YOU A LITTLE...
DAK DAK DAK DAK
DAK DAK DAK DAK
... HARDER.
DAK!!
I'M STAGE ZERO.
A GENIUS CHOSEN BY THE DARK TRIAD.
NO MATTER HOW MANY OF YOU PEONS THERE ARE...
...YOU'LL NEVER WIN.

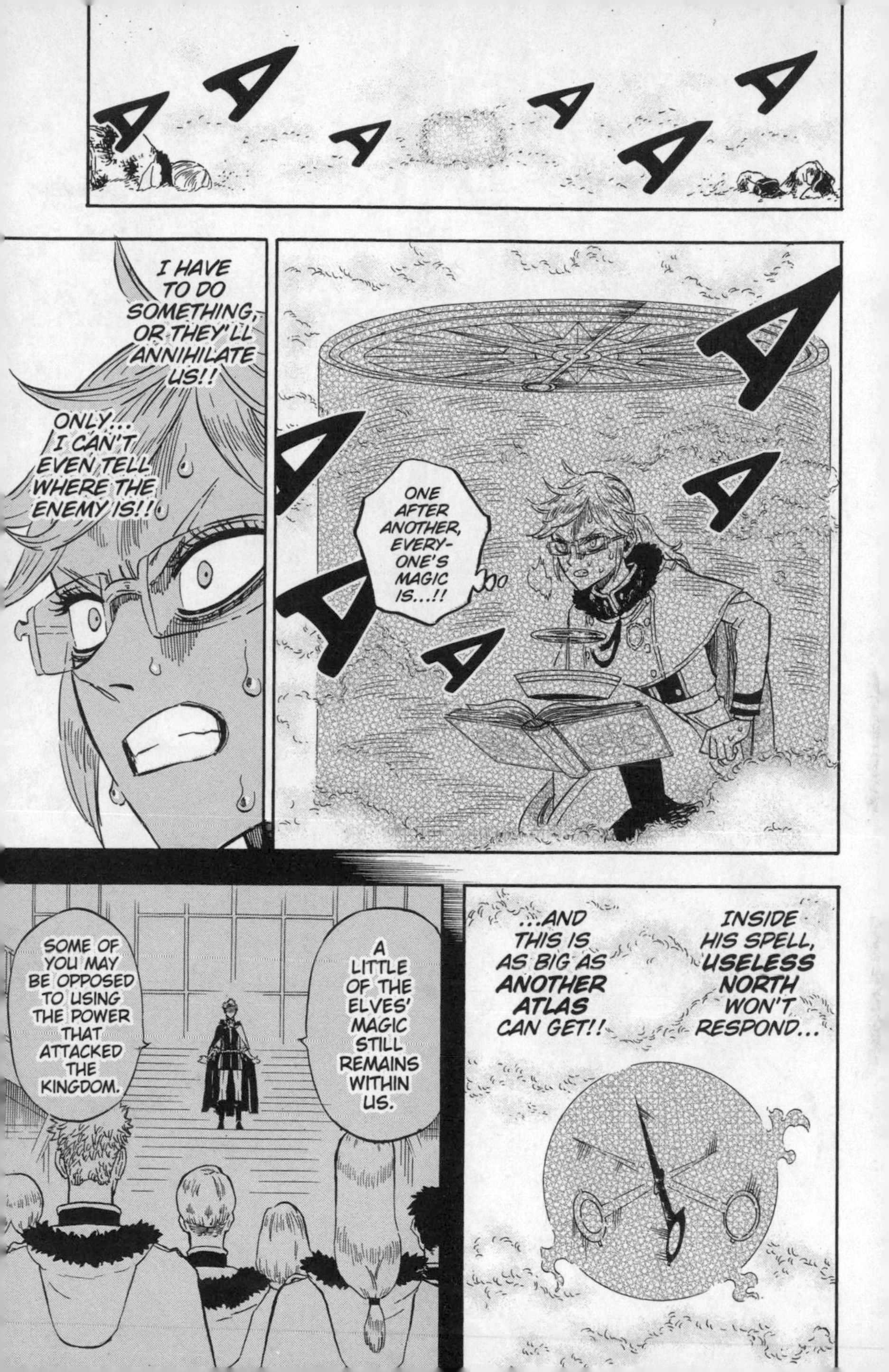

A A A A A A A
A A A A A A
ONE AFTER ANOTHER, EVERYONE'S MAGIC IS...!!
I HAVE TO DO SOMETHING, OR THEY'LL ANNIHILATE US!!
ONLY... I CAN'T EVEN TELL WHERE THE ENEMY IS!!
INSIDE HIS SPELL, USELESS NORTH WON'T RESPOND...
...AND THIS IS AS BIG AS ANOTHER ATLAS CAN GET!!
A LITTLE OF THE ELVES' MAGIC STILL REMAINS WITHIN US.
SOME OF YOU MAY BE OPPOSED TO USING THE POWER THAT ATTACKED THE KINGDOM.

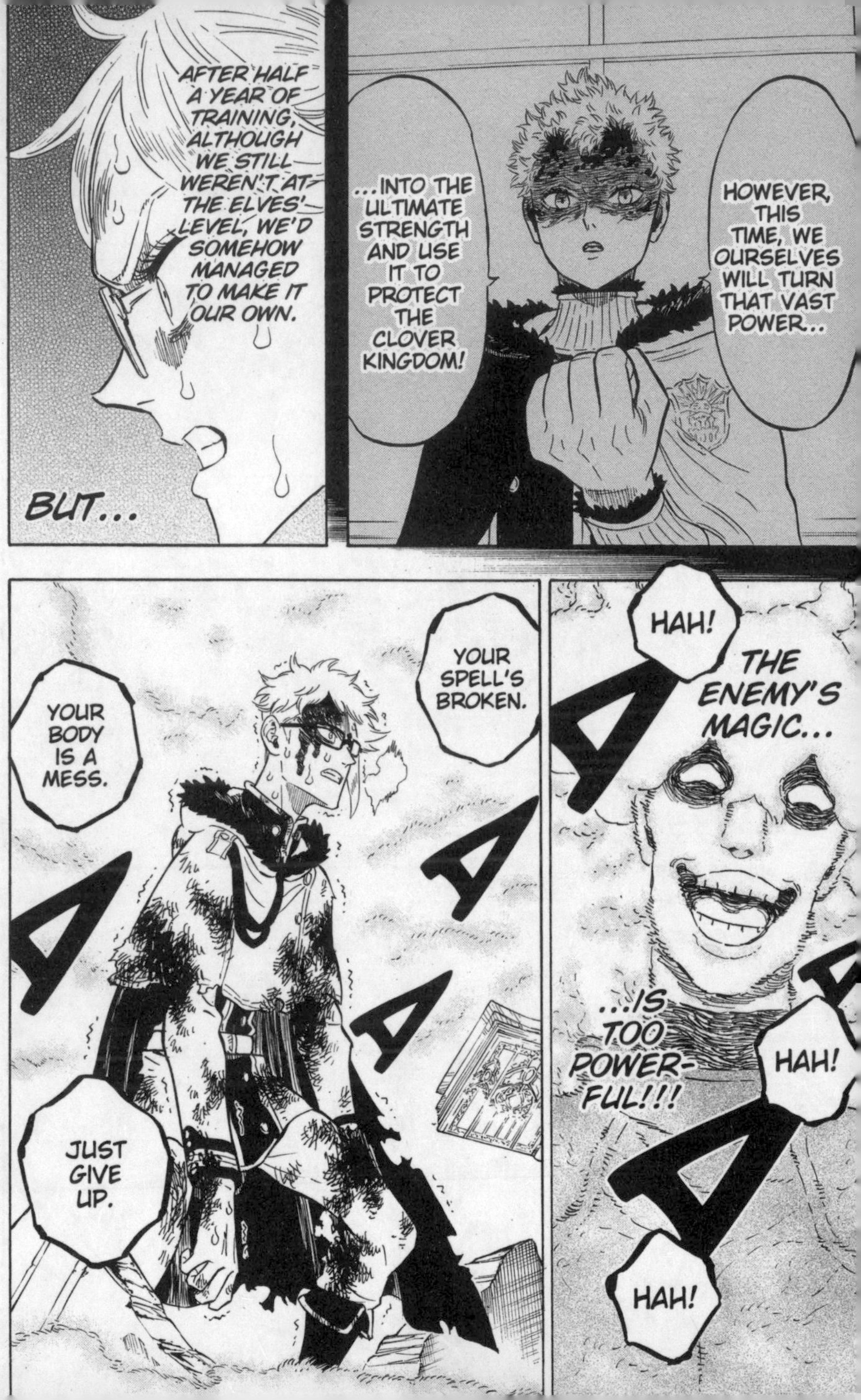
HOWEVER, THIS TIME, WE OURSELVES WILL TURN THAT VAST POWER...
...INTO THE ULTIMATE STRENGTH AND USE IT TO PROTECT THE CLOVER KINGDOM!
AFTER HALF A YEAR OF TRAINING, ALTHOUGH WE STILL WEREN'T AT THE ELVES' LEVEL, WE'D SOMEHOW MANAGED TO MAKE IT OUR OWN.
BUT...
HAH!
THE ENEMY'S MAGIC...
...IS TOO POWER-FUL!!!
HAH!
HAH!
YOUR SPELL'S BROKEN.
YOUR BODY IS A MESS.
JUST GIVE UP.

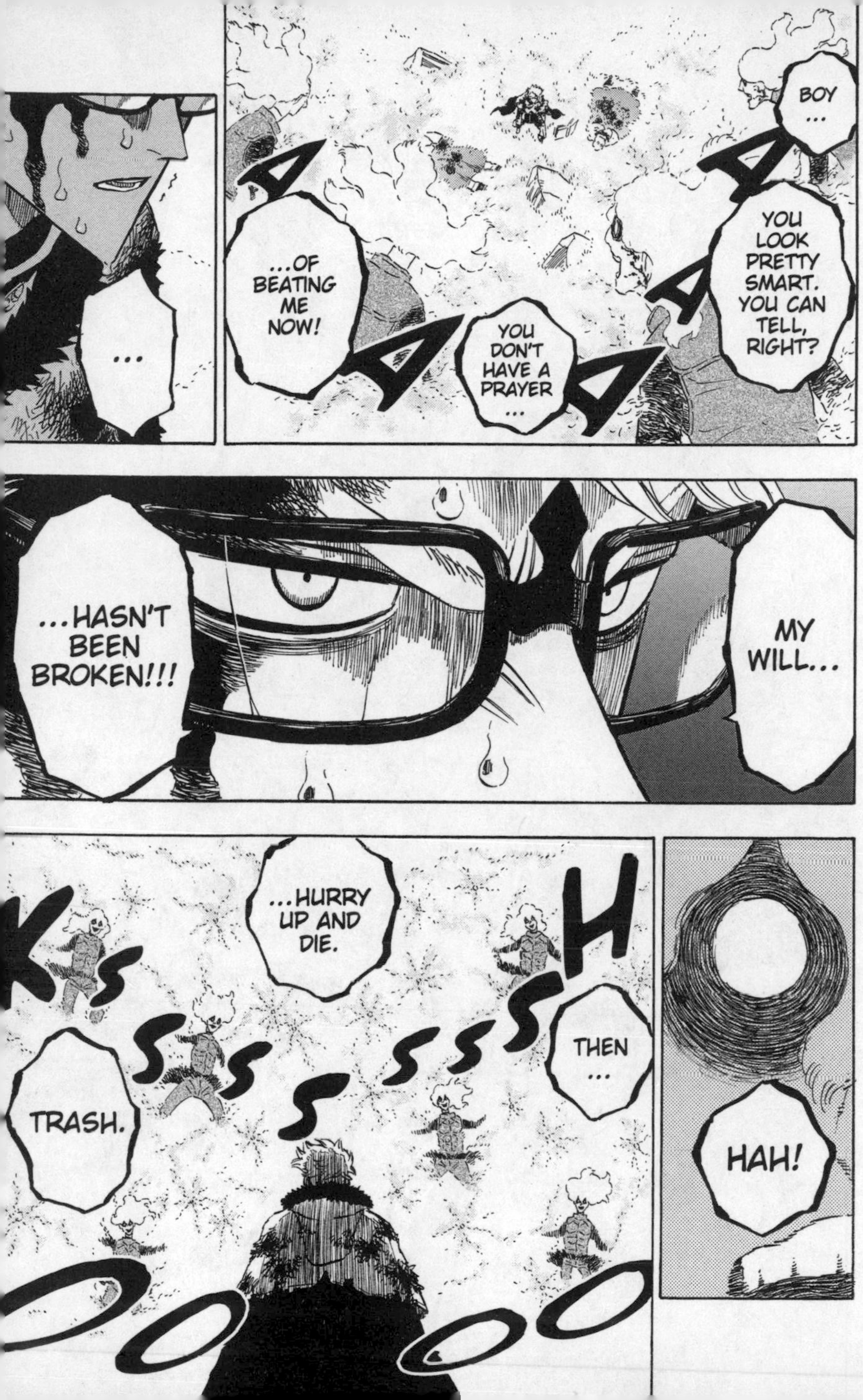
BOY...
YOU LOOK PRETTY SMART. YOU CAN TELL, RIGHT?
YOU DON'T HAVE A PRAYER...
...OF BEATING ME NOW!
AAAAA
...
MY WILL...
...HASN'T BEEN BROKEN!!!
HAH!
THEN...
...HURRY UP AND DIE.
TRASH.
KSSSSSSSH
OOOO

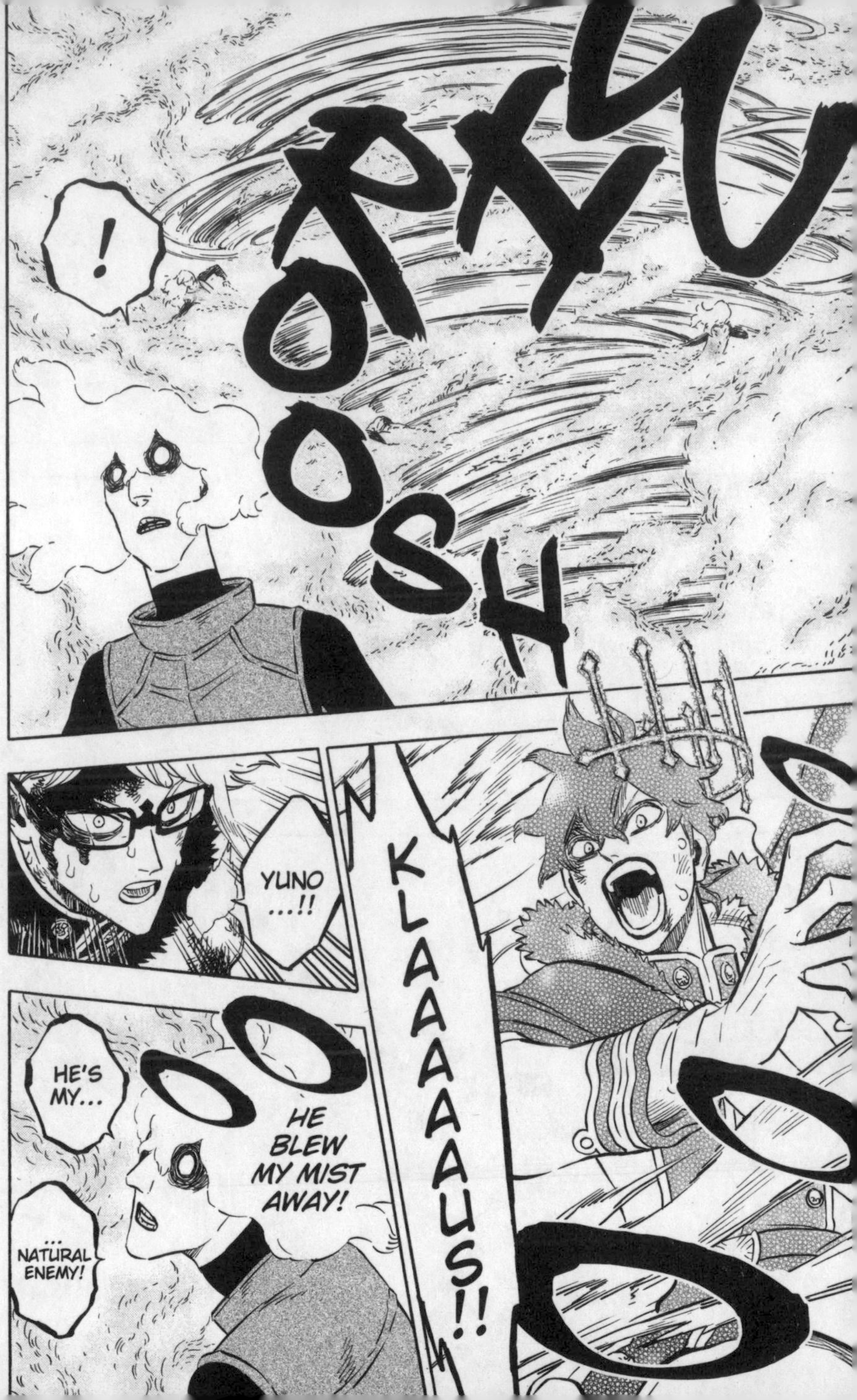
!
KLAAAAAAUS!!
YUNO ...!!
HE BLEW MY MIST AWAY!
HE'S MY...
...NATURAL ENEMY!

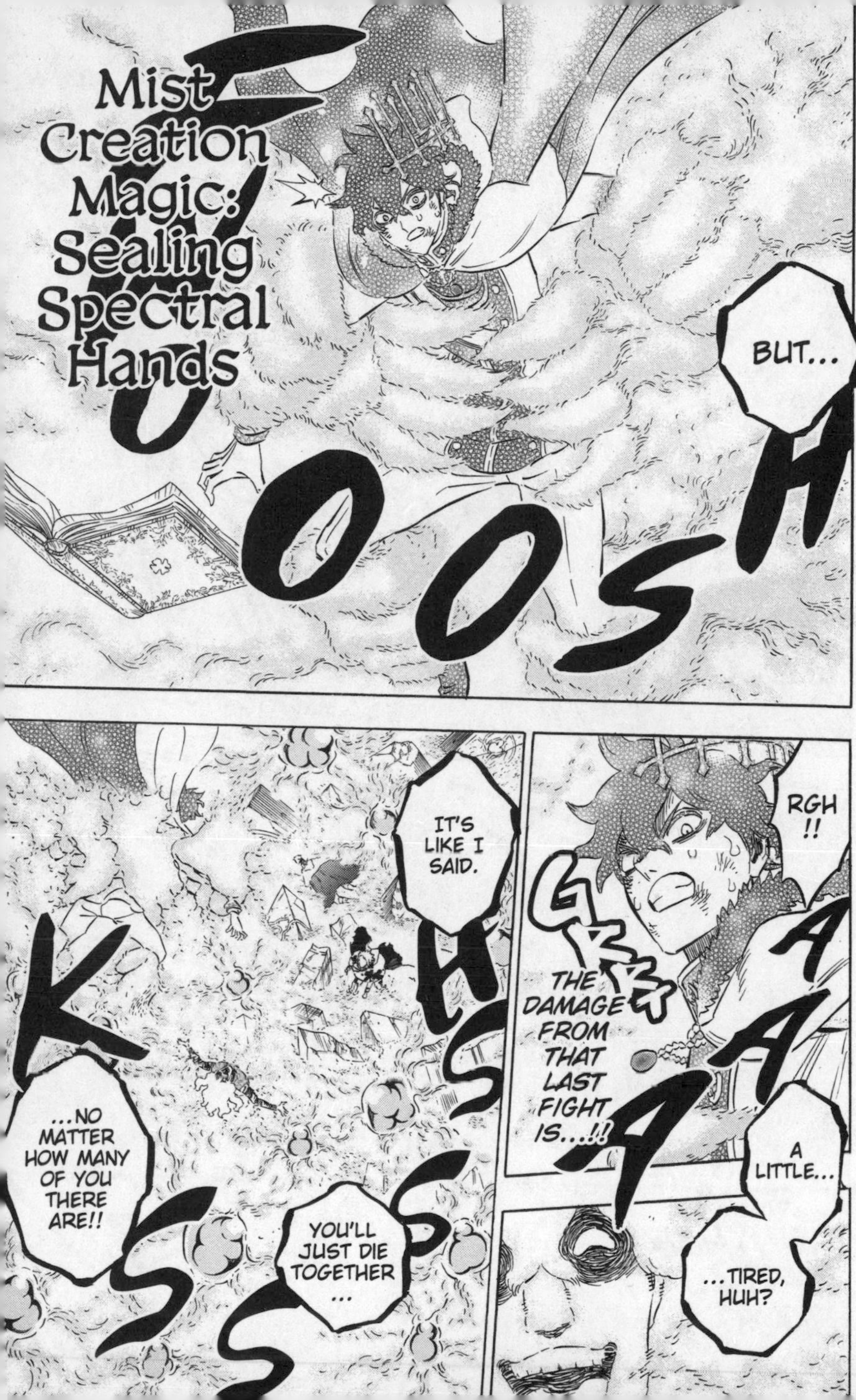
BUT...
Mist Creation Magic: Sealing Spectral Hands
OOSH
RGH!!
THE DAMAGE FROM THAT LAST FIGHT IS...!!
A LITTLE...
...TIRED, HUH?
IT'S LIKE I SAID.
...NO MATTER HOW MANY OF YOU THERE ARE!!
YOU'LL JUST DIE TOGETHER...

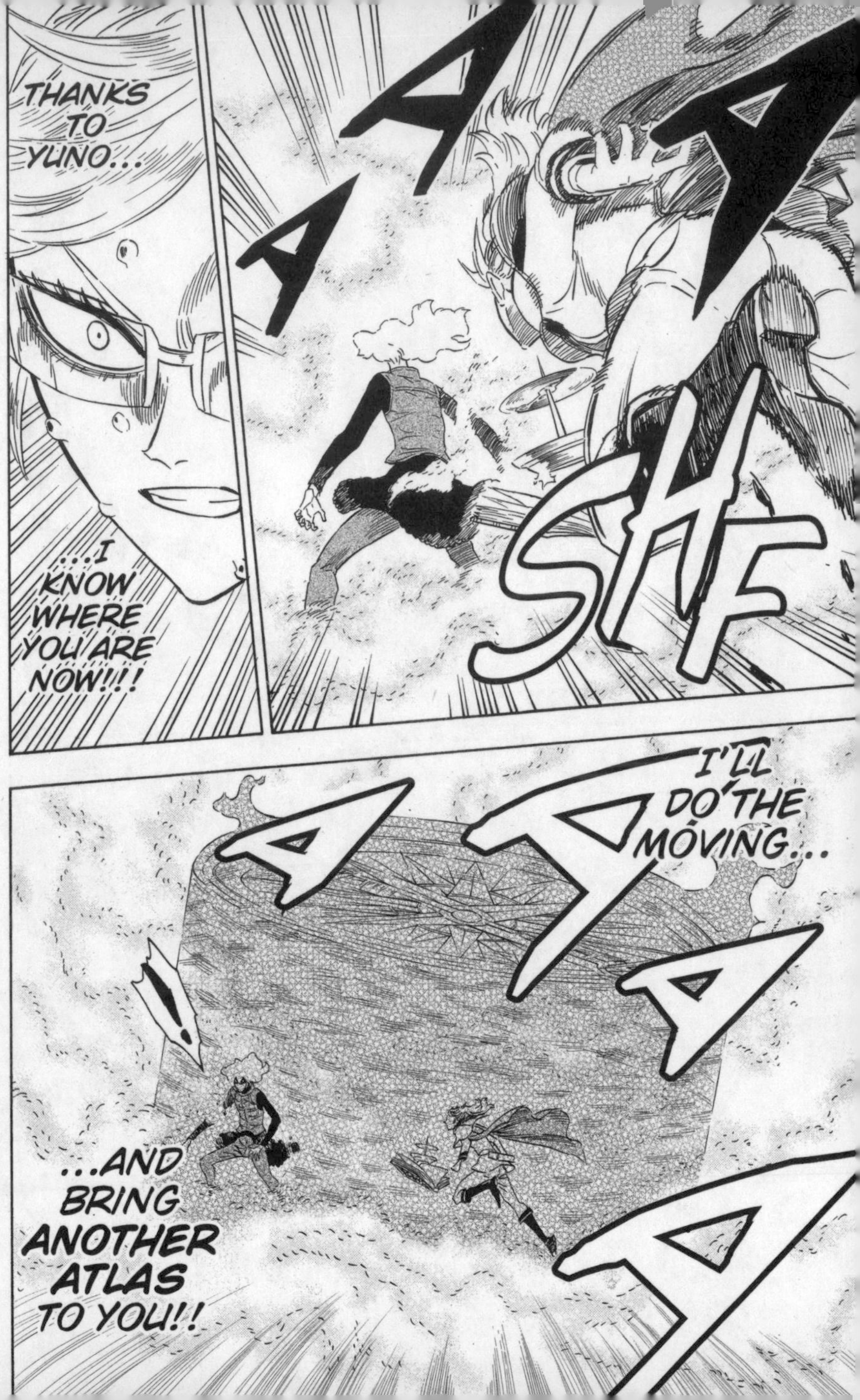
AAAA
SHF
THANKS TO YUNO...
...I KNOW WHERE YOU ARE NOW!!!
I'LL DO THE MOVING...
AAAAA
!
...AND BRING ANOTHER ATLAS TO YOU!!

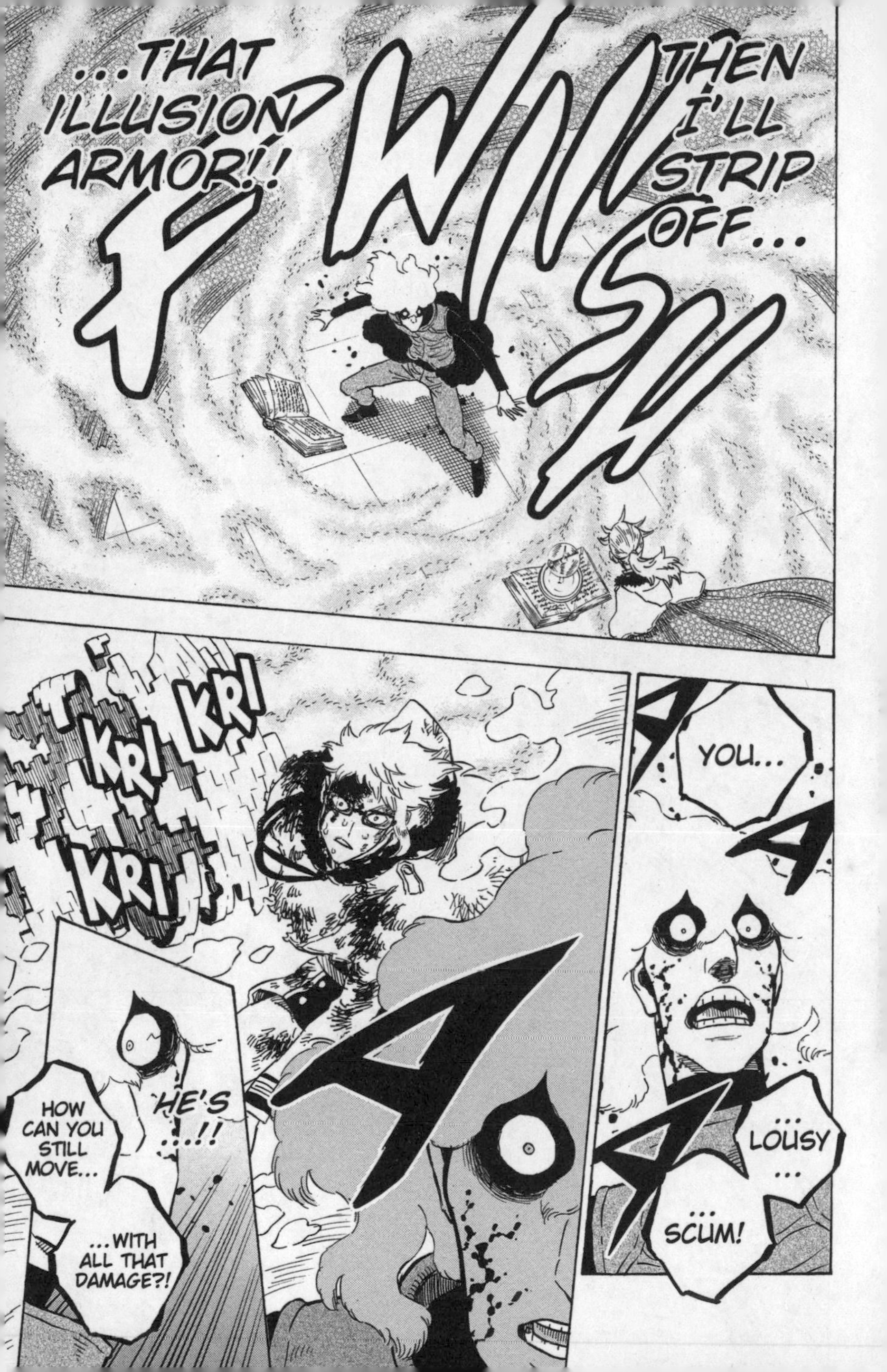
THEN I'LL STRIP OFF...
...THAT ILLUSION ARMOR!!
YOU...
...LOUSY...
...SCUM!
KRI
KRI
KRI
HE'S ...!!
HOW CAN YOU STILL MOVE...
...WITH ALL THAT DAMAGE?!

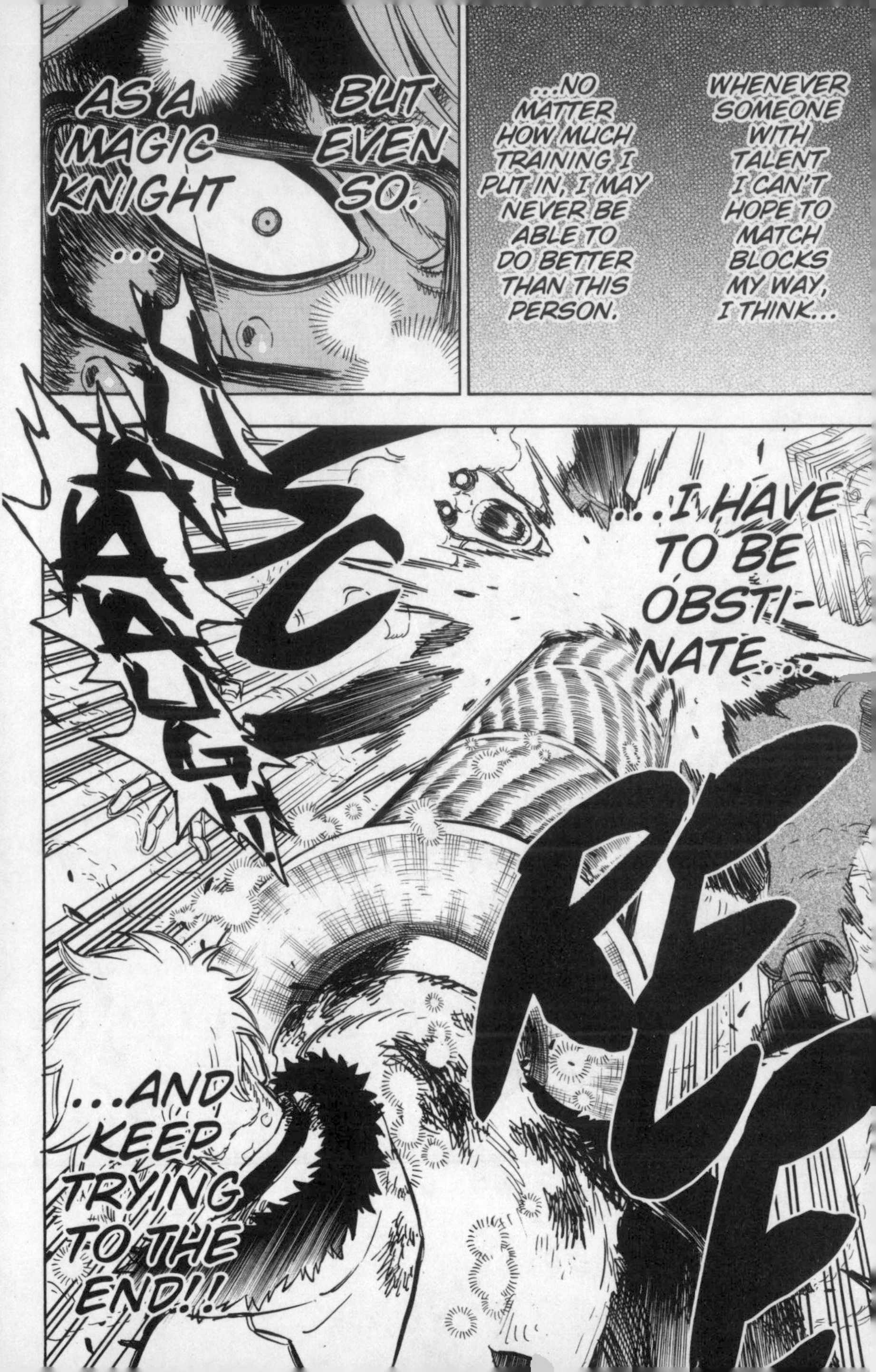
WHENEVER SOMEONE WITH TALENT I CAN'T HOPE TO MATCH BLOCKS MY WAY, I THINK...
...NO MATTER HOW MUCH TRAINING I PUT IN, I MAY NEVER BE ABLE TO DO BETTER THAN THIS PERSON.
BUT EVEN SO.
AS A MAGIC KNIGHT...
...I HAVE TO BE OBSTI-NATE...
...AND KEEP TRYING TO THE END!!

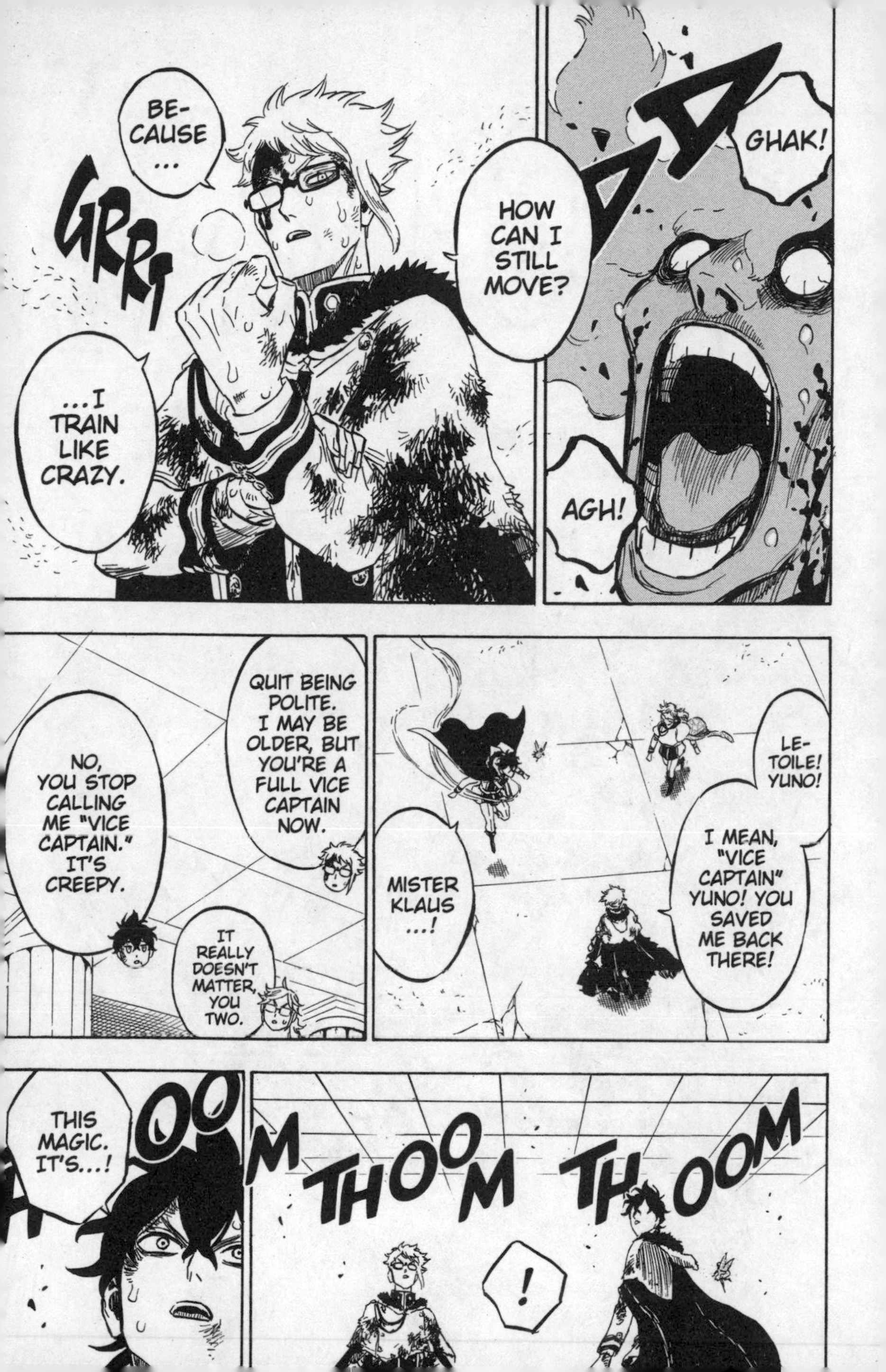

GHAK!
HOW CAN I STILL MOVE?
AGH!
BE-CAUSE ...
GRRR
...I TRAIN LIKE CRAZY.
LE-TOILE! YUNO!
I MEAN, "VICE CAPTAIN" YUNO! YOU SAVED ME BACK THERE!
MISTER KLAUS ...!
QUIT BEING POLITE. I MAY BE OLDER, BUT YOU'RE A FULL VICE CAPTAIN NOW.
NO, YOU STOP CALLING ME "VICE CAPTAIN." IT'S CREEPY.
IT REALLY DOESN'T MATTER, YOU TWO.
THOOM THOOM
!
THIS MAGIC. IT'S...!

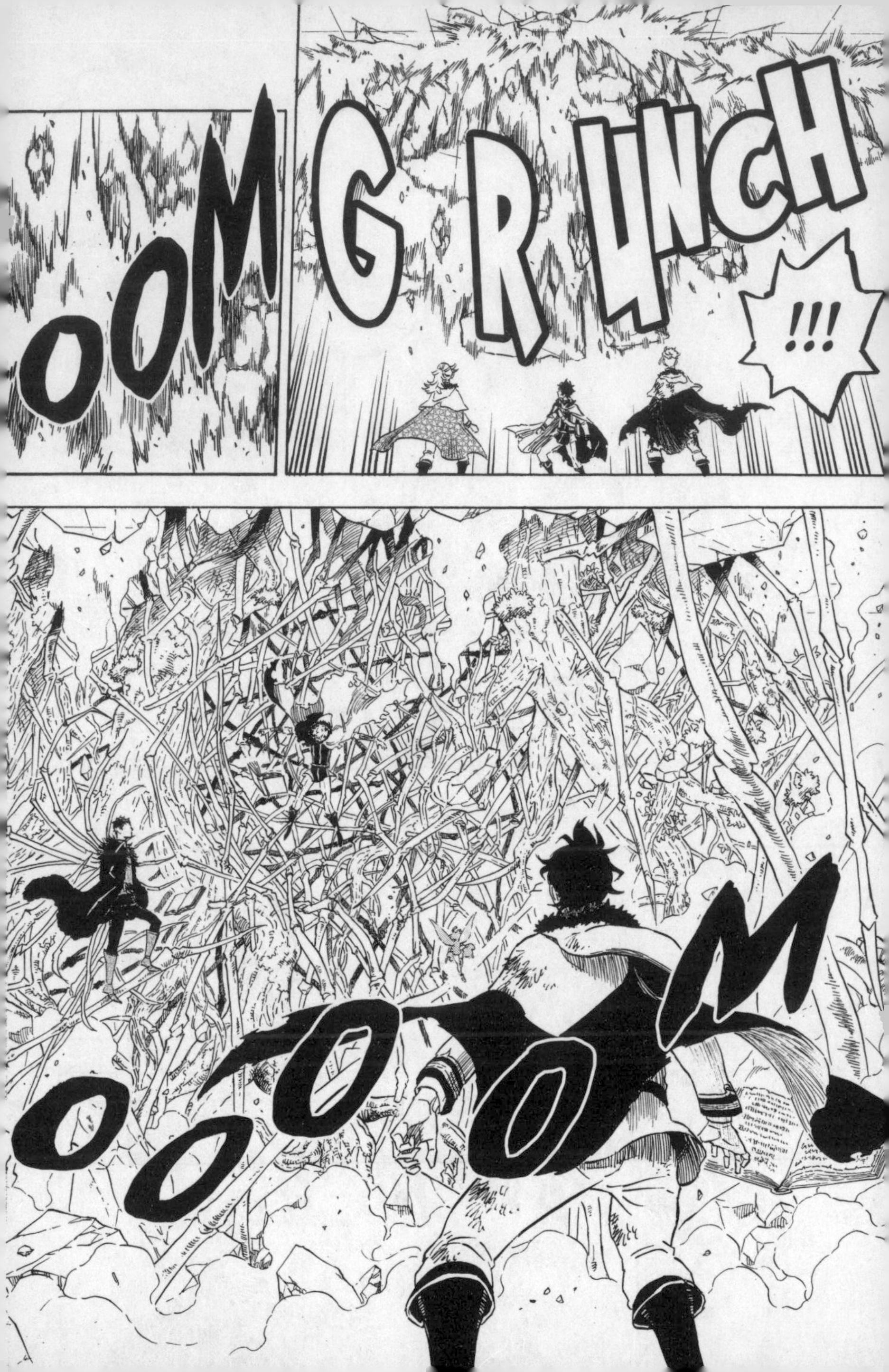
GRUNCH
!!!
OOM
OOOOM

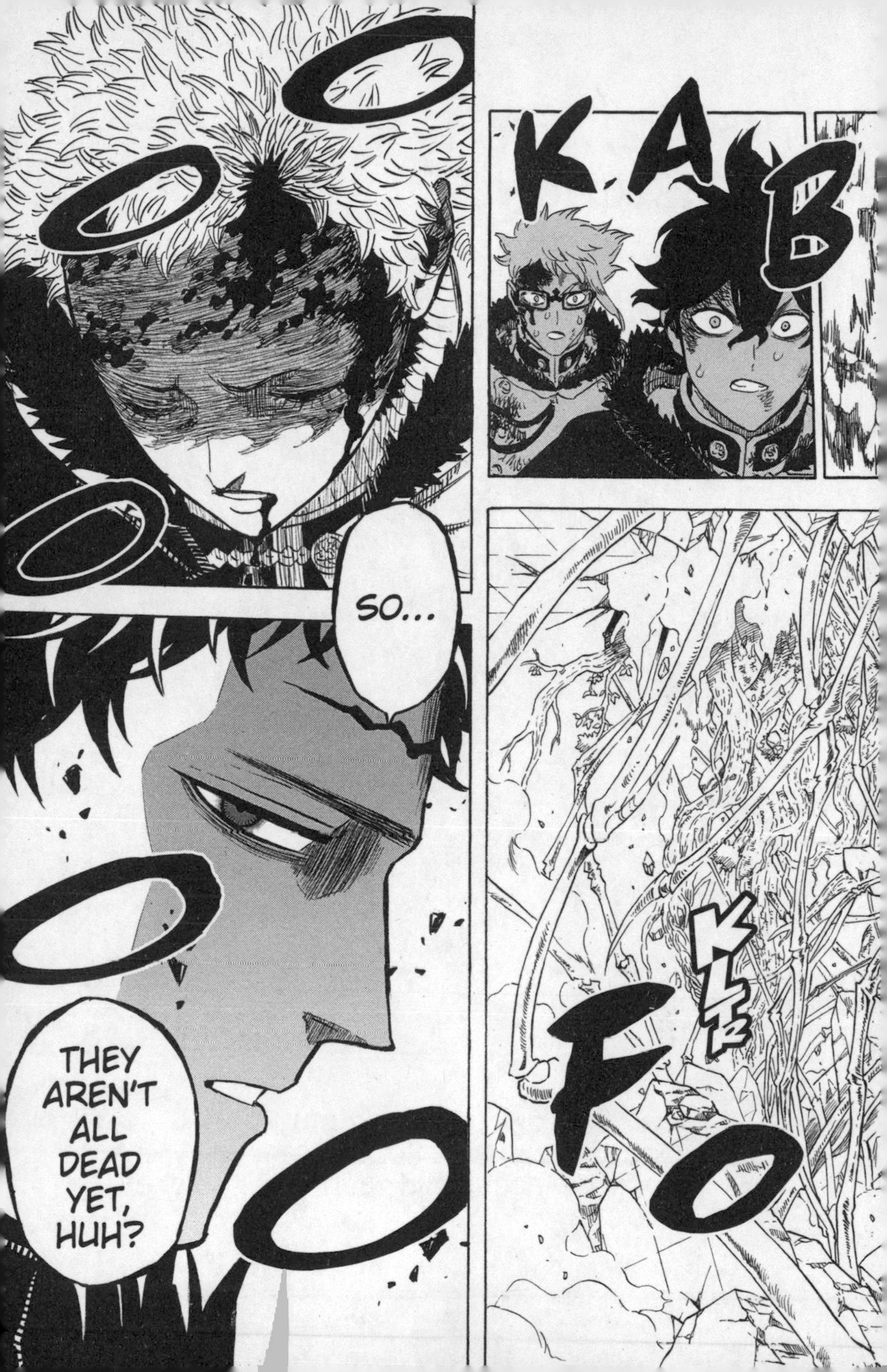
KAB
FO
SO...
THEY AREN'T ALL DEAD YET, HUH?

Foyal Migusteau

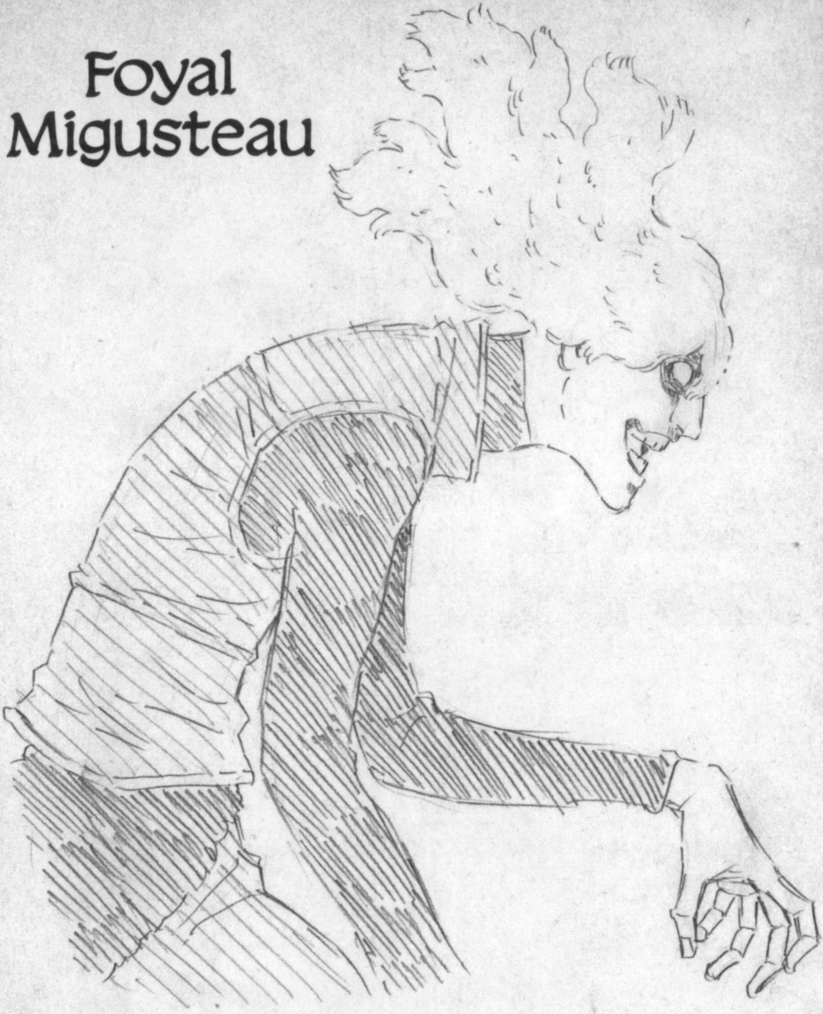

Age: 25 Height: 182 cm
Birthday: October 28 Sign: Scorpio Blood Type: AB
Likes: Gloomy places, mild-tasting fish dishes

Character Profile

Page 238: Zenon's Power

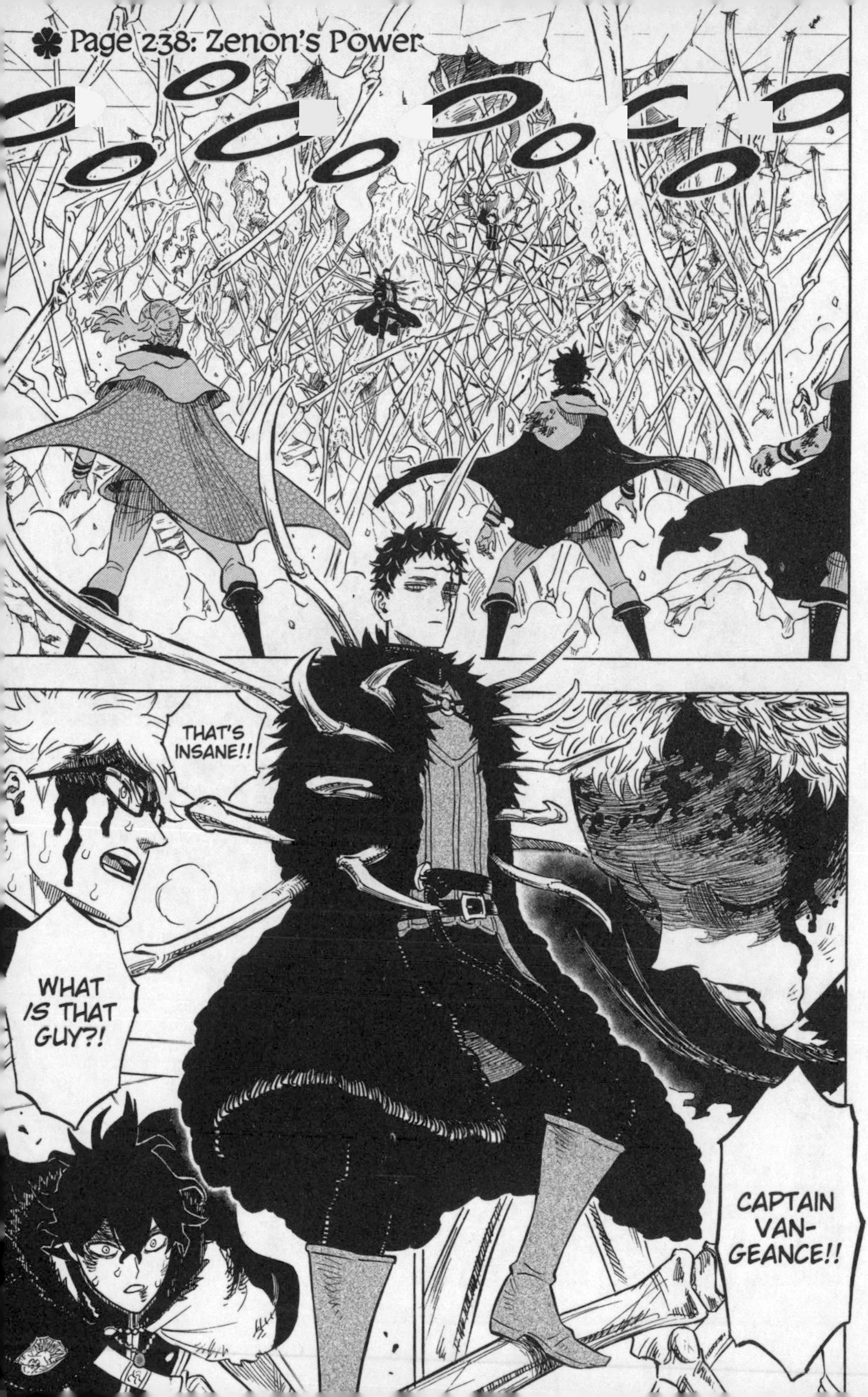
THAT'S INSANE!!
WHAT IS THAT GUY?!
CAPTAIN VAN-GEANCE!!

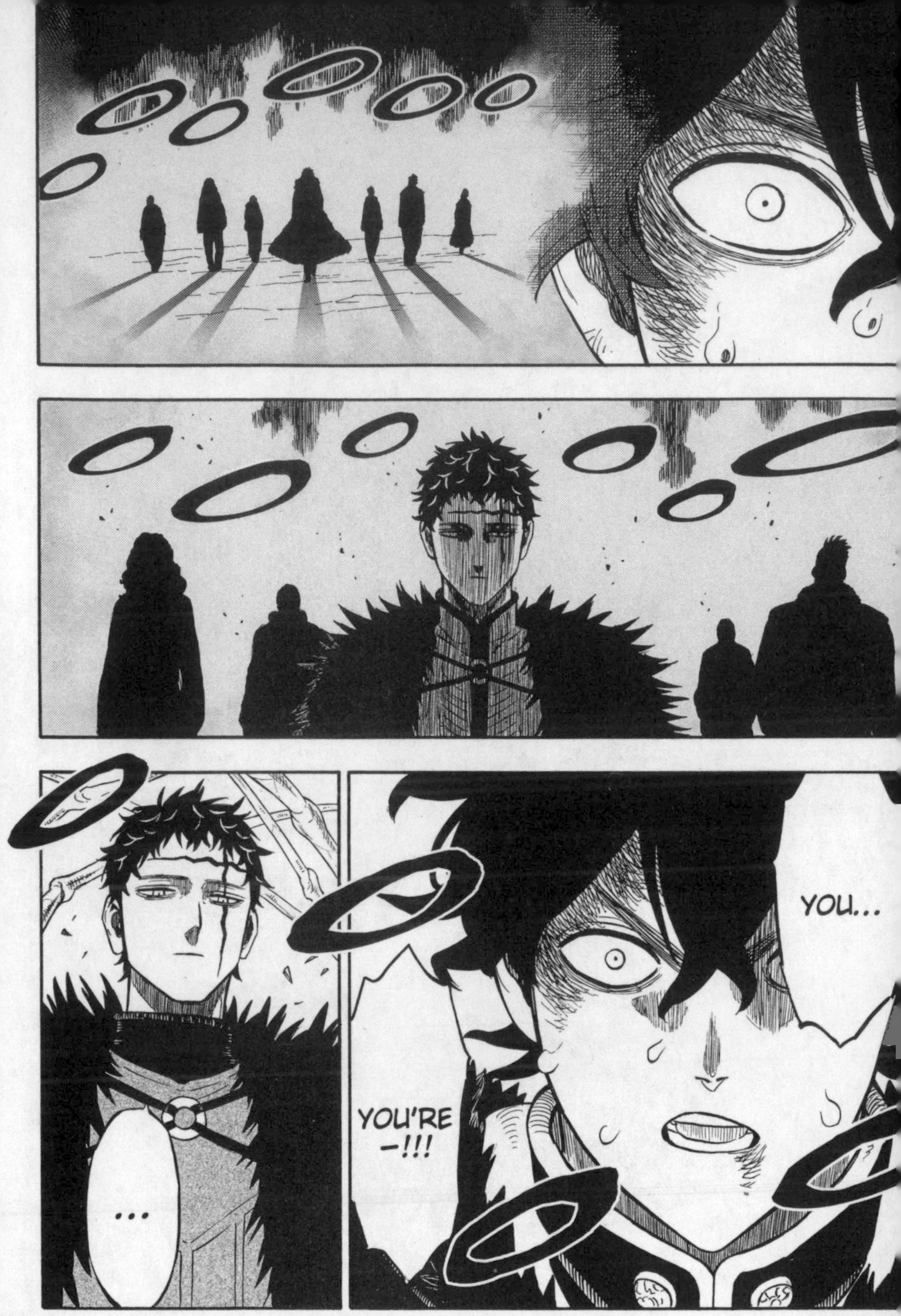
YOU...
YOU'RE—!!!
...

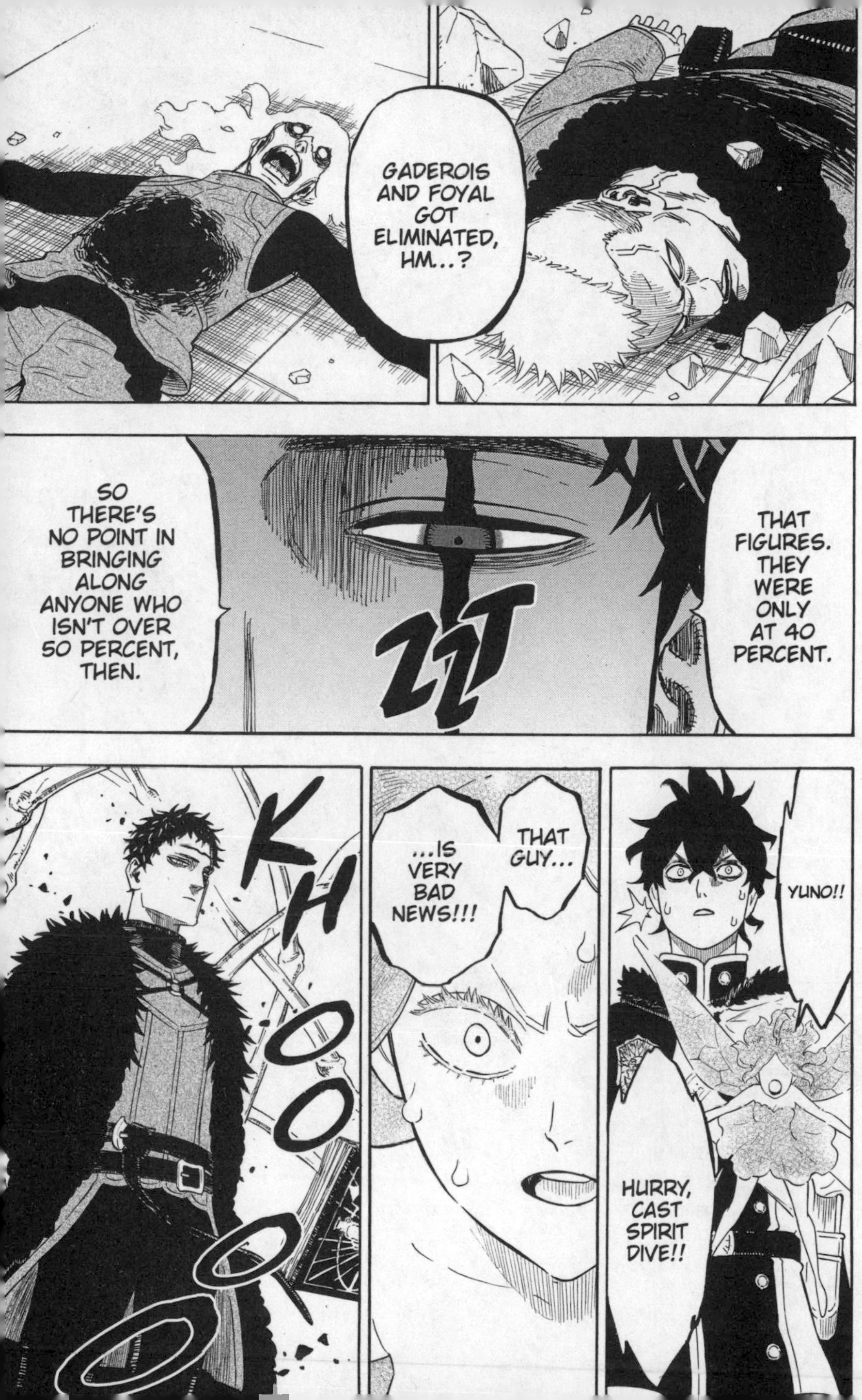
GADEROIS AND FOYAL GOT ELIMINATED, HM...?
THAT FIGURES. THEY WERE ONLY AT 40 PERCENT.
ZZT
SO THERE'S NO POINT IN BRINGING ALONG ANYONE WHO ISN'T OVER 50 PERCENT, THEN.
YUNO!!
HURRY, CAST SPIRIT DIVE!!
THAT GUY...
...IS VERY BAD NEWS!!!
KHOOOO

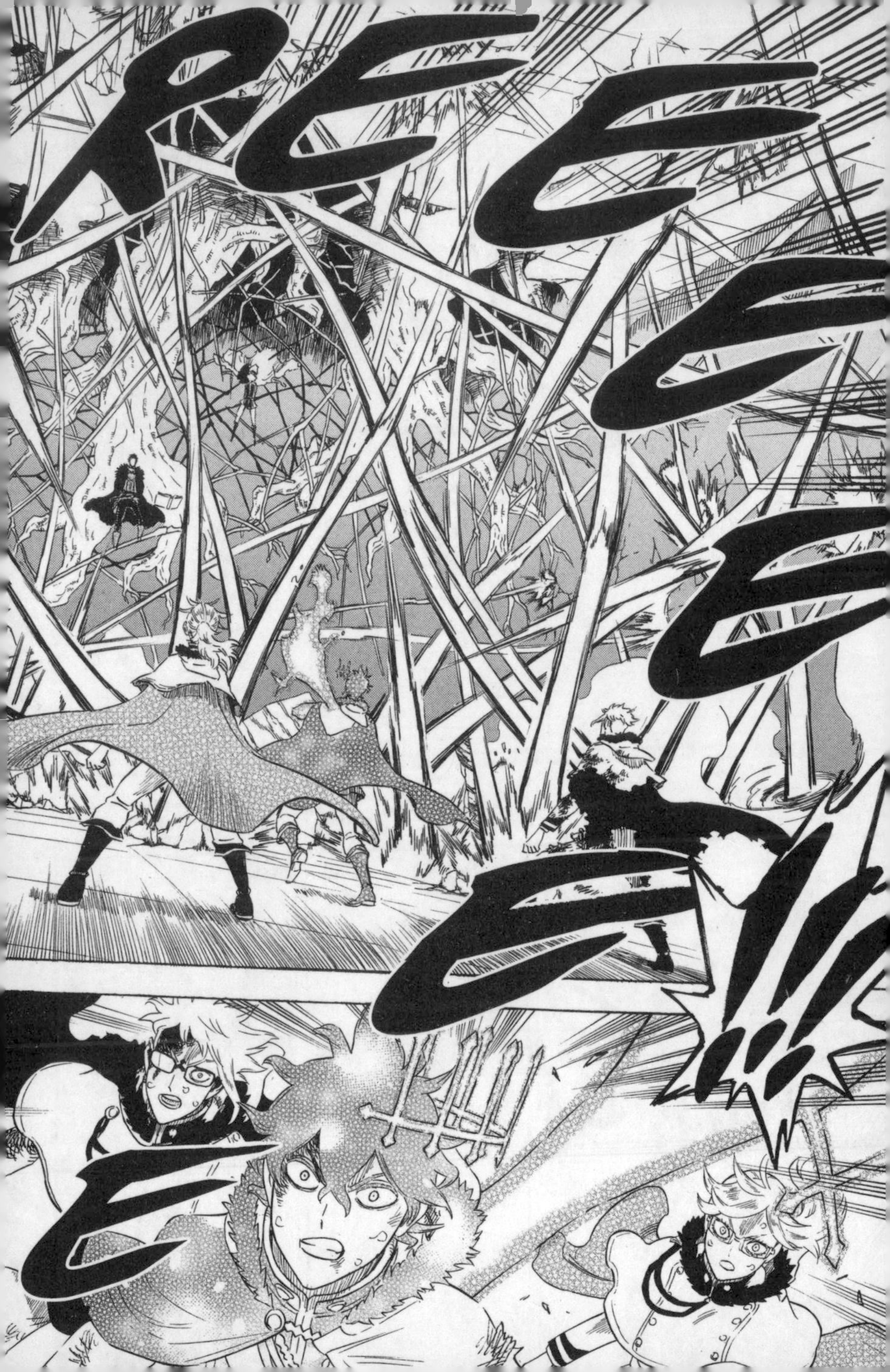
REEEEEE!!

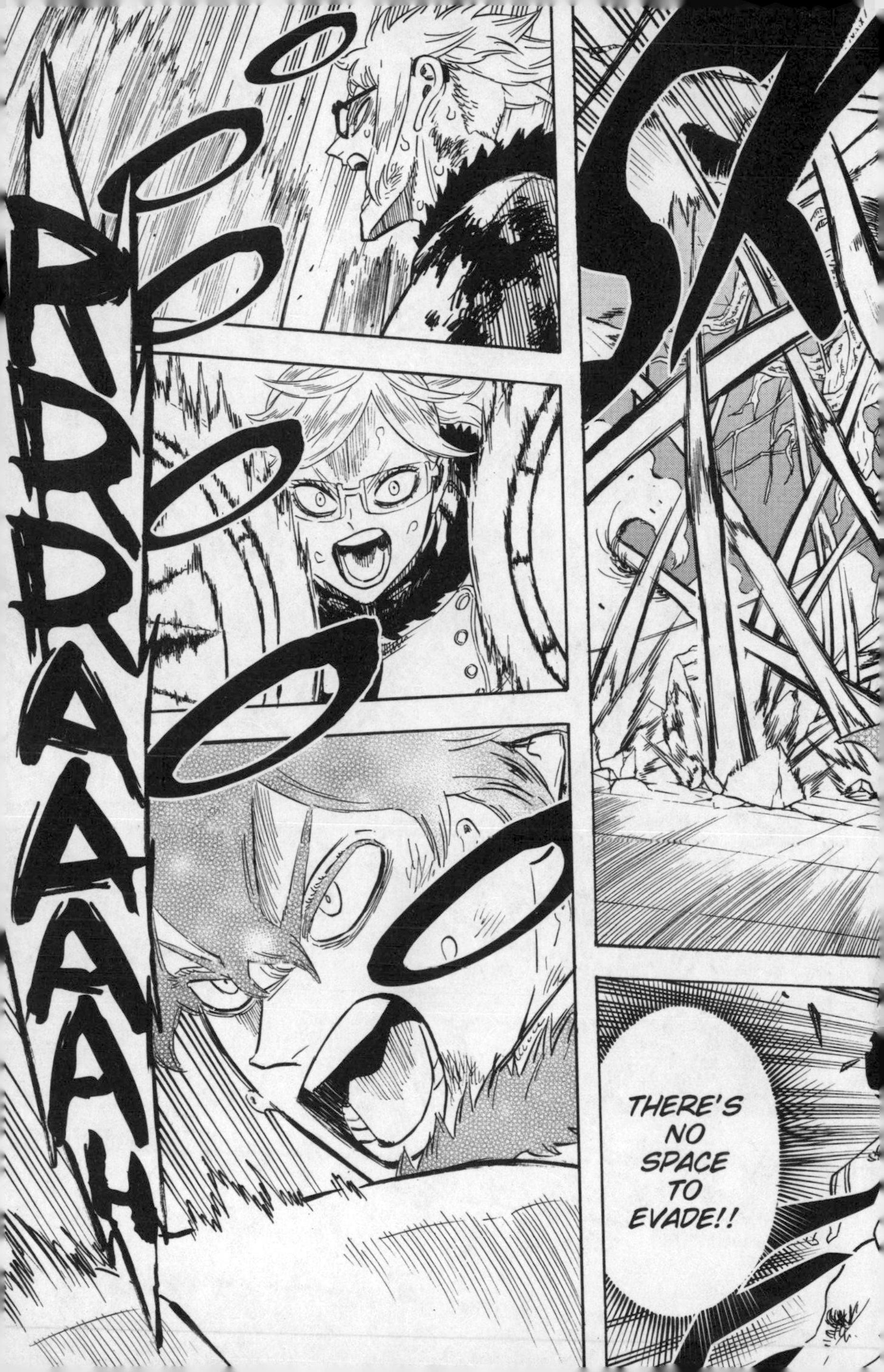
THERE'S NO SPACE TO EVADE!!
RRRAAAAH

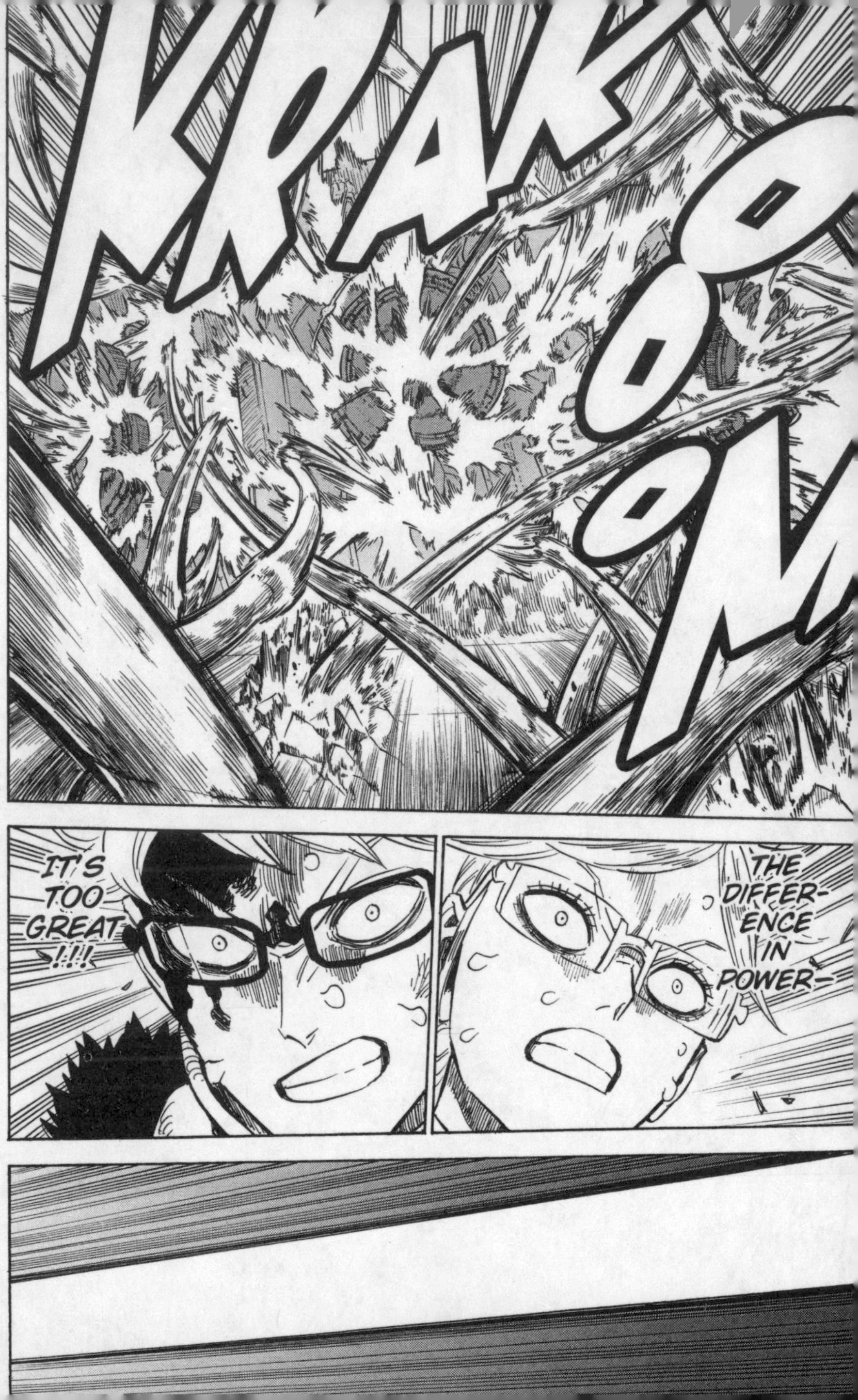
THE DIFFER-ENCE IN POWER—
IT'S TOO GREAT!!!

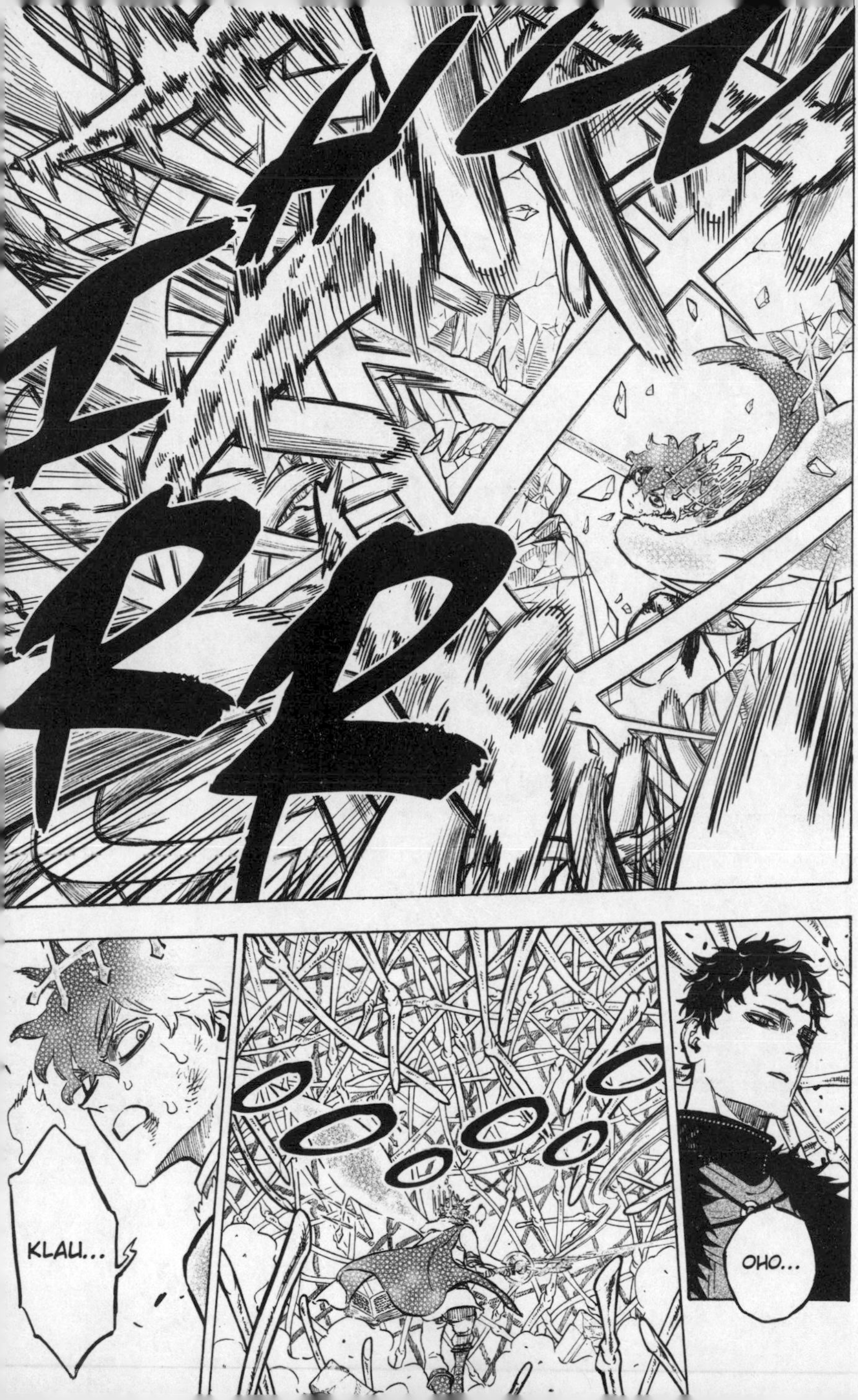
OHO...
KLAU...

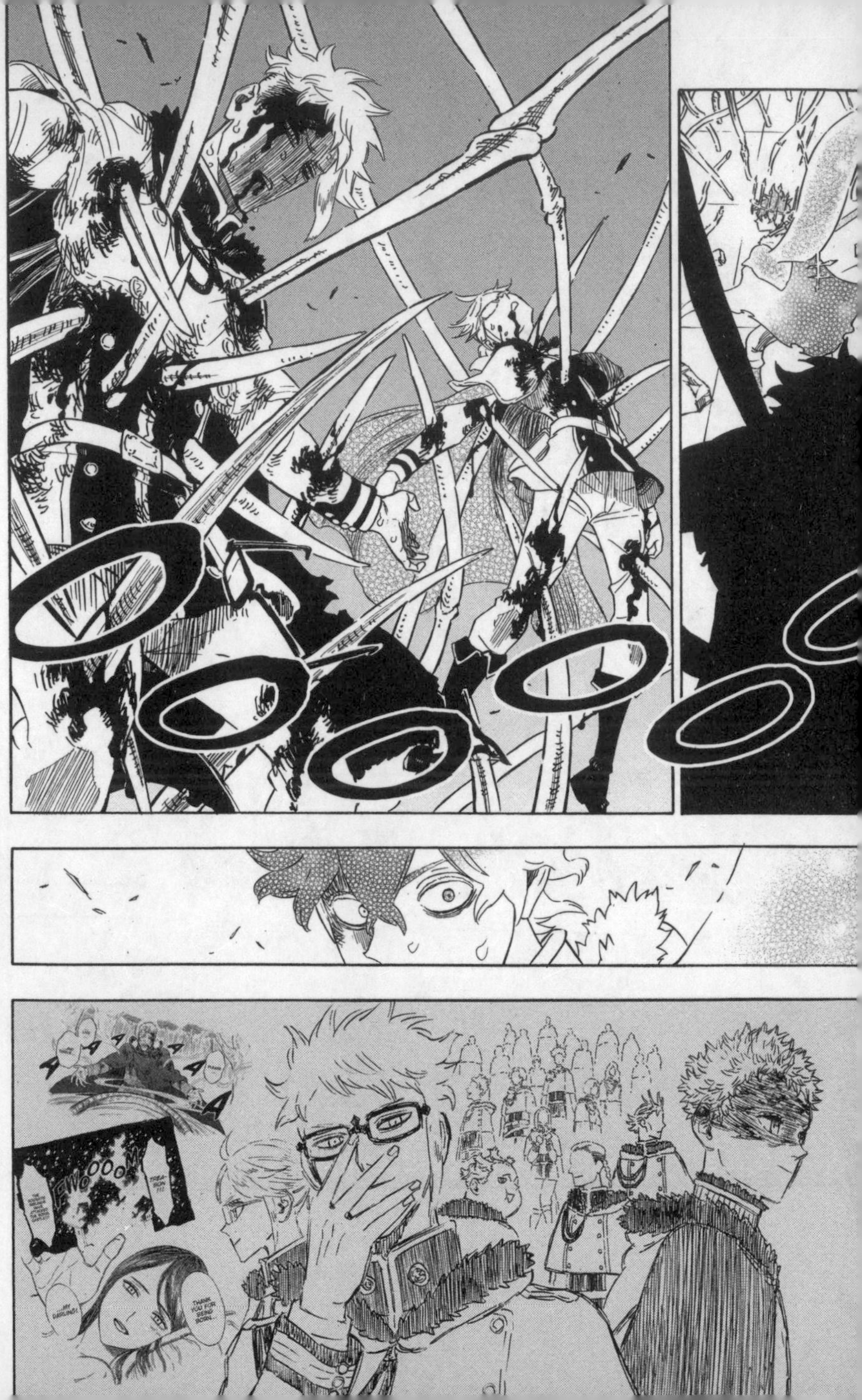
TREA-SON!!!
FWOOOOM
THANK YOU FOR BEING BORN...
...MY DARLING!

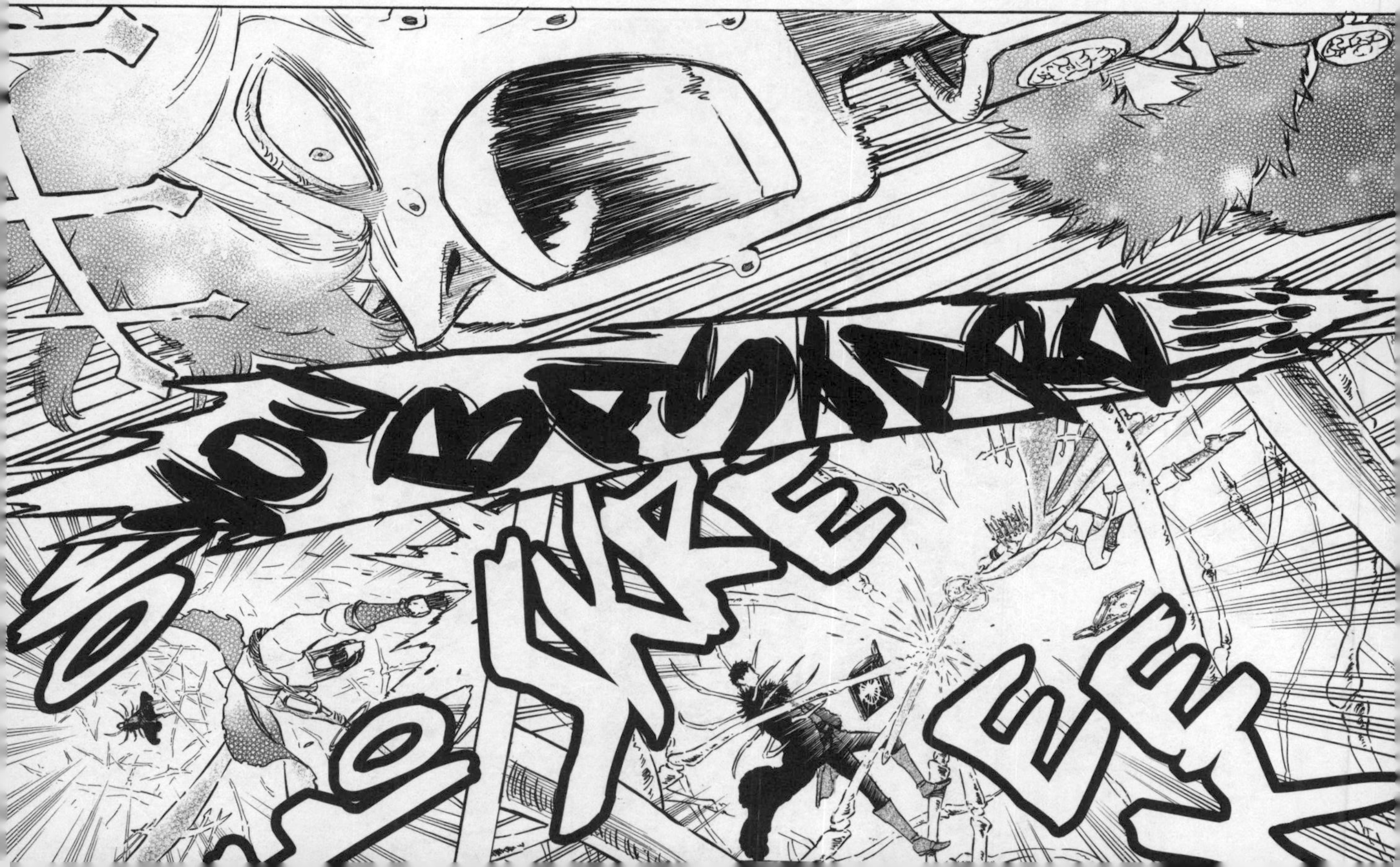
YOU BASTARD!!

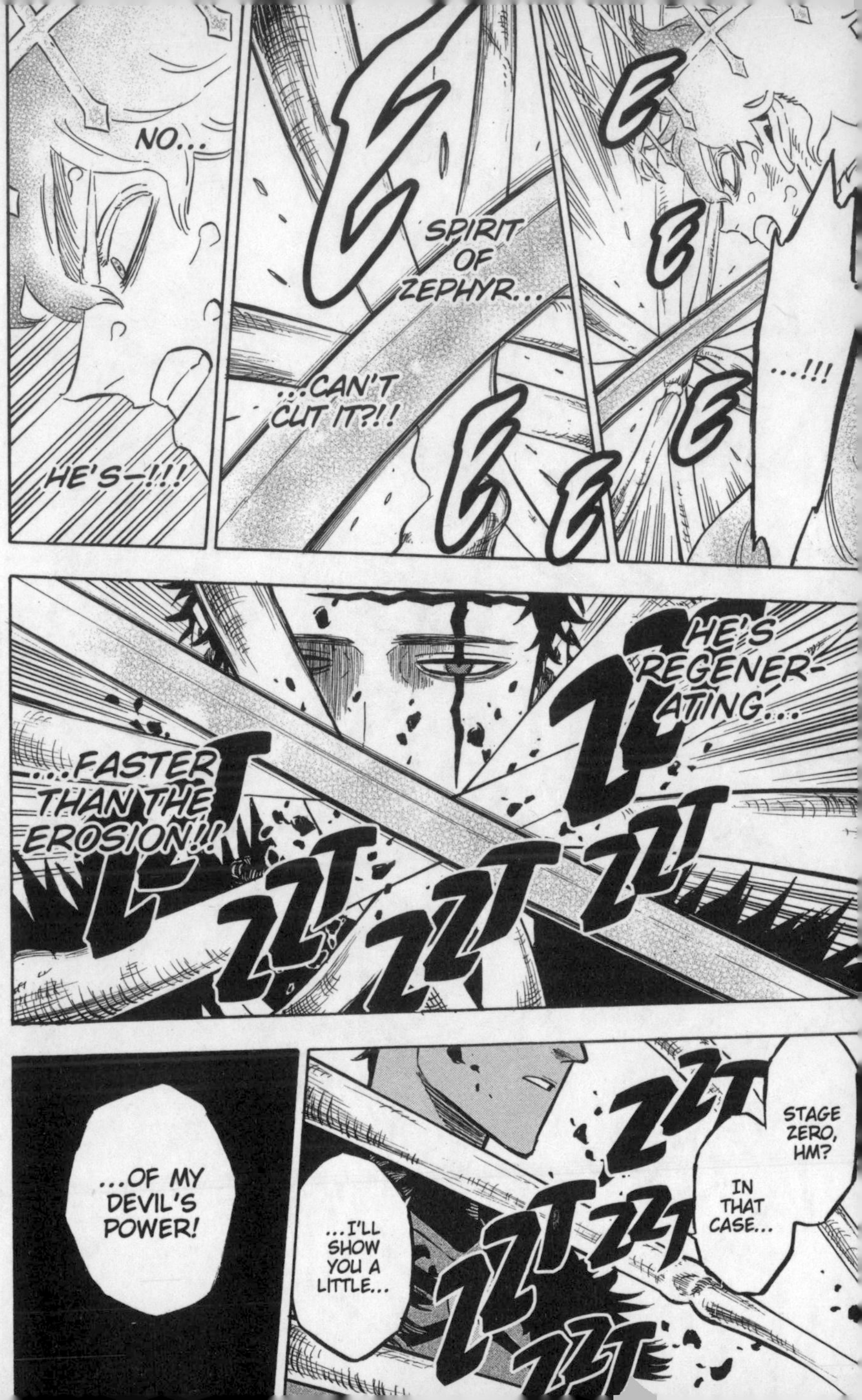
...!!!
SPIRIT OF ZEPHYR...
...CAN'T CUT IT?!!
NO...
HE'S—!!!
HE'S REGENER-ATING...
...FASTER THAN THE EROSION!!
STAGE ZERO, HM?
IN THAT CASE...
...I'LL SHOW YOU A LITTLE...
...OF MY DEVIL'S POWER!

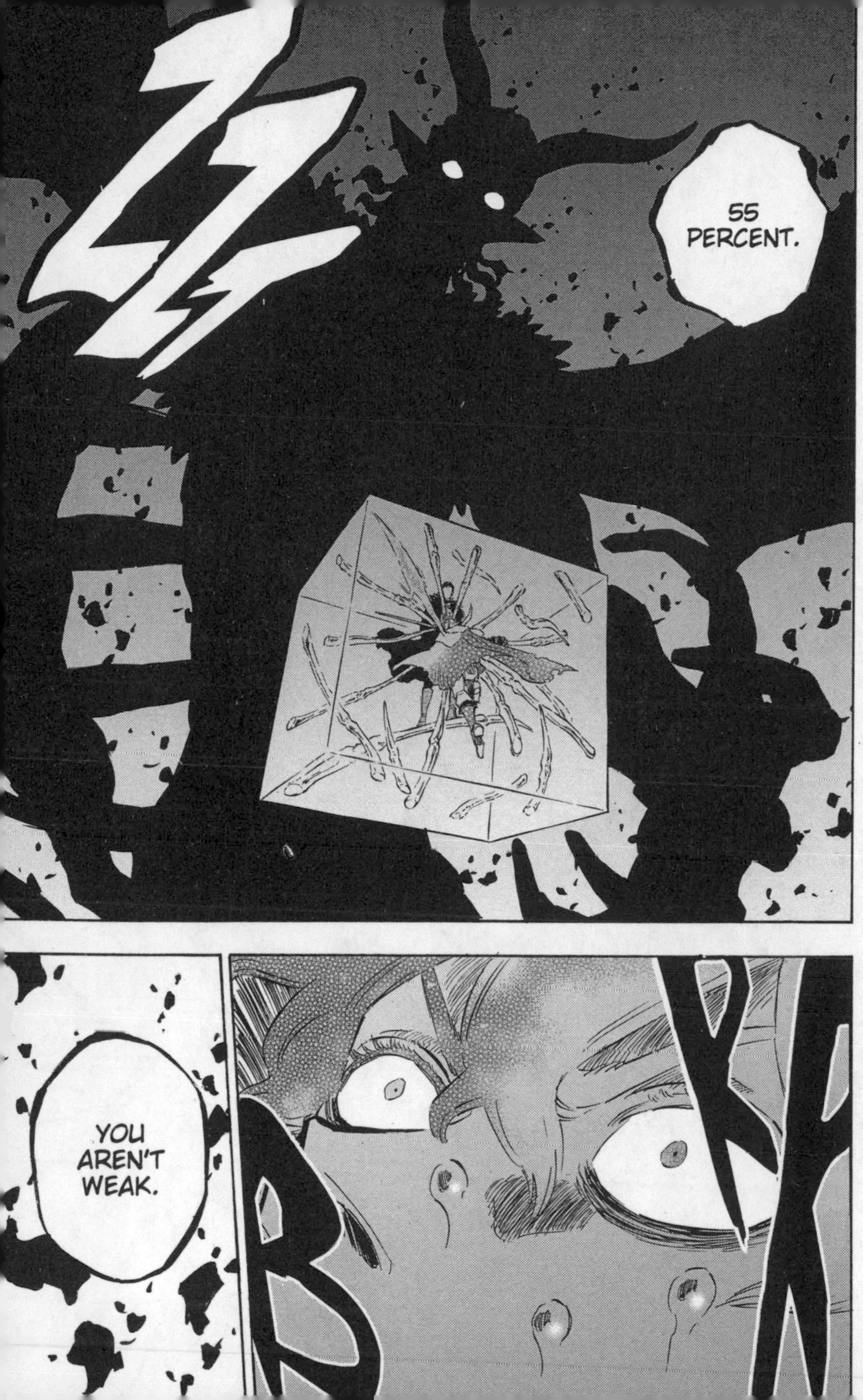
55 PERCENT.
YOU AREN'T WEAK.

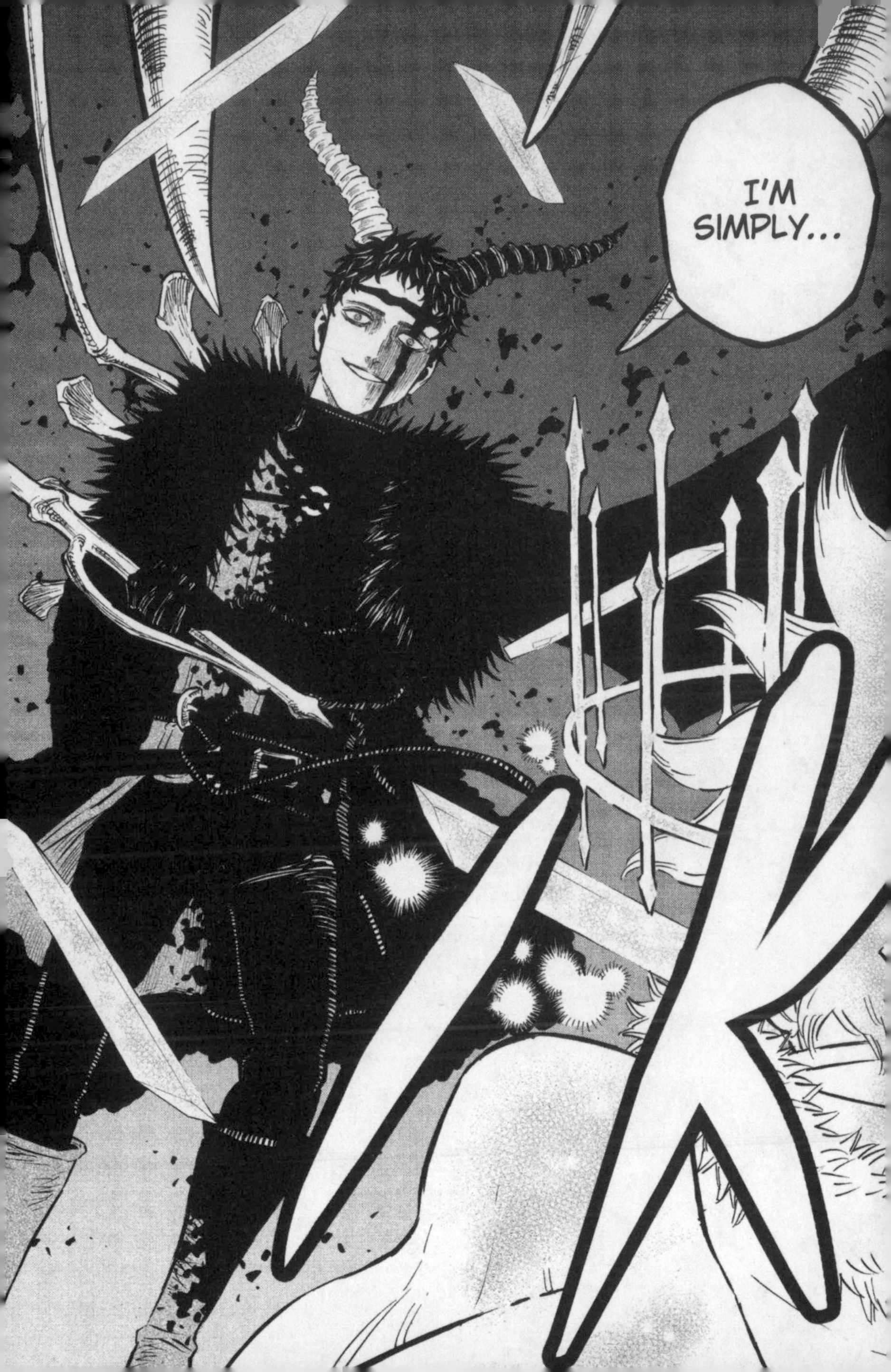
I'M SIMPLY...

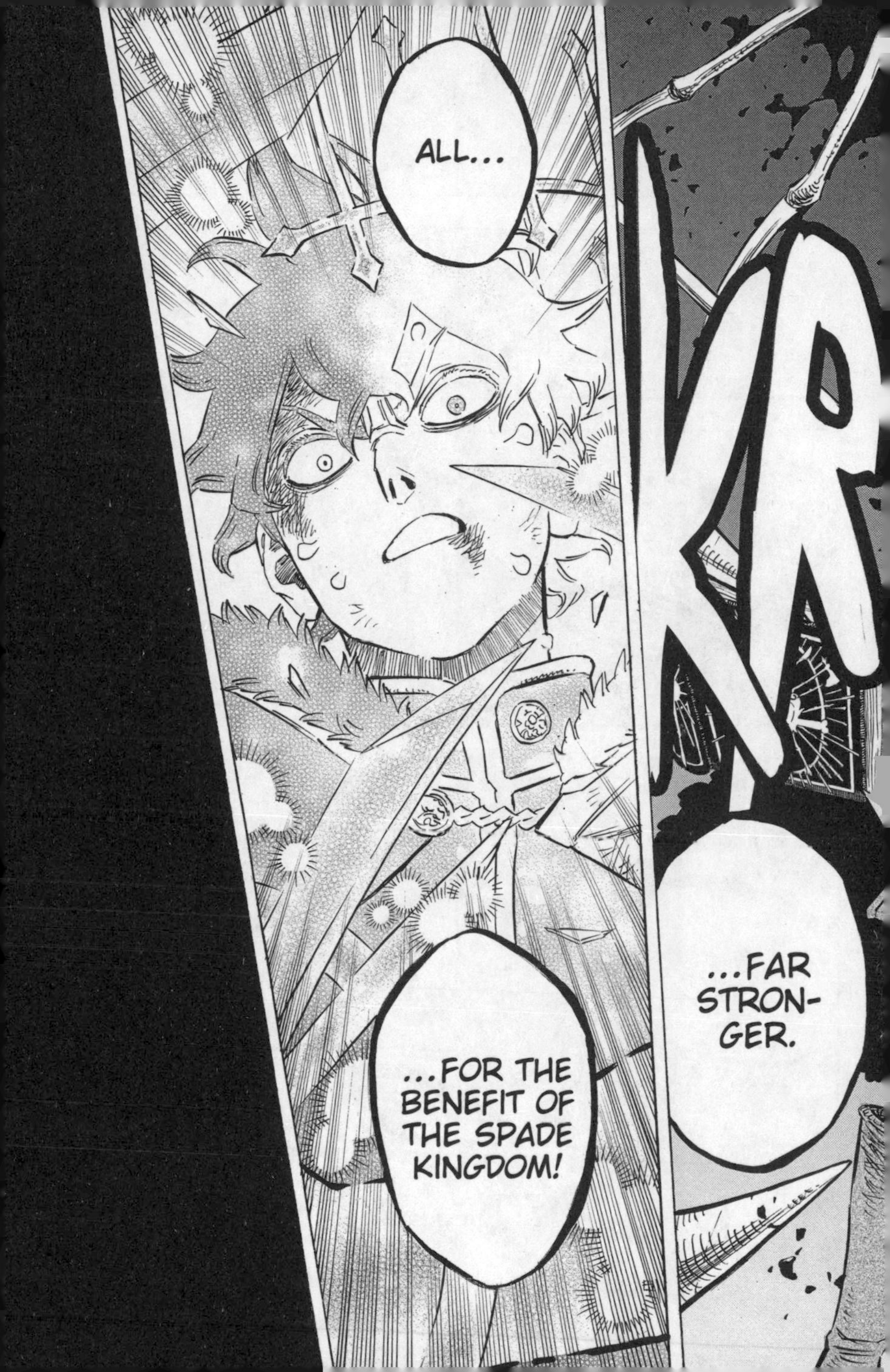
...FAR STRON-GER.
ALL...
...FOR THE BENEFIT OF THE SPADE KINGDOM!

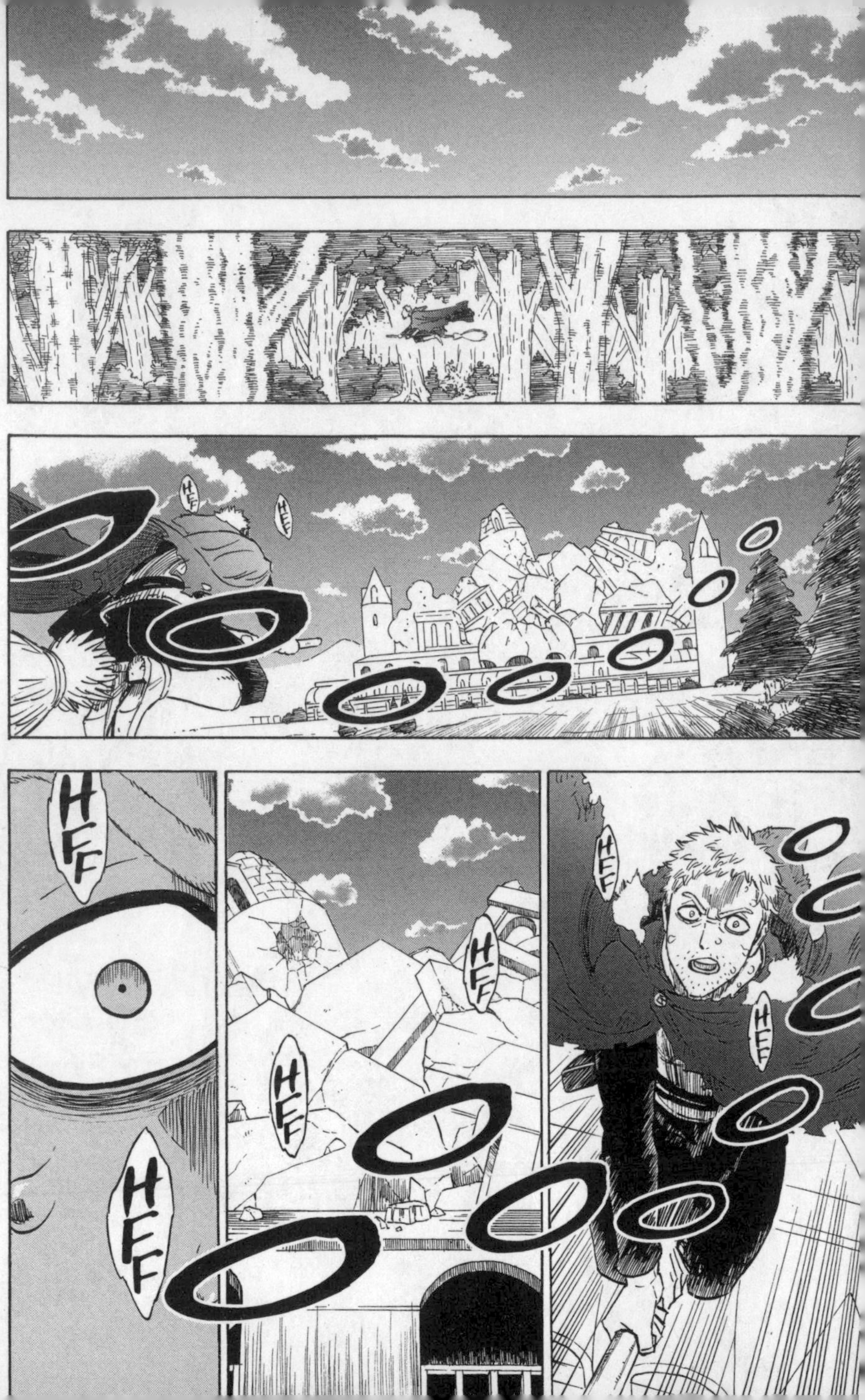
HFF
HFF
HFF
HFF
HFF
HFF
HFF
HFF

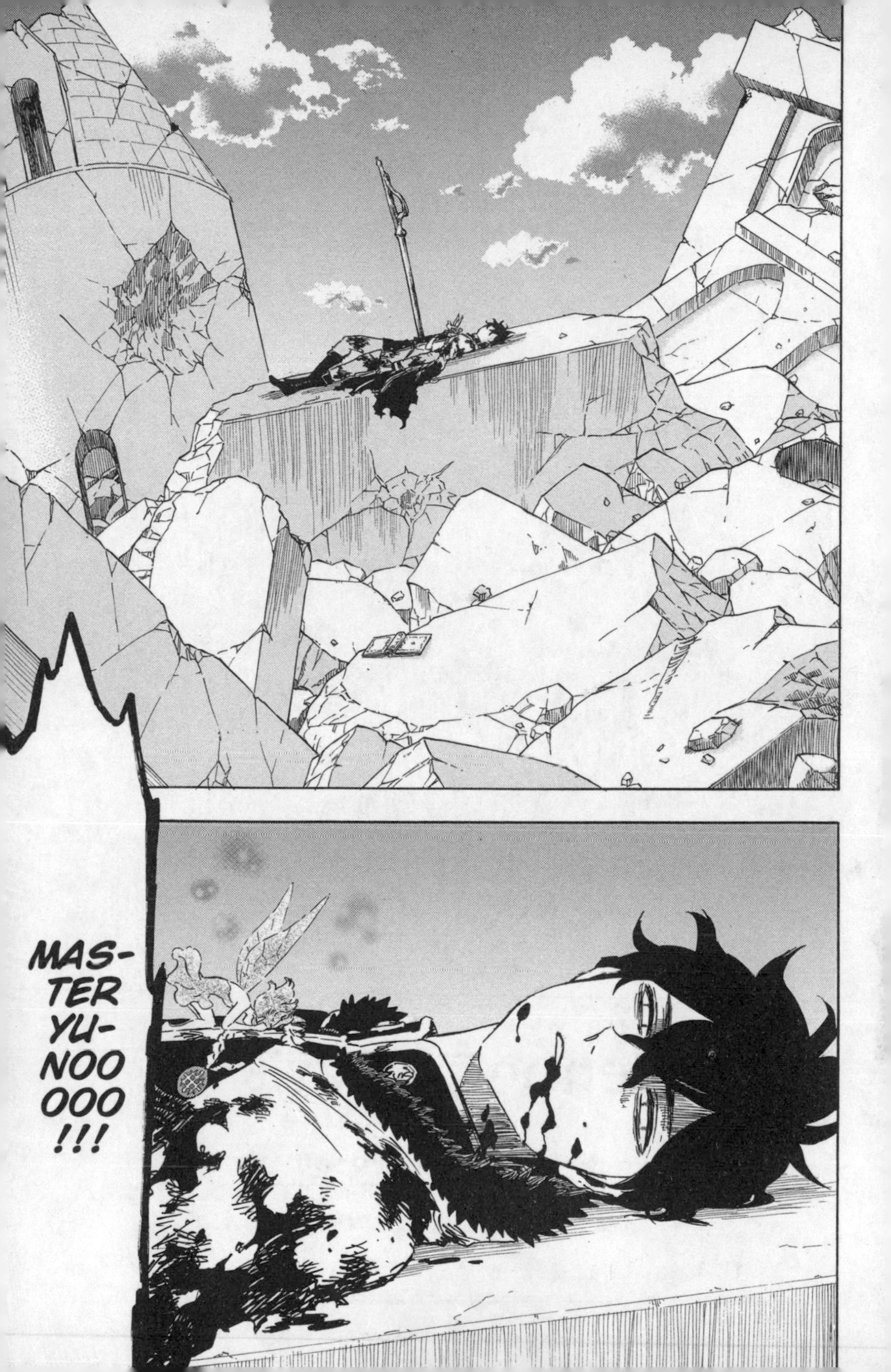
MAS-
TER
YU-
NOO
OOO
!!!

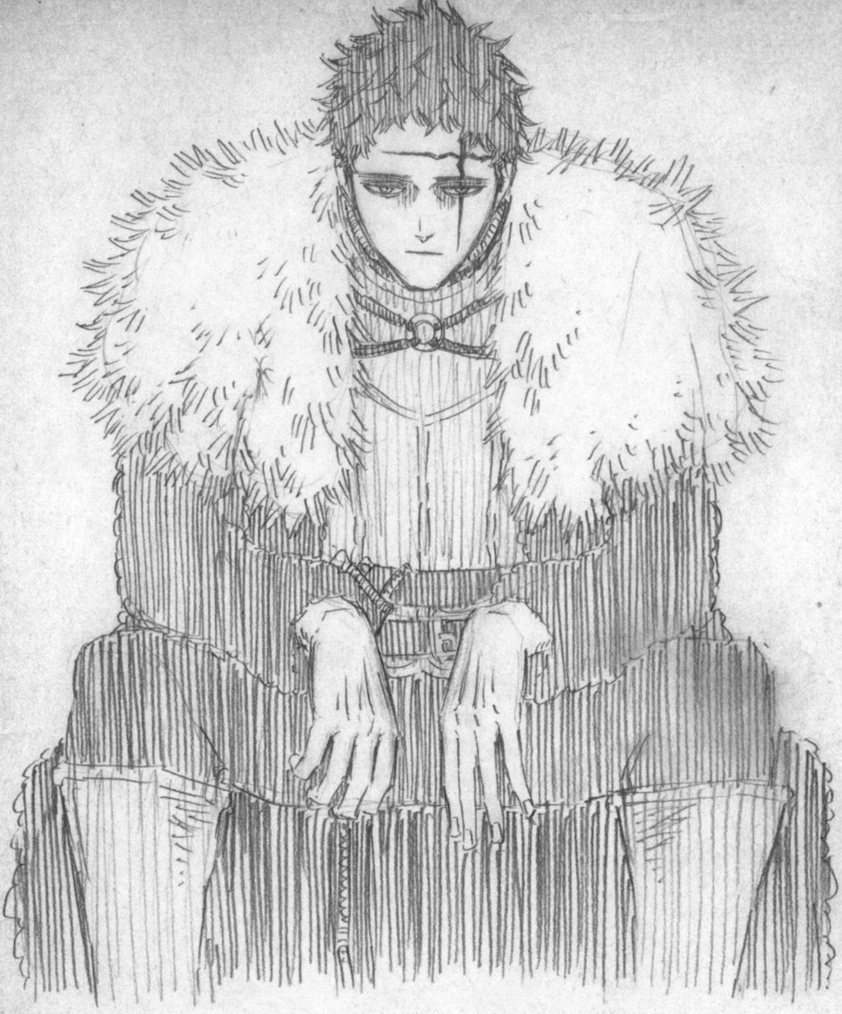

Zenon Zogratis

Age: — Height: 178 cm
Birthday: December 28 Sign: Capricorn Blood Type: A
Likes: Nothing in particular

Character Profile

Page 239: Budding of Yggdrasil

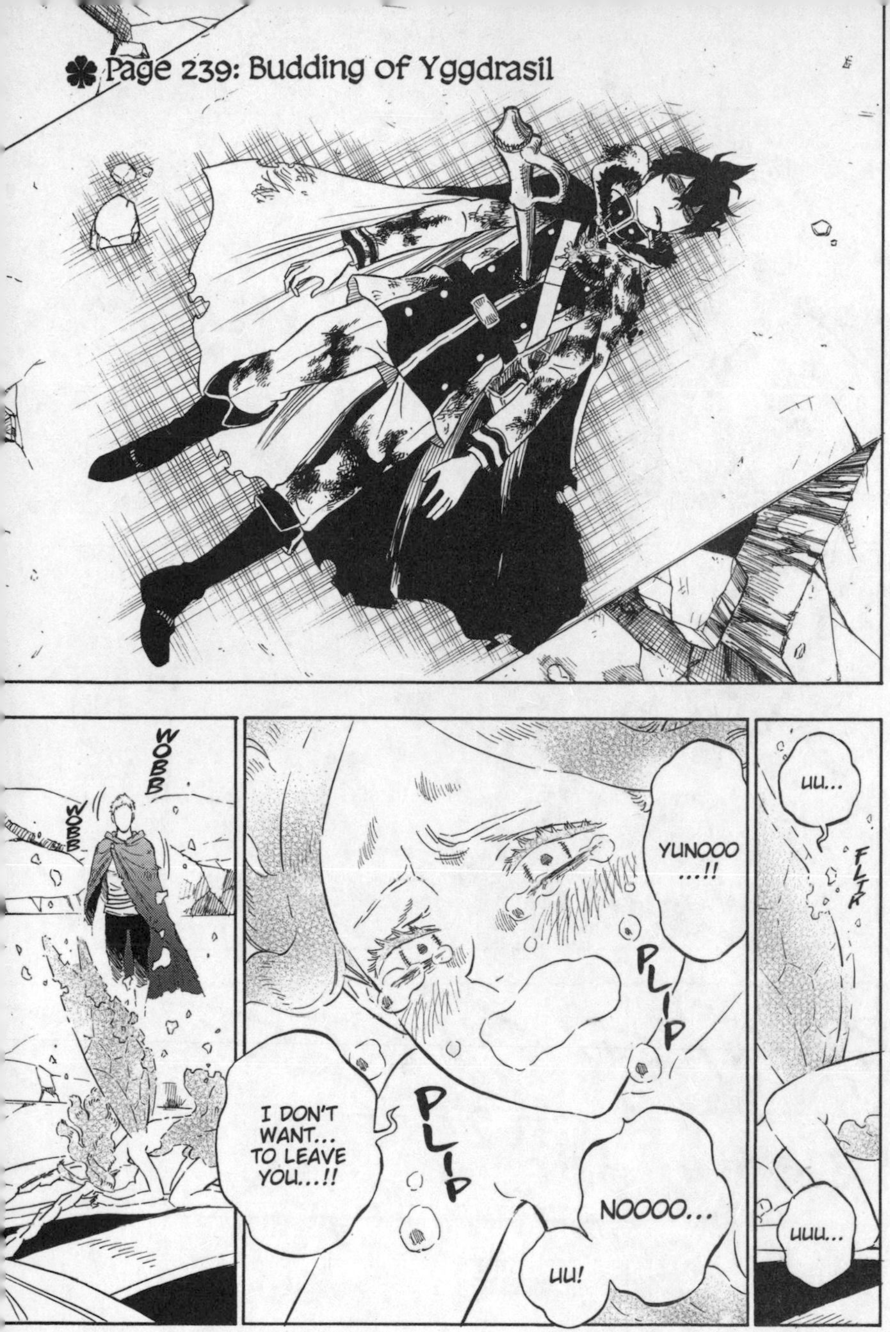
UU...
FLIK
UUU...
YUNOOO ...!!
PLIP
I DON'T WANT... TO LEAVE YOU...!!
PLIP
NOOOO...
UU!
WOBB
WOBB

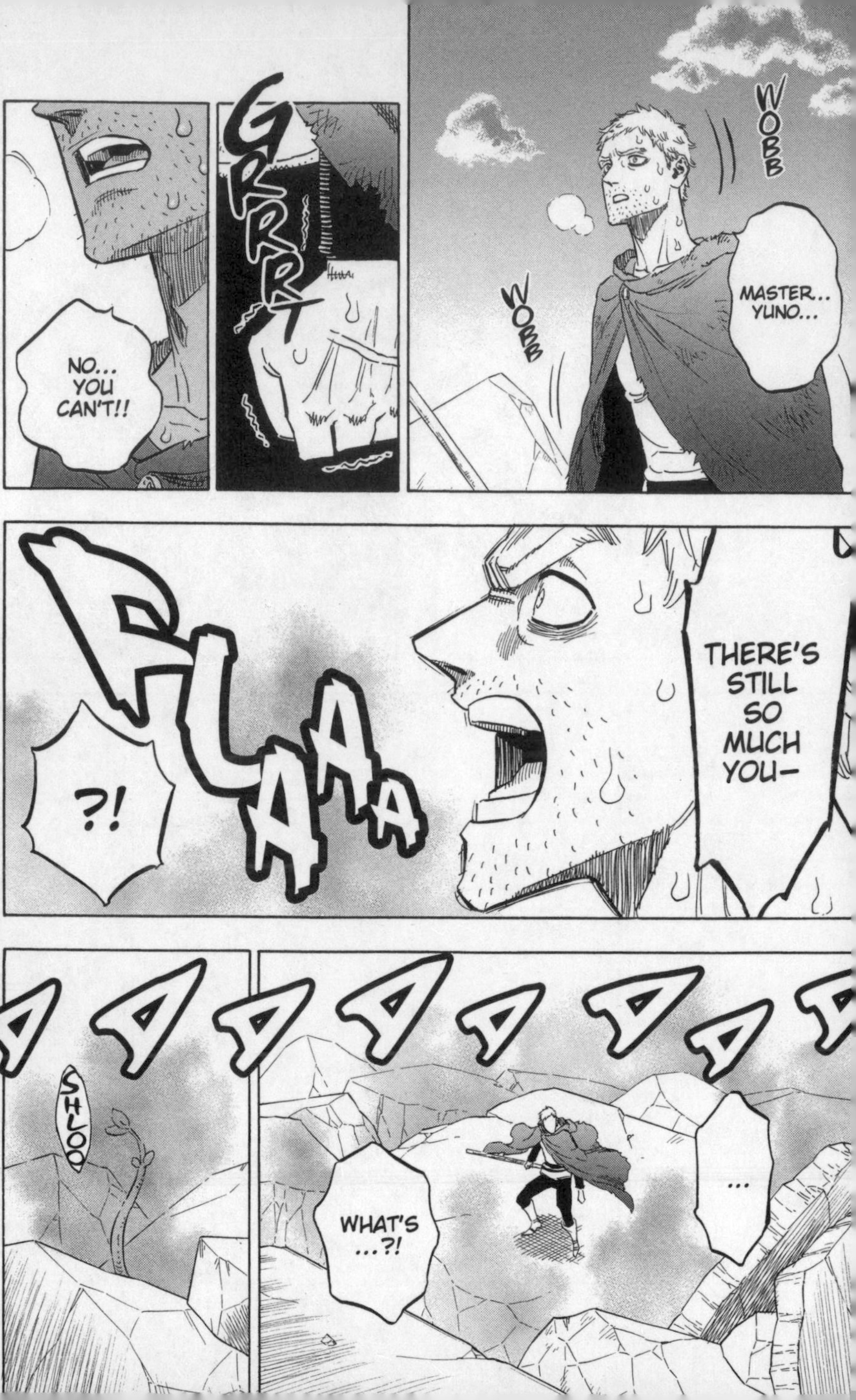
WOBB
MASTER... YUNO...
WOBB
GRRRT
NO... YOU CAN'T!!
THERE'S STILL SO MUCH YOU-
BLAAAA
?!
AAAAAAAA
...
WHAT'S ...?!
SHLOO

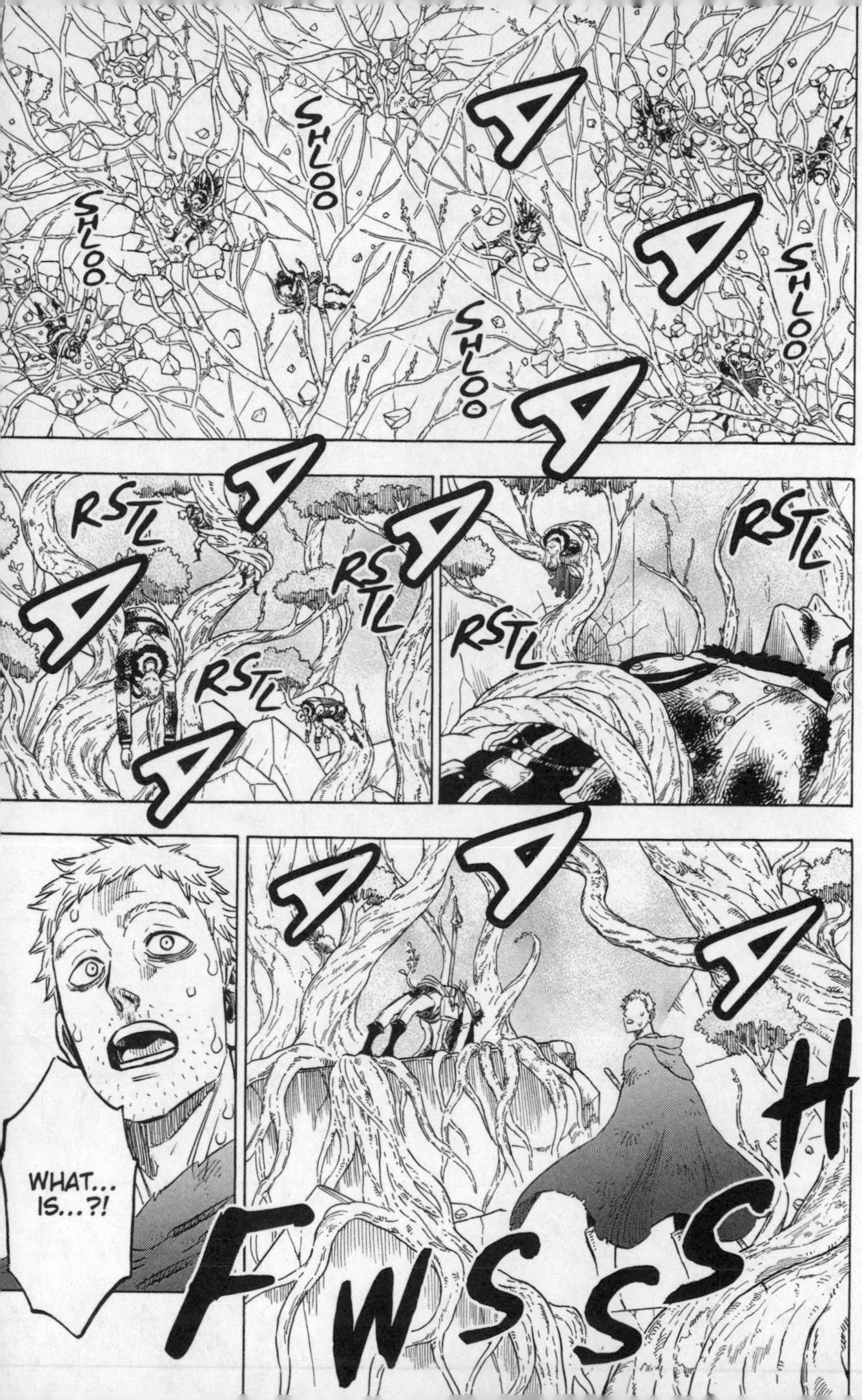
AAAAAAAAAA
SHLOO
SHLOO
SHLOO
SHLOO
RSTL
RSTL
RSTL
RS TL
RSTL
FWSSSH
WHAT... IS...?!

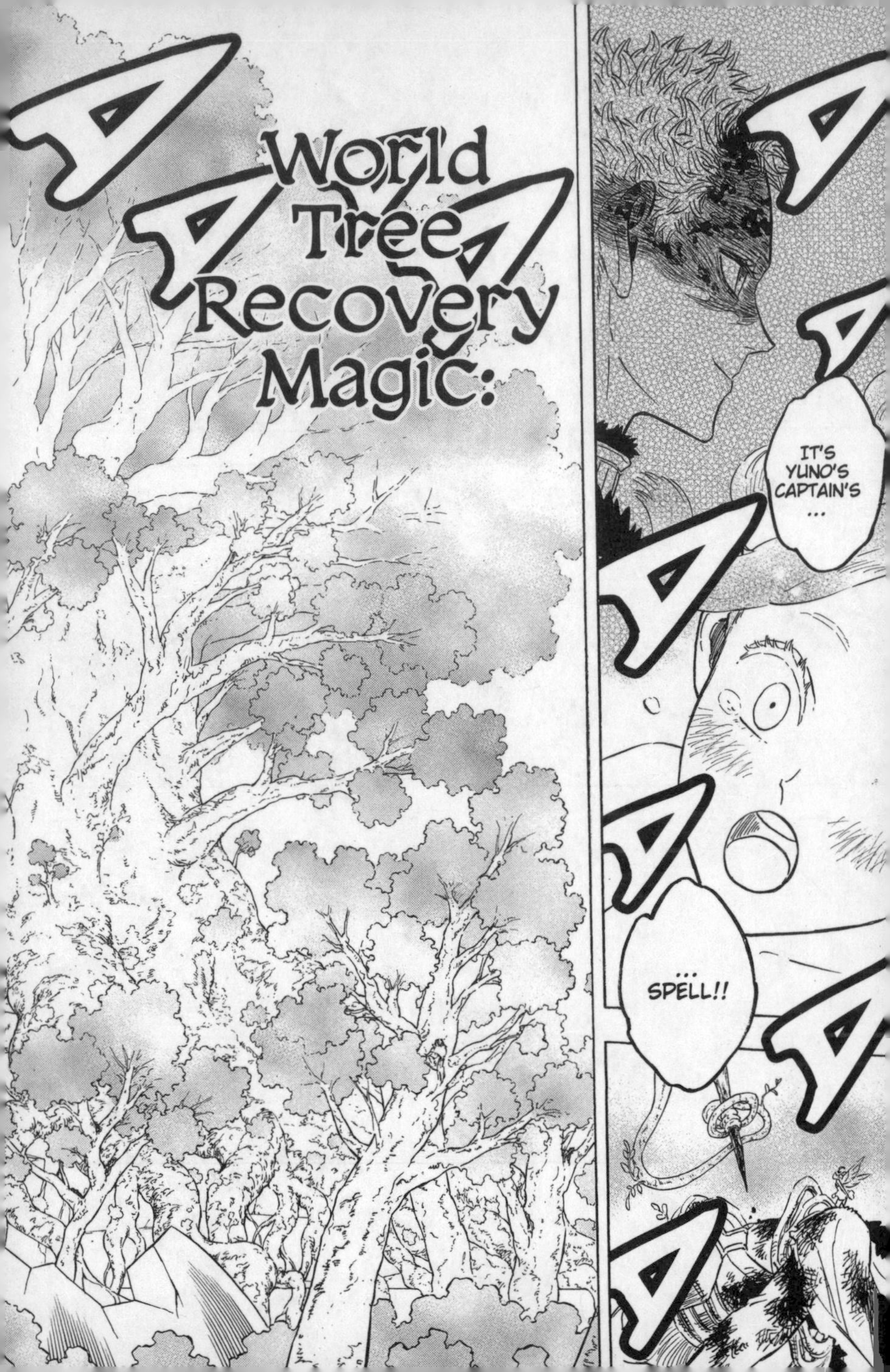
IT'S YUNO'S CAPTAIN'S ...
... SPELL!!
World Tree Recovery Magic:

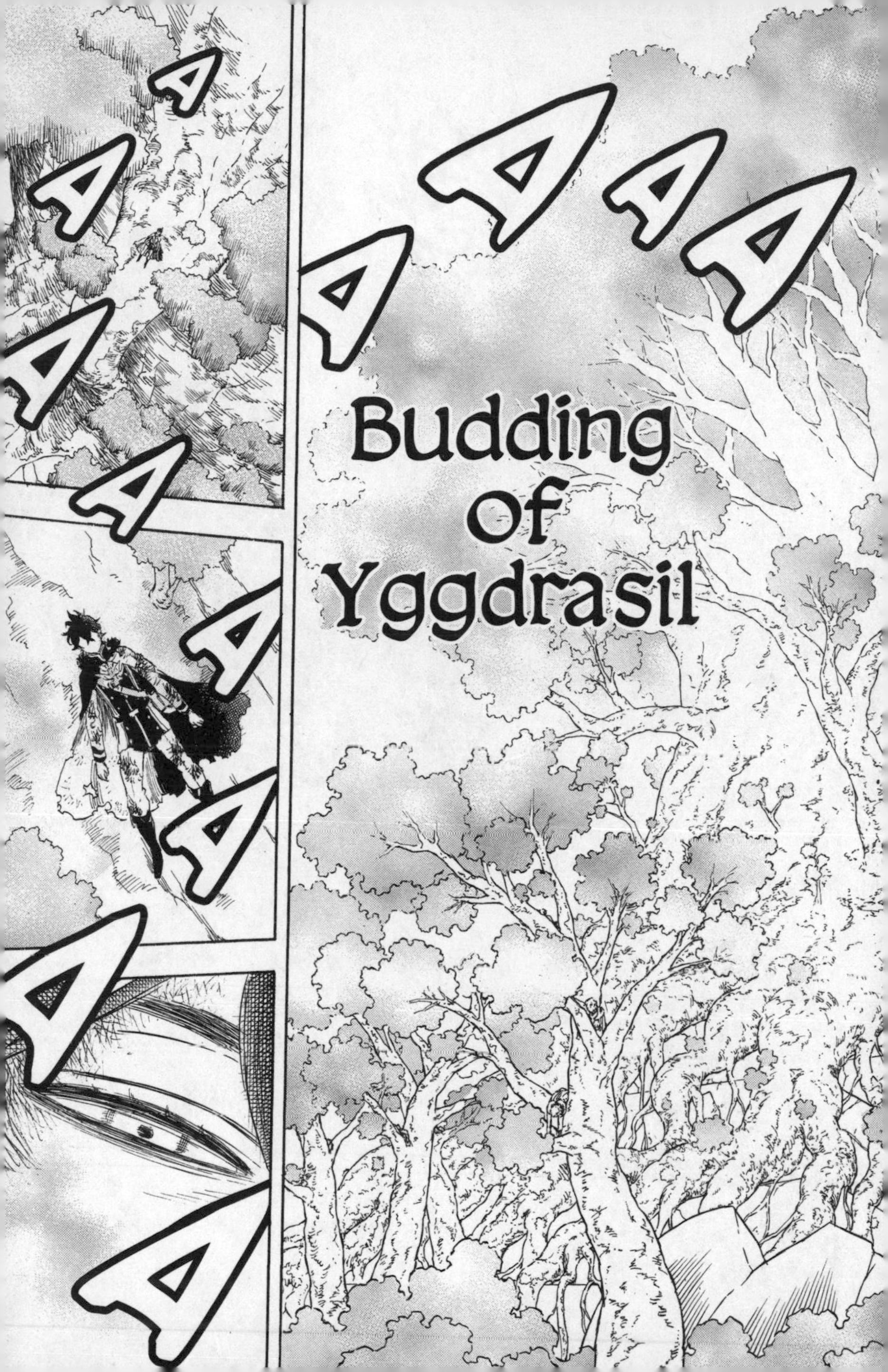
AAAAA
Budding Of Yggdrasil
AAAA
AA
AA

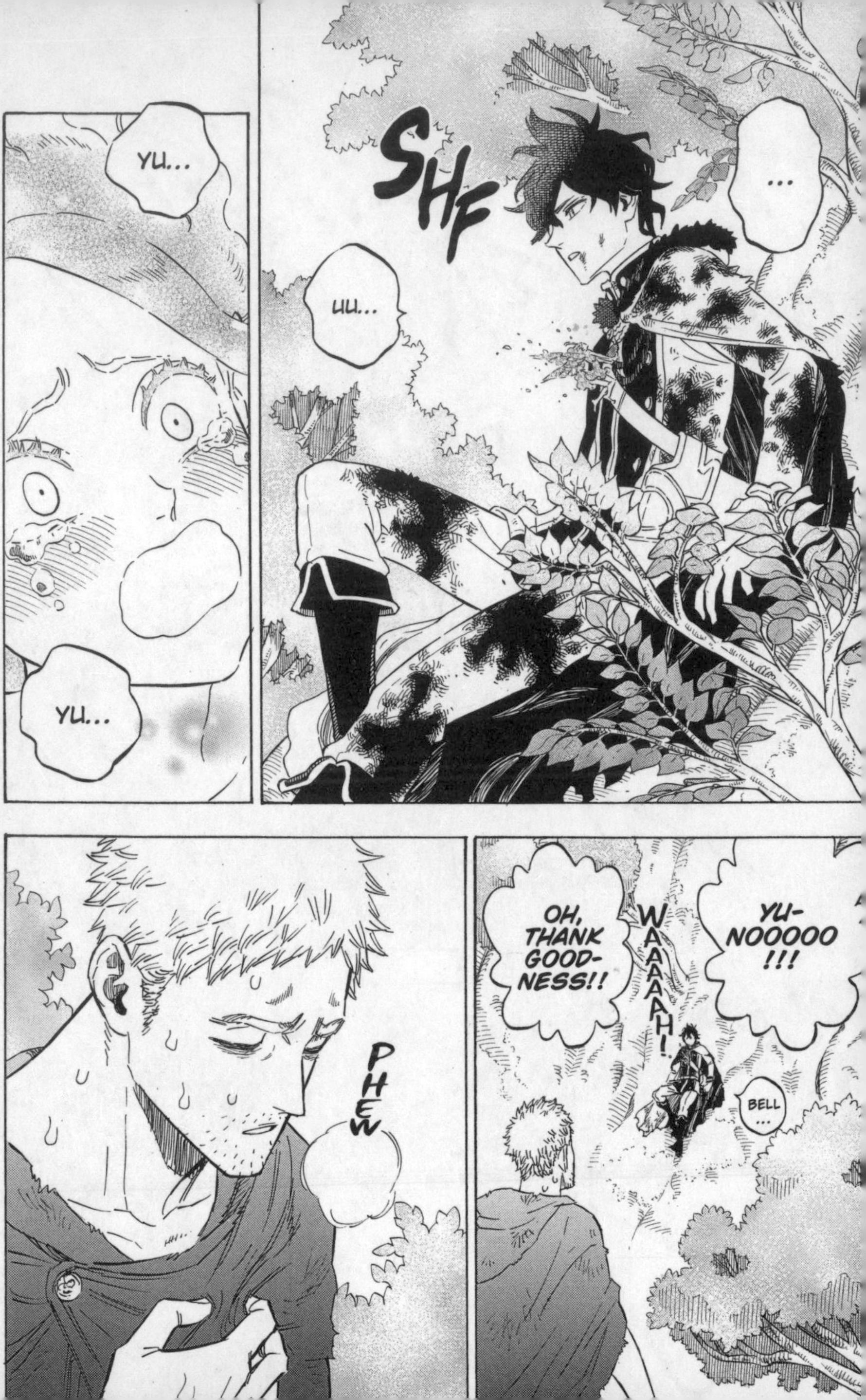
...
SHF
UU...
YU...
YU...
YU-NOOOOO!!!
WAAAAAH!
OH, THANK GOODNESS!!
BELL...
PHEW

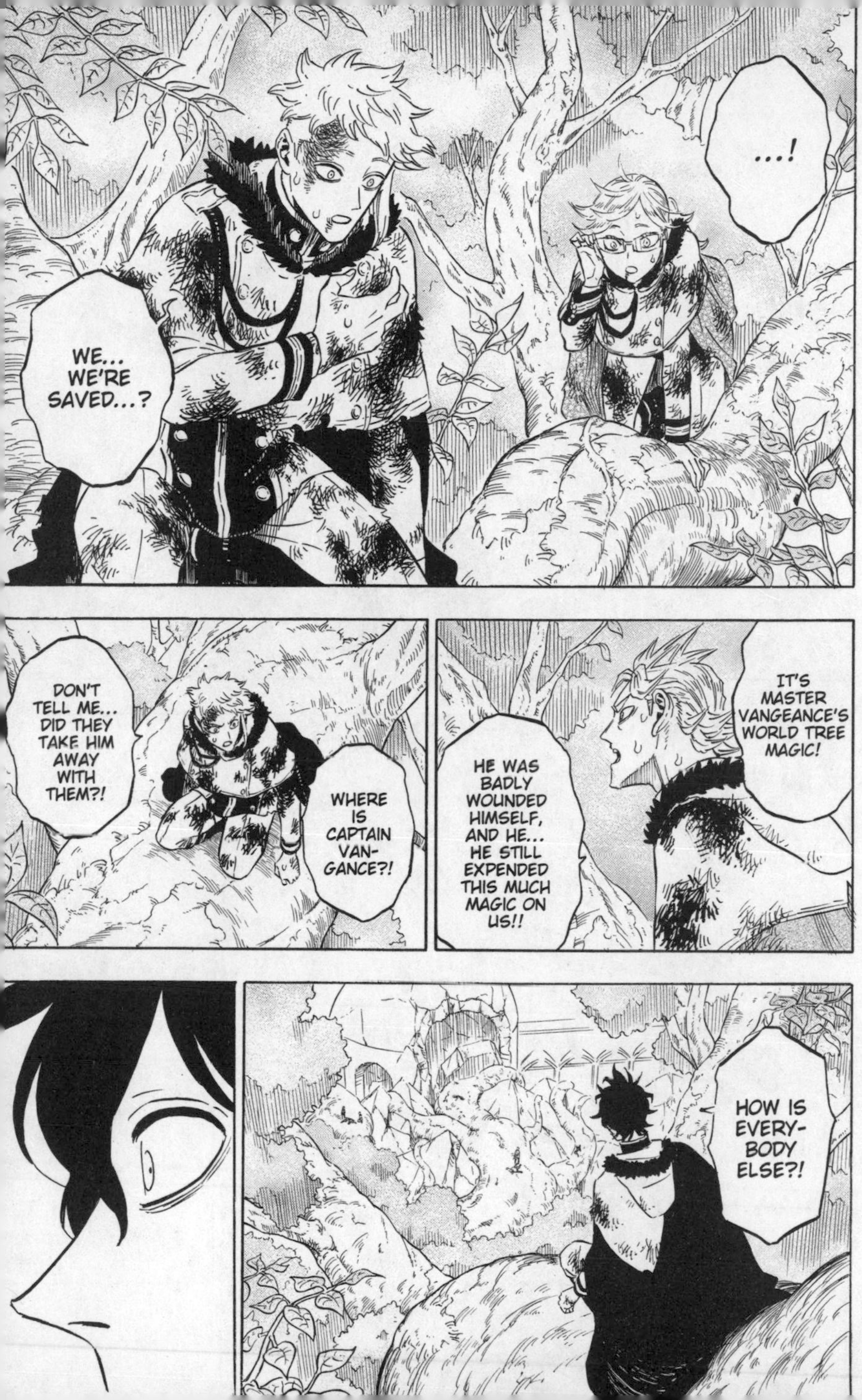
...!
WE... WE'RE SAVED...?
IT'S MASTER VANGEANCE'S WORLD TREE MAGIC!
HE WAS BADLY WOUNDED HIMSELF, AND HE... HE STILL EXPENDED THIS MUCH MAGIC ON US!!
WHERE IS CAPTAIN VAN-GANCE?!
DON'T TELL ME... DID THEY TAKE HIM AWAY WITH THEM?!
HOW IS EVERY-BODY ELSE?!

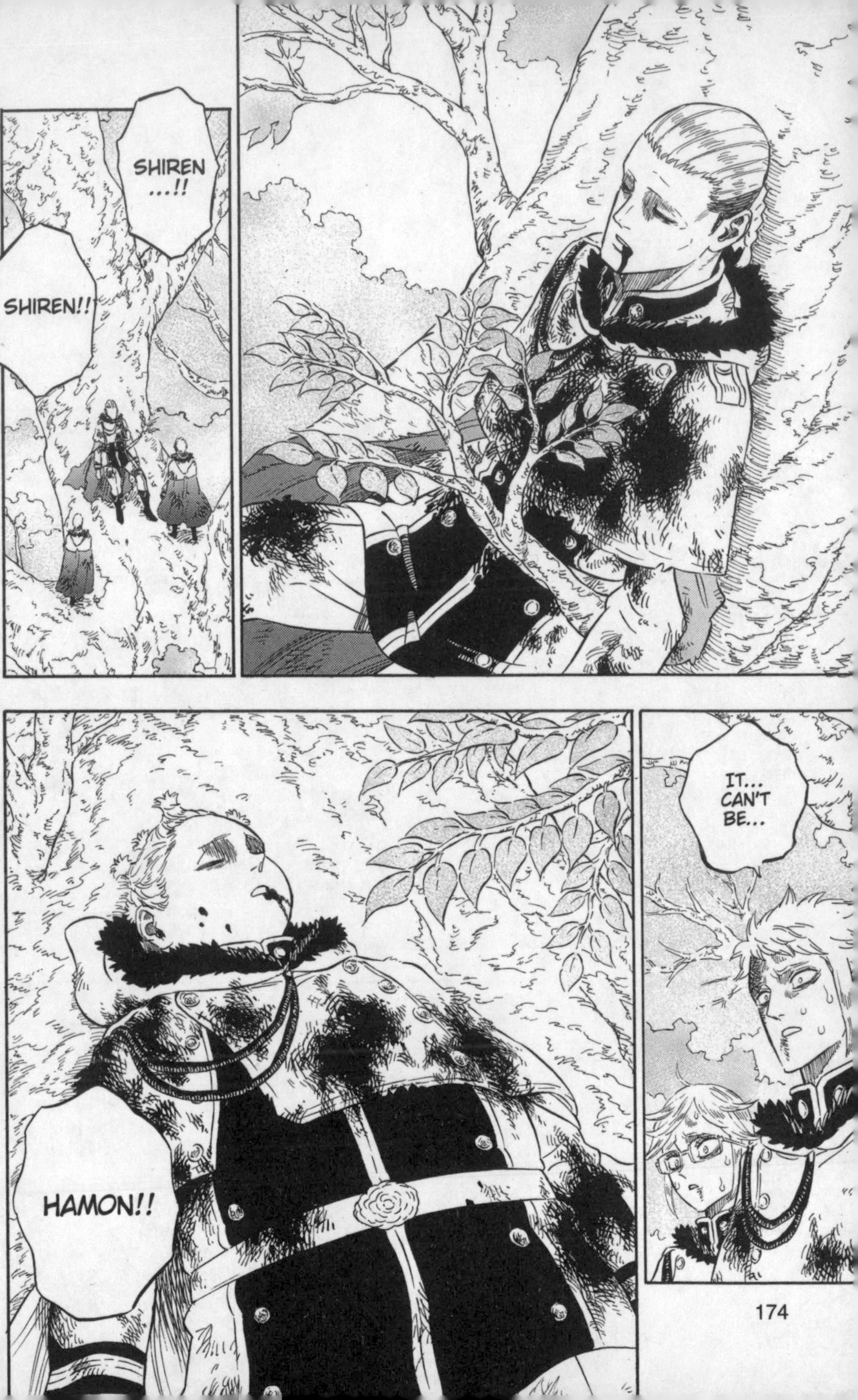
SHIREN ...!!
SHIREN!!
IT... CAN'T BE...
HAMON!!

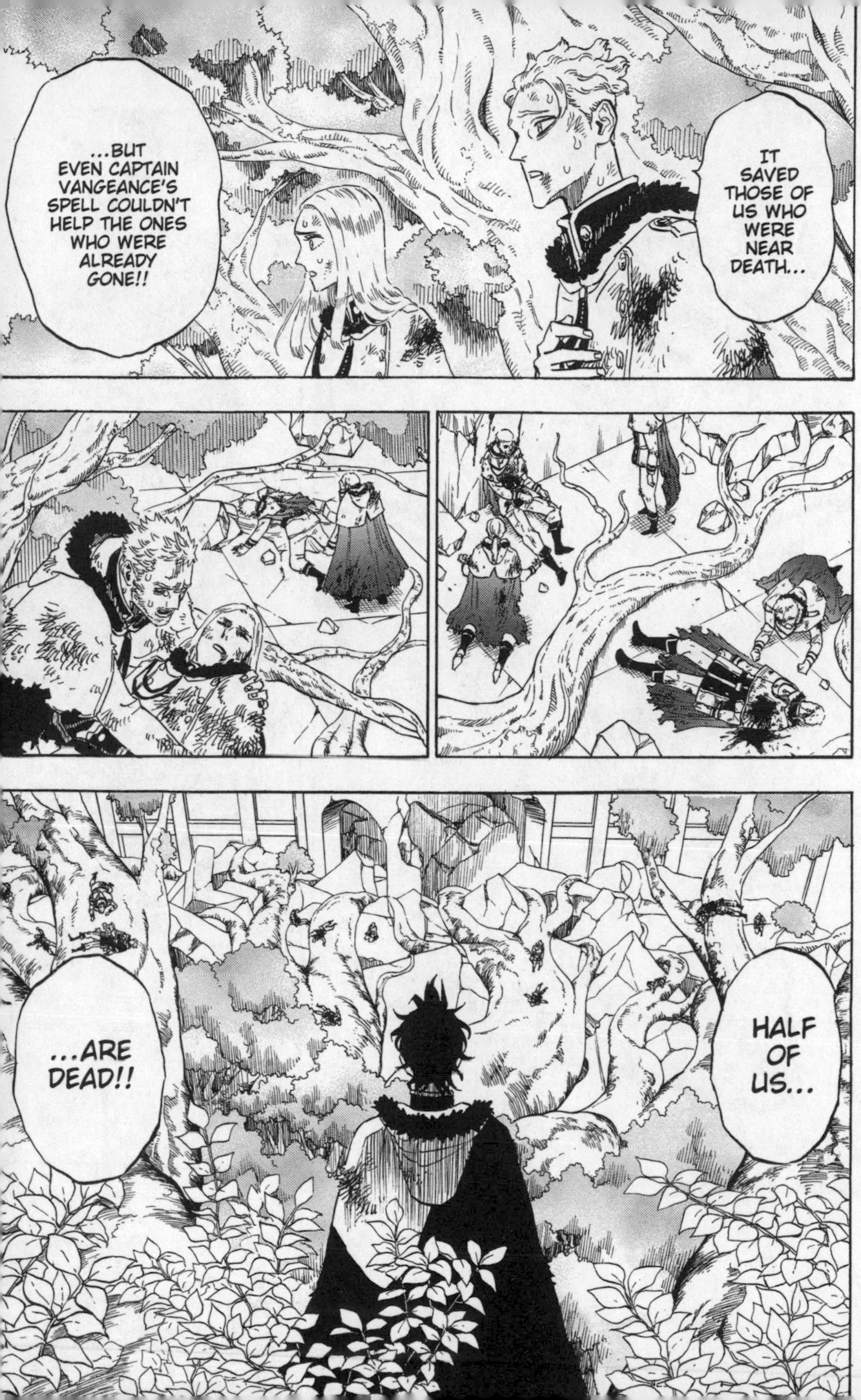
IT SAVED THOSE OF US WHO WERE NEAR DEATH...
...BUT EVEN CAPTAIN VANGEANCE'S SPELL COULDN'T HELP THE ONES WHO WERE ALREADY GONE!!
HALF OF US...
...ARE DEAD!!

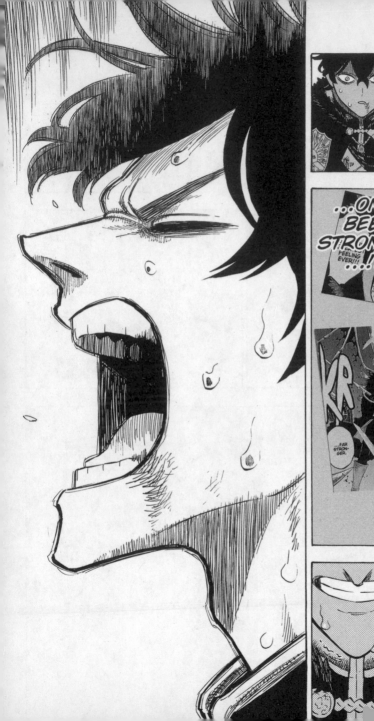

IF I'D...

...ONLY BEEN STRONGER...!!!

LIKE I'M ELEC- TRIFIED!

HUH

I'M SIMPLY...

KR IK K

...FAR STRON- GER.

...

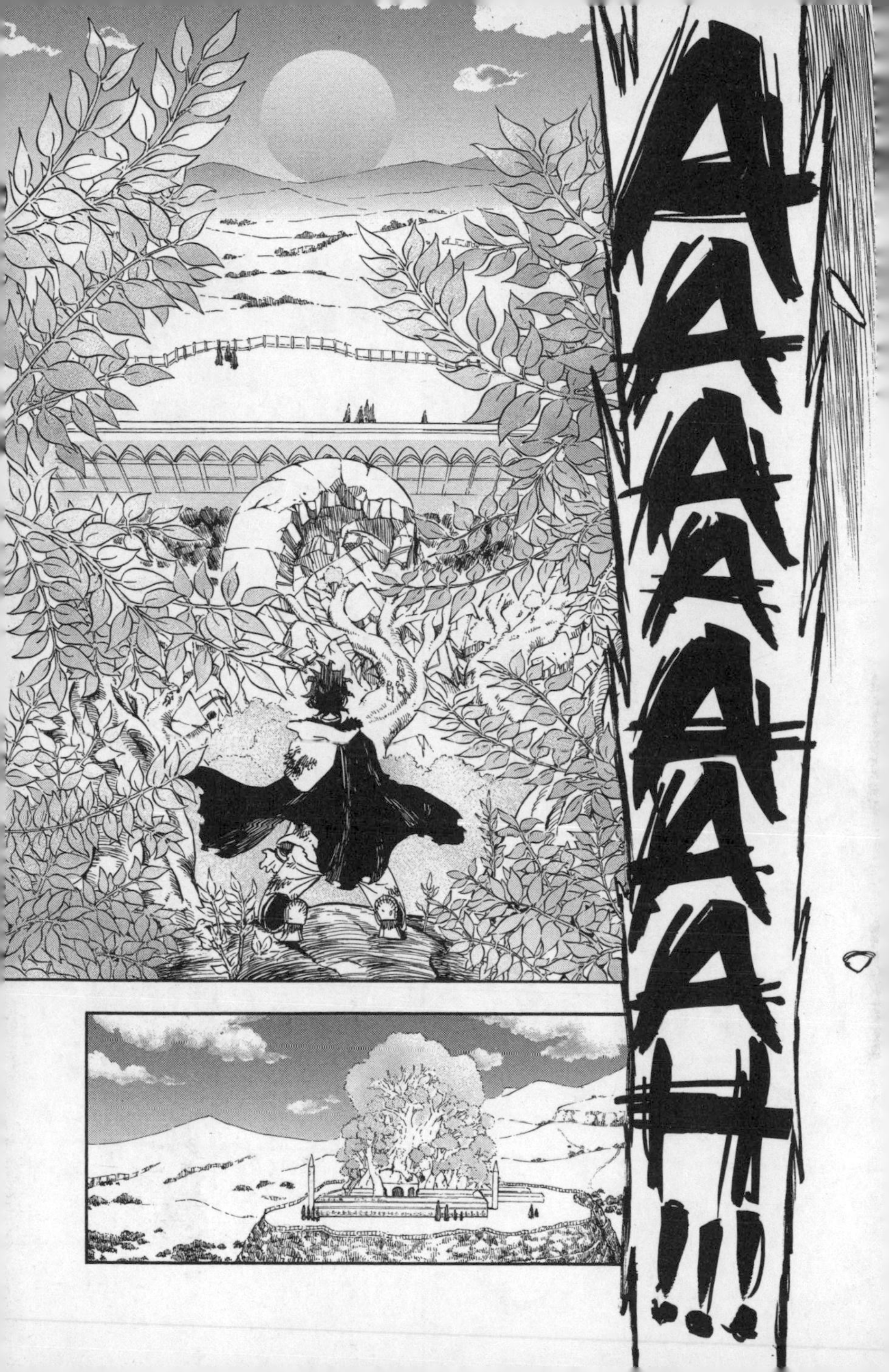
AAAAAAAH!!!

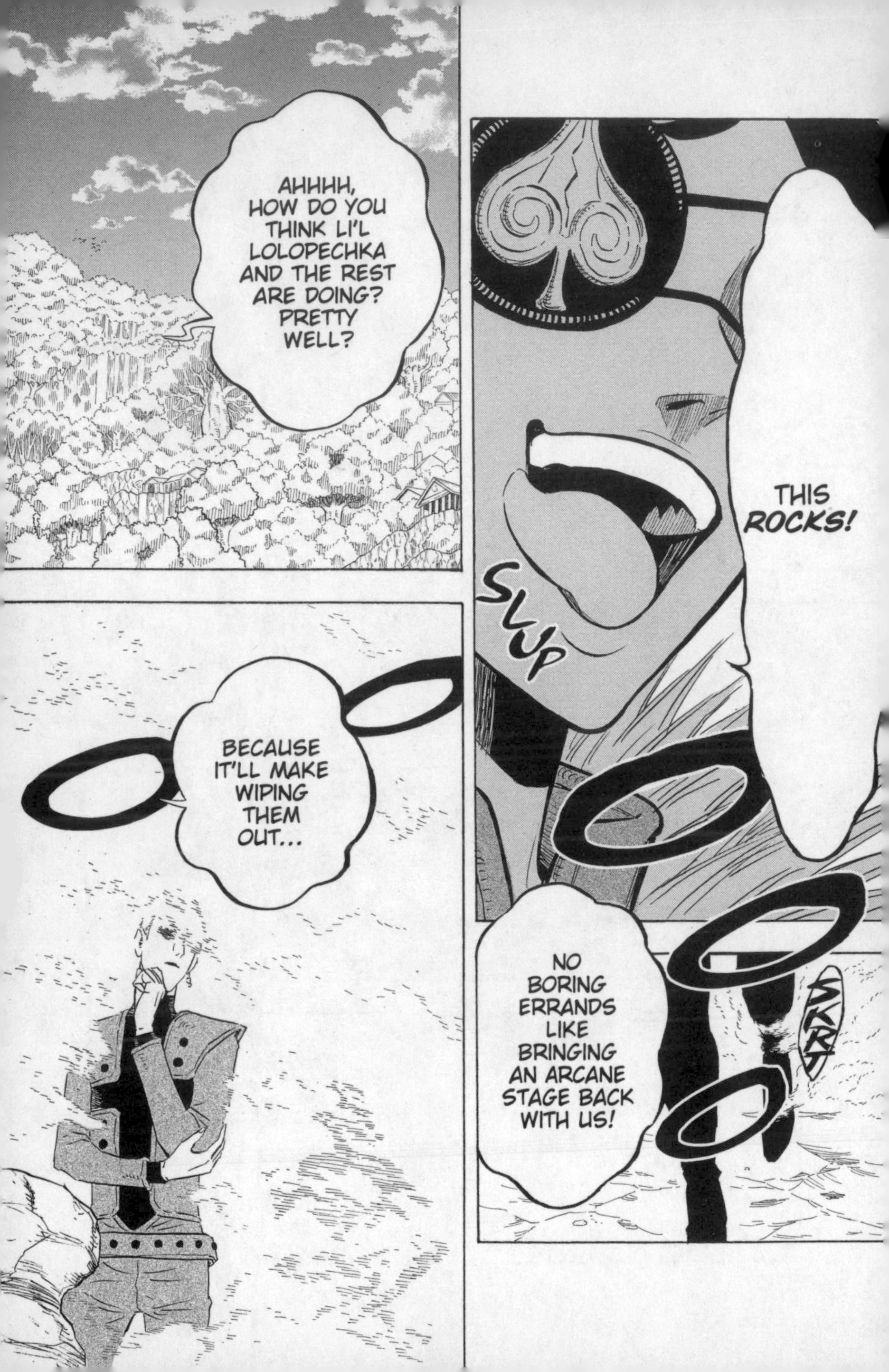
THIS ROCKS!
SLUP
NO BORING ERRANDS LIKE BRINGING AN ARCANE STAGE BACK WITH US!
SKRT
AHHHH, HOW DO YOU THINK LI'L LOLOPECHKA AND THE REST ARE DOING? PRETTY WELL?
BECAUSE IT'LL MAKE WIPING THEM OUT...

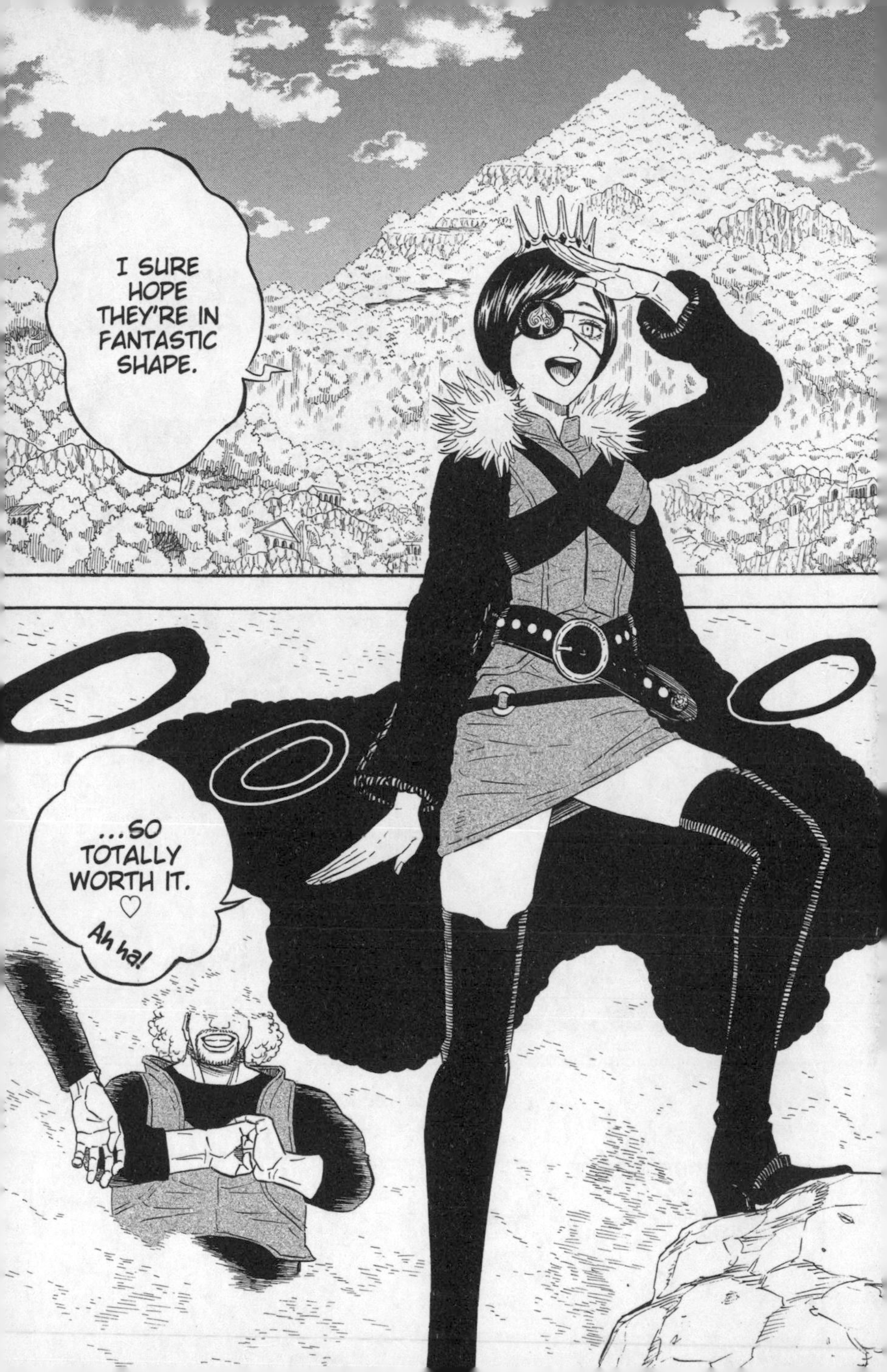
I SURE HOPE THEY'RE IN FANTASTIC SHAPE.
...SO TOTALLY WORTH IT. ♡
Ah ha!

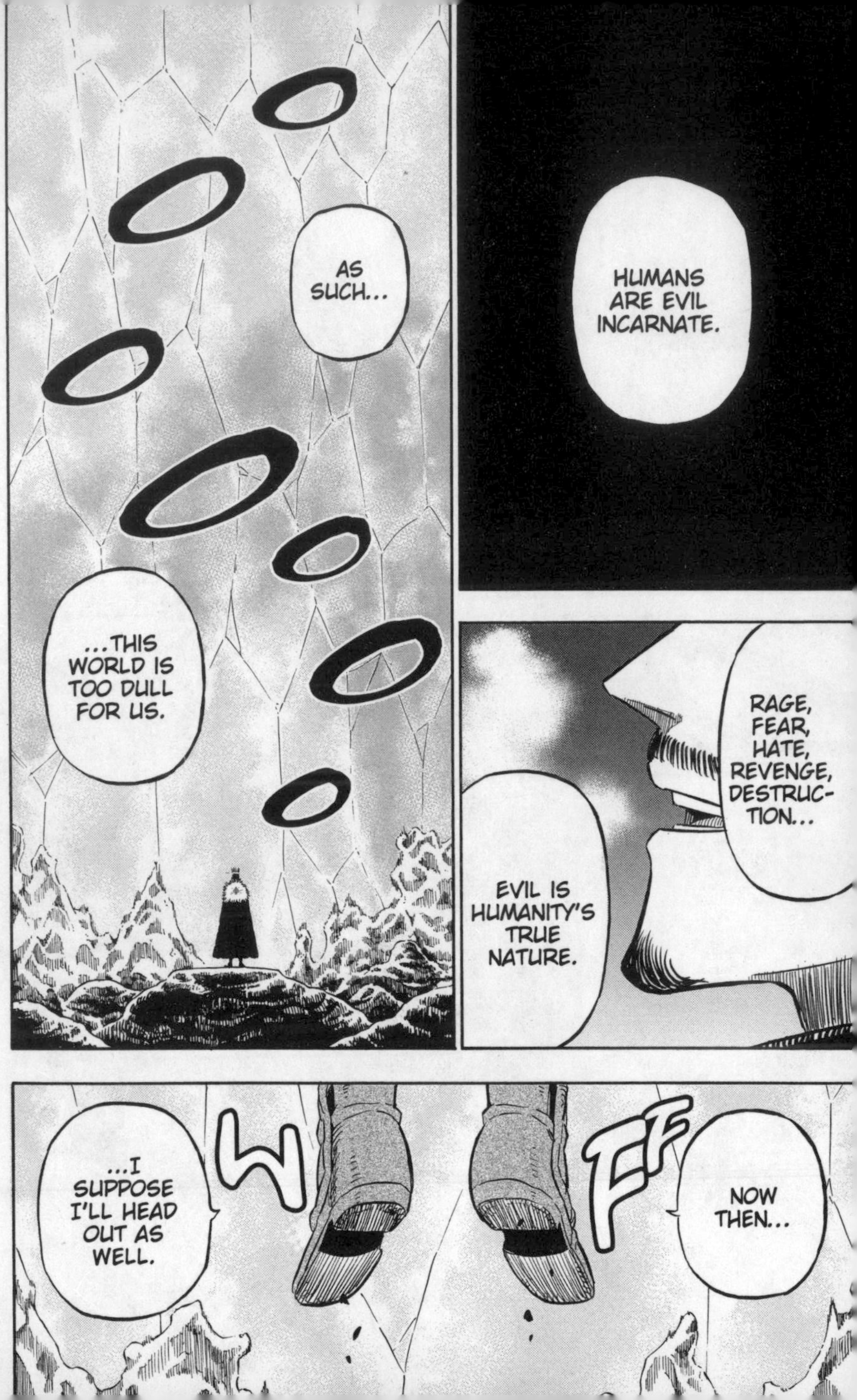
HUMANS ARE EVIL INCARNATE.
RAGE, FEAR, HATE, REVENGE, DESTRUC-TION...
EVIL IS HUMANITY'S TRUE NATURE.
AS SUCH...
...THIS WORLD IS TOO DULL FOR US.
NOW THEN...
FF
W
...I SUPPOSE I'LL HEAD OUT AS WELL.

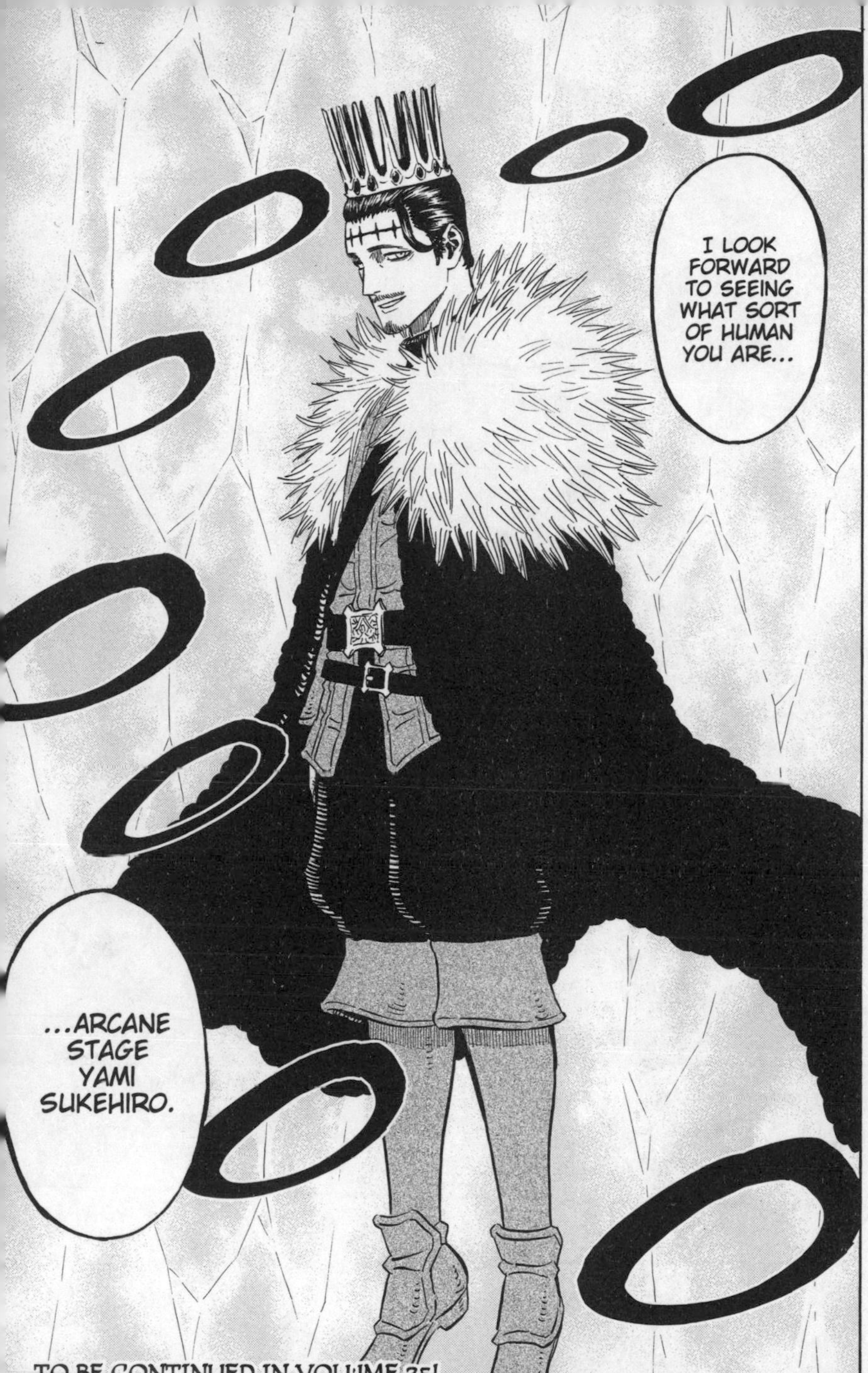
I LOOK FORWARD TO SEEING WHAT SORT OF HUMAN YOU ARE...
...ARCANE STAGE YAMI SUKEHIRO.

TO BE CONTINUED IN VOLUME 25!

The Blank Page Brigade

This volume's topic:
What are your three favorite snacks?

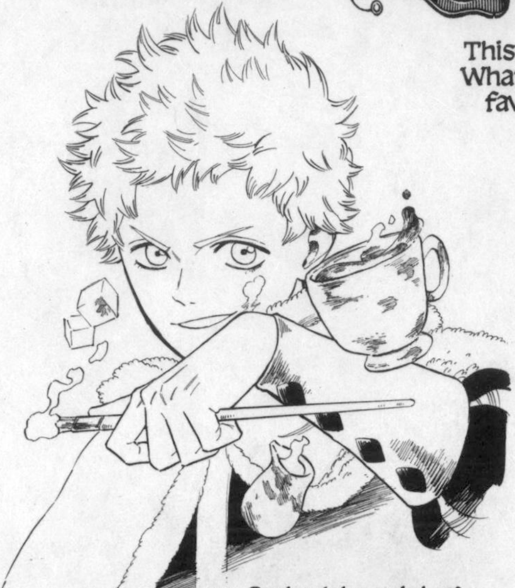

1. Sasha (chocolates)
2. Don Tacos (tortilla chips)
3. Wasabeef (potato chips)

Kazuhiro Wakao

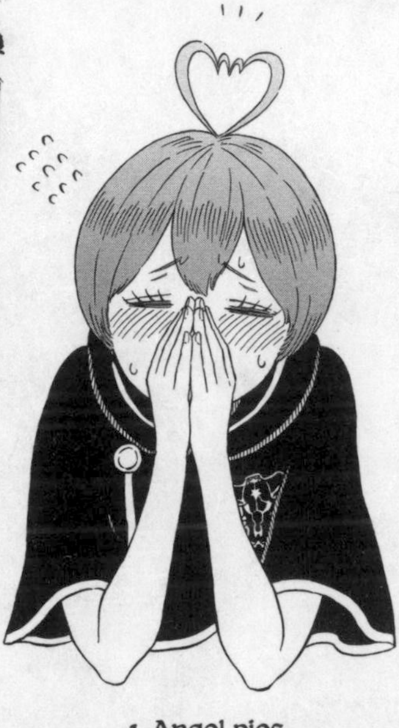

1. Angel pies
2. Black Thunder (candy bars)
3. Potato chips

Yagasa

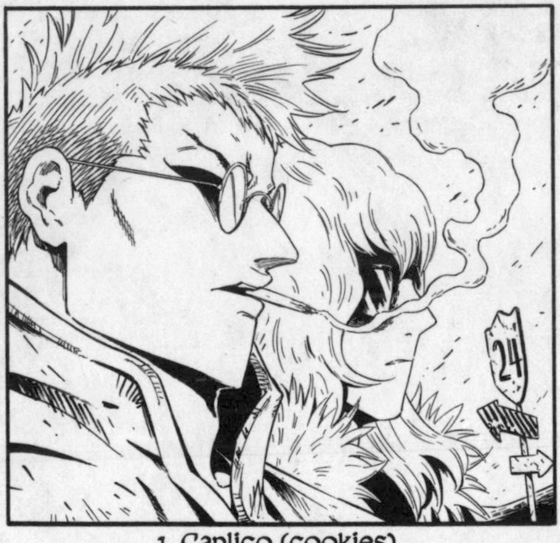
24

1. Caplico (cookies)
2. Pie no Mi (chocolate cookies)
3. Takenoko no Sato (chocolates)

Seiya Miyamoto

1. Kaki no Tane (rice crackers)
2. Alfort (chocolate cookies)
3. Potato chips, "lightly salted" flavor

Masayoshi Satosho

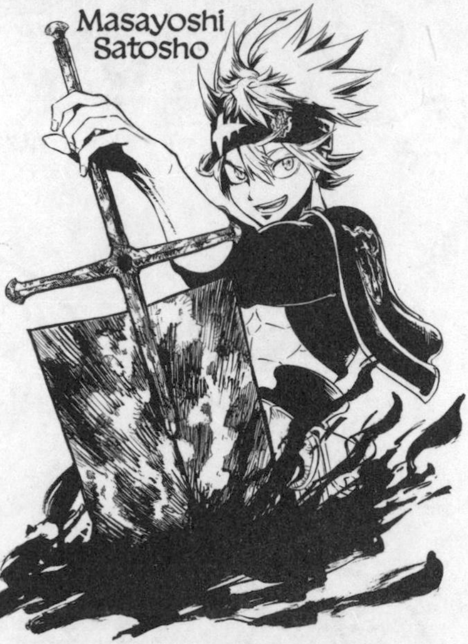

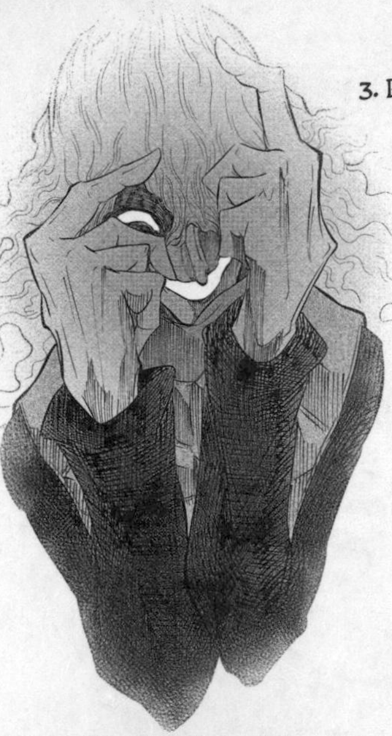

1. Crunky chocolate
2. Kata-age potato chips
3. Kit-Kat

Sōta Hishikawa

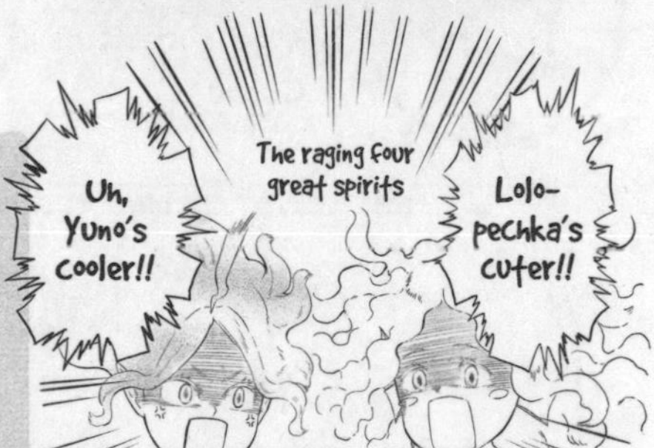
Lolo-pechka's cuter!!
The raging four great spirits
Uh, Yuno's cooler!!
Grrrr...

1. Suppa Mucho potato chips (brisk plum flavor)
2. Alfort (chocolate cookies)
3. Ramune

Yōtarō Hayakawa

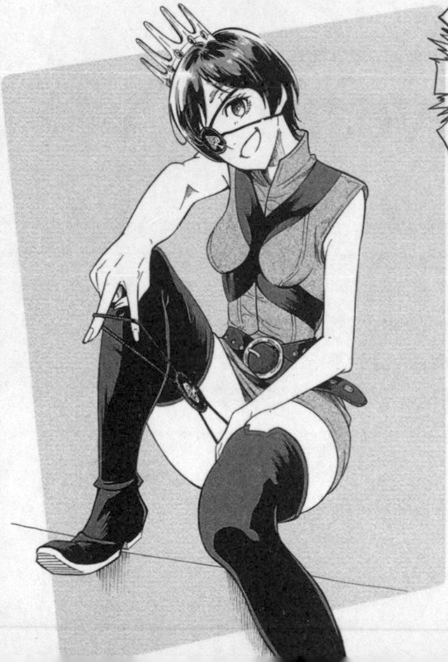

1. Choco Pies
2. Kara Mucho (potato chips)
3. Country Ma'am (cookies)

Hayato Gotō

The Blank Page Brigade

This volume's topic: What are your three favorite snacks?

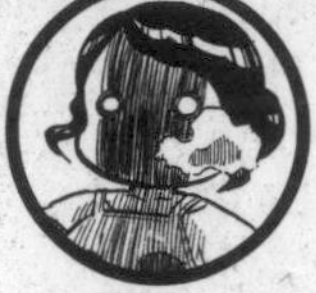

1. Lumonde (cookies)
2. Jagabee potato snacks, happy butter flavor
3. Pie no Mi (chocolate cookies)

©

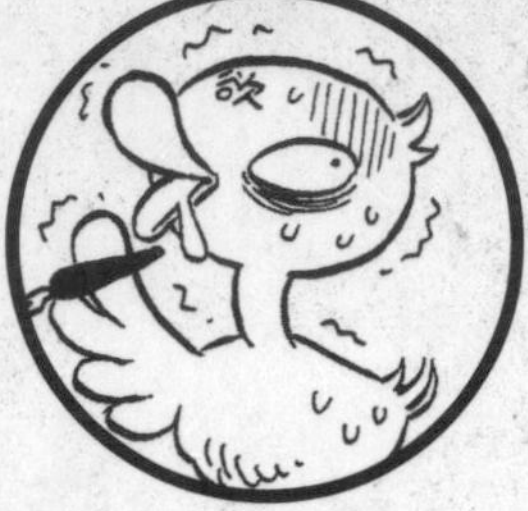

1. Jagarico potato snacks, buttered potato flavor
2. Potato chips, happy butter flavor
3. Pizza potato chips

Captain Tabata

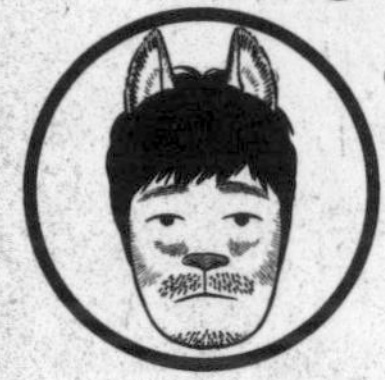

1. Kaki no Tane (rice crackers), wasabi flavor
2. Chip Star (potato chips), "lightly salted" flavor
3. Galbo (chocolates)

Comics editor Fujiwara

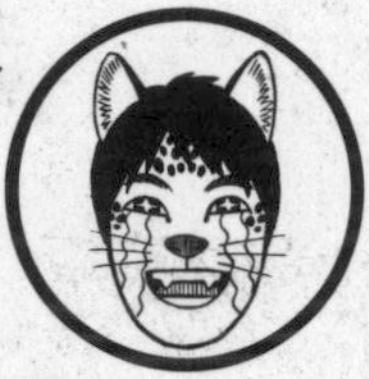

1. Kit-Kat
2. Alfort (chocolate cookies)
3. Poifull (jelly beans)

Editor Iwasaki

AFTERWORD

Half a year has gone by in the manga, and things have changed a bit. As for the Tabata family, I'm as sloppy as ever, but thanks to my wife's valiant efforts, the baby is growing fast. Possibly because she's jealous of the baby, our dog is constantly begging for attention, and this grungy old guy just doesn't know what to do with all the cuteness around him.

Special Bonus Material!

Charmy's maxim!!

Do not
eat to live...
Live to eat!!!

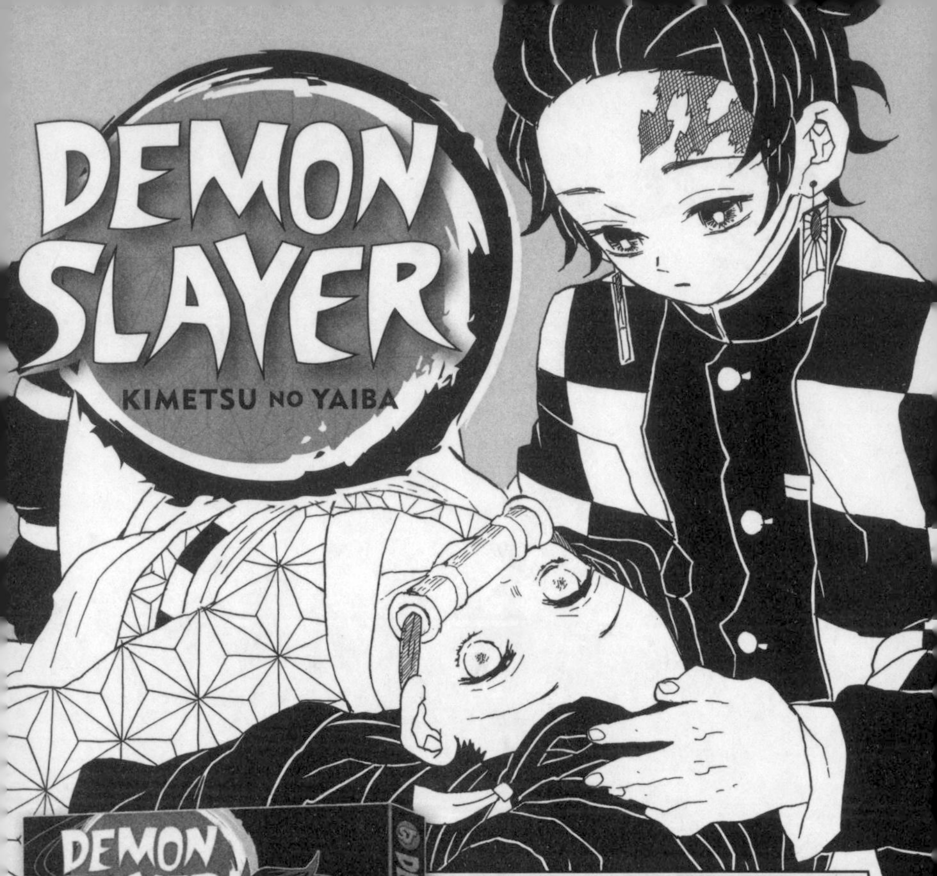
DEMON SLAYER
KIMETSU NO YAIBA

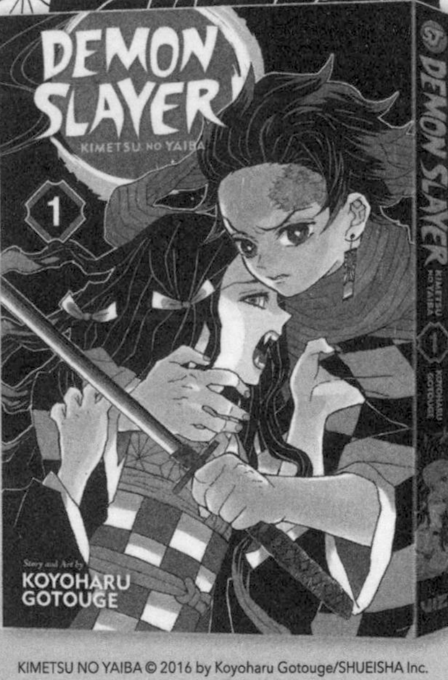
DEMON SLAYER
KIMETSU NO YAIBA
1
Story and Art by
KOYOHARU GOTOUGE
VIZ

Story and Art by

KOYOHARU GOTOUGE

In Taisho-era Japan, kindhearted Tanjiro Kamado makes a living selling charcoal. But his peaceful life is shattered when a demon slaughters his entire family. His little sister Nezuko is the only survivor, but she has been transformed into a demon herself! Tanjiro sets out on a dangerous journey to find a way to return his sister to normal and destroy the demon who ruined his life.

RATED T TEEN

VIZ

BORUTO

-NARUTO NEXT GENERATIONS-

CREATOR/SUPERVISOR **Masashi Kishimoto**
ART BY **Mikio Ikemoto** SCRIPT BY **Ukyo Kodachi**

A NEW GENERATION OF NINJA IS HERE!

Naruto was a young shinobi with an incorrigible knack for mischief. He achieved his dream to become the greatest ninja in his village, and now his face sits atop the Hokage monument. But this is not his story... A new generation of ninja is ready to take the stage, led by Naruto's own son, Boruto!

SHONEN JUMP

VIZ MEDIA
viz.com

ASTRA
LOST IN SPACE

CAN EIGHT TEENAGERS FIND THEIR WAY HOME FROM 5,000 LIGHT-YEARS AWAY?

It's the year 2063, and interstellar space travel has become the norm. Eight students from Caird High School and one child set out on a routine planet camp excursion. While there, the students are mysteriously transported 5,000 light-years away to the middle of nowhere! Will they ever make it back home?!

ASTRA
LOST IN SPACE
Story and Art by KENTA SHINOHARA

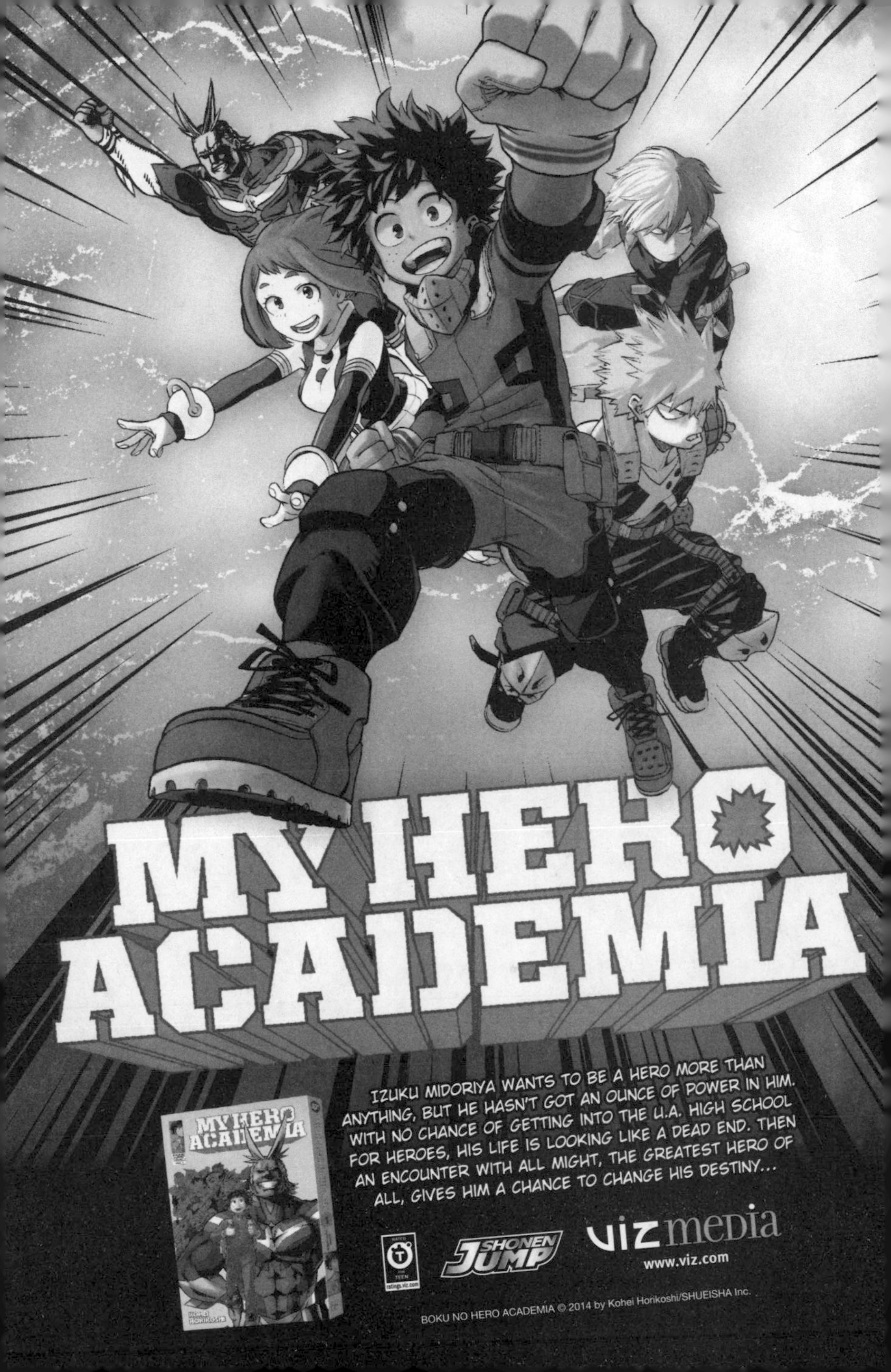
MY HERO ACADEMIA
IZUKU MIDORIYA WANTS TO BE A HERO MORE THAN ANYTHING, BUT HE HASN'T GOT AN OUNCE OF POWER IN HIM. WITH NO CHANCE OF GETTING INTO THE U.A. HIGH SCHOOL FOR HEROES, HIS LIFE IS LOOKING LIKE A DEAD END. THEN AN ENCOUNTER WITH ALL MIGHT, THE GREATEST HERO OF ALL, GIVES HIM A CHANCE TO CHANGE HIS DESTINY...
MY HERO ACADEMIA
KOHEI HORIKOSHI
RATED T FOR TEEN
ratings.viz.com
SHONEN JUMP
VIZ media
www.viz.com
BOKU NO HERO ACADEMIA © 2014 by Kohei Horikoshi/SHUEISHA Inc.

Dr. STONE

STORY BY
RIICHIRO INAGAKI

ART BY
BOICHI

One fateful day, all of humanity turned to stone. Many millennia later, Taiju frees himself from petrification and finds himself surrounded by statues. The situation looks grim—until he runs into his science-loving friend Senku! Together they plan to restart civilization with the power of science!

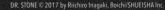

www.viz.com

Stop

YOU'RE READING
THE WRONG WAY!

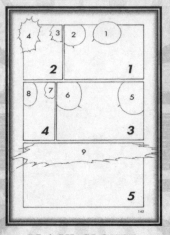

BLACK CLOVER

reads from right to left, starting in the upper-right corner. Japanese is read from right to left, meaning that action, sound effects, and word-balloon order are completely reversed from English order.